PROTEST AND SURVIVAL

PROTEST AND SURVIVAL

ESSAYS FOR
E. P. THOMPSON

EDITED BY JOHN RULE AND
ROBERT MALCOLMSON

© The Merlin Press Ltd, 1993

Published in the United Kingdom by
The Merlin Press
10 Malden Road
London NW5

Published in the United States
by The New Press, New York
Distributed by W.W. Norton & Company, Inc.
500 Fifth Avenue
New York, NY 10110

Library of Congress Cataloging-in-Publication Data

Protest and survival : essays for E. P. Thompson /
    [edited] by John Rule and Robert Malcolmson.—1st ed.
        p. cm.
    Includes bibliographical references (p.).
    ISBN 1–56584–114–X
    1. Working class—History.   2. Labor movement—History.
    3. Social classes—History.
    4. Thompson, E. P. (Edward Palmer), 1924–   .
    I. Rule, John, 1944–   .   II. Malcolmson, Robert W.
    III. Thompson, E. P. (Edward Palmer), 1924–   .
    HD4841.P76   1993
    305.5′62—dc20   93–15823
                              CIP

Printed in the United States of America
93 94 95 96   9 8 7 6 5 4 3 2 1

Contents

Preface   vii

Chapter 1   1

Edward Thompson as a Teacher: Yorkshire and
Warwick
Peter Searby and the Editors

Chapter 2   24

An Eighteenth-Century Peasantry
J.M. Neeson

Chapter 3   60

The Laws of God and the Laws of Man: Lord
George Gordon and the Death Penalty
Douglas Hay

Chapter 4   112

Trade Unions, the Government and the French
Revolution, 1789–1802
John Rule

Chapter 5   139

William Blake and the Great Eastcheap Orthodoxy
Alec Morley

Chapter 6   174

A Little Jubilee? The Literacy of Robert
Wedderburn in 1817
Peter Linebaugh

Chapter 7   221

The Fabrication of Deviance: 'Dangerous Classes'
and 'Criminal Classes' in Victorian England
Victor Bailey

Chapter 8   257

'Our Party is the People': Edward Carpenter and
Radicalism in Sheffield
Sheila Rowbotham

Chapter 9   279

The Forward March of Labour Started? Building a
Politicized Class Culture in West Ham, 1898–1900
Leon Fink

Chapter 10   322

Feminist, Socialist, Antiwar Agitator: Sylvia
Pankhurst and the Great War
Barbara Winslow

Chapter 11   355

On the Waterfront: Black, Italian and Irish
Longshoremen in the New York Harbour Strike of
1919
Calvin Winslow

Chapter 12   394

Fear and Hope in the Nuclear Age
Robert Malcolmson

E.P. Thompson: A Select Bibliography   417
Harvey J. Kaye and Keith McClelland

Contributors   422

Preface

Potential contributors to a festshrift for E.P. Thompson are legion. No other historian has had such a wide, deep and international influence on the writing of social history. The contributors to this volume were all directly influenced by him at the beginnings of their careers in history. Accordingly the volume pays tribute to Edward Thompson as a teacher and research supervisor and it fully reflects his significant impact on historical scholarship on both sides of the Atlantic. It is all the more appropriate for appearing when the publication of *Customs in Common* in 1991 marked the return of Edward Thompson to historical writing after his decade in the fore-front of the peace movement.

Acknowledgements are due to various people who offered advice, information and encouragement. Robert Malcolmson received valuable assistance from Sandra den Otter, Harold Mah and Bryan Palmer. He is grateful to Yvonne Place for her efficient and attentive secretarial support. John Rule is similarly grateful to the Departmental secretaries at Southampton. He also wishes to thank the British Academy for a grant assisting his research into early trade unionism. John Harrison gave valuable advice at one stage. Martin Eve is quite the most appropriate publisher for this volume and his enthusiasm has been sustaining. Dorothy Thompson was in on things from the beginning and gave us support, advice and critical reaction from time to time.

Polity Press and the authors kindly allowed the reprinting of the select bibliography which first appeared in *E.P. Thompson, Critical Perspectives*, edited by Harvey J. Kaye and Keith McClelland in 1990. Material from the Public

Record Office appears by permission of the Controller of H.M. Stationery Office. Acknowledgements for the use of copyright material in the essay by Sheila Rowbotham are due to the Director of Sheffield Libraries for the Caprenter correspondence; to the Board of Trustees of the Victoria and Albert Museum for the Journal of Charles Ashbee; and to Yale University Library for the William Harrison Riley Papers.

Chapter One

Edward Thompson as a teacher: Yorkshire and Warwick*

Peter Searby & the Editors

In 1948, at the age of 24, Edward Thompson became a staff tutor in English in the department of Extra-Mural Studies in the University of Leeds, after reading history and English in his three years at Cambridge.[1] He was quickly teaching both subjects, and continued to do so until he left for the University of Warwick in 1965. He very soon was at home in the idiosyncratic Yorkshire milieu. 'People who got to know him', writes an old class-member, 'admired and trusted him and that is quite an achievement. People in the West Riding do not normally open up to a middle-class academic from the South I'm afraid.'[2] Students recall, across forty years, the friendly welcome from Edward and Dorothy Thompson at their Halifax home. Huge cakes were offered after pay-day while cats scampered about and slid through a hole cut in the solid front door; sometimes an attempt would be made to press a kitten into a visitor's pocket as a parting gift. The Thompsons'

---

*In this essay the pages on Yorkshire were written by Peter Searby and those on Warwick by Robert Malcolmson and John Rule.

1. I wish to offer my gratitude to members of the Leeds department for their advice and help, and particularly to Malcolm Chase who guided me through its copious archives. I have also learnt much about the Leeds background in the 1950s and 60s from talking to John F.C. Harrison and Roy and Gwen Shaw. The paper could not have been written without the help and testimony of Edward Thompson's onetime students – Dorothy Greenald, Iris Inison, Colin Palmer, Oliver Swift and Peter Thornton – and I tender my thanks to them. I stress that the views I express are entirely mine.

2. Colin Palmer to PS, 22 August 1992.

many political activities anchored them in the community and drew some people to Edward Thompson's classes. Joining a peace march in Leeds in 1953, Oliver Swift noticed that

> At the head of the column sharing the lead was a tall rangy sort of fellow. The march ended at the museum, since demolished, and one of the speakers was Edward. He struck me then as a person devoid of dogma, which was something that could not be said about myself at that time. Some weeks later I happened to enter Batley Public Library and noticed a poster advertising a WEA class on social history to be given by Edward. I signed up at once and have not looked back since. . . Three years of social history followed by three years of English Literature changed my life, after an education which though expensive was more concerned with sport than academic achievement.[3]

The Leeds Department of Extra-Mural Studies was responsible for university-level adult education in most of the North Riding, the coastal strip up to Redcar being Hull's province, and shared the West Riding with Sheffield. Throughout each session, from autumn to spring, each tutor taught four or five tutorial classes, parts of three-year courses that strove to achieve the standards of degree courses. There were also shorter summer schools and weekend and day-release classes. Tutors had to travel long distances; in the session of 1954–5, for example, Edward taught in Middlesbrough, Batley, Keighley, Northallerton and Halifax. Colleagues did not live near each other. There was a staff meeting every month or so, and also branch and district WEA committee meetings, held on Saturday afternoons. But professional life was not dominated, as it increasingly is in higher education now, by the pressure of a host of committees. The Leeds staff tutors gathered for annual conferences that were marked by lively and sometimes contentious debate over matters of educational principle. Discussion continued through lengthy papers duplicated for postal consumption among the score or so of tutors. For good and ill, life for a staff tutor was very different from a lecturer's in an internal department, being more concerned with fundamental principles and much less marked by group solidarity. In their comparative isolation tutors had to sustain pressures that a more closely-knit community would have helped to diffuse, but there was also much private time for other activities. In these Yorkshire years

---

3. Oliver Swift to Dorothy Greenald, August 1992.

Edward Thompson gave much energy to Left politics, and wrote *William Morris* and *The Making of the English Working Class*.

The Leeds Extra-Mural Department[4] was founded in 1946, part of the large university expansion in this field that resulted from postwar idealism. Its director was Sidney Raybould, a robust Yorkshireman with a meagre sense of humour, and no more lacking in contentiousness than some of his colleagues. He was an economist with much experience of extramural work and firm ideas about its nature and purpose. Quickly winning the confidence of the university authorities, he recruited many tutors in a few years and eventually there were thirty. In the 1950s and 60s Leeds was one of the largest extramural departments in the country, and Raybould was the best-known administrator and publicist in the field, spreading his views in a host of books and articles. His attitude towards Edward Thompson was complex. Academically insecure himself, he was proud of his young colleague with a Cambridge First, who went on to publish two very distinguished books while serving in his department. On the other hand until 1956 Edward Thompson was a member of the Communist Party. Nothing could have been more openly avowed than Thompson's political beliefs, and Raybould was fully aware of them when he appointed him – which was much to Raybould's credit. Uneasiness remained; after all, these were the days of the Cold War and McCarthy's crusade in America, and Raybould was naturally apprehensive when at an early staff meeting Edward Thompson announced that his aim in adult teaching was 'to create revolutionaries'.[5] Raybould was perturbed by the left-wing views of two other tutors also, and his concern was shared by some colleagues. Though personal relationships within the department were generally cordial enough, there were some wide-ranging disputes, essentially provoked by political differences, in which

---

4. In 1951 it was renamed the Department of Adult Education and Extra-Mural Studies.

5. The issue is discussed in Roger T. Fieldhouse, *Adult Education and the Cold War: Liberal values under siege 1946–51* (University of Leeds Department of Adult and Continuing Education, 1985), pp. 15–18. His contention that it led 'to the isolation of, if not discrimination against' the three men does not seem to be supported by the evidence.

Edward Thompson does not seem to have been at his most persuasive. But more important was the quality of Edward Thompson's *teaching*; and witnesses agree that it was far more balanced and restrained than his polemical utterance might suggest – though it is also true that of course his sympathies were always apparent in the lecture room, not least in his choice of topic. One strong impression, when one reads of these distant departmental wrangles, is that much argument was in fact truly redundant, between people who failed to realise their agreement on underlying liberal fundamentals.

Much of the department's teaching was in partnership with the Workers' Educational Association, and there were differences in attitude towards it between Edward Thompson on the one hand and Raybould and some of his colleagues on the other. Raybould was active in an age when universities were more autonomous and more clearly separated from other agencies in the educational hierarchy than they are now; universities had a more sharply defined sense of their own nature. Raybould revered it, or what he thought it was.[6] He was anxious for his extramural department to enjoy the same status as internal ones, which meant that its work had demonstrably to be equivalent to theirs. In addition he had a disinterested affection for the WEA's original purpose, to bring university education within the reach of working-class adults by part-time study. So his social hopes were consistent with his institutional ambitions. Both focused on the three-year tutorial class, where (to quote the Board of Education Regulations he often referred to) 'the standard of work must correspond with that required for university degrees in honours'. To effect this 'university standard' was one of Raybould's chief aims as director, and it was frequently reiterated to colleagues. WEA students were older than most undergraduates, and they brought to their studies, Raybould said, 'experience of life which in the nature of things is lacking in children and adolescents, however able, in an intellectual

---

6. This paragraph is based on the following works by S.G. Raybould: *University Standards in W.E.A. Work* (1948), *The Approach to W.E.A. Teaching* (1949), *The English Universities and Adult Education* (1951), and *University Extramural Education in England 1945–6: A Study in Finance and Policy* (1964).

sense, some of these may be'.[7] Still, reading his many papers on adult education thirty or forty years later, one is struck by his sense not of what students might bring to their classes, but of what the tutor had to do for them. He assumed a contrast between the intellectual inadequacy of WEA students and the university that would succour them – the centre of impeccably disinterested learning, Olympian, beneficent and detached.

Raybould's views were widely shared in the department, and led to a vigorous debate with those who found them antipathetic. Among these was Edward Thompson, who made his opinions clear in a paper of 10,000 words duplicated in 1950 for circulation to colleagues.[8] Its climax is a quotation from *Jude the Obscure*. As Jude passes by an Oxford stone-mason's yard, 'For a moment there fell on Jude a true illumination: that here in the stone yard was a centre of effort as worthy as that dignified by the name of scholarly study within the noblest of the colleges'. The highest task for the Extra-Mural Department was to support the aims that the Workers' Educational Association had had since its foundation in 1903:

> In the first place, they are limited by its title and policy-statements to an emphasis on the educational needs of a class in society denied by economic circumstances or social environment a full share in the use of other institutions for higher education. In the second place, they are directed to a specific emphasis – 'education for social purpose' – on making this section or class more effective in social activities. In the third place, through the tutorial class movement, they are concerned specifically with healing the divorce between the institutions of higher education and the centres of social experience – between 'workers by hand and brain' – existing in our society.[9]

The intentions of the original members of the WEA were still valid:

> They demanded knowledge in order to act more efficiently in relation to those issues which their experience of life prompted as being urgent.

---

7. *University Standards in W.E.A. Work*, p.32.

8. University of Leeds Department of Extra-Mural Studies Archives, Adult Education Papers, vol.1, 4 (July 1950), E.P. Thompson, 'Against "University" Standards: Comments upon the Reflections of Messrs Baxandall, Shaw and McLeish', pp.16–39. The following paragraph is based on this paper, from which the quotations are taken.

9. p.31.

Their attitude was a class-conscious attitude, that is they were conscious at all times, in the pursuit of truth and in social activity, of the interests of their own class in its struggle for social emancipation.[10]

In the pursuit of true partnership the university should be humble: encouraging WEA classes to take decisions over essential issues of policy and not just trivia such as the booking of rooms; stressing the importance of high academic standards of rigour and balance, certainly, but emphasising that the concern for these values came from within the WEA itself by referring to 'tutorial standards' rather than 'university standards'. The tutor too should live and teach in a spirit of true fraternity; learning from his students while at the same time using his knowledge to help them to deepen their understanding. Referring again to the original aims of the WEA he so respected, he wrote:

The tutor . . . was prepared to have hitherto accepted academic judgements corrected in the light of the student's experience: but not to abandon his teaching to the over-simplifications or distortions liable to arise from the limitations of this experience. He could not permit social-purposiveness to replace study, desire to master discipline. Thus, in the healthy tutorial class, a struggle constantly took place between the scholarship of the tutor and the social dynamic of the movement.[11]

This special function of the WEA was being undermined by inexorable processes analysed in detail at the time by Edward Thompson's sympathetic colleague John F.C. Harrison.[12] In the twenty years after the war there was a decline in WEA membership and self-generated income, while the number of its students in tutorial classes was at best stationary at a time when the demand for extramural education was rising. (Because of the ebbing in the WEA's strength as a recruiting agent Raybould and others were perforce driven to expand autonomous university provision, much as this move was criticised by some.) Perhaps most important of all was the decline in the proportion of WEA students that were manual workers, from 24 per cent in 1945 to 16 per cent in 1956. A redefinition of 'working class' in terms of those with minimal

10. p.35.

11. p.35.

12. 'The WEA in the Welfare State', in S.G. Raybould, ed, *Trends in English Adult Education* (1959), pp. 1–29.

formal education did not truly compensate for the lessening of this core, while all these changes underlined how difficult it was to see the WEA as the credible agent of the social emancipation its founders had dreamed of. In the 1950s there seemed to observers to be an inevitable trend towards accommodating with capitalism rather than towards conquering it. In the words of John Harrison:

> It is obvious to any tutor in the field that the quality of the response which he now normally gets from the average WEA branch and class could never have built and sustained a movement with a reputation as great as that of the WEA in the past. Clearly something has been lost. This situation is not primarily the result of wrong-headedness or weak leadership or the apathy of the rank and file, but rather of the profound social and educational changes since the early days of the WEA, more especially since 1939. In the new social democracy of the fifties the operative ideals of the WEA do not appeal as strongly as they once did to the sort of people whom they previously attracted.[13]

Edward Thompson was aware of these changes, as we shall see. Indeed, his uneasiness at them helps to explain the urgency he felt as a teacher and some of the reasons for his success in that role.

II

Leeds tutors each year wrote detailed reports on the progress of their tutorial classes for the enlightenment of Raybould and the university. These duplicated papers exist in abundance in the department's archives – a record of approaches, successes and failures that is invaluable for the historian (and which one wishes were paralleled for internal university faculties). Almost all Edward Thompson's reports survive for his sixteen years of teaching in Yorkshire: about 30,000 words concerning some 60 tutorial classes – commentary that is wry, self-critical, pragmatic, and above all generous and enthusiastic.[14]

Extramural teaching was quite unlike lecturing on a BA course or supervising graduate students. Tutorial classes

13. J.F.C. Harrison, 'The WEA in the Welfare State'. p.26.

14. What follows is largely based on these documents: Leeds University Department of Extra-Mural Studies Archives, Joint Tutorial Classes Committee, Reports by Tutors on Classes.

suffered handicaps that 'internal' students rarely had to face in those days (whatever afflicts them today). Rooms were often unsuitable and unwelcoming, and Edward Thompson's wish to offer novel and arresting material to students was sometimes frustrated by the department library's inability (for example) to find working-class autobiographies for the book-box. Learning had to be 'for its own sake' entirely; tutorial classes did not work towards a material reward – even a certificate – though students were expected from the outset to attend for three years. Yet novices were not likely to guess what the course would really entail from the brief advertising they saw, though a strong WEA branch in the locality might help to prepare them. A more fundamental problem was that the previous educational experience of the recruits was often limited, so that they were unsure of what they really wanted or foresaw from the mortgage of their winter evenings.

In class they found that the regulations for tutorial classes attached a great importance to writing, and many found the pressure of composition disconcerting. In these circumstances it is not surprising that all WEA classes tended to suffer dropouts in the first few months, though to some extent this was counterbalanced by latecomers. Despite their implicit undertaking to study for three years students attended, of course, just as they wished, and during the winter Edward Thompson found that numbers might be reduced for many fortuitous reasons – compulsory overtime, courtship, marriage and childbirth for younger members, and illness and death for the oldest. A common pattern was that an initial recruitment of 14 or 15 lost 6 or 7 members during the autumn but gained 2 or 3 latecomers. Although not one of Edward Thompson's classes seems to have been closed because it was felt to have fallen below the viability threshold, the threat was often there. The vitality and very existence of a class depended on the flair and enthusiasm of the tutor far more than it would have done in an internal department.

Some typical challenges to the tutor, and Edward Thompson's adroit responses to them, are suggested by his report on a history class in Batley in 1953–4:

> This class – part original, part added – has an excellent core to it, of about ten or eleven members, and a further five or six students on the register who blow in and out irregularly, take a vigorous part in

discussions, but are not fulfilling stipulated requirements of reading, writing or attendance. While three of the latter will be taken off the register next year, there seems to be no good reason for excluding any of them from the meeting room, since everyone likes to see them and they manifestly have no ill effect on the morale or quality of work of the rest. Batley is a small town where everyone knows everyone else: the community sense extends to the W.E.A. and to the class, and is reinforced by it: the most admirable regulations of the most enlightened administrators must bend before the facts of life in Batley. Anyway, how can the tutor exclude the President of the Branch – so busy with his voluntary work for his union, school, chapel, and the W.E.A. itself that he cannot write an exercise when it is required? Class discussions have been extremely vigorous, but one very old member (thundering the table in defence of Gladstone's integrity) has tended always to lead them into the swamp of local reminiscence. Nevertheless, both the tutor and the class feel that this is the kind of thing we have got to expect and to put up with, and no one would dream of asking the old gentleman to stop describing his speech at the School Board election of 1877. After all, we cannot have our cake and eat it. If we want academic tidiness, we will not also have the variety of experience and the informal non-vocational spirit to which we give lip-service. Between the Ideal and the Reality falls the Shadow of Compromise. And if Compromise be accepted, then Batley is a fairly good tutorial class.

Edward Thompson's social history teaching focused on Britain from the Industrial Revolution to the twentieth century, and its interaction with the research for *The Making of the English Working Class* is very evident. As he several times recorded, he learned much from his classes, and his comment on his Morley students in 1963–4 reveals how his own insight might be enhanced by such grassroots contact:

The work has been in the late 18th and early 19th centuries, and discussion has elicited a surprising and gruesome fund of memory among the older students. Within living memory in Morley, it seems, miners have worked lying down in eighteen-inch seams, children have been in the mills at the age of nine, urine has been collected from pub urinals for scouring, while the brother of one of the students still uses teazles to raise the 'nap'. It is difficult to believe that the Industrial Revolution has yet occurred in Morley, and next year's syllabus (in the later 19th century) will seem like a tour through the space age.

Students were given copies of original documents from his research in progress (occasionally they seem to have been given the originals themselves), and they were encouraged to collect similar material from local repositories and to compile 'reminiscence books'. In his English literature teaching (about half the total) the way to get class involvement was more readily to hand. The range of texts studied was very wide, from Ben Jonson to John Braine. Above all others Shakespeare was preferred by Edward Thompson: 'contemporary literature is pitiful stuff compared with Shakespeare', was his scathing comment on the lacklustre response of the Bingley class, in 1952–3, to T.S. Eliot, W.B. Yeats, Sean O'Casey and Graham Greene. After the Morley class of 1961–2 his judgement was that

> a class of this kind responds best to Shakespeare; the distance stimulates application, the in-bred respect keeps philistinism at bay, and it is difficult to graft onto Falstaff a discussion on the Morley local elections.

To stimulate the clash of argument was a constant aim. Outside lecturers were brought in to

> enable the students to gain the benefit of meeting scholars with different viewpoints, grinding different axes or hacksaws, and carrying different bundles of chips on their shoulders – an advantage which the internal student usually has over his extra-mural counterparts.[15]

Recording what seems on the face of things to have been a quite successful literature class in Bingley, Edward Thompson wrote in 1952:

> In sum, then, this group is keen, conscientious, but not brilliant. The best are good-average tutorial class students, lacking a little perhaps in boldness or originality. There is too little rebellion in the class, and they are too content to be *taught*. It looks as if the whole course of the class might be run without one good earnest row between the students.

But in fact the quality of the argument in Edward Thompson's classes is very well remembered by ex-students. Perhaps recklessly, Peter Thornton once accused him of romanticising the working class, and was compelled to justify his statement at length. 'You could disagree with Edward, but you'd got to prove your point.' Dorothy Greenald does not believe that 'you could have got away without discussion. There was the same amount of time given for discussion as for the lecture. People weren't reluctant to discuss because they had plenty to say because of the views he'd put forward and the inspiration.'[16]

---

15. Reports 1954–55, no.33, Keighley social history.

16. Dorothy Greenald and Peter Thornton: taped conversation, 12 September 1992.

Despite his respect for a class's particularity, he could sometimes be very directive indeed, as is apparent from his account of the first year (1959–60) of a literature class in Harrogate (which contrasts in several striking ways with the Batley report quoted earlier). From a total of 20 students in attendance at some time during the session only 11 were sufficiently conscientious to qualify as satisfactory attenders; and the same number qualified in written work. In a trenchant yet subtle assessment he asked:

What has happened to give us this serious fall-out, between those on the register and those completing the class requirements? Quite possibly some of the responsibility is mine: but this is always difficult to assess. But a large part of the explanation lies in the different composition of this class and more 'traditional' classes like Halifax and Morley; and the different recruiting methods of the W.E.A. branches. The social composition of the class is very much what might be expected in Harrogate – several civil servants, a bank official, a social worker, housewives, teachers, a commercial traveller, and so on: some of these very good students indeed. The Harrogate W.E.A. has a deservedly high reputation, for its imaginative and vigorous recruiting policy and general publicity. But in consequence of these two factors, a great number of people passed through the first few class evenings – about 28 were temporarily placed on the provisional register – with no experience of sustained study, and with the expectation of attending a series of lectures – at 'university level' – which would combine the functions of intellectual stimulation and of a social occasion. *These are not unworthy motivations*: there is certainly a place for such diffuse needs in the adult education movement. But they also can lead to difficulties in establishing the discipline of tutorial work: I encountered in the first weeks . . . some quite vocal opposition from some of the newcomers to written work, class exercises, and to the three-year undertaking. Two couples proposed to attend, husband and wife, on alternating weeks, and were indignant at my adverse comments: another student persisted, despite my veto, in attending my class and a class in comparative religion on alternate weeks – with the appalling consequence that she refused (on the alternate week when she put in an attendance) to discuss Lawrence or Hopkins except in terms of Jung or Buddhism.

The fact is, that with a provisional register overflowing in a manner I had not encountered for ten years, I decided to adopt a tougher policy than I would have dared at the usual class: actively to discourage the more dilettante students by setting standards high from the very start, by selecting fairly difficult texts, and by dispensing almost altogether with lectures in favour of close textual discussion. It is possible I carried this policy too far: and on one evening, about six weeks into the year, when I was slogging hard at an exercise taken from a contemporary newspaper, there was something like a rebellion from several class members who exclaimed indignantly that this was not what they had expected of a literature course. At the same time, in this first ten or eleven weeks average attendance fell away from the 20s to 13 or 14.

But if this shock-treatment is certainly not to be recommended as a general practice, and was probably unfair to a few students who might have been won by gentler methods, it has resulted in a first-rate class which in the second half of the year it has been a pleasure to teach.

Two years later the same 11 were registered, of whom 9 qualified in attendance and 7 in written work too. So 7, out of an original enrolment three times as large, completed the tutorial class satisfactorily – about the average. Edward Thompson's comment was that:

> This has been a good class. One student wished to discuss Jung, and another Aneurin Bevan, but all the others wished to study literature all the time, and that is a high percentage. Even the Aneurin Jung faction became converted to literary studies, and contributed life to the class work. It has been a delightful class to teach because there has been no need to push it at any point. The students have read widely enough to keep the tutor on his toes. Several have been in the habit of bringing essays without waiting for the tutor's suggestions. . . There were few class meetings in which the tutor did not find himself being taught.
>
> But it was scarcely a traditional tutorial class, a certain teacher-civil-servant bias being evident.[17]

It is hard to judge Edward Thompson's impact on his classes. Fortunately, we have several helpful sources. One is a commentary on a session in his Bingley literature class in November 1949 by W. P. Baker, another extramural tutor, briefed to observe and advise young colleagues and report back to Sidney Raybould. Though Edward Thompson's comment on this session was merely that there was a 'good discussion' in a 'promising' start to the year, Baker wrote that

> in many respects this was one of the most satisfactory classes that I have ever visited. Thompson's work was quite first-class, both in his introduction of the subject (Dickens's *Hard Times*) and in stimulating the discussion. . . It was really all very good indeed, and I only wondered whether the students had been rather specially selected for the course, but I gather that this was not so. . . . They all took an active part in discussion, they all knew the text which was being considered . . . and as far as I could tell they had all done other reading conscientiously. . . The class clearly appreciated Thompson; one keen member told me in a conversation how much he was getting out of the course.[18]

---

17. Reports 1961–62, no.21, Harrogate literature.

18. His report, dated 26 November 1949, is in the archives of the Leeds

A member of his early Cleckheaton classes, Iris Inison, recalls:

> When I first met Edward Thompson I was struck by his sheer enthusiasm, also a little bit awed by his undoubted intellect, which, combined with his humour, and his articulate and graphic method of expression, made his classes fascinating. The mixture of students, old, young, verbose, set the stage for an evening – unpredictable, exciting. Anything could happen. . . .
>
> Once in his social history class he asked us to try and find a very old person to interview about their younger days. Usually I am not keen on homework, but he was so compelling, so enthusiastic, that one felt one must make the effort! I did! I found a charming 93 year old lady and got a great deal of information about her past, and as she was intelligent and articulate, I was able to do quite a good write-up. I got my reward! Edward was so pleased and interested, it was better than winning the Booker prize.[19]

Dorothy Greenald, a member of the first Cleckheaton class in 1948–51 and several others later, also vividly recalls a very enthusiastic young tutor.

> Edward was a fantastic stimulating lecturer. You laughed and you enjoyed every minute of it, and you were ready to go the next week. I can't recall that we ever missed a class ever. . . We went for the enjoyment and the stimulation and the discussion, and the value to ourselves in opening up ideas and making you look at things differently, or really looking deeper into things more. . . It was like going to the cinema really except that it was more informative. You had to read too to do the written work, but most people were readers and were interested. I can't recall that we had in the class any people who were shiftless and just went for a night out.[20]

Edward Thompson, she recalls, was careful not to obtrude his left-wing views into his teaching. His nervous energy was so abundant that he would pull constantly at his sweater till, before his students' mesmerised gaze, it was seen to unravel. Peter Thornton, another member of an early Cleckheaton history class, recalls that 'He had a technique of involving you and getting the personal picture of people. You always felt

---

department.

---

19. Iris Inison to Dorothy Greenald, August 1992.
20. Dorothy Greenald, taped conversation, 12 September 1992.

that he was talking about individuals with feelings and problems and backgrounds that were like yours.'[21] Student testimony shows that one of the things they most valued in Edward Thompson's classes was the enhancement of self-awareness that they brought.

Even the most committed students are sometimes reluctant to write, and Edward Thompson was constantly pressing them to do so. All WEA tutors faced the same difficulty, and students say that he got a better response than some of his colleagues 'because the stimulation was there . . . and there was something to write about. But he was very critical when you did write. He didn't let you off by soft words. He praised you but he also said what he thought, suggesting what you might look at a bit deeper. People learned from these critical notes.'[22] One example of a student's written work that has been traced bears his meticulous and helpful appraisal.[23] The assignment is a piece of practical criticism of about 500 words, and deals with an unnamed writer, whose utterance is described by Edward Thompson as 'a filthy piece of literary demagogy'. His commentary amounts to 350 words, and balances careful encouragement with searching criticism very gently expressed.

Disavowing the role of lecturer, however much he was pushed into it, Edward Thompson continually praised the 'WEA spirit'. For example, he said of Cleckheaton's 1948–9 literature class: 'Altogether, the tutor believes he has learnt as much as he has imparted . . . and in spite of some initial mistakes, the class has learnt to work in the spirit so desirable in the WEA – not as tutor and passive audience, but as a group combining various talents and pooling differing knowledge and experience for a common end'. Wherever he found this spirit, he celebrated it. Concerning the first year of a Northallerton social history class with 10 committed members (1954–5), he wrote that

---

21. Peter Thornton, taped conversation, 28 February 1992.

22. Dorothy Greenald, taped conversation, 12 September 1992.

23. It comes from a member of a Cleckheaton literature class, Kathleen Hey; it has been retrieved by Dorothy Greenald, to whose kindness I owe it.

This class presents a strange contrast with the class in Halifax started in the same year and in the same subject. While the latter contains a number of those people whom the W.E.A. especially desires to serve (several of whom are slowly becoming very good students), it has been almost devoid of W.E.A. spirit. This Northallerton class, however, has a very good W. E. A. spirit, has responded very well to co-operative methods of work, and is largely made up of civil servants, housewives, retired persons (including two active in the Conservative Party) and 'white-collar' workers.

This has been a good class . . . particularly satisfying has been the response to my invitation to the students to prepare special interventions in class on the basis of first-hand contemporary sources which I have loaned them. . . Finally, this is the first class at which, in response to my request for written work, I have been asked to read the MS of a full-sized book.

This report underlines the social changes of the 1950s that were altering the function of the WEA – not that Northaller-ton had a vast untapped market for tutorial classes. In its third year the committed membership was down to 6, although it was written, 'It has been a sophisticated class, and one which has embraced extremes of faith and opinion amicably enough: a Tory councillor has rubbed shoulders with a Labour county councillor; Catholic and Methodist have argued the Educa-tion Acts.' The active members of the WEA branch were nearing retirement, and Edward Thompson hoped that it would be given help to continue.

His sympathies were especially drawn to classes in commu-nities quite different from Northallerton. In 1948–9 (his first year, and he admits to mistakes as an inexperienced tutor) he ran into difficulties with a literature class of manual workers and housewives in Shepley. Having patchy results with three novels he tried poetry 'but met with so little response that he found he was losing weight'. Most of the men (the women were more appreciative) 'persisted in regarding poetry as a luxury the labour movement could do without'. 'It might be suggested', he concludes,

that this class, with its small prospect of development, does not justify the provision of tutorial work. But the students are extremely loyal to the movement, and have made a serious effort to comply with the external manifestations of good class work. Every student read, or attempted to read, the novels discussed, and some further reading was done. Nearly every student did written work, of indifferent value, but giving evidence of painstaking effort. For several students – including the pillar of the class, a retired manual worker with a wide background of reading and a lively and penetrating mind – the class has come to assume a most important place in their scheme of life. It is the tutor's opinion that such classes as this should be both continued and encouraged. Certainly the class would benefit from an infusion of fresh blood and younger members. But even as it is, it may be performing a more worth-while function than a class of far higher standards confining its membership to the professional section of a large centre of population. In the latter case the result may only be to encourage an intellectual elite. At Shepley, a small industrial valley, it is necessary to grapple more realistically with problems of standards and popular culture. It is unlikely that the active trade-unionist will find in himself a specialist interest in problems of literary criticism or 'intellectual climate'. Must he therefore be denied an opportunity to gain acquaintance with major works of literature under qualified guidance? Even if the going is hard and the results unspectacular this sort of class *must* be kept alive, with the proviso that the work should always be at the top capacity of the better students. Any other course might mean the abandonment of working-class education in favour of (an easier job for the tutor!) the further isolation of an elite.

The following year the record at Shepley was no better, yet redemption was implied by an essay by a manual worker over 60 years old on *King Lear* 'showing a most thorough knowledge of the play'. The essay's 500 words,

> were the result of several evenings' work, and of a great deal of thought and reading, re-reading and puzzling over difficult passages. The essay (the tutor has been allowed to take a copy) might be so much waste paper within a university's walls: the first page is a record of false starts and every phrase is marked with painful effort: but if every student had produced work of the same standard in relation to his training and abilities, the tutor would have held this up as an exemplary class.

A few years later Edward Thompson had to conclude that another tutorial class, in social history, had not been a success, yet 'on the other hand, the years have not been wasted effort: . . . in Todmorden, one of Gradgrind's fortresses, a centre of lively, informed and intelligent discussion has been kept alive, which may bear fruit in more serious educational work in the future'.[24]

We find here Edward Thompson's commitment to the historic role of the WEA, and it is apparent, refracted through a student's memory, in Peter Thornton's account of a more successful social history class in another of Gradgrind's fortresses, Cleckheaton:

---

24. Reports 1953–4, Todmorden social history

Edward Thompson's classes . . . had this effect of making you realise that history wasn't something separate and apart; it was a progression that you were part of. I've felt this ever since. And when he did things like the handloom weavers of Yorkshire, the Luddites, the social developments of the Industrial Revolution in this part of the world, you very quickly realised how much you and your people were part of it. We'd had these things at school; we knew about the Luddites but it was something that had happened in the past and it had gone over our heads. If anyone ever used the term 'Luddite' it meant somebody out to destroy things, not that they had a terrible problem that they were trying to solve and that they lived in a society that they found depressing. Edward brought all this home to us.[25]

Dorothy Greenald emphasises a more personal, existential gain. A child from a miner's home which, she remembers, possessed only one book, she started as a half-timer in a woollen mill during the First World War, at the age of 12. Refused permission to attend night school by her mother, she knew no literature till a workmate introduced her to Balzac and Zola, whose accounts of life in the lower depths she read keenly. She graduated from a Sunday evening forum on ethics to the WEA in the 1930s, and so came to Edward Thompson's tutorial classes. *Sons and Lovers* was a revelation to her. 'You could relate to it; you lived it as you read it. Miriam stayed with me.' She was reluctant to talk about her background in class, it having been instilled into her that 'though other children were alright there was something wrong with us'. But Edward Thompson 'brought it out that your background wasn't anything to be ashamed of . . . that changed me really'.[26] The alchemy that occurred in his classes remains mysterious, like the achievements of many exceptional teachers, and helps to explain why he is so well remembered by his students of many years ago. 'The warmth and affection past students still have for him is not because of what he has become, but for what he was as a friend and tutor, happy, friendly and helpful, who treated all students as equals'[27]

---

25. Peter Thornton, taped conversation, 28 February 1992

26. Dorothy Greenald, taped conversation, 12 September 1992

27. Dorothy Greenald to PS, 29 September 1992

III

In 1965, two years after the publication of *The Making of the English Working Class*, Edward and Dorothy Thompson moved to the West Midlands. They did so in order that he could take up a position at the newly-established University of Warwick, located on the outskirts of Coventry, as Director of the Centre for the Study of Social History. It was at Warwick, during the years 1965–1970, that he started to supervise the work of research students and it was then that most of the contributors to this volume first met and studied with him.

Research in social history at Warwick began modestly enough, with four postgraduates working with Edward in 1965–66. By the end of the 1960s the Centre for the Study of Social History was a busy and vibrant place; it had attracted a number of students from North America; academic visitors were often present; and a lot of original research was under way. One or two of these research projects were complete or nearing completion before Edward left Warwick in 1970, others were well launched, and others still were just beginning and would be intensively pursued through the 1970s. Much of this research was later published, and the University of Warwick, thanks especially to Edward's initiatives and energies, became highly regarded as a place for lively and creative research into social history.

From the beginning seminars (usually fortnightly) were crucial to the vitality of the Centre for the Study of Social History. Edward established a two-session pattern for scheduling these seminars: a visiting speaker would give a paper in the evening and was often persuaded to reappear at the second session the following morning, when one of the students would present on a subject connected to the visitor's interests. Thus, for example, John Rule was able to receive directly the criticisms of John Saville on his first paper on Cornish Chartism. Invitations to speak at the seminar appear to have been rarely declined. Students and others heard papers from prominent labour historians, including Asa Briggs, Royden Harrison, and Eric Hobsbawm; from important writers in the expanding field of social history, including Richard Cobb, Brian Harrison, Raphael Samuel, and Keith Thomas; and from members of a younger generation of scholars who were researching at other universities, such as Iorwerth Prothero, Gareth Stedman Jones, Eileen Yeo, and Stephen Yeo. The seminars were regularly augmented by the active presence of other historians, including Robin Clifton and Fred Reid, both of the University's History Department; Dorothy Thompson, who in 1968 took up a full-time position at the University of Birmingham; Barrie Trinder, who taught adult education in Shropshire; and David Montgomery, now at Yale University, who for two years was a visiting lecturer at Warwick in American labour history. Many of the regular participants in Warwick's seminars remember them as among the best they have ever attended: as occasions that were intellectually exciting and enriching, and distinguished by a style that was notably inclusive, friendly, and non-hierarchical. Edward's students learned a lot from these seminars, both in substance and in respect of humane values.

One was struck at the time and still is by the range of this intellectual discourse – a diversity that Edward Thompson actively promoted. Some speakers came from outside social history proper, such as Hugh Clegg, a specialist in industrial relations and also a member of Warwick's faculty, sociologist Stuart Hall, and the radio-producer Charles Parker. Occasionally visits were arranged to other places, which allowed the Warwick postgraduates to meet Mabel Ashby (author of *Joseph Ashby of Tysoe*) in her home village of Bledington, Gloucestershire, and to attend joint seminars with the Centre for Contemporary Cultural Studies at the University of Birmingham, the local historians working with W.G. Hoskins at the University of Leicester, and the researchers associated with Max Hartwell at Nuffield College, Oxford. All this was testimony to the quality and breadth of the intellectual experience at Warwick. Some speakers held views that were close to Edward's own, but others emphatically did not.

Studying with Edward Thompson made for some intense experiences. The writing of history was for him a serious and demanding vocation, not to be confused with the limiting notion of a career, with its various symbols of status and advancement. Writing history was a life-enhancing activity. It was done with a deep sense of commitment. It involved a rigorous apprenticeship in method, criticism, craftsmanship, and a study of sources. Good social history – probing history,

attentive history, scrupulously-researched history – was vital
to the health of society. His research students felt strongly
that they were embarking on intellectual missions of
importance.

There were certainly flashes of brilliance in Edward
Thompson's teaching. We remember his penetrating and
clarifying contributions to seminars; his making of imaginative connections between some apparently minor topic that
was under discussion and issues of larger importance; his
arresting statements offered in reaction to some orthodoxy,
statements that pressed the other people present – students,
colleagues – to reconsider what they had thought they had
understood, to think more critically, and to be less intellectually complacent. Such occasions are recalled by most of his
students from the 1960s and early 1970s, and they were often
memorable moments, fixing in our minds fresh vantage points
of interpretation and alternative readings of important texts
or past experiences. At these times his students, mostly men
and women in their early and mid twenties, apprentices to the
craft, felt a sense of creative engagement and excitement in
committing themselves to the study of history and in trying to
make better sense of the past and uncover some of its concealed meanings. Much of this learning had a long-lasting
impact. One of us, Alec Morley, a member of a younger
academic generation who in 1992 was working in South Africa
on development issues, remarked then that 'In my head I
keep hearing Edward Thompson giving his lectures on
eighteenth-century paternalism. His voice inspires me still –
even in this very different place.'

But this acuteness and originality were only a part of
Edward Thompson's presence as a teacher. For he was also
exceptionally attentive, painstaking, and rigorous. He prodded, he encouraged, he advised on sources, he introduced us
to people whom he thought could help our work, he kept in
regular contact, he asked to see our drafts (often before we
wanted to display them). He sent us references that he had
turned up in the course of his own research, which, as well as
being valuable in themselves, often drew our attention to
promising new evidence and archival holdings. A postcard in
his hand to one of us might suggest a lead worth pursuing (a
locality likely to be rich in relevant material, an antiquarian

text that would be worth mining); another of us would get a note mentioning the interesting work of another scholar or a newspaper clipping that referred to some legal case that should be tracked down and studied. For aspiring young historians, working a lot on their own, this was all very helpful and supportive. Edward Thompson demonstrated in all sorts of practical ways a degree of care and concern for the welfare of his students that was truly extraordinary. Perhaps at the time we did not always appreciate in full the remarkable access we enjoyed to his time and his mind. Certainly we, his research students, were less at risk than some of our peers of slipping into a malaise of self-isolation.

Edward Thompson was a marvellous critic of his students' written work, those draft chapters and papers for seminars that we were all obliged to produce. He was a tough critic – often very tough. Some of our most vivid memories are of the comments that most of us received on our early efforts at original historical composition. Actually, 'comments' is too weak as a description. For what he was likely to put in our hands (some of us still retain these documents in our files) were eight, ten, or twelve pages of single-spaced typescript that left little cause for self-satisfaction. He exposed flaws in our arguments, deplored sloppy research and inadequate documentation, pinpointed muddled and defensive thinking, regretted the mechanistic use of good material, and suggested better and more creative ways of marshalling and interpreting our findings. To receive such (as it seemed to the recipients) root-and-branch critiques was not, at the time, the greatest experience. But the criticisms were almost always warranted. They forced us back to the drawing board; they made us return to the archives, or interrogate our sources more thoughtfully, or reconsider our language of explanation, or simply correct certain slovenly tics or self-indulgent scholasticisms of which we had been previously unaware. This was often a humbling experience. It was also salutary. It made us better, more reflective, more probing historians. We were taught a lesson in how to take strong criticism and benefit from it. Over the years we have frequently appreciated the virtue of this constructive severity.

Edward Thompson did not smother his students with his own opinions. He was undogmatic in his guidance, open to new ideas and approaches, wide-ranging and eclectic in his intellectual involvement in the past and the present. Of course, research students were usually drawn to him because of a liking for his political commitments, or a likeminded concern to help create a new social history, or an admiration for *The Making of the English Working Class*. Those who were content with the status quo would probably have sought guidance elsewhere. But the fostering of ideological conformity was not part of his pedagogical brief. His students were to a large extent expected to follow their own muses, to formulate and pursue their own questions, to read widely and work hard, and to eschew inordinate intellectual deference – in short, to find and discipline their own intellectual voices and to make the best of their allotted capacities. There was no party line – though there were, of course, some collaborative enquiries (most notably, perhaps, *Albion's Fatal Tree*, published in 1975), and there was in a general way a common set of historical concerns, sensibilities, and questions concerning social relationships to be explored. But this commonality was sufficiently tolerant and generous to allow plenty of scope for diverse, even divergent, styles and approaches and political engagements, as the research he supervised and (we hope) the contents of this volume serve to demonstrate.

The research culture that Edward Thompson fostered among his students and exemplified through his own conduct was admirably unstuffy and cooperative. His students got in the habit of exchanging findings, passing along references they had come across, and reporting to one another on new books and articles. There was a marked commitment to intellectual sharing. We did not feel that we were competing against each other. Moreover, there was also a sense that our teacher benefitted from – he certainly warmly acknowledged – the work of his students: the new knowledge they produced, the sceptical and unexpected questions they raised, the new perspectives they espoused such as those drawn from feminism. At the University of Warwick and its Centre for the Study of Social History there was a healthy sense of community and mutuality, reinforced by egalitarian premises. Intellectual authority could be earned and was to be respected, but discourse was conducted in a highly democratic mode. Such openness and tolerance, when combined with tactful guidance, permitted apprentices to prosper, though sometimes only after a little painful learning from their own naiveté and mistakes.

Edward Thompson is known largely by his works in the public realm. These works include his books and extended essays, on a wide range of subjects – William Morris, crime, the moral economy, paternalism, William Blake, wife sales, class relations, Louis Althusser, forest economies, early Hanoverian Whigs, the labour movement, libertarian traditions, the Cold War. This literary corpus of historical enquiry and dispute and reconstruction is likely to be read and reread well into the future. Also among his works is his political activism on behalf of several causes, most notably, perhaps, the peace movement in the 1980s. These contributions to public debate helped to call into question some stultifying (and dangerous) ideologies of political animus. They also enlarged his sphere of commentary and influence, in Britain and on the continent especially, the character and significance of which are sure to be accorded future analysis and assessment.

In addition to this much-observed public realm was the intimate community of teacher and students, and it is from this lesser-known realm that the contributors to this volume are drawn. All are former students of Edward Thompson, with one exception (Sheila Rowbotham) students in a formal as well as a looser sense. They are all most emphatically beneficiaries of his teaching, his example, his stimulus and encouragement, his criticism and advice. All are his friends. We came from different backgrounds, had different casts of mind, and have developed in different and not always predictable directions. But there is among us a common sense of intellectual and personal indebtedness; a common sense of good fortune to have been able to work with a historian of such creative powers; and a common desire to offer some suitable expression of our respect and affection. *Protest and Survival* is both a reflection of the breadth of Edward Thompson's interests and testimony to the many corners he has brightened. It is also a token of our appreciation for the importance he attached to teaching and the skill and sensitivity he brought to it. His career as a university teacher, as conventionally defined, was short but impressive, and we who were part of his circle of enquiry wish to acknowledge the impact of his deeds, his words, and his kindnesses.

Chapter Two

An Eighteenth-Century Peasantry

J. M. Neeson

English historians have trouble with peasants: trouble defining them, trouble dating their disappearance, trouble seeing them at all.[1] Currently we argue three cases: England never had peasants; England had them but they disappeared before industrialization; England had them far into the nineteenth century.[2] In this article I want to argue against the first two propositions: England did have peasants; they did not disappear before industrialization. And I want to qualify the third: in common-field England parliamentary enclosures, taking place from the 1760s to the 1820s, reduced the numbers of small landholders, expropriated landless users of commons, and radically transformed the economy and culture both had shared with richer tenants and freeholders. As a result the disappearance of English peasants from common-field England occurred after 1750 but before 1830.

Peasants and Historians

In *Captain Swing*, their study of agricultural labour and rural

1. I am grateful to Cambridge University Press for permission to use here parts of my argument in *Commoners. Common Right, Enclosure and Social Change in England, 1700–1820* (forthcoming, Cambridge 1993)

2. Alan Macfarlane, *The Origins of English Individualism* (Oxford, 1978); J.D. Chambers and G.E. Mingay, *The Agricultural Revolution 1750–1880* (1966); Robert C. Allen, *Enclosure and the Yeoman* (Oxford, 1992); Mick Reed, 'The Peasantry of Nineteenth-Century England: a Neglected Class?', *History Workshop Journal* Issue 18 (1984); Mick Reed and R.A.E. Wells, eds., *Class, Conflict and Protest in the English Countryside, 1700–1880* (1990); and see below.

riot in 1830, Eric Hobsbawm and George Rudé argued that the English peasantry had gone by 1750. Not only did a transition from feudalism to agrarian capitalism not take place in the eighteenth century, but not even so much as a transition from family subsistence cultivation to wage dependency took place then either.[3] Naturally, Ireland was an exception: peasants *did* surviive in Ireland. They survived too in the 'thinly-populated' parts of Wales and Scotland, 'perhaps in parts of Northern England', and in 'local concentrations' elsewhere. But in most of England the rural proletariat was in place by 1750. Any peasants or smallholders hanging on later than this were, in Hobsbawm and Rudé's words, only 'unimportant minorities'.[4]

As evidence for this proposition they cited a rare convergence of opinion between most contemporary historians and Karl Marx. [5] And indeed it is true that, while citing Marx, Hobsbawm and Rudé were at the same time expressing what had become, by the 1960s, the orthodox view of English landed society in the eighteenth century. The ultimate success of this orthodoxy was the work of J.D. Chambers and G.E. Mingay. Although they identified the survival of large numbers of *smallholders* into the mid-nineteenth century, Chambers and Mingay argued that the disappearance of the peasantry occurred before 1760. Thus early in the eighteenth century crippling wartime taxation and low agricultural prices led to debt. Then harvest failure, disease, and the competing attractions of trade and industry accelerated decline. For some time small owners' land had swelled the estates of the great landlords, but the trend became marked in the first half of the century, and again in the depression after the Napoleonic Wars. Mingay fixed the date more firmly in *Enclosure and the Small Farmer in the Age of the Industrial*

3. On an eighteenth-century transition see Charles Searle, 'Custom, Class Conflict and Agrarian Capitalism: the Cumbrian Customary Economy in the Eighteenth Century', *Past and Present* no.110 (1986) pp.106–33. See also Reed, 'The Peasantry', pp. 54–5, 58–9.

4. E. J. Hobsbawm and George Rudé, *Captain Swing* (1969), pp.23, 27, 21; see also Hobsbawm, *Industry and Empire* (1968), p.78.

5. They note Marx's agreement that the landlord/tenant/labourer structure had been established before the start of the Industrial Revolution on p.27, the reference is to Marx, *Werke*, xxiii, p.750.

Revolution: 'The major decline of small owners and of small farmers in general must have occurred before 1760, probably between about 1660 and 1750'.[6]

Coupled with the older work of Johnson, Davies, Gonner and Clapham, Chambers and Mingay, with the help of W.E. Tate, managed to uproot the Hammond thesis that Parliamentary enclosure starting in the second half of the eighteenth century was a major cause of the disappearance of the English peasantry.[7] The popularization of this view was so complete that ten years after *The Agricultural Revolution*, in a discussion of rural social protest from 1700 to 1850, Roger Wells could call it 'an elementary fact in English agricultural history' that the 'vast bulk of the inhabitants of the English countryside since the mid-eighteenth century were landless agricultural labourers and their families'. This view was shared by Corrigan and Sayer, sociologists otherwise aware of the 'remarkable continuities' of English history. It was the view too of Harold Perkin, who considered peasantry to be the antithesis of progress and found none in Britain except on the 'Celtic fringe' where they lived 'still half-immersed in tribalism, dominated by near-feudal or alien landlords . . . and almost without the varied, prosperous, energetic 'middle ranks' which characterized Anglo-Saxon England'.[8] Even

6. Chambers and Mingay, *Agricultural Revolution*, pp.19, 20. Mingay, *Enclosure and the Small Farmer in the Age of the Industrial Revolution* (1968), pp.9, 31–32; the evidence cited came from Mingay's study of estates in Nottinghamshire, Staffordshire, Bedfordshire and Sussex published in 'The Size of Farms in the Eighteenth Century', *Economic History Review*, xiv (1961–2), pp. 469–88.

7. A.H. Johnson, *The Disappearance of the Small Landowner* (1909, new ed. Merlin, 1963); E.C.K. Gonner, *Common Land and Inclosure* (1912, 1966 ed.); J.H. Clapham, *Economic History of Modern Britain*, i (Cambridge, 1926, 2nd ed., 1930, reprinted 1950); W.E. Tate, 'Parliamentary Counter-Petitions during the Enclosures of the Eighteenth and Nineteenth Centuries', *English Historical Review*, lix (1944); Tate, 'Opposition to Parliamentary Enclosure in Eighteenth-Century England' *Agricultural History*, xix (1945); J.L. and Barbara Hammond, *The Village Labourer* (1911, 1966 ed.).

8. Wells, 'The Development of the English Rural Proletariat and Social Protest, 1700–1850', *Journal of Peasant Studies*, vii (1979), p.115, citing J.P.D. Dunbabin, *Rural Discontent in Nineteenth-Century Britain* (1974), p.286. In their discussion of the slow progress of enclosure

K.D.M. Snell, in a vindication of the Hammonds' interpretation of enclosure's 'social effects', remained unsure of the relationship between enclosure and peasant disappearance. His concern was with the 'cottager and other labouring classes'. Apart from a rejection of the Land Tax, which ignored the work of J.M. Martin and Michael Turner, he did not talk about land at all.[9]

And if historians of the eighteenth and nineteenth centuries have described them as centuries without peasants, historians of the seventeenth have assumed that the end of the English peasantry occurred then too. Robert Brenner argued his case for the determining power of class politics in effecting the different development of England and the rest of Europe partly from an assumption that the English peasantry not only lost political power in the sixteenth and seventeenth centuries but also ceased to exist.[10] In part this is due to the way agrarian history has been written as the history of individual villages. Thus in the last twenty years we have read that Terling, Chippenham, Orwell and Kibworth Harcourt all lost their

---

between the sixteenth and the nineteenth, even twentieth, centuries Philip Corrigan and Derek Sayer nevertheless found Wells' article 'very useful'; see *The Great Arch: English State Formation as Cultural Revolution* (1985), p.96, note 9. Another example of the influence of this view is James Obelkevich, *Religion and Rural Society: South Lindsey 1825–1875* (1976), p.25, which cites Hobsbawm and Rudé, *Captain Swing*, Chambers and Mingay, *Agricultural Revolution*, and John Saville, 'Primitive Accumulation and Early Industrialization in Britain', in R. Miliband and J. Saville, eds., *Socialist Register* (1979). Harold Perkin, *The Origins of Modern English Society, 1780–1880* (1969), pp.91, 97: this repudiation of peasantry as an un-English phenomenon almost augurs Alan Macfarlane's *Origins of English Individualism*; on this see Philip Abrams, *Historical Sociology* (Shepton Mallett, 1982), pp.322–25. Finally, Allen, *Enclosure and the Yeoman*, is the latest assertion of a decline before enclosure of family farmers (defined as those holding about sixty or seventy acres), in this case in the south midlands. He is not concerned with the enclosure experience of occupiers of less land.

---

9. K.D.M. Snell, *Annals of the Labouring Poor. Social Change and Agrarian England 1660–1900* (Cambridge, 1985), pp.143–44.

10. Robert Brenner, 'Agrarian Class Structure and Economic Development in Pre-Industrial Europe', *Past and Present*, no.70 (1976), pp.63–64, 70.

peasants early. And we generalize their experience to the rest of England.[11]

If I overstate the case, if I ignore the work of W.G. Hoskins on the peasants of Wigston Magna, a village only a few miles from Kibworth, of Joan Thirsk on the Lincolnshire peasantry, of E.P. Thompson on the history of the field labourers, and of Alan Everitt on farm labourers-with-land, it is because others have done so too.[12] The examples I have given (the most widely-used textbook on the agricultural revolution, an influential study of rural social protest in the early nineteenth century, one of the most provocative recent historical debates, and the most detailed monographs of sixteenth and seventeenth-century lowland English villages) are themselves evidence that the work of Hoskins, Everitt, Thirsk, and Thompson, in this respect, has been bypassed. In Hobsbawm and Rudé's terms they have described the histories of unimportant minorities found only here and there in local concentrations.

And yet there are at least two reasons why we owe the question more attention. First, it is possible to show that a large landholding population *did* survive in much of eighteenth and early nineteenth-century common-field England. Second, a majority of these landholders shared an economy grounded in communal land use until parliamentary enclosure. England may well have had an eighteenth-century peasantry after all.

---

11. Keith Wrightson and David Levine, *Poverty and Piety in an English Village: Terling 1525–1700* (1979); Margaret Spufford, *Contrasting Communities. English Villagers in the Sixteenth and Seventeenth Centuries* (Cambridge, 1974), esp. pp.50, 118, 165–66; Cicely Howell, *Land, Family and Inheritance in Transition. Kibworth Harcourt 1280–1700* (Cambridge, 1983), p.69; see also A.C. Chibnall, *Sherington: Fields and Fiefs of a Buckinghamshire Village* (Cambridge, 1965).

12. W.G. Hoskins, *The Midland Peasant. The Economic and Social History of a Leicestershire Village* (1957), esp. p.215; Joan Thirsk, *English Peasant Farming. The Agrarian History of Lincolnshire from Tudor to Recent Times* (1957), and 'Agriculture and Social Change in the Seventeenth Century', in Thirsk, ed., *Land, Church and People. Essays presented to H.P.R. Finberg* (Reading, 1970), pp.172, 176–77; E.P. Thompson, *The Making of the English Working Class* (1963, 1968 ed.), ch.7; Alan Everitt, 'Farm Labourers', in Thirsk ed., *The Agrarian History of England and Wales, iv, pp.396–465*.

Peasants and Land

More than thirty years ago W.G. Hoskins showed that in Wigston Magna, Leicestershire, on the eve of enclosure in 1765, one third of the population occupied land, and half of the population owned it.[13] But Wigston Magna, though large and located in an area typical of much of the land lying along the borders of Leicestershire, Warwickshire and Northamptonshire, is only one village, and it was enclosed in 1765. It could be a local concentration, and one not surviving much after Hobsbawm and Rudé's mid-century terminus. It seems important then to look at larger numbers of villages and to look at them later in the century.

Until Mingay's criticism of Johnson's use of Land Tax returns was published in the mid 1960s, this would have been a relatively simple thing to do using studies like Johnson's, Gray's on Oxfordshire and Davies' national survey. But Mingay's discovery that different parishes had different tax rates, coupled with Chambers' observation that small owners appearing on the Land Tax after enclosure were untaxed cottagers and commoners before, and more recent criticism, makes using earlier work hazardous.[14] Since then landholding history has necessarily become parish rather than county based, leading to a fragmentation of information that makes generalization difficult. With this in mind I have looked at

13. The number of occupiers was at least 72; when the smallest occupiers were included, 99 families out of 200 owned land, Hoskins, *Midland Peasant*, pp.227, 217–18.

14. E. Davies, 'The Small Landowner, 1780–1832, in the Light of the Land Tax Assessments', *Economic History Review*, 1st series, i (1927); Johnson, *Disappearance of the Small Landowner*; H.L. Gray, 'Yeoman Farming in Oxfordshire from the Sixteenth Century to the Nineteenth', *Quarterly Journal of Economics*, lxiv (1910); G.E. Mingay, 'The Land Tax Assessments and the Small Landowner', *Economic History Review*, xvii (1964); J.D. Chambers, 'Enclosure and the Small Landowner', *Economic History Review*, v (1953); J.D. Chambers, 'Enclosure and the Small Landowner in Lindsey', *The Lincolnshire Historian*, i (1947); J.M. Neeson, 'Parliamentary Enclosure and the Disappearance of the English Peasantry, Revisited', in George Grantham and Carol S. Leonard, eds., *Agrarian Organization in the Century of Industrialization: Europe, Russia and North America*, Research in Economic History, Supplement 5, 1989, Part A, pp.105–7.

landholders in a relatively large number of unenclosed Northamptonshire villages (twenty-three), with a variety of agricultures. And I have looked at them in the late eighteenth and
early nineteenth centuries – a time when, as English peasants,
they should have disappeared.[15]

They suggest that landholding was still relatively common
at the end of the eighteenth and the beginning of the nineteenth centuries in open-field Northamptonshire. In fact,
proportions of occupiers and landlords ranged from a minimum of 22% of the population of a parish to a maximum of
73%. Expressed as a proportion of the total population of
these villages in 1801, landholders were 53%, or, as in
Wigston Magna, roughly half of the population.[16] Largest
proportions occurred in fenland parishes. But if fen parishes
are excluded the proportion of landholders in all the other
parishes falls no further than to 49%, so proportions were
high outside the fens too.[17] The numbers of landholders in
Nene valley parishes, for example, often exceeded half.[18] The

15. The study used Land Tax returns and enclosure Awards to look at the
landholding profiles of about 1100 landholders, holding rather more
than 1100 parcels of land in the period 1778–1815. Fifteen parishes
were randomly selected from total of 54 enclosed between 1778 and
1802. They were located in a variety of clays and loams, mostly given
over to mixed farming, in the valleys of the Nene and Welland, on the
higher land between the valleys, and in or around Whittlewood and
Rockingham Forests. Two more parishes were added in order to look at
the fenland: they were enclosed between 1809 and 1815. The final six
parishes were not enclosed until after 1815; they were selected to match
the agricultural regions represented in the other data. For a discussion
of the use of the Land Tax in this essay see Neeson, *Commoners:
Common Right, Enclosure and Social Change in England 1700–1820*
(forthcoming, Cambridge, 1993), Appendices A, B and C.

16. Total population of the twenty-three villages, using the 1801 census,
was 9087; divided by a (conservative) family size factor of 4.3 this
becomes 2113. Total landholders on the Land Tax returns for the
parishes was 1112, or 53% of the total population.

17. Total population in 1801, excluding the three fen parishes of Eye,
Maxey and Helpston, was 7972 or 1854 families. Total landholding
families was 909 or 49% of the population.

18. They were Wollaston (67%), Hargrave (73%), Stanwick (60%), Lut-
ton (58%). Large proportions were also found in villages on the scarp
(Kilsby, West Haddon, Yelvertoft – other evidence); and in Abthorpe
(69%) and Roade (55%) on the boundaries of Whittlewood and

size of this landed population indicates how deeply landholding was still imbricated in the rural economy. If proportions like these were observed of shoemakers or weavers instead of landholders we would consider the economy to be dominated by rural manufacturing.

The impression of a lasting connection between population and land strengthens when we consider *small* landholders separately. I shall define 'small' to be fifty acres or less, an amount large enough to include family farms providing subsistence, but not the farms of substantial owner-occupiers or large tenants.[19] It is also a category which includes the smallest occupiers and users of common right who were only partly supported by their holdings, and it would include some landed artisans and tradesmen too. Defined like this, small landholders were 35% of the total population; small occupiers were 22%. And these average figures underestimate the degree of sub-50 acre occupancy in a third of the villages in the study.[20]

There are obvious shortcomings in a calculation like this and these figures are offered as no more than very rough estimates. Quite apart from the deficiencies of the 1801 census, numbers of landholders taken from the tax returns may be inflated by the inclusion of absentee landlords and non-resident occupiers. They are deflated by the omission of sub-tenants and some poor owners of less than three acres or so.[21] And they are deflated again because the landholding

---

and Salcey forests. But not all forest parishes were populated by large numbers of landholders: Whitfield and Whittlebury, both in Whittlewood forest, had below average numbers.

---

19. See also R. C. Allen, 'The Growth of Labour Productivity in Early Modern English Agriculture', University of British Columbia, Department of Economics, Discussion paper no.86–40, pp.5–6: Allen suggests here that mixed agriculture farms worked with largely family labour were no bigger than fifty to sixty acres.

20. Total of sub-fifty acre occupiers was 467 (22%); total of sub-fifty acre landlords was 282 (13%). For the range from parish to parish see Neeson, *Commoners*, Appendix D.

21. For the deficiencies of the Land Tax in omitting sub-letting and the poorest owners see Neeson, *Commoners*, ch.2, and Appendix A.

figures of some parishes pre-date the census significantly: the chances are good that their populations had grown by 1801.[22]

Having said that, the Northamptonshire evidence still suggests that there was a substantial number of small owners and occupiers among the roughly fifty per cent of the population who held land in late eighteenth-century open-field villages. And evidence from some nineteenth-century villages corroborates this. Mick Reed has gone so far as to argue that a substantial peasantry survived well into the second half of that century, and that, again, it was not one confined in the outer darkness of the 'Celtic fringe'.[23] And there are other reasons why a peasantry might survive into the nineteenth century: Ian Carter's work on Aberdeenshire describes a Scottish peasantry living into the 1870s in symbiosis with much larger tenants who needed them in order to reclaim land.[24] It should be noted that none of these places was enclosed by Act of Parliament.

Although a substantial *number* of peasants lived in open-field England in the eighteenth and early nineteenth centuries it is clear that they were not the occupiers of most of the land.

---

22. The parishes were Rushden (1774), Bugbrooke (1774), Wollaston (1783), Roade (1786), Wadenhoe (1788).

23. Where this peasantry survived, and the strength of its relationship to labouring families, both need elaboration. Certainly it was smaller than its eighteenth-century counterpart. But it seems reasonable to assume that in areas of unenclosed waste, or in still-open common-field villages where land remained cheap and both landed and landless commoners were numerous, a peasant economy could continue. Bourne's Surrey heathland village survived as late as 1900, George Bourne, *Change in the Village* (1912). Mick Reed, 'Nineteenth-Century Rural England: A Case for 'Peasant Studies'?' *Journal of Peasant Studies*, xiv (1986) pp.78–79 and 'The Peasantry of Nineteenth-Century England'. For the use of common land by nineteenth-century labourers and small farmers see also Brian Short, '"The Art and Craft of Chicken Cramming": Poultry in the Weald of Sussex', *Agricultural History Review*, xxx (1982), p.17. For unenclosed forest commons and their effect on landholding in neighbouring enclosed villages see Neeson, 'Parliamentary Enclosure and the Disappearance of the English Peasantry, Revisited', pp.97–98; for the importance of landless and landed commoners for the working of mutual aid see Neeson, *Commoners*, ch.6.

24. Ian Carter, *Farm Life in North-East Scotland 1840–1914: the Poor Man's Country* (Edinburgh, 1979), pp.52–60.

The rural economy was not primarily a peasant one in 1750 for a number of reasons. First, the middling peasant occupiers of forty to eighty acres were relatively few. Second, the small peasantry that remained, though numerous, did not control a majority of the land. Owner-occupiers and tenants of fifty acres or less usually held no more than perhaps a quarter or a third of all the land in open-field villages. For example, in Wigston a large majority of occupiers (of the order of 75%) held less than fifty acres each, and most worked less than twelve. Together they held a little more than 20% of the land in the parish. In Cumbria the proportion was about a third. In Oxfordshire Gray noted that one third of the county was in the hands of owner-occupiers of all sizes. Hunt calculated that in Leicestershire 32% of the land in forty-four enclosures belonged to small owners.[25] But even these proportions are larger than the ten to twenty per cent sometimes assumed to be general, and would rise were small tenants included.[26] Arguably, proportions were not much smaller than in parts of France at the same time: Arthur Young estimated that one third of France lay in the hands of peasant proprietors in the 1780s.[27]

The evidence from these counties makes it clear that small occupiers did not hold most of the land, although they did

---

25. Hoskins, *Midland Peasant*, p.219: peasant farms of 100a or less comprised 30% of the parish. Searle, 'Custom, Class Conflict and Agrarian Capitalism', p.1; H.G. Hunt, 'Landownership and Enclosure 1750–1830', *Economic History Review*, xi (1958–9), pp.499–501.

26. Citing F.M.L. Thompson's interpretation of Gregory King's figures of income from land Mingay suggests that owner-occupiers received about one third of the income from land at the end of the seventeenth century. His own investigations suggest that 10 to 20% of the cultivated acreage was in the hands of owner-occupiers at the end of the eighteenth century. A rough alignment of income and landownership suggests a fall in landownership or landed income to owner-occupiers of from 30% in the 1680s to 20% or even 10% in the late eighteenth century. Northamptonshire evidence of owner-occupancy in the later eighteenth century suggests that owner-occupiers still held a third of the land or more on the eve of enclosure. Mingay, *Enclosure and the Small Farmer*, pp.13–16.

27. Arthur Young, *Travels During the Years 1787, 1788 and 1789; undertaken more particularly with a view of ascertaining the Cultivation, Wealth, Resources, and National Prosperity of the Kingdom of France* (2nd ed., 1794), i, p.412.

hold more than we have supposed. In terms of productive power, in Northamptonshire, Oxfordshire and Leicestershire, most production came from farms of at least one hundred acres in the hands of tenants or freeholders. But it is equally clear that access to land was not restricted to these farmers. Instead, a substantial proportion of a village held land, fed itself to some degree, and supplied young stock to farmers and food to local markets.[28]

How would historians who describe a relatively peasantless eighteenth century view these commoners? They would argue that, although commoners were more numerous than they had thought, they were not peasants. Instead, they were one of two distinct groups: they were either smallholders, or they were labourers-with-land. In the case of smallholders there is some disagreement about both their numbers and the nature of their economies.[29] The disagreement need not detain us here; what matters is that both agree that smallholders in no way resemble a peasantry in English villages by the middle of the eighteenth century.

They would also agree that the second group, the labourers with land, were more numerous than smallholders. Nevertheless, in their case, *poverty* rules them out as contenders for peasant status. Holding less than a farm, and working for wages, seemingly disqualify small landholders from peasant status in England (though not apparently in Ireland) despite the fact that peasants have often needed multiple sources of

28. On the late survival of peasantry and its coexistence with capitalism in agriculture see the review essay by Harold Newby, 'Rural Sociology and its Relevance to the Agricultural Economist: A Review' *Journal of Agricultural Economics*, xxxiii (1982), pp.141–42.

29. Chambers and Mingay, for example, have argued that although they had declined in the early eighteenth century and could no longer be called a peasantry they were still numerous and were real farmers, if small. Hobsbawm and Rudé, Harold Perkin, J.M. Martin, and others have argued that there were relatively few of them and that they were largely involved in trade, using land only as an adjunct to it. Hobsbawm and Rudé go on to say that these men did not think of themselves as farmers: Chambers and Mingay, *Agricultural Revolution*, pp.88–9; Hobsbawm and Rudé, *Captain Swing*, p.24; Perkin, *Origins of Modern English Society*, pp.91, 97; J.M. Martin, 'Village Traders and the Emergence of a Proletariat in South Warwickshire', *Agricultural History Review*, xxxii (1984), pp.179–88.

income, including wages, from whatever source.[30] Hobsbawm
and Rudé describe a more abject poverty, an independence
that was only precarious, and, again, survival on the meagre
proceeds of labour and the right to keep sheep, pigs, a cow or
some geese on the common waste. Enclosure, when it came,
would administer the *coup de grace*. Dissipating 'the haze
which surrounded rural poverty', it would leave that poverty
'nakedly visible as propertyless labour.'[31]

But the evidence of petty landholding offers a different
view. A large number of families in common-field England
lived, in part, off the income from working or letting very
small amounts of land: at least a third of the population of the
open-field Midlands did so. It seems unlikely that they were
confined to this region alone. Within open-field England the
same kinds of small peasant economies probably stippled the
clays, the loams and downs; and they characterized heathland, forest and fen more thoroughly. Outside the lowlands,
the more plentiful common waste of highland England and
Wales supported more again.

But the question for these historians is 'Were they poor?'
We must forget for the moment that peasants often *are* poor
and instead assess the value of a couple of acres in the
eighteenth century. (If we take as small an acreage as this we
can assume that larger holdings were correspondingly more
useful.)

First, a couple of acres would keep a cow, if the cow could
be bought. A cow in the middle of the eighteenth century cost
anything from forty-five shillings to eight or nine pounds,
depending on quality and age.[32] The cost and risk could be
reduced by sharing cows between households.[33] Calves cost

---

30. Chambers and Mingay, *Agricultural Revolution*, p.88.

31. Hobsbawm and Rudé, *Captain Swing*, p.35.

32. William Squire of Wigston, Leicestershire, left two cows on his death in
    1678 each worth about 45s, Hoskins, *Midland Peasant*, p.308. The cost
    of cows in the middle of the eighteenth century ranged from around £4
    in Cheshire and Lancashire to £5 to £8 or more in Hertfordshire and
    Buckinghamshire, John Broad, 'Cattle Plague in Eighteenth-Century
    England' *Agricultural History Review*, xxxi (1983), p.109.

33. The inventory of Edward Brown of Kilsby made in April 1769 included
    'Part in a Cow' worth three pounds: Northamptonshire Record Office

much less, between one and two pounds each, again depending on age. A calf bought by a farm servant or a labourer could be raised by a neighbour or a friend. Once grown, she could be fed on only an acre and a half of grassland if her owner kept half a dozen ewes to help manure it.[34] With generous commons, in fenland for example, she could survive and give milk on even less. During the winter, hay and straw were expensive fodder, and a cow in calf needed as much as fifteen pounds a day, but cows were turned into the stubble and fallow fields, and they were fed on straw and chaff supplemented with fodder from commons in the shape of furze and browse wood, and all manner of woodland foliage. Rivers provided weed: one Hampshire parson wrote to the *Annals of Agriculture* in 1803, in praise of the weeds in his local river which fed many commoners' cows.[35] Villages near the coast used seaweed – a substance high in calcium and magnesium.[36] Robert Trow-Smith argues that the calving percentages on good medieval farms were 'extraordinarily high', suggesting that 'winter keep for the cow was in fact more adequate than many modern historians . . . would have one believe'.[37] These medieval cows were fed in much the same way as eighteenth-century commoners' cows.

The value of the cow lay in her calves and in the milk she gave. In season, between spring and autumn in each year, she would give anything from under one to three gallons of milk a

Rd(K) 10.

34. Testimony to Henry Pilkington, Poor Law Assistant Commissioner, in 1832, cited in Hoskins, *Midland Peasant*, p.270.

35. The Rev. Willis of Sopley, Hants, 'On Cows for Cottagers', *Annals of Agriculture*, x1 (1803), pp. 555, 564–67.

36. John Seymour, *The Smallholder* (1983), p. 63: 'We do buy fertilizer, but it is organic natural seaweed fertilizer which can be spread on the land to about five hundredweight to the acre, for pastures. The cows can eat it, so you can leave the cows in while you are spreading – unlike the chemical fertilizers where you have to take the cattle off. And if the cows lick at the seaweed they are getting the added calcium and magnesium which they need. The reports from other farmers, who have used it for long periods, are that they get no milk fever or magnesium deficiency; it is staggering.'

37. Robert Trow Smith, *A History of British Livestock Husbandry 1700–1900* (1959), p.117.

day. Owning more than one cow would bring winter milk too if one of them was set to calve after Christmas.[38] In the late eighteenth century Arthur Young put the value of three gallons a day at five pounds a year.[39] In the hungry 1790s Nathaniel Kent put it higher at 3s 6d a week, or £9–2s a year, if the value of the calf was included.[40] A recent estimate of the average yield of poor cows before enclosure suggests an annual output of 330 gallons or 3 cwt of cheese. This is substantial, but even the most conservative estimate (and perhaps the most likely for a cottager's cow) of a gallon of milk a day in season would bring in the equivalent of half a labourer's annual wage. Milk was turned into butter too, and cheese, which was readily sold; the whey was drunk or fed to pigs.[41] Finally, the price of the calf in the autumn would go some way to paying the rent and Land Tax.

But if a cow was too expensive, if its cost could not be shared, or if it died and could not be replaced, a few acres easily supported sheep, which were cheaper to buy than cows, and produced wool, ewe's milk, lambs and meat. Ewes gave milk (one to three pints a day) from the end of lambing to some time in August; then milking ceased, to give the ewes time to strengthen before they went to the ram in late autumn, and at the onset of winter. Lambing began again after

38. B.A. Holderness, 'Prices, Productivity and Output', in G.E. Mingay, ed. *Agrarian History of England and Wales* vi (Cambridge, 1989), p.162; Dorothy Hartley, *Lost Country Life* (New York, 1979), p.102.

39. Howell, *Land, Family and Inheritance*, pp.165–66, cites G. Fussell, 'Four Centuries of Leicestershire Farming', *Transactions of the Leicestershire Archaeological Society*, xxiv (1949), p.164, quoting Arthur Young on Leicester longhorns fed on hay in winter, producing three gallons of milk a day, worth £5 a season. Inferior cows produced less milk hence the estimate here of £2 and up. Howell also notes that in 1623 Gervase Markham reckoned on a gallon a day from Whit to Michaelmas (p.165).

40. Nathaniel Kent, 'The Great Advantage of a Cow to the Family of a Labouring Man', *Annals of Agriculture*, xxxi (1798), p.22: 'setting the profit of the calf versus the loss sustained when the cow is dry'. He assumed a high rent of thirty shillings per acre but still reckoned on a profit of thirty per cent.

41. Holderness, 'Prices, Productivity and Output', pp.162–63.

Christmas.[42] The small common-field breeds were hardy, and thought to eat less in proportion to their size than the larger breeds. They were said to bear extreme hunger with less of a reduction in flesh than the larger sort, and when turned onto poor land would fatten faster.[43]

Livestock may have been the easiest and most profitable way to use a very small acreage, but even strips amounting to as little as two or three acres were sown with barley, rye, oats, wheat, peas and beans, and, increasingly, with potatoes. Small commoners at Maulden in Bedfordshire grew all these and turnips or rape too. Those tithed in 1775 included one who grew two acres each of wheat, barley and beans; another who grew this and two acres of rye and two roods of potatoes. Others grew only an acre each of oats, rye and potatoes.[44] Petitioners against the enclosure of Wilbarston in Northamptonshire, a parish in wood pasture not arable, claimed that their few acres provided 'Bread corn for their severall families' in years of dearth.[45] Cicely Howell has calculated that, to feed itself, a family needed at least twelve acres in south-east Leicestershire in the middle ages. Because corn yields doubled between the middle ages and 1800 as little as two or three acres would provide as much as a third or a half of a family's food, in the mid-eighteenth century.[46] William Pitt,

42. Howell, *Land, Family and Inheritance* (1983), p.166; Hartley, *Lost Country Life*, p.61.

43. Mr Price of Appledore, Kent, in *Annals of Agriculture*, xxxi (1798), p.344; John Morton also noted the hardy small sheep of the Northamptonshire scarp, in *Natural History of Northamptonshire* (1712), pp.9–10; for an opposing view see J. Wedge, *General View of the Agriculture of the County of Warwick* (1794), pp.34–36.

44. Bedfordshire Record Office P31/3/7 (1775); on cereals, vegetables, flax and hemp in the mixed farming of small peasants in Staffordshire see Angus McInnes, 'The Village Community 1660–1760' *North Staffordshire Journal of Field Studies*, xxii (1983) pp.52–53. Even a rood or two was useful: typically half of a labourer's allotment in Flora Thompson's enclosed Oxfordshire village was sown with wheat or barley, Thompson, *Lark Rise to Candleford* (1939, 1973 ed.), p.63.

45. Northamptonshire Record Office: Rockingham Castle MSS. B.7.55, photostat no.752.

46. Howell, *Land, Family and Inheritance*, p.152; Christopher Dyer, *Standards of Living in the Later Middle Ages* (Cambridge, 1989),

the Reporter to the Board of Agriculture for Northamptonshire agrees: four acres would feed a family in the
1790s. This was a substantial contribution to an economy in
which the overwhelming expense was food. And unlike enclosed smallholdings, strips of land in open fields suffered
little dis-economy of scale because they could rely on external
sources of common pasture to some degree.

This is only the beginnings of a description of the value of
even very small acreages to the smallest peasants who also
depended on wage work, those whose seeming poverty has
deprived them of peasant status in the literature. The value of
a couple of acres suggests that this poverty is only relative: it
was far better to hold land, even land burdened with debt,
than not. Moreover, English peasants, whether landholders
or not, had common right too, which brings me to the second
part of the argument.

Peasants and Common Right

At common law common right was the right to share the
produce of land, not the ownership of the soil, but the right to
pasture over it (common of pasture), to cut peat or turf for fuel
(common of turbary), and to collect firewood and repair wood
(common of estovers).[47] But this common law definition
ignores the complexity of local custom and usage. In reality,
on the ground, the range of common produce was magnifi-
cently broad, the uses to which it was put were minutely
varied, and the defence of local practice was determined and
often successful for a time, at least.

The obvious example is the gleaning by women and children of corn and straw from wheat fields after harvest. In

---

pp.127–31, discusses the varied regional productivity of medieval
peasant holdings. Holderness, 'Prices, Productivity and Output',
p.138; Mark Overton, 'Estimating Crop Yields from Probate
Inventories: An Example from East Anglia, 1585–1735', *Journal of
Economic History*, xxxix (1979) p.375. An anonymous correspondent
to the *Annals of Agriculture* in 1799 argued that when well dunged and
fed with lucerne and turnips a two-acre plot in Hertfordshire had
produced 124 bushels and half a peck of barley, xxxiii (1799), p.302.

---

47. *Halsbury's Laws of England*, (2nd ed., ed. Viscount Hailsham, 1932),
    iv, p.531, s.983.

some places they gleaned peas and beans too. Gleaning was a
common practice, universally regarded as a common right.
Indefensible at common law after 1788, in most villages with
some arable fields it survived and prospered nonetheless.
Commentators reckoned that gleaned corn would provide
enough flour for at least a couple of months' bread in the
autumn, usually enough to last till Christmas. In Canterbury
gleaning brought in a 'whole winter's corn'.[48] Long Buckby
gleaners were said to store their gleaned corn up in the
bedrooms when the space downstairs ran out.[49] At Atherstone in the 1760s gleaning was worth fifteen shillings, more
than half a woman's harvest wage.[50] F.M. Eden calculated
that gleaners in Roade, Northamptonshire, gathered enough
corn after harvest to make bread to last the rest of the year,
worth about six per cent of the family's annual income.[51] The
value of this was even greater in the 1790s when flour for a
family cost from five to eight shillings a week. Besides the
corn, the straw could be burnt on cottage hearths, or used to
fire bread ovens, to dry malt or to brew. If long it was turned
into thatch or thrown into stalls and yards to be mixed with
dung and used for manure. Gleaning persisted longer than
any other right or custom. In the 1870s in more than fifty
Northamptonshire parishes the gleaning bell still rang out to
open and close the fields.[52]

---

48. Margaret Baker, *Folklore and Customs of Rural England* (1974), p.162.

49. Anon., 'The Folklore of Long Buckby' *The Library List*, v, no.54
    (January, 1939), Northampton Public Library No.49.

50. Warwickshire Record Office: Compton Bracebridge HR/35: women's
    wages were twenty-five shillings.

51. F. M. Eden, *The State of the Poor* (1797, 1966 ed.) ii, p.547.

52. Anon., 'A Letter from a Vale Farmer to the Editors, On the Disadvan-
    tages of Plowing in Stubble', *Museum Rusticum et Commerciale*, vol.ii,
    lxxii (1764), pp.35–36; on peas and beans see Northants. R.O.
    Fitzwilliam Misc. Vol.746, p.25, November 1722; FH 991, Great
    Weldon bylaws, 1728; Thomas North, *The Church Bells of
    Northamptonshire* (Leicester, 1878), *passim*. For the regulation of
    gleaning see Neeson, 'Common Right and Enclosure', pp.72–75. For
    an explanation of the longevity of gleaning see Peter King, 'Gleaners,
    Farmers and the Failure of Legal Sanctions in England 1750–1850', *Past
    and Present*, no.125 (1989) pp.116–50; cf. Neeson, 'Common Right and
    Enclosure', pp.405–8.

But *uncultivated* commons in forest, fen, heath and even on the smaller wastes of arable parishes, or in the common fields at particular times, are the best example of the variety of advantages, besides grazing, that were won from shared land use. They offered not one but many harvests. They included hazel-nuts and chestnuts, often sold for city markets; herbs for cooking and healing (wild chervil, fennel, mint, wild thyme, marjoram, borage, wild basil, tansy); mushrooms for soups and stews; all manner of young leaves for salads and vegetables (watercress, young hawthorn and nettle, wild sorrel, chicory, salad burnet); crab-apples for cider; elderberries, blackberries, barberries, raspberries, wild strawberries, rosehips and haws, cranberries and sloes for jellies, jams and wines; not to mention rabbits and hares for stews and for sale, or the fish and fowl of fenland villages caught in the autumn when the land was lost under water.

Commons might provide sand for cleaning and turf for fires; furze, reeds and weeds for fodder and litter, and also for firing ovens, bakehouses and woolcombers' pots; and teazles for their combs. They offered bulrushes and flags for baskets, hats and chair-seats, besoms and brooms. There was dry, fallen wood in forests and woodlands for fuel and for charcoal; and, on heathland, a fern harvest for ash to make lye for soap, and a beechmast harvest and acorns for pigs. Commons offered space too, for football pitches a mile long, and for weavers' tenters. They gave wood for walking-sticks and hurdles for folding sheep; wood too for bowls and spoons. Even the loose wool caught on thorn bushes lived again in blankets and suits of clothes.[53]

Despite this abundance, the value of common right in the eighteenth century, like the existence of a small peasantry, is in doubt. Eighteenth-century critics thought it was worth less than regular employment in an enclosed village, though they also said that it was widespread and tenaciously defended. Chambers and Mingay agreed that common right had only limited value and argued that few people enjoyed it. Garrett Hardin theorized that the end of common right was due to its

---

53. For a longer discussion see Neeson, *Commoners*, ch.6.

inevitable overuse, itself a result of sharing property in common. Hobsbawm and Rudé, and Chambers, with their metaphors of hazes and squalid curtains, thought it was better than nothing, but not a lot better.[54]

This interpretation is already under attack: from E. P. Thompson's *Whigs and Hunters* where the successful defence of forest commons is described, from Charles Searle's account of customary tenure in Cumbria, and from Jane Humphries' description of the value of common right to women and children. I want to continue their argument here by looking at common of pasture, the right most supportive of peasant economies; and I want to look at it in the Midlands, an area close to the heart of agrarian capitalism and industrialization.

Common of pasture was the right to graze horses, cattle and sheep in the commonable places of a manor – not only on the common waste but also on the fields in due season, the meadows, the lanes and roadsides and village greens. Most pasture rights were attached to land as *common appendant*, or they belonged to particular cottages as *common appurtenant*.

Can a cash value be put on access to common pastures in the eighteenth century? Some observers thought that it could. When Henry Homer, no defender of commons, assessed their retail value in the late 1760s he put it at a quarter to a third of the rent.[55] Obviously value varied from place to place, and no average figure will do, but Homer did not exaggerate. Here are some contemporary estimates made in woodland, fen, marsh, hill and vale.[56] First, woodland: Mrs Barbara Welch, a

---

54. On eighteenth-century critics see Neeson, *Commoners*, ch.1. Garrett Hardin, 'The Tragedy of the Commons', *Science*, clxii (1968); Hobsbawm and Rudé, *Captain Swing*, p.35; J.D. Chambers, 'Enclosure and Labour Supply in the Industrial Revolution', *Economic History Review* v (1953), reprinted in E.L. Jones, ed., *Agriculture and Economic Growth in England, 1650–1815* (1967), p.117.

55. Henry Homer, *An Essay on the Nature and Method of Ascertaining the Specific Shares of Proprietors, upon the Inclosure of Common Fields. With Observations upon the Inconveniencies of Open Fields, and upon the Objections to their Inclosure Particularly as far as they relate to the Publick and the Poor* (1766, 2nd ed. Oxford, n.d.), p.76.

56. For an overview of village by-laws and a discussion of common rights from domesday to the seventeenth century in the East Midlands, see Joan Thirsk, 'Field Systems of the East Midlands', in A.R.H. Baker

tenant to the Duke of Montagu, estimated the value of her common right in his two hundred-acre wood in 1716 at 'almost one third of the value of the estate'. In other words, in her opinion her lands were effectively one third larger than their actual acreage.[57] In the fenland common right was, if anything, more useful. Common pastures in fen villages were in themselves sufficient for raising a household cow or some sheep, and common pasture rights belonged to resident householders without land as well as those with. Substantial husbandmen there might hold no land at all. The most conservative estimate of value – made by the Cambridgeshire Reporter to the Board of Agriculture – put the right for a cow common in the fen at thirty to forty shillings a year. He thought this was derisory but noted that commoners did not: 'a surveyor would be knocked on the head, that went with a view to enclosure'.[58] Marsh villagers had some of the same advantages. William Stout thought the value of marsh common for his family's sheep worth a quarter the value of the holding:

> My father then could have kept one hundred sheep all summer on that marsh; and about the seventh month yearly the high tides brought the sheep's dung and sea tangle to the side, which was gathered by the Inhabitants, every house at the sand Knowing how far their liberties for gathring extended.[59]

and R.A. Butlin eds., *Studies of Field Systems in the British Isles* (Cambridge, 1973), pp.232–80.

57. Northamptonshire Record Office: Boughton papers W28; also B67 (Brooke of Great Oakley) notes on Robinson's case (n.d. probably 1790s): Ossory calculated the value of field pasture at ten shillings per acre; wood pasture at two shillings per acre or five shillings per head of cattle. Open-field rents were from seven to ten shillings per acre at this time, William Pitt, *General View of the Agriculture of the County of Northampton* (1809), p.38.

58. Spufford, *Contrasting Communities*, p. 165, on the ability to stock without having much land in the fen parish of Willingham which remained a peasant village in the eighteenth century. W. Gooch, *General View of the Agriculture of the County of Cambridge*, cited by Arthur Young in *Annals of Agriculture*, xliii, pp.92–93, discussing Cottenham.

59. William Stout, *The Autobiography of William Stout of Lancaster, 1665–1752* ed., J.D. Marshall (Manchester, 1967), p.67.

Forest, fen and marsh commons such as these were often generous, but hill and vale parishes benefitted from common right too. In Long Buckby on the Northamptonshire scarp the rent of meadow with common right was higher than that of meadow without.[60] Cottage commoners in the Warwickshire village of Atherstone refused compensation of twenty shillings a year each for their commons in the open fields in 1738. They thought they were worth more than a cash payment could cover. They also enjoyed grazing rights over another eight hundred acres of uncultivated common waste. The value of this in the market was the equivalent, in cash terms, of fifteen percent of a labourer's annual income, perhaps more.[61] In practical terms its value was greater because it saved some of the rent of pasture land, perhaps as much as a third of the rent of an average holding. Finally, two examples taken from downland. On the Wiltshire downs Thomas Davis, Reporter to the Board of Agriculture, noted in the early 1790s that the sheep and corn economy of small farmers was devastated when they lost their commons at enclosure because they could no longer keep enough sheep to manure their arable land. And at Bucklebury in the Berkshire downs in 1834 almost two hundred petitioners against enclosure argued that the value of their common was substantial and gave as evidence the fact that 'renters of small pieces of land adjoining the Common' paid rents fifty per cent higher than tenants of farms in the parish because they had the right to common their stock.[62] The value of commons varied across this range of agricultures from a quarter to a half or more of the rental paid for the land.

---

60. Northamptonshire Record Office: SG 235, rental of the lands of Mrs Peyto.

61. On Atherstone see Warwickshire Record Office: HR 35/25 and E.P. Thompson, *Customs in Common* (1992), pp.152–58. R.W. Malcolmson, *Life and Labour in England, 1700–1780* (1981), p.37. I have assumed a generous working year of 250 days at an average one shilling a day.

62. T. Davis (Senior), *A General View of the Agriculture of the County of Wiltshire* (1794), p.80, quoted in J.A. Yelling, *Common Field and Enclosure in England 1450–1850* (1977), p.102; Berkshire Record Office: D/E Hy E9/1, Bucklebury Petition, 1834, 47 were identified as freeholders, 124 as 'occupiers'.

If common of pasture was valuable in as wide a range of locations and agricultures as this then it becomes important to know who actually enjoyed it in the eighteenth century. Was the right to keep a cow rare? And were cottagers with common right few?

Common right was more widely enjoyed than historians have thought. In Northamptonshire, customary court by-laws, presentments and stinting agreements show that all occupiers of commonable land, and all or most householders in forest, fen, and some heathland parishes, enjoyed the right to pasture cows or sheep in the eighteenth century. Pasture rights in common-field arable villages outside the forest and fen were restricted to those with land or cottage rights, but they may have been of little use without land or a cottage close anyway. To pasture a cow here the poorest commoners often had to occupy as much as six to ten acres by the end of the century or to occupy a cottage to which common right was attached. Occupiers with no more than an acre or two might make up any shortfall with a payment of about sixpence an acre. Of course pasture rights for sheep required less land, only an acre per sheep, and sheep were also easy to place with a farmer so even landless labourers could (and did) keep a few. Rights to pasture pigs and geese were rarely tied to land or cottage-holding; they existed where pasture and custom allowed.

I have suggested that a quarter or more of the population of open-field villages in Northamptonshire were small occupiers in the late eighteenth century. It is likely, then, that all of these, even the smallest, were entitled to pasture rights to some degree. But counting numbers of *cottagers* who had access to commons by virtue of their occupancy of a common right cottage is difficult. Whereas rights appendant to land were inseparable from it, those appurtenant to cottages could be bought and sold. So, although cottages with common rights were often a half or a third of a parish's housing stock, and were well provided with grazing rights, they were also vulnerable to tenementisation, to engrossment, to the permanent removal of their rights through sale, and to the separation of the use of their rights from occupancy.

On the face of it there was plenty of scope here for the devaluation of cottage rights long before the late eighteenth century, and with it the dispossession of cottagers themselves. Yet, despite engrossment, these rights were not easily marketable. In several parishes manorial court orders explicitly forbade the separation of occupancy from use: whoever occupied a cottage was alone allowed to stock for the rights. In any case cottages let *with* rights were more valuable to their owners than cottages let *without* them. This is because they brought in higher rents and at the same time remained clearly eligible for compensation at enclosure. Only in royal forests, or on substantially consolidated estates, were these advantages outweighed by the value of ridding the waste of cottagers' cattle by buying up cottages. Finally, evidence of the separation of cottages from their rights is almost always coincident with enclosure, when, because common right was about to end, cottagers began to sell their rights to speculators. There is only a little evidence of earlier separation. Cottage commons were likely to remain intact then, though cottages were bought up by farmers and landlords, and they were often divided to create two or more dwellings sharing the original rights – thereby increasing the number of cottage commoners eligible for right.[63]

Common of pasture was more valuable than contemporary pro-enclosure opinion admitted, and more widely enjoyed than some historians have thought. If it was not everywhere the patrimony of the poorest, it was critically important to the economies of small occupiers. Combined with rents lower than those in enclosed villages, and relatively easy access to land, it gave some independence of prices and wages. Even for landless labouring families it held out some hope for the future: 'an Inability to stock at present', wrote an Atherstone opponent of enclosure, 'does not necessarily imply the same for the future'.[64] In fact hoping for land was in the very nature of commoners, as we shall see.

---

63. For a fully referenced account of access to common right before enclosure see Neeson, *Commoners*, chs.2 and 3.

64. Warwickshire Record Office: HR 35/14, 15.

The Social Meaning of Common Right

I said at the beginning of this essay that there is an historical orthodoxy that the English peasantry had disappeared by 1750 at the latest. I went on to say that the survival of petty landholding and common right into the first half of the nineteenth century might show that this orthodoxy was wrong. Then I added that the survival until enclosure of common right in particular was evidence of a peculiarly peasant economy. I want to return to that point now, looking first at common-field agriculture and village relations and then at reactions to enclosure.

Before enclosure, but not after it, Midland peasant agriculture required co-operation and the protection of common interests. Sharing common pasture and working plots scattered over the length and breadth of a parish each called for collective regulation. Every spring and autumn occupiers made bylaws to set aside pasture, to throw fields open to commonable beasts, to impose stints, to brand the herd and arrange its coming and going, to provide bulls and impound sick animals, and to clear water-courses. They set rotations (and departures from them), they punished trespass and overstocking. They elected officers to enforce the bylaws, and employed pinders and haywards to summarily fine offenders or to bring them to court.

And, although the jurors were almost certainly the most substantial commoners,[65] the interests of the smallest commoners were usually considered: their grazing rights were relatively secure. Thus, when new stints reduced the levels of stocking, juries often aimed them at the larger herds, leaving the smallest occupiers' rights relatively untouched. Equally, they upheld the poorest commoners' rights to fuel or browse wood. Sometimes we can hear common need and the obligations of neighbours in the language of field orders. At Sowe in Warwickshire no man was to bring waggons, carts or any other implements onto any baulk and 'Damnify his Nieghbour thereby'; there would be no riding along any

---

65. For a recent discussion of the Laxton jury see J.V. Beckett, 'The Disappearance of the Cottager and the Squatter from the English Countryside', in B.A. Holderness and Michael Turner, *Land, Labour and Agriculture. Essays presented to Gordon Mingay* (1991), p.65.

baulks except one's own so that no man may 'do his Neighbour Damage'; no grass borders should be left in any of the fields to 'defraud the Common herd'.[66] And in every parish at least once a year commoners heard the words of the Bible make the same point. Rogation – after the Reformation the only procession left in the Anglican calendar – was a progress around the parish boundaries of minister and congregation to give thanks to God for the fruits of the earth and to proclaim 'Cursed be he that removeth his neighbours land-mark' to which all the people should say Amen.[67]

Common-field villages did not house serenely self-regulating democratic communities. Economic and political changes affected the behaviour of open-field farmers, divided their interests, and led them to act independently in all kinds of ways. In some parishes the workings of the land market, or the ability of landlords to consolidate holdings, reduced the number of small peasants to nothing long before enclosure. In others, large owners and substantial tenants may have been more eager than small commoners to innovate and to consolidate land. In still others they may have tried to overstock the commons. The point is that they did not deny common pasture to small occupiers and cottagers. Landlords did not annul leases and raise rents two or three times over in the space of a year; nor did they drive land sales up to record levels. It took a parliamentary enclosure to do all this. Before enclosure the larger owners could (and did) alter the terms of landholding relations in this or that respect, but they could not tear up the contract. This limit to agrarian capitalism favoured the small and middling occupiers most. They took from it vitally-important pasture, some risk-sharing, a sense of common purpose with richer men – however tenuous – , and a tradition of mutual aid. The *social* efficiency of this common-field collectivism is overlooked by historians who consider enclosure's efficiency in narrowly economic terms –

66. Warwickshire Record Office: CR 556/299 (5).

67. H. Crossman, *An Introduction to the Knowledge of the Christian Religion* (S.P.C.K., new ed., n.d.) [pre-1841], pp.64–65. The verse is Deuteronomy xxvii.17, King James version; earlier the words were more specific 'Curseth is he that translateth the bounds and doles of his neighbour'.

measuring only what Keith Snell has called 'growths-manship'.[68]

That commoners recognized their mutual dependence on this shared economy is evident in their reaction to enclosure. I have argued elsewhere than an alliance of small occupiers and landless commoners resisted parliamentary enclosure in Northamptonshire. They contested enclosure Bills with petitions, threats, foot-dragging, the theft of new landmarks, surveys and field books; with riotous assemblies to destroy gates, posts and rails; and with more covert thefts and arson. It is entirely possible that a similar search of estate correspondence, enclosure papers, newspapers and court records would turn up evidence of opposition in other Midland counties too. Opposition was long-lived, successful in impeding and delaying enclosure Bills, and not confined to 'special case' places where common lands were unusually large.[69]

I think we can recognise a shared consciousness in collective action like this. But it is also evident in the forum commoners chose for their resistance. They rarely took their opposition to Parliament, and then only as a last resort. Resistance was intensely, and most successfully, a local matter. This was not due to any restricted peasant world view but rather because commoners saw Parliament itself as part of the problem. In the Midlands its value as a defender of their economy had waned ever since the late sixteenth century when it allowed anti-enclosure statutes to lapse.[70] Peasants,

---

68. On the bonds forged by collective agriculture see Marc Bloch, *French Rural History* (1966), p.180. Eric Wolf emphasizes the dependence of small and middling peasants on mutuality, and their consequent vulnerability, Eric Wolf, 'On Peasant Rebellions', *International Social Science Journal* xxi (1969). See K.D.M. Snell, 'Agrarian Histories and Our Rural Past', *Journal of Historical Geography* xvii (1991), pp.195–203.

69. Neeson, 'The Opponents of Enclosure in Eighteenth-Century Northamptonshire', *Past and Present* no.105 (1984) pp.114–39. Cf. 'In order for enclosure to be undertaken at all, agreement had first to be reached among the owners of the majority of the community's land, and that left the people without property politically isolated', John Bohstedt, *Riots and Community Politics in England and Wales 1790–1810* (Cambridge, Mass., 1983), p.197.

70. On the evolution of parliamentary attitudes to enclosure see D.C.

more than their pamphleteer defenders, knew they mattered very little to the state. At enclosure they understood very well where Parliament stood, and enclosers underlined it: 'It wou'd be tedious to reckon up the inconveniencys of open Fields', they said to Atherstone commoners; 'it hath been long the avow'd sense of Parliament that they are the occasion of frequent Trespasses and disputes and a hindrance to Industry & Improvmts: of Land'.[71] Commoners were up against a Parliament of enclosers and they knew it.

Accordingly, they directed their opposition to the *local* enclosers and couched it in revealing terms. Notions of sufficiency and accusations of greed filled the language of enclosure's opponents. West Haddon peasants argued that their lands supported them well *enough*, that they needed no more; that enclosing itself was a wicked thing, unjust, it could not answer to conscience. It promoted private profit not public welfare. Brigstock commoners accused the Duke of Grafton of unseemly and unnecessary greed. They expected better of him. At Atherstone commoners claimed the purpose of the enclosure was 'to serve the Particular end of two or three Private Persons whereas Lands in Common duely consider'd are as they was first design'd a Benefit to the Publick without Exception'. They asked the Lord of the Manor to act in that spirit and so:

> restore to the Town that peace and tranquillity which your attempt to the contrary has made such Melancholy breaches upon; the more opposite this is to your Interest the more Noble and Generous wou'd be the Sacrifice you make for so valuable a blessing and the higher wou'd it raise you in the esteem and good will of all wise and Vertuous Persons.[72]

Coleman, *The Economy of England* (Oxford, 1977), pp.175–78; on the failure of crown protection in the 1630s see John E. Martin, *Feudalism to Capitalism. Peasant and Landlord in English Agrarian Development* (1983, 1986), pp.144–50. Parliament rejected the last bill to regulate enclosure in 1656.

71. Warwickshire Record Office: H35/11 'Answer to the Paper of Grievances' n.d., probably 1760s; *Northampton Mercury*, 20 Jan. 1777; Berkshire Record Office: D/EHy08/1 'The History of a Secret Committee' [n.d. c. 1768].

72. Warwickshire Record Office: HR 35/15, beginning 'We have before us a Paper entitled the Inclosure Vindicated . . . .'; HR 35/14 'Some Observations upon a Paper entitled The inclosure Explain'd and

Commoners continued a dialogue with enclosers that was older than the present crisis. They expected to be heard.

I have said that the expectation sprang in part from the negotiation and argument of daily routine in common-field agriculture – the constant dealing of neighbours working the same land. But surely the expectation was shared by those who were not yet commoners too. Farm servants and day labourers who were children of commoners expected to become commoners themselves. Others who stood little chance of inheritance perhaps hoped to get land or rights through saving, skill or good luck. In the meantime they behaved as if this was likely: they lived in hope. George Cornewall Lewis noticed this living-in-hope when he described Irish labourers in the early nineteenth century as men who worked on the assumption that they would have land at some point: 'though they may not have a present, yet they have a future interest in the matter; though they may not be personally concerned, yet their kinsmen and friends and fellows are concerned.' Fewer English labourers could be as certain of land as the Irishmen Lewis described, but in common-field villages more looked forward to it than we have allowed.[73] Their 'future interest' made commons their business. It made an attack on common right more difficult: it had to withstand the resistance of commoners *and* those who would become commoners. Not only commoners' spoke on common right's behalf: their children and neighbours did too.

This web of connection could have some eminent threads woven into it. In early seventeenth-century Orwell Margaret Spufford noted that the prosperous and poor sides of families did not drift apart:

Vindicated'. See also Everitt, 'Farm Labourers', pp.439–40, for examples of sixteenth-century gentry willing to go to law to defend their labourers' commons.

73. George Cornewall Lewis, *Local Disturbances in Ireland* (1836), p.188, I am grateful to Dorothy Thompson for this reference; and see D. Walker, *General View of the Agriculture of the County of Hertford* (1795), pp.52–53 describing a village in which very few cottagers could afford to buy a cow: 'if the cottager cannot purchase now he cherishes the hope that he may be able to purchase thereafter'; and Beckett, 'The Disappearance of the Cottager and Squatter', p.66, for the conclusion that labourers in Laxton climbed the 'farming ladder' until the 1950s.

There seems to have been a close family network, and a remarkably unexclusive amount of give-and-take between cousins, one group of whom were acquiring plate, books, university education, and ex-monastic lands, and the other group of which were continuing to live in Orwell on between fourteen and thirty-five acres apiece.

Similarly at Wigston on the eve of the eighteenth century gentry families were related to peasant farmers and even cottagers.[74] Here is another reason why juries protected small commoners' rights, why they allowed the local poor to glean but not the certificate poor from outside, why the landless as well as the landed signed counter-petitions, why some gentlemen supported them too, and why labourers as well as landowners pulled down fences.

Kinship and sharing the same fields and commons in as intimate a way as common-field agriculture demanded, probably discouraged overt displays of social difference too. Clothes, houses, language and leisure divide or unite people of different wealth and social standing. But when farmers dressed as plainly as husbandmen and put pewter on their tables not silver, when their wives and daughters worked with other women, and when they ate with their labourers and servants at the same table every day, and drank too, when contact was as regular and as personal as this perhaps a sense of obligation and connection was there too. Clare's poem *The Parish* describes the polarization at enclosure of labourers and the landed; in particular he describes the decline of farmers like Ralph Wormstall, 'a very rich plain and super-stitious man'. Clare remembered his thrift (he went to market himself, sold even the apples and pears from his orchard when he had a bumper crop, and after forty years still wore his wedding suit every Sunday) but he also remembered his meticulous observation of ceremony:

he was always punctual in having the old bowl of frumitory at sheep-shearing ready in time for the shepherds suppers and never let the old year go out without warming the old can of ale for the ringers well pepperd with ginger and he woud always have his Yule cake cut at Twelfth night for the Morris dancers to taste of with their beer let the old dame mutter as she might he always got the fattest goose for Christmass and a couple of the best ducks in the yard for lammass tide and he kept

74. Spufford, *Contrasting Communities*, pp.111, 299; David Cressy, 'Kinship and Kin Interaction in Early Modern England', *Past and Present*, no.113 (1986), pp.50, 68; Hoskins, *Midland Peasant*, pp.199–200.

almost every Saint day in the almanack with an additional pitcher after dinner and another pipe at night with the Vicar which he called 'honoring the day'[75]

Clare remembered him after enclosure when the customs he honoured survived in a changed social setting, and on a short lease, but the same celebrations (and more) occurred before enclosure in a village full of commoners. To Christmas, Twelfth Night and Lammas they added beating the bounds, feasts at the division of lot meadows, and the hundred smaller and more private occasions when labour was shared and rewarded with food, drink and evenings spent together.[76] Village celebrations were acknowledgments that wages alone could not pay for labour. They brought together those with very little land or commons and those with the lion's share. They mediated an otherwise strictly economic relationship. They made it harder to dance with people on Saturday night and overstock their common pastures on Monday morning.[77] After enclosure the occasions for celebrations like these declined. It is not surprising that complaints of superciliousness among the farmers grow strongest at the end of the eighteenth century and in the first decades of the nineteenth. Doubtless they were the bitter fruits of dearth

---

75. John Clare, in *Selected Poems and Prose of John Clare*, ed. Eric Robinson and Geoffrey Summerfield (Oxford, 1967), p.28.

76. The division of Warkworth lot meadows was marked by a weekend-long feast, Thirsk, 'Field Systems of the East Midlands', p.248, citing John Bridges, *History and Antiquities of Northamptonshire* ed. P. Whalley (Oxford, 1791), i. p.219; commoners from several parishes rioted against Warkworth's enclosure, *Northampton Mercury* 16 Sept. 1765; Public Record Office, London, War Office papers 4/7, pp.420–21 (I am grateful to Bernice Clifton for this reference). On smaller celebrations marking the sharing of labour see Hugh Brody, *Inishkillane. Change and Decline in the West of Ireland* (1973, 1986 ed.), pp.27, 134.

77. This is not to deny social hierarchy, rather to describe how its unequal power relations were managed in a society sharing commons, cf. Beckett, 'The Disappearance of the Cottager and Squatter', p.65. Celebration had other functions too, of course; see R.W. Malcolmson, *Popular Recreations in English Society 1700–1850* (Cambridge, 1973), pp.83–84.

and the denial of moral economy, but they came too from the experience of parliamentary enclosure.[78]

By the middle of the eighteenth century any kinship between gentry, yeomen and commoners may have failed. In Northamptonshire the absence of middling farmers of sixty to a hundred acres is striking, and those who did survive often supported enclosure when it came.[79] But there is little reason to think that the kinship of smaller peasants and labourers changed. Moreover, related to them or not, they still shared a history of collaboration with the very men who would decide to enclose the village, a history of past favours, common interests and daily routines. We can see this when commoners reminded gentry that they had stood together against common enemies, or reminded them of their obligations: for example Brigstock commoners' terse assertion that:

> antient rights given to the Poore for the generall good of a Towne ought to be safely preserved & keept to their owne proper use and uses but not to be perverted by the richer Sort of ye same to private Ends and Sinister Respects.[80]

But collaboration transcended mere emergencies; it was a way of life. Commoners collaborated with 'the richer Sort' not only for a particular, finite end – a piecemeal enclosure or the removal of the lord's flocks from the common, for example – but as a general insurance policy. They worked at building a connection, a mutuality that emphasized common interests. How they did it is no more than suggested here but common-field agriculture, sharing common waste, living-in-hope of getting commons or land, kinship, ceremony and celebration were important parts of it, together with an assertive local

---

78. John Clare 'The Parish: A Satire' in *Selected Poems* (Everyman ed., 1965) pp.140–67. For a defence of the historical specificity of both nineteenth-century ballads and pastoral poetry see Alun Howkins and Ian Dyck, 'Popular Ballads, Rural Radicalism and William Cobbett', *History Workshop Journal* issue 23 (1987), pp.22–23, and John Barrell and John Bull, *Penguin Book of English Pastoral Verse* (1974, 1975, 1982 ed.), pp.380–81; as an example of the decline of celebration see the prosecution of mop and pail day at Rushden in 1846, *Northampton Mercury* 23 May 1846, which provoked the complaint that 'We shan't be allowed to play at marbles next'.

79. Neeson, 'The Opponents of Enclosure', p.132.

80. Northamptonshire Record Office: Box X360.

consciousness, the provision of skilled and timely labour, and votes.[81] Even a lord's duty to keep a bull for the commoners' cows, or to contribute to the ale the jury drank after the court adjourned, was a point of contact that could be turned by commoners into a relationship of obligation.[82]

This explains why, as enclosures went through and protest letters and petitions were ignored, the tone of opposition changed. There is increasingly about it a sense of the violation of expected behaviour, an accusation that the customary rights and needs of commoners had once been acknowledged but were now denied. 'Where is *now*', ran a letter sent to the Marquis of Anglesey, 'the degree of virtue which can resist interest?'

> . . . Should a poor man take one of Your sheep from the common, his life would be forfeited by law. But should You take the common from a hundred poor mens sheep, the law gives no redress. The poor man is liable to be hung for taking from You what would not supply You with a meal & You would do nothing illegal by depriving him of his subsistence; nor is Your family supplied for a day by the subtraction which distresses his for life!. . . . Yet the causers of crimes are more guilty than the perpetrators. What must be the inference of the poor? when they see those who should be their patterns defy morality for gain, especially when, if wealth could give contentment, they had enough wherewith to be satisfied. And when the laws are not accessible to the injured poor and Government gives them no redress?

But the Marquis was unmoved and from Uxbridge House he announced the end of dialogue:

> Excepting as to the mere fact of the Inclosure, the forming of which no one has a right to contest, All your statements are without foundation &

---

81. On voting behaviour and its reward in Whittlewood and Salcey forests, see John Edward Linnell, *Old Oak: the Story of a Forest Village* (1932), pp.89–90.

82. Ian Carter notes the same in Aberdeenshire: 'a systematic blurring of class lines was a central element of peasant defensive tactics, and hence an important element in the culture generated by that peasantry', *Farm Life in North-East Scotland*, p.5. The relationship worked both ways of course, especially at enclosure: when, at the second attempt to enclose Atherstone in the 1760s, the commoners asked Justice Littleton of Tamworth to intercede on their behalf he wrote to the enclosers that he would put *their* side of the case to the commoners, though privately, for if he did so publicly he would lose the commoners' trust, Warwickshire Record Office: HR 35/19, 22.

as your language is studiously Offensive I must decline any further communication with you.[83]

At Atherstone commoners asked:

What must we think of those who can Cloak themselves with Indifference and Neutrality while an affair of such importance to the said Town is depending what must we look upon those to be who byass'd by some sinister and selfish ends and views will give their vote for such an Inclosure?[84]

And at Ashill in Norfolk:

you have often times blinded us saying that the fault was all in the Placemen of Parliament; but now you have opened our eyes, we know they have a great power, but they have nothing to do with the regulation of this parish.[85]

The call to remember the old peasant community went unheard. John Clare's poetry is full of fury at the repudiation of customary expectation, the denial of connection between the strong and the weak: he called it 'the kindred bond'. His charge to the enclosers, the 'petty tyrants', the 'spoilers', was that they were turning their backs on the major part of the village. He wrote, 'Old customs usage daily disappears'. Another poet agreed and took as his example the end of celebration: 'Feast of the happy Village! where art thou?', wrote Ebenezer Elliott,

Phsaw! thou wert vulgar – we are splendid now.
Yet, poor man's pudding – rich with spicy crumbs,
And tiers of currants, thick as both my thumbs, –
Where art thou, festal pudding of our sires? –
Gone, to feed fat the heirs of thieves and liars.

Much later, a peasant in another village put it this way:

---

83. Staffordshire Record Office: D603/K/16/104, C. Landor to the Marquis of Anglesey 26 Apr. 1824, and 3 May 1824 Anglesey to the Rev. C. Landor.

84. Warwickshire Record Office HR 35/14; see also *The Case of the Major Part of the Owners and Proprietors of Lands in the Common Fields, Commonable Cow Pasture, Common Meadows, Lammas Grounds, and Waste Grounds, of Sympson, in the County of Bucks.*, Goldsmith's Library, 1770 fol.

85. Public Record Office: H.P. 42.150, Anonymous letter enclosed in the Rev. Edwards to Sidmouth, 22 May 1816.

Do you know . . . what the trees say when the axe comes into the forest?. . . . When the axe comes into the forest, the trees say: 'Look! The handle is one of us!'[86]

Perhaps peasant consciousness, lived daily in the routines and expectations of common-field agriculture and common right, was never so well-expressed as when peasant economy and society was in the process of being extinguished.

To conclude: we may have to call a substantial proportion of eighteenth-century English society peasants. This is not sentimental.[87] On the contrary, it defines a large part of rural England more accurately. It frees it from the marginal, minority status associated with terms like poor cottagers, or labourers-with-land, or smallholders. The first two are terms which define only the poorest parts of the peasantry, and ignore their connection to those with a bit more land, to whom they were related, with whom they shared common right and a common agriculture. It ignores the stages in a peasant's life, from farm servant or labourer to husbandman. It disregards the effect of relatively easy access to land on this kind of mobility. Unless we recognise the connections between small and very small landholders, the poorest commoners remain no more than a proto-proletariat, a stage in a process, only two-dimensional, and the larger commoners became 'smallholders' with all the sense of apartness and individualism so inappropriate to common-field villages.

Calling eighteenth-century common-field landholders and landless commoners peasants would also acknowledge that relatively easy access to land, common right, and common-field agriculture, provided the determining framework of their social relations and their way of life. Land and common right came first. They were considered the most desirable, most satisfactory basis for a living. Agricultural labour or rural trade and manufacture enhanced or even enabled this economy to continue, but land itself came first. Long after

---

86. John Clare 'Remembrances', in Robinson and Summerfield, eds., *Selected Poems and Prose of John Clare*, p.175; 'The Parish', in Elaine Feinstein, ed., *Selected Poems of John Clare* (1968) p.70, line 845; Ebenezer Elliott, 'The Splendid Village', in Barrell and Bull, eds., *Penguin Book of English Pastoral Verse*, p.421 (my italics); John Berger, 'Boris is buying horses', *Once in Europa* (1983), p.69.

87. Mingay, *Enclosure and the Small Farmer*, p.10.

enclosure had created compact farms, and renting more than an allotment had become almost impossible, labourers still felt a longing for land. Well into the second half of the nineteenth century, in Edward Thompson's words, 'the ground-swell of rural grievance came back always to access to the *land*'.[88]

Finally, the survival of this peasantry until enclosure in many common-field villages also helps establish the social meaning of parliamentary enclosure in more dramatic terms than the orthodox version of a much earlier peasant disappearance allowed. Between 1750 and 1820 20.9% of England was enclosed by Act of Parliament, or some 6.8 million acres; as a proportion of agricultural land the area was much greater, perhaps 30% of the total. Moreover, in the midlands, enclosure affected the most densely populated rural areas.[89] It was no small event; it affected large numbers of men, women and children who lived and worked in what was still the largest sector of the economy – agriculture. Ann Kussmaul and Keith Snell have argued that enclosure seriously disrupted the employment patterns of farm servants, labourers and women.[90] Now it is clear that enclosure transformed the customary economies of occupiers and cottage-commoners as well. Moreover, enclosure was an institutional or political intervention. No other attack on common right succeeded as well as enclosure. No other means could be found to raise rents as far

88. Thompson, *Making*, p.253, and a sense of time itself came out of the changes enclosure brought: 'Times used to be better before Bledlow was enclosed'; Malcolm Chase, *The People's Farm: English Radical Agrarianism 1775–1840* (Oxford, 1988); Snell, *Annals*, p.12, on letters from rural emigrants: 'After the family, almost every letter voiced another major concern – land.'

89. Michael Turner, *English Parliamentary Enclosure* (1983), p.32. Hoskins suggests that perhaps half of the arable land in England in 1700 later came to be enclosed by Act, W.G. Hoskins, *The Making of the English Landscape* (1955, 1970), p.178. A more recent sample of 10% of the enclosure Awards in England estimates a total of 7.25 million acres enclosed by Act. Of this 61% was common waste but in the midlands roughly 75% was common arable, John Chapman, 'The Extent and Nature of Parliamentary Enclosure', *Agricultural History Review*, xxxv (1987), pp.28–30.

90. Ann Kussmaul, *Servants in Husbandry in Early Modern England* (Cambridge, 1981), pp.15, 120–1; Snell, *Annals*, ch.4.

or as fast. Enclosure, sanctioned by law, propagandized by the Board of Agriculture, and profited in by Members of Parliament, was the final blow to peasants in common-field England. The result was a memory of expropriation that informed, legitimized, and sharpened the class politics of nineteenth-century villages.

Chapter Three

The Laws of God and the Laws of Man: Lord George Gordon and the Death Penalty

Douglas Hay

The Crisis of the 1780s

In a few decades, between about 1780 and 1820, there was a marked erosion of sacral significance in English criminal law.[1] The word sacral itself was invented about a hundred years ago by the anthropologists, and it has some advantages over other words (sacred, divine, religious) in denoting the awe, mystery, and power of what is meant to be revered, and thus marked by ritual observance.[2] I shall use the word in considering some central mysteries of monarchy, and of law. The focus is an important trial that took place in 1787. Lord George Gordon, a younger brother of the fourth Duke of Gordon, was already notorious for his role as a Member of Parliament in the events leading to the great 'Gordon riots' of June 1780.

---

1. Passages in this article appear also in my forthcoming book, in which I consider the argument for the longer period. I wish to thank E.P. Thompson, J. M. Neeson, Nicholas Rogers, Christopher Hill, Robin Clifton, and the Colloquium on Punishment held by the Society of Fellows in the Humanities, Columbia University, in May 1990, for comments; and Evelyn Bogie, Norma Eakin, Laird Meneley, Carey Nieuwhof, Ruth Paley, Marianne Rogers, and Earl Stuart for assistance in obtaining materials.

2. 'Of or pertaining to sacred rites or observances'; F.W. Maitland used the term in connection with trial by battle. *Oxford English Dictionary*; *Social England*, ed. H.D. Traill and J.S. Mann (London, 1901), vol. 1, p.415.

Seven years later the Attorney General prosecuted him for a new outrage: criticizing the capital statutes and their administration by the judges, in a pamphlet that argued that both were in contempt of the law of God. Gordon was convicted and sentenced to imprisonment, with a requirement for sureties so enormous that his sentence became one for life. He died in Newgate of typhus in 1793, a convert to Judaism, and a believer in the Revolution.

The significance of his political trajectory and his punishment is that Gordon was one of the last to voice a very old critique of the death penalty, one which was particularly threatening to the state in the late 1780s. Gordon conjured with the laws of God, in a tradition reaching back four centuries, and in a manner profoundly disturbing to those in power. His radically religious attack on the death penalty tested the connections between monarchy, capital punishment, religious justification, and social inequality. The libel expressed not only Gordon's own obsessive preoccupations, but also beliefs and attitudes widespread among the London poor. His trial focuses our attention on the sacral meanings of the criminal law, to both its supporters and its most radical critics. It also may mark the last period in which such meanings had wide currency. Utilitarian arguments dominate the discourse of defenders of capital punishment from the 1780s, and within a few decades of Gordon's death the parliamentary attack on capital punishment now familiar to us had supplanted most religious arguments. Bentham and those associated with him set out to disinfest man's laws of sacral mysteries altogether, and largely succeeded.[3] Gordon's trial thus stands at an intersection of different spheres of understanding about justice, religion, and law. It is not a coincidence that his trial took place during the greatest crisis in the administration of justice in the eighteenth century.

The mid-1780s occupy an unusually significant place in the history of capital punishment in England. Both the rate and the absolute number of executions for theft were the highest in the eighteenth century. The hanging of a considerable

---

3. The masculine form seems appropriate, and not only from contemporary usage: most convicts and most prosecutors, and without exception all electors, legislators, magistrates, jurymen, lawyers, judges, and monarchs in this period were male.

number of adolescents who had participated in the Gordon riots in 1780 aroused both contemporary comment and the fear (in Burke, among others) that too many executions would harden the hearts of the mob and provoke resentment rather than awe.[4] But the number of executions in London and Middlesex in 1780, for riot and more ordinary crimes, was dwarfed by the numbers in almost every later year of that decade. There was a continuous increase from 1782, and in 1785 there were twice as many hangings as in 1780. On the Home circuit, the next largest jurisdiction, there were four times as many as in 1780. In those two jurisdictions alone, London and its nearest counties, almost 150 people were hanged in 1785. These numbers were unprecedented in living memory: there had not been so many hangings in England since some time before the beginning of the eighteenth century. Most important for the argument that follows, 85% of the executions throughout the country were for offences against property. That proportion was higher than it had been at any time in the preceding thirty years.[5]

There were some clear institutional reasons for this pattern.[6] The usual post-war increase in crime appeared after the end of the American war and was exacerbated by dearths in 1782–3 and 1787. Very high committal rates generated high numbers of death sentences. But the number of executions was being determined also by a greater propensity of the judges and the government and the King to let condemned men and women hang, rather than save them through pardons conditional on transportation. We know that they did so in part because the jails were filled to overflowing: in the absence of transportation, due to the American war and before the first fleet left for Australia in 1787, more hangings made sense to the judges partly as deterrence, partly as an administrative necessity. At this juncture, a sense of both crisis and opportunity prompted or made more prominent

---

4. Cited in Hay, 'Property, Authority and the Criminal Law', in D. Hay, P. Linebaugh, E.P. Thompson, *Albion's Fatal Tree: Crime and Society in Eighteenth-Century England* (New York, 1975), p.50.

5. The statistical basis for these figures, the sources, and the material in the following paragraph appear in my forthcoming book.

6. See also J. M. Beattie, *Crime and the Courts in England, 1660–1800* (Princeton, 1986), ch. 10.

some of the best known Georgian polemics on capital punishment. Among those published within a few months, at the height of the crisis, were the arguments of the Reverend Martin Madan, demanding more executions; Sir Samuel Romilly's reply; and Archdeacon William Paley's celebrated discussion of the functioning, and functionality, of the death penalty in England.[7]

All were cast in rationalist terms, and largely within the same field of discourse: deterrence, humanity, the intentions of the legislature, the practices of the judges, the possibilities of reform. Paley's, the best-known justification for the existing system, was a persuasive argument about the assumptions of legislators that probably best represents the reasoning of conservative contemporaries: that many crimes were punishable by death not because many criminals would be so punished, but so that if circumstances required, they could be; that the deterrence of the many required the sacrifice of a few. Romilly was anxious to urge replacement of capital punishment by imprisonment, and to defend the judge's use of mercy. He did so because he was answering the Reverend Martin Madan, who had criticized judicial discretion and pardons as policies that weakened the impact of necessary terror. Although two of the three were clerics, all were lawyers or men who had been interested in the law. Their arguments have a modern ring; we share their universe of debate.

The two divines had no doubts about the place of capital punishment in English jurisprudence, and in this they were certainly representative also of the great majority of Anglican clergymen. A recent summary of the language of men of the cloth over a century of assize sermons, and polemical writings, identifies both a (predominantly Anglican) defence of

---

7. Martin Madan, *Thoughts on Executive Justice, with Respect to our Criminal Laws* . . . (1785); Samuel Romilly, *Observations on a late Publication, Intituled, Thoughts on Executive Justice* (1786); William Paley, *Principles of Moral and Political Philosophy* (1785), Book VI, ch. 9. In general, see Leon Radzinowicz, *A History of English Criminal Law and Its Administration from 1750* (London, 1948), vol. 1, for summaries, although important points are ignored, and the interpretation is misleading.

capital punishment, and (more tentatively) a rationalist dissenting critique.[8] It is a suggestive survey of one of the chief sources of justification for punishment in English society in this period, but because it creates a general account from writings spread over roughly the century 1720–1820, it is less sensitive to the degree to which each of these productions, as well as upholding a general idea, was also part of an historically specific polemic. Apart from an attack on the notion of hell in the 1740s and an eruption and then decline of controversy in the 1790s, the chronology is unclear.[9]

Reading many of the clerical justifications for the existing law, whether as assize sermons or in the pages of Paley and Madan, who were apologists for the system of capital punishment, or even reading Romilly's essay of 1785, it is easy to forget that something unprecedented for the eighteenth century was happening in these years. The flesh and blood context of these reasonable texts was hundreds of public hangings – nearly 300 in London alone in the years 1784–87 – almost all of them for offences against property. The spectacle of state-decreed death was enhanced by the sufferings of one of the last women burned at the stake, Phoebe Harris, who died in 1786. And by January 1787 hundreds of convicts awaited transportation on the first fleet to Botany Bay, which would take them to the uttermost ends of the earth. The language of the classic texts of the mid-1780s expresses little of the pain, suffering, fear, despair, insolence, defiance, repentence, expiation, wild hope, and agonized death, enacted in the criminal courts and the teeming jails and prisons, and on the gallows. Those emotions were suddenly given voice in 1787 in a quite different kind of religious text: *The Prisoners Petition to the Right Honourable Lord George Gordon, to*

---

8. R. McGowen, 'The Changing Face of God's Justice: The Debates over Divine and Human Punishment in Eighteenth-Century England', *Criminal Justice History*, vol. 9 (1988), pp.63–98; McGowen, '"He Beareth Not the Sword in Vain': Religion and the Criminal Law in Eighteenth-Century England", *Eighteenth-Century Studies*, vol. 21 no. 2 (1987–8), pp.192–211.

9. A decline in the later 1790s might be explained by the sudden drop of capital prosecutions on the outbreak of war in 1793.

preserve their Lives and Liberties, and prevent their Banishment to Botany Bay.[10]

'Lord George Blaze', Incendiary

Polite opinion concurred with the judgement of the *Gentleman's Magazine* on Gordon's pamphlet: 'a farrago of vague reasoning, and absurd reference, interlarded with a great number of Scripture phrases.'[11] Its main argument was that the word of God showed conclusively that He did not sanction death for theft; rather, the Old Testament explicitly prescribed restitution.[12] If the text seemed to some gentlemen to be eccentric in the extreme, Gordon's behaviour in producing it was no less so.[13] Pondering a small theft by one of his own servants, he had looked into the law of God and discovered the discrepancy with the capital statutes of England. Since the latter appeared not to deter thieves, he tried to talk to Lord Mansfield, the Lord Chief Justice. He was not admitted, but Mr Justice Gould of Common Pleas breakfasted with him, and, according to Gordon, with tears in his eyes suggested that Gordon write down his sentiments, for the judges were bound by the existing law of the land.[14]

Gordon made frequent visits to Newgate, in October, November and December 1786, asking to be admitted to talk

10. London: Printed by Thomas Wilkins, no. 23 Aldermanbury, 1787; hereafter *Petition*. I have used the copy filed with the Treasury Solicitor's prosecution brief, Public Record Office (hereafter PRO), TS/11/388.

11. Vol.61, p.531. Compare *The Times*, 13 Nov. 1786, commenting on his statements in 1780: 'a farrago of scriptural perverted dogmas.'

12. *Petition*, pp.20–21: 'Let not our blood fall to the earth before the face of the Lord for the pardonable trespasses of thievery, for which the Saviour does not require our blood. . . . A true law hath the Almighty given to his people, by the hand of Moses his servant, the faithful in his house.'

13. Unless otherwise noted, the following account is from the evidence given at trial: 22 *State Trials* 175–209; PRO TS 11/388; *The Times* 4, 9, 12, 17, 24, 26 Jan. 1787.

14. Gould himself used passages from Leviticus to justify gleaning and to favour the poor in a dissenting judgement the following year: below, n.122.

with the condemned convicts, and engaging the turnkey in debate about the capital statutes. He asked, 'Don't you think it is cruel that so much blood should be spilt?' 'Don't you think it is very hard so many should suffer?' He argued 'that it was too much to take away the life of any man for being guilty of shoplifting, stealing or any such trifling offences': 'No man ought to suffer death without he spilt blood.' He was refused permission to talk to the prisoners. Once the pamphlet was written, his footman appeared at Newgate with copies for the two chief turnkeys and Mr Villette, the Ordinary (chaplain) of the prison. One copy was given to the sheriff, who passed it to the Attorney General. Gordon then sent two persons to try to take copies into Newgate; they failed to gain entry, and gave them out to passersby at the entrance to the prison.

This episode, striking as it is, with a brother of one of the wealthiest peers of the realm purporting to speak on behalf of thieves to the government and to the judges, and quoting scripture to do so, was nonetheless a recapitulation of a pattern in Gordon's behaviour through the 1780s, a continuing career of popular agitation that led the press to refer to him often as 'Lord Blaze', the man who had set London alight in the Gordon riots and might do so again. Through the press and other sources we can trace the way in which popular opinion granted Gordon a standing that his social equals were anxious to deny.

Gordon had been acquitted of high treason in 1781. He was not held responsible for the actions of the rioters who had sacked London for five days in June 1780 following the anti-Catholic petitioning that he was prominent in organizing.[15] Throughout the 1780s he kept his anxiety about a Catholic threat to the constitution before the eyes of the public. When Shelburne's government confirmed Rockingham's grant of incomplete but still substantial legislative and judicial autonomy to Ireland in 1783, Gordon sent a 'blasphemous, un-

---

15. The aim of the Protestant Association in England was repeal of Sir George Saville's Catholic Relief Act (18 George III c.66); the prosecution of Gordon was for high treason in encouraging the mobs that besieged the House of Commons and destroyed many public buildings. See 21 *State Trials* 485; the most recent account is Nicholas Rogers, 'The Gordon Riots revisited,' Canadian Historical Association, *Historical Papers* (1988), pp.16–34.

moral, treasonable, schismatical, seditious and scandalous letter' to Lord Shelburne hinting at impeachment for corruption, accusing him of giving treasonable advice to the King, and lauding the wisdom and honesty of the English judges.[16] He continued the campaign by urging support for Protestant Holland in its quarrel with Emperor Joseph II.[17] Gordon published a pamphlet in which he dared to quote a personal interview he had with the King to show the monarch's insufficient warmth in defence of Protestantism, demanded protection from the government because of threatening letters he claimed to have received from Irish Catholics bent on his destruction, and denounced the proposed terms of the Dutch-Austrian treaty as deserving burning by the common hangman.[18]

Gordon identified Catholic regimes with tyranny, but it was British complicity in tyranny that he emphasised. The opposition to the extension of Catholic relief to Scotland in 1779 was in part based on the belief that it would enable Catholic Scots to be enlisted to fight the American revolutionaries, whose cause Gordon supported.[19] And Gordon made a succession of popular causes on other subjects his business. In January 1783 he intervened on behalf of some soldiers of the Atholl Highlanders, who had rioted and refused to embark for India once peace was announced; not a single man was punished and they

---

16. HMC Kenyon p.513; *Public Advertiser*, 14 Jan. 1783.

17. See also n.92.

18. The Protestants of Trieste, under Austrian rule, were supposed to be asking his protection. He persuaded the guard at St. James to present arms to the Dutch ambassador, but later turned on the Dutch for naming a Catholic commander-in-chief. 10 June 1783; 3 Feb., 7 April 1785; 2, 17, 18 May 1785; 16, 20 June 1785; 10, 15, 20 October 1785; 27 Feb. 1787; [Lord George Gordon], *Innocence Vindicated, the Intrigues of Popery and its Abettors Displayed, in an Authentic Narrative . . . Part I* (London: 2nd ed., R. Denham, 1784), *Part II* (2nd ed., London, R. Denham and C. Bremner, 1783); *DNB*. Dates are references to *The Times* unless otherwise noted.

19. Gordon suggested instead that Catholic Scots had enlisted to fight the Americans and that the perjury of swearing they were Protestant must have required a dispensation from the Pope: *Innocence Vindicated . . . Part I*, p.8.

celebrated Gordon in a ballad.[20] In 1785 he unsuccessfully petitioned Parliament on behalf of Glasgow weavers opposed to a tax on calico, and opposed a tax on horses (for which he published the thanks voted him by some Scots farmers) and a shop tax, which some argued would make shop girls into prostitutes. In the latter case he apparently attempted to organize a strike of shopkeepers and an association to oppose the tax, an association that *The Times* suggested would be illegal. The paper also reported an Irish rumour that Gordon had headed a violent mob in the agitation.[21] Later that year he met the King at his levee with a petition from 500 debtors in King's Bench prison, and the debtors in Newgate reportedly asked him to present their petition also to the King.[22] Both those prisons had been broken open and severely damaged during the Gordon riots, and *The Times* probably expressed the reaction of many gentlemen to the effrontery of this 'incendiary':

> . . . this man to whose turbulent spirit and persecuting fanaticism the lives of hundreds were sacrificed, has the audacity to demand audience of his King, and to present petitions to the throne from vagrants of various descriptions.

If mad, he should be confined, but *The Times* thought there was evidence of cunning 'more dangerous than outrage.'[23]

There was a crescendo of denunciation in that paper in 1786, as Gordon added to his reputation for religious controversy by opposing the church courts, achieving the distinction of a highly publicized excommunication. He had been called as a witness in a probate case and had refused to attend, denying the jurisdiction of the Archbishop of Canterbury in what he considered a temporal matter.[24] Such heterodoxy was profoundly disturbing in the brother of a peer: it was clear that

20. J.M. Bullock, *The 'Mutiny' of the Atholl Highlanders & an Account of the Sheelagreen Gordons* (Buckie: privately printed, 1911), pp.10–20.

21. 8, 10, 18 Feb., 16 June, 4 July, 30 Sept 1785; below, n.93. On the agitation surrounding the shop tax, see Susan Brown's forthcoming Oxford D.Phil. thesis.

22. 10 Oct., 4 Nov. 1785.

23. 18 Nov. 1785.

24. 8, 10 Nov., 13 Dec. 1785, 18, 19 May, 16, 24 June, 1, 12 July 1786; *Gentleman's Magazine* (1786), p.993.

Gordon was contesting established authority.[25] He was involved that year in a number of other controversies, always calling into question the good faith of the government.[26]

More important, he trifled again with the mob. During his campaign against a proposed commercial treaty with France in early November 1786, he distributed handbills in the West End, and announced at the door of the Prime Minister that he proposed a public burning of the treaty at the door of the French ambassador (where he also appeared) on the significant night of Guy Fawkes. The Attorney General, Pepper Arden, sent the Solicitor General to the ambassador for further information, and worried about how best to prevent a riot. The Home Secretary and other ministers were absent, and Arden was not convinced that Sir Sampson Wright, the head magistrate at Bow Street, appreciated the dangers. The Attorney General gave instructions through the Home Office that the London magistrates were not to act without advice from the government: 'a matter of this sort requires much consideration.' The press reported that the Law Officers and the Home Office spent several hours on the 4th deciding what to do. General Fawcett, commander of the guards, was consulted, and they were called out on the 5th; the London magistrates sat up through the night to deal with the emergency, which came to nothing.[27]

Clearly the echoes of 1780 were alarming. The Attorney General was perhaps already rattled: a few days before, a

---

25. It may also be a sign of his increasing adherence to millenarian sectarianism: see below.

26. See below, n.135.

27. Gordon's objection was that the agreement was in part secret, and that 'instead of affording a market for our manufactures, it was designed as a cloak for transplanting the principles of Versailles to England.' Pepper Arden expressed his intention of consulting with the Solicitor General and some of the King's Counsel about the best way of dealing with Gordon; he favoured binding Gordon to keep the peace in order to stop the demonstration before it began, if affidavits of his threats could be got, and deprecated what appears to have been the simple announcement of the magistrates that they would use force: PRO, HO 42/10 fols.306–9, Arden to Nepean(?), 4 Nov., and memo at Windsor, 5 Nov. re General Fawcett; *The Times*, 3, 7, 8, 17 Nov. 1786; Watson, p.74.

woman escaped from Bedlam and took refuge in his house, in Lincoln's Inn Fields. When she was taken to him,

> a report was instantly spread through the neighbourhood, that Lord George Gordon had assisted Margaret Nicholson in her escape from Bedlam, and that she was now come to *open* her *case* to the Attorney General, and to have his opinion on the legality of her confinement. A great crowd gathered around the house to know the truth of the circumstances, which Mr Pepper Arden perceiving, and hearing the *ominous* name of Lord George, it is said he actually – .[28]

The significance of the incident was not only the gathering crowd: Margaret Nicholson had attempted to assassinate the King in August, and had been committed as insane. Gordon was reported to have protested that her incarceration was a life sentence without trial.[29]

It seems likely that the government decided at this point that Gordon had to be controlled. *The Times* of course denied his importance, 'so little are the actions of this madman attended to now, even by the lowest and most ignorant of the people', but it nonetheless began a sustained attack on Gordon's reputation immediately after Guy Fawkes. In five letters from 'An Englishman' it reviewed his entire career, questioning his integrity, sanity, and loyalty to the Hanoverians in the most pungent terms, branding him a fanatic, accusing him of trampling 'on the laws of God and man', and warning him to beware awakening 'the sleeping anger of insulted justice.'[30] In late November it was reported that the apparently abandoned prosecution for contempt of the ecclesiastical courts was about to begin; conviction could mean indefinite imprisonment. But there were doubts about the wisdom of incarcerating Gordon for a church court offence. The implications for religious toleration were unwelcome, and the Archbishop had been reported to be seeking to have the law changed.[31] Instead, the Attorney General prepared to

---

28. 4 Nov. 1786.

29. *The Times* 12 Aug. 1786, which ridiculed the suggestion. She died in Bedlam in 1828; *Dictionary of National Biography*; Nigel Walker, *Crime and Insanity in England*, vol.1 (Edinburgh, 1968), p.185.

30. 8, 10, 13, 15, 21 Nov. 1786; see also 7, 9, 11 Nov. There was one defence of Gordon, denying his connection with the mob in 1780: 'A Petitioner', 14 Nov. 1786.

31. 19 May, 16, 24 June, 1, 6, 12 July, 25 Nov. 1786; see below, n.135.

begin a prosecution against Gordon for libelling the French ambassador and the Queen of France, three months before, in the *Public Advertiser*. He did not act, however, until Gordon gave the government exactly what it needed.[32] He was apparently under surveillance (as he had claimed since 1785), and when in late 1786 and early 1787 he turned his interest to the convicts in Newgate and to other prisoners (including destitute blacks awaiting deportation to Sierra Leone) the government was soon informed.[33] *The Times* reported his visits to Newgate scornfully, 'Lord George Crop knows not

32. The French ambassador may have requested action as a result of Gordon's opposition to the treaty, or because of his advertised friendship with, and defence of, Count Cagliostro and the attack on the French court: below, n.134. This information was exhibited 28 Nov. 1786, the last day of Michaelmas term, but Gordon was not apprized of it by the Attorney General until 22 Jan., after the government learned of the Botany Bay *Petition*; process began on 25 Jan., and Gordon learned the details of the charge of libelling the French Queen on 30 Jan. or 1 Feb. It is possible that this first prosecution would not have proceeded had Gordon not provided grounds for the second information by publishing the *Petition* in early January. Exhibiting an *ex officio* information was the usual first step in a state libel prosecution, but it was not uncommon for an Attorney General to use such an information as a threat, without acting upon it. For the subsequent proceedings on both informations, see n.35. *Public Advertiser*, 22, 24 Aug. 1786; PRO, KB 10/45 pt.2 no.79; KB 21/44 p.274; *The Times*, 9, 22–7, 30 Jan., 1, 2 Feb. 1787.

33. The City authorities authorized a round-up of vagrant blacks to be forcibly sent with those petitioning for passage to Sierra Leone on the west coast of Africa, and poor relief payments were stopped to try to force more to join the expedition. Gordon criticized the entire proposal as a penal colony, a Botany Bay for blacks, not in accord with God's laws. On a visit to the Poultry Counter lockup he talked with one of the imprisoned men. John Kirby, Keeper of the Wood Street Counter and perhaps a relative of William Kirby, the chamber-keeper in the Home Office, reported this conversation to Evan Nepean, the Undersecretary of State for the Home Office: 'his name is Newton, his Lordship did not stop long the business I have not yet learn'd.' Christopher Fyfe, *A History of Sierra Leone* (Oxford University Press, 1962), p.17; PRO, HO 42/11/17, John Kirby to Nepean, 16 Jan. 1787; *The Times*, 2 May, 3 Dec. 1785; *Public Advertiser*, 6, 18 Dec. 1786; R.R. Nelson, *The Home Office, 1782–1801* (Durham, N.C.: Duke University Press, 1969), pp.55–6; J.C. Sainty, *Home Office Officials 1782–1870* (1975), pp.35, 53; David Brion Davis, *The Problem of Slavery in the Age of Revolution 1770–1823* (Ithaca, 1975), p.382 n.50.

what to do, or where to turn himself – *Newgate prisoners, Botany Bay convicts*, and *vagabond blacks*, solicit his divided and distracted attention.'[34] The Attorney General then informed Gordon that he would be prosecuted for the libel on the Queen of France, and also privately began preparations for the prosecution of the Botany Bay *Petition*. As Gordon pestered the court with technical objections to the first charge, the government quietly secured its last proofs for the second. On 12 February Gordon finally learned the full dimensions of his troubles, when the second information was read to him in court.[35]

To make the issue of criminal punishments a popular one, as he had with the issue of Catholicism and the constitution, to tell the poor at the height of the penal crisis of the 1780s that God condemned English criminal law, and to agitate in the streets, was unpardonable. The London prisons and jails were desperately overcrowded with capital prisoners and other convicts, and those awaiting deportation to Sierra Leone. The government was receiving reports of overcrowding and threatened escapes from throughout the country; large num-

---

34. 9, 12 Jan. 1787; cf. 20 Nov. 1786, suggesting he organize the prostitutes, aggrieved by the late opening of Parliament. One account suggests that Gordon, as a young midshipman visiting Jamaica sometime before 1772, discussed with the Governor there the cruelties and injustice of slavery; I have not been able to verify this story. Israel Solomons, *Lord George Gordon's Conversion to Judaism (A Paper read and illustrated by slides, before the Jewish Historical Society of England, June 2, 1913, at the University College, London)* (London, A.M.5674), p.3. Also published in *Transactions of the Jewish Historical Society of England*, vii (1911–1914; r. 1971) 222–71.

35. The government initially lacked one proof of the latter offence. It sent the jailer to Gordon for evidence that he had written the pamphlet, evidence which he willingly supplied; his printer was then arrested, and the press reported at the end of January that the pamphlet was said to be treasonable. Gordon appeared in court 12 Feb., when the charge was read to him. PRO TS 11/388; *The Times*, 24–30 Jan., 13 Feb. 1787; PRO, KB 10/45 pt.2, Hilary 27 George III no.40, information for the first libel, exhibited 23 Jan. 1787 (the first day of term, probably nominal). The subsequent process in KB, for both informations, is to be found in KB 21/44 pp.302, 307, 310, 314, 352, 471, 472, 473, and in KB 29/446 Easter 27 George III. On the libel against the Queen of France, and the relative importance of the two prosecutions, see also below, n.134.

bers of hangings presented constant problems for the maintenance of public order.[36] The government now had both the motive and the means to imprison Gordon on a criminal charge, after a trial that would sustain the authority of the criminal law, the judges, and the King. When Gordon began spreading reports in April that the convicts on the first fleet to Australia were all ill, dying, or dead, the Attorney General, Pepper Arden, had every reason to proceed with a vigorous prosecution. The jury was very carefully vetted, as it had been for Gordon's 1781 treason trial, when he was acquitted.[37] But this time the charge was not capital, Gordon had been execrated and satirized for months in the press, and Erskine, the brilliant barrister who had defended him in 1781, was on the side of the prosecution.[38] Conviction was inevitable.

The Attorney General clearly believed what he said when he opened the government case on 6 June: Gordon's purpose was

> to infuse into the minds of those unhappy wretches whose lives or liberties were forfeit to the law of their country, that those who pronounced the sentences upon them had no right to pronounce such sentences, and . . . to provoke his majesty's subjects to rise in defence of what he calls those injured subjects, and to oppose the execution of those laws to which their crimes have made them subject.

He reminded his audience (to Gordon's protest) that 'It is but seven years ago since the three great gaols of this kingdom were sapped to their foundation, and every prisoner set at liberty.' The reference, of course, was to the riots of 1780, attributed to the accused. He now threatened a repetition of 'the same outrages'. Gordon was the worst of subjects, 'for it would be impossible that government should subsist, if such notions were admitted to be disseminated among the people.'[39]

---

36. *The Times* 1 Feb. 1787; HO 42/10, 11 *passim*; Beattie, pp. 593–6.

37. The lists of jurors for both trials, marked for reliability by the prosecution, are in TS 11/388.

38. *The Times*, 26, 29, 30 Jan., 5 Feb. 1787. Gordon conducted his own defence, except for final pleas in mitigation. I describe his experience with King's Bench procedure elsewhere.

39. *Trial*, cols.183–4, 187.

The claim that Gordon's 'farrago' of scriptural quotation could undermine government was plausible in 1787, but the reasons are not apparent in accounts of the trial itself. It inevitably was an arena for presenting some of the rationalist arguments about capital punishment. The Attorney General argued (for the benefit of 'any men so weak as to be affected by arguments like these with respect to the power of taking away life') that executions were more frequent in England than elsewhere because 'the laws are milder': there was no torture, and criminal procedure was so perfect 'that it is hardly possible to suppose a conviction where innocence can exist.' In his own defence, Gordon made clear that he believed that the laws were not only too bloody, but had not deterred thieves. Prompted by a theft in his own household, he said, he had considered the law of God and of England. The latter, of course, provided for capital punishment for the theft of 40 shillings in a dwelling, a penalty enacted primarily with servants in mind. The law of God was clearly opposed: it did not require the shedding of blood for theft, and in many countries this was the law of the state as well. The law of England was unsanctified not only in that respect, for those transported to Botany Bay found themselves in a military dictatorship (Gordon's words): 'there is neither judge, jury, nor counsel allowed to the prisoners, whatever offences they may commit, at Botany-Bay.'[40]

Gordon's defence at the trial was rather cautious, legalistic, whiggish: he emphasised his humanitarian concerns for the condemned, his constitutional concerns for those about to be transported to a penal colony beyond the reach of English justice, and his objection to the fact that he was prosecuted by the contentious proceeding of an *ex officio* information, after a delay of many months.[41] He recapitulated some of the current constitutional arguments about the law of libel, and gave evidence that the prosecution had attempted to entrap him into sending copies of the pamphlet to another prison and

---

40. *Trial*, cols.189, 197. The statute 12 Anne st.1 c.7, to which Gordon referred, was used in over 150 capital convictions in London and Middlesex in the 1780s. About a third of these convicts were hanged.

41. This last was a common argument of advanced Whigs; Gordon quoted extensively from Blackstone: cols.200–201.

that the Home Secretary had him spied upon continually.[42] He denied that he fomented unrest, emphasizing that he had sent the pamphlet to the judges, the Recorder, and the Keeper and Ordinary of Newgate. His argument about Mosaic law is hardly mentioned in his testimony.

He elaborated this defence from Holland, where he fled after his conviction on 6 June 1787, but before sentence, customarily passed on the last day of term. The new pamphlet recapitulated many of the points made more briefly at his trial, and from much the same perspective.[43] It dealt in part with the constitutional rights of jurors in libel trials, as he had at his own trial. The text was witty and scurrilous in some of its other themes[44], but nonetheless again subordinated the religious argument (there was but one scriptural passage) to constitutional claims or humanitarian sentiments more acceptable to most gentlemen.[45]

At one point only is there a more personal and poignant note, a reference to two of the score of hangings that followed the riots of 1780:

> I shall never sufficiently lament the scandalous exhibition in Bow-street; where an infant boy, whose weight being insufficient, was strangled by the strength of ruffians. I can never forget the untimely death of another

---

42. Cols.203–6. On this belief, and some evidence that Gordon was right in accusing Nepean of paying spies to follow him everywhere, see above, n.33.

43. *A Letter from the Right Hon. Lord George Gordon to the Attorney General of England, in which the Motives of his Lordship's Public Conduct, from the Beginning of the Memorable Year 1780 to the Present Time, are Vindicated Upon Principles of Religion, Morality, and sound Policy* (Amsterdam 1787), dated 4 July 1787.

44. See below at n.134.

45. He repeated the accusation that the celebrated Dr Dodd, executed for forgery in 1777, was convicted on an indictment that was fraudulent. The style of the pamphlet, and relative emphasis, compared to some of Gordon's other publications, suggests that parts may have been revised by another hand, but most of it is entirely congruent with his argument at trial. (For the purposes of my argument, I have accepted all other attributions to Gordon of works bearing his name: his public persona is the issue in most cases.)

unhappy *infant girl*, convicted upon the evidence of being seen giddily dancing with an old cloak of Lady Mansfield about her shoulders.[46]

These memories of those hanged in his name may have been what finally led Gordon to the side of the condemned in Newgate in 1786; we cannot know.[47] But the idiom in which they are expressed, the language of a humane gentleman, is very different from that of the *Prisoner's Petition* itself, the publication with which government and judiciary chose to destroy Gordon. To make sense of it, we must see his provocative activities in the 1780s in a longer perspective, one that comprehends the use of religious argument in both English popular politics and English law. For the man who fought papacy as the whore of Babylon, and repudiated the authority of the Archbishop of Canterbury, was stirring resonances once common in England, and now becoming common again in the later eighteenth century, in both the streets and the courts.

Israel Bar Abraham George Gordon, Prophet

The Prisoner's Petition is cast in the idiom of prophecy and in the words of scripture:

---

46. *A Letter*, p.12. The house in Bloomsbury Square of Lord Chief Justice Mansfield (Gordon calls him 'my thin-visaged countryman') was destroyed by the rioters; his country residence was also threatened. Among the three executed in Bloomsbury Square in July was Laetita Holland, who had in her possession a green petticoat and aprons belonging to Lord Mansfield's niece: she said that she was given them by the mob, but a witness testified to her being in the house earlier. In an earlier trial, witnesses described Richard Roberts's role in destroying the staircase in the residence of Sir John Fielding, the Bow Street magistrate, and also testified that he had been given drink by a nearby publican who enticed him to participate. In testimony and the press he is referred to repeatedly as a lad or 'a little boy': 'that youth, a child I call him' said one witness. The jury recommended mercy on account of his age, 17. He was reported to cry all the way to the gallows, and to warn some boys near the place of execution to mind their masters' business and avoid his fate. He was hanged 12 July 1780 in Bow Street. Old Bailey *Proceedings*, 1780, pp.358–63, no.292; pp.548–9, no.382; *Aris' Birmingham Gazette*, 3, 17 July 1780.

47. See also below, n.99.

. . .we have reason to cry aloud from our dungeons and prison-ships, in defence of our lives and liberties, in this advanced period of the world (when many kingdoms and common-wealths affect holiness unto the Lord, and profess to take hold out of all languages of the nations, even to take hold of the skirt of him that is a Jew, saying, We will go with you, for we have heard that God is with you) that the just punishment ordained by God for our trespasses of thievery, is profanely altered by men like ourselves, that his adequate judgment of our offences mingled with mercy, is not executed upon us in righteousness; that the everlasting law of his statutes is changed and perverted to our destruction, and the true record of the Almighty, is falsified and erased by the lawyers and judges (who sit with their backs to the words of the living God, and the fear of man before their faces) till the streets of our city have run down with a stream of blood, instead of righteousness, as it is at this day. . . . How long, O Lord! shall these white walls of council, who sit to judge the people after the law, command us to be hanged, contrary to the law? They tithe Mint and Rue and all manner of herbs, by making long charges to the juries, with a shew of justice and religion, and afterwards pass over judgment and the love of God, by pronouncing the sentence of death upon us, and shedding our innocent blood for expiable trespasses which do not require our cutting off from the people. Surely then shall the blood of our lives be required at their hands, life for life, banishment for banishment. Whoso sheddeth man's blood, by man shall his blood be shed; for in the image of God made he man.

There is now but a step between us and eternity; it behoves us therefore to be instant in speaking the truth and to demand speedy justice: the Hangman and the scaffolding of the New Drop, is already prepared for our executions on one hand, and Governor Phillip, and military tyranny, at Botany Bay, awaits us on the other. . . .

We look with concern and abhorrence on the bloody hue of the felony laws, and the frequent executions in England, in this reign, under a nominal administration of justice, since the time our eyes have been opened to the expectation of salvation, pardon, expiation and deliverance, in this world, through the divine providence, justice, and mercy of God's holy law, in favour of our cases, annuling the rigour of our sentences, and in arrest of the perverted judgments pronounced upon us. It would be blasphemy to compare the laws of the nations with the laws of GOD, or to set up the rebellious judgment of men against the decree of the Almighty. . . .

These passages were those chosen by the government for prosecution, as the clearest libel on His Majesty's judges.[48] The rest of the pamphlet excoriated the Draconian nature of the laws, the 'pride and stubbornness of the hearts of the Kings, their Ecclesiastics, and Sycophants', and warned of the

---

48. Pp.8–10, 13–14; marked in the copy filed with the prosecution brief, and recited in the information: *Trial*, PRO, TS 11/388.

consequences of so defying God. His punishments for England for such bloody injustices were 'rebellions, plots, tu-
mults, discontents, corruption, revolt of colonies, fires,
dearness of provisions, factions, loss of trade, grievous taxes,
felonies, murders, perjuries, evil counsellors about the
Throne, and a general diminishing' of the nation. 'Behold the
mighty men are as nothing before God, and the most famous
Kings as if they were not. . . .'[49] Contemporaries surely read
into these words: the loss of the American colonies, the
political divisiveness of that issue, many recent protests
against taxes, and the dearth and extensive food riots of 1782
and 1783.

The main argument, as we have seen, was also directly
based on scripture: that the laws of England that punished
theft with death were void because they explicitly contradicted the Mosaic law, the Old Testament punishments for
theft.[50] The most relevant passages were those in Exodus 22,
providing that theft should be punishable by restitution.[51] The
equivalent offences were all punishable by death in England
in the 1780s.[52] The *Petition* thus called into question most
executions that took place under English law.[53]

---

49. Biblical passages quoted or paraphrased (although not identified by
    Gordon) include Genesis 2:7, 9:6; Exodus 5:2, 7:14, 21:24;
    Deuteronomy 6:5; Joshua 2, 6:22–27; Psalms 2:10, 9:8, 19:7–9, 25:14,
    79:3–11, 91:4–8, 10–11, 106:21–38 and 47, 127:1; Isaiah 22:2, 30:18,
    33:22; Matthew 5:18, 6:10; Luke 11:42, Acts 23:3; James 4:11–12.

50. Above, n.12.

51. Exodus 22: five-fold restitution for stolen and killed or sold oxen,
    four-fold for stolen sheep; or double if caught red-handed (verses 1,4).
    Double restitution for theft of money or goods from a house to which
    they had been delivered for safekeeping (v.7). Housebreaking by day
    appears to demand restitution only – or slavery for non-payment (v.3).

52. 14 Geo. II c.6 (1741); 15 Geo. II c.34 (1742); 12 Anne st.1 c.7 (1713);
    39 Eliz. c.15 (1597), are the equivalents of those cited in the preceding
    note, depending in part on values. In some other respects, the Old
    Testament was as harsh or more so than English law. Murder is capital
    in both, of course (Numbers 28). Burglary appears to be punishable by
    death in both, in the sense that Exodus makes it permissable to kill the
    intruder (v.2; 18 Eliz. c.7 (1576)); bestiality is a capital offence in both
    systems (v.19; 5 Eliz. c.17 (1562)); witchcraft, capital in Exodus, had
    ceased to be so in England in 1736. See also n.61.

53. I.e., all capital property offences except burglary.

The power of this denunciation, and the danger it represented to the government, arose partly from the contrast it
presented to the conventional religious defences of English
law. We can see, from the evidence that clerics were in the
forefront of justifications for the existing state of the law and
constantly concerned with the theological foundations of the
regime, why the arguments of Gordon were considered both
an outrage and dangerous in the extreme.[54] Their very sim-
plicity, their reliance on specific scriptural passages, their
appeal to the ordinary person's understanding, their warnings
to kings and the mighty, and the assumption of absolute
equality in the eyes of God – all were strikingly different from
the arguments of the divines who promoted their professional
advancement with published assize sermons addressed primarily to judges and grand jurors.[55] The assize sermon typically relied on either Romans 13:1–7: 'For rulers are not a
terror to good works, but to the evil . . . if thou do that which
is evil, be afraid: for he beareth not the sword in vain, for he is
the minister of God'; or Peter 2: 13–18 'Submit yourselves to
every ordinance of man for the Lord's sake, whether it be to
the king as supreme; or unto governors, as unto them that are
sent by him for the punishment of evildoers, and for the praise
of them that do well. . . . Fear God. Honour the king.'[56] They
were, in short, justifications for the regime and its legitimacy.
But for the most part the usual assize sermon took the form of
a rationalist exposition of social hierarchy, deterrence, and
the need for obedience: the lessons crystallized in Archdeacon Paley's lectures and most famous book. Eighteenth-
century gentlemen were acutely aware that too much Biblical
quotation could encourage biblical literalism, which could be

54. McGowen; Robert Hole, *Pulpits, Politics and Public Order in England 1760–1832* (1989).

55. We do not yet know very much about who were either the intended, or actual, audiences of such sermons.

56. Hole, pp.12–13, and *passim*; Paley cited these as the only scriptural passages relevant to civil rights and obligations. See *Moral and Political Philosophy*, Book 6, ch.4, where he argued that they must be understood not as injunctions to passive obedience, but as general statements, to be modified by all the usual Lockean and other whig caveats against obedience to unjust power.

used to justify revolution. It had been used to do so little more than a hundred years before.

Gordon was in that revolutionary tradition, and to understand both popular and governmental reactions to his attack on the capital statutes, we must examine some of the resonances of his argument. If clergymen addressed grand jurors and judges and the condemned in the language of legitimate power, Gordon's language is that of 'enthusiasm', biblical citation, direct instruction from the Lord in the most literalist of traditions. He repudiates the power of the Hanoverian state as illegitimate and indeed as blasphemous. For some at least of his contemporaries, *The Prisoner's Petition* was a recapitulation of a very old radical critique of the injustice of English law.

From at least the fourteenth century, opponents of capital punishment for theft had pointed to the laws of Moses (and by extension, the laws of Christ) as their authority for declaring most of the English capital statutes contrary to the law of God.[57] Sir Thomas More's *Utopia* (1516; first English translation 1551) imbedded the Mosaic scriptural authority within a social argument, but the most powerful attraction it had was to millenarians intent on making the laws of man correspond as closely as possible to the divine will. It seems likely that those Lollards who were scriptural literalists made the claim in the fifteenth century, and it was a focus of religious controversy in England and on the continent in the sixteenth. Luther and Calvin utterly rejected the Mosaic code as binding on Christians (although sometimes citing its provisions), but there was also a radical stream of reformation theology that called for the implementation of the express word of God in the Old Testament, including the 'judicials', the criminal penalties. Anabaptists and others united evangelical mysticism with a biblical literalism that extended to the law of Moses. The uncompromising exponents of Mosaic law were in the tradition of medieval radical sects and movements, and some of this tradition came to inform the British separatists

---

57. B.S. Capp, *The Fifth Monarchy Men: A Study in Seventeenth-century English Millenarianism* (London: Faber and Faber, 1972), p.169, quoting Walter Brute (1392), reprinted by the Marian exile John Foxe, *Acts and Monuments* (1563).

and puritans, the most famous of whom were Thomas Cartwright, William Perkins, and John Knox.[58]

Most of these men were concerned above all with the failure of English law to punish with death the capital offences of scripture: adultery, witchcraft, blasphemy, incest, dishonouring parents, sodomy, sabbath-breaking were held to be among them. Faced with the Mosaic law of theft, some of them were prepared to admit modifications. Thus William Perkins defended English law's death penalty for theft because Englishmen were much poorer than the ancient Jews, therefore theft was 'farre more grievous' a sin in England, where a small theft from a poor man did more harm; moreover, 'the people of this country are of a more stirring and fierce disposition. . . .' But the ideas of the more radical biblical literalists in England created much alarm. Archbishop Whitgift scorned Cartwright's call for Mosaic law in the courts as unthinkable revolution:

> . . . the prince must be abridged of that prerogative which she hath in pardoning such as by the law be condemned to die: the punishments of death for felony must be mitigated according to Moses' law. . . . To be short, all things must be transformed: lawyers must cast away their huge volumes and multitude of cases, and content themselves with the books of Moses: we of the clergy would be the best judges; and they must require the law at our hands. . . .[59]

The orthodox position was that with the destruction of ancient Israel, the judicials of Moses, designed by God for the ancient Jews, had perished also, and that in any case the law of restitution for theft had to yield to different circumstances. But the radical separatist position (represented by Henry Barrow) was that Mosaic law was binding on Christians, and that included not only capital penalties for blasphemy and the other religious offences of the Old Testament, but also the

---

58. Capp, pp.168–70; George Lee Haskins, *Law and Authority in Early Massachusetts: A Study in Tradition and Design* (New York: Macmillan, 1960), p.265 n.65; P.D.L. Avis, 'Moses and the Magistrate: a Study in the rise of Protestant Legalism,' *Journal of Ecclesiastical History*, vol.26 (1975), pp.152–6, 158–169; Donald Pennington and Keith Thomas (eds.), *Puritans and Revolutionaries* (Oxford: Clarendon Press, 1978), pp.98–102, 269–72. For the discussion in *Utopia*, see the translation by Paul Turner (Harmondsworth, 1965), p. 50.

59. Avis, p.166; C.H. and K. George, *The Protestant Mind of the English Reformation 1570–1640* (Princeton University Press, 1961), pp.229–30.

penalties for theft. It was therefore unlawful to hang a thief. 'He that maketh any new lawes taketh unto him the office of God, who is onlie lawmaker.' For this, and his other heresies, Barrow was condemned and executed in 1593.[60]

In the 1640s the argument re-entered English public debate with new vigour. In 1636 John Cotton of Massachusetts had drafted a code of laws for the colony that copied almost all features of the Mosaic law, including restitution for theft, and published it in London in 1641; in 1644 the colony of New Haven declared Moses' laws to be in force; and in 1648 Massachusetts adopted a code of laws that preserved the Mosaic laws for punishment of theft. The theologues of the New England colonies were prepared to admit that man might perhaps enact lesser penalties than those in scripture, but they believed that man certainly had no authority to demand death where God had not. That position was strongly reinforced in some of the vast popular literature of the interregnum: in the 1640s Levellers and some Independents rested the argument against capital punishment for theft upon it, and some radicals cited the Lollards and celebrated Moses as the supreme voice on earth of God's law. The Fifth Monarchy Men, a millenarian sect that came close to real power in 1653, were influenced by the New England codes and insisted on the absolute primacy of Mosaic law, both in matters of theft and personal morality. Cromwell and most propertied men were appalled.[61]

No equivalent printed literature appeared once press controls were re-imposed, but the tradition did not die.[62] Fifth Monarchy Men and other radical millenarians continued

---

60. Avis, pp.167, 170–71, *DNB*.

61. Haskins, pp.124–6, 144–51, 153–4; Capp, pp.140, 162–171, 182; *Examen Legum Angliae: or, the Laws of England Examined by Scripture, Antiquity, and Reason* (London, 1656), preface, and pp.8, 16–17, 65, 98, 147 (Moses); 28, 50, 57 (Lollards); 53–55, 65 (punishment for theft). The author was consistent in supporting the death penalty for adultery, witchcraft, and the other capital offences of the Old Testament. The work is cited by Fifth Monarchists, although Capp does not consider it to be written by one of them.

62. Robert Zaller, 'The debate on capital punishment during the English Revolution', *American Journal of Legal History*, vol.31 no.2 (1987), pp.126–44; Capp, p.195.

some activity into the 1660s and then dispersed into other groups, including Baptists, Congregationalists, and (perhaps for the radical fringe) the Quakers.[63] Chapbooks and a popular prophetic tradition, the availability of some of the pamphlet literature of the interregnum among radical and religious groups, and the persistence of biblical literalism and millenarian interpretation throughout the eighteenth century in both Anglican and dissenting groups, are the avenues through which the radical ideas of the seventeenth century were transmitted into the eighteenth.[64]

Certainly Gordon was aware of some of the old arguments in favour of the Mosaic law: he cites Beccaria, but also Sir Thomas More.[65] His friend and biographer, the Jacobin Dr Robert Watson, wrote that Gordon was well-acquainted with the history of the Commonwealth, 'and seemed to have our republican ancestors constantly in his view', as did many late-eighteenth-century radicals and democrats.[66] Some other ideas of the Fifth Monarchy Men in particular may have attracted him.[67] He also had one personal connection that may have been particularly important. In the 1760s and 1770s James Murray of Newcastle, a Presbyterian Scot like Gordon,

---

63. Capp, p.225.

64. On the continuities see J.F.C. Harrison, *The Second Coming: Popular Millenarianism 1780–1850* (London: Routledge & Kegan Paul, 1979), pp.13ff and *passim*, and Deborah M. Valenze, 'Prophecy and Popular Literature in Eighteenth-Century England', *Journal of Ecclesiastical History*, vol.29, no.1 (January, 1978), pp.75–92 for chapbooks that reiterated levelling traditions, encouraged literalist study of the Bible, and heightened millenarian expectations. See also Malcolm Chase, *The People's Farm: English Agrarianism, 1775–1840* (Oxford, 1988).

65. *Petition*, p.12.

66. Robert Watson, *The Life of Lord George Gordon: with a Philosophical Review of his Political Conduct* (London: H.D. Symonds and D.I. Eaton, 1795), p.76; J. Ann Hone, *For the Cause of Truth: Radicalism in London 1796–1821* (Oxford, 1982), pp.54, 57, 411. In his 1783 attack on Lord Shelburne, Gordon cited a number of the state trials of the interregnum: *Public Advertiser* 14 Jan. 1783.

67. His firm support for the Dutch (republican and protestant) is anticipated by the Fifth Monarchists (Capp, p.155, 236); other points in common are his affirmation at trial (Fifth Monarchists usually refused to take oaths as a misuse of God's name, Capp, p.180), and the Jewish content of his millenarianism, discussed below.

attacked the North ministry, the Church, the American war, corruption, taxes, kings and aristocrats in a constant stream of democratic invective in both his sermons and printed pamphlets. He praised Oliver Cromwell, he preached violently anti-Catholic sermons in the 1770s, and he wrote a two-volume work on Revelations.[68] His emphasis on scriptural literalism and individual interpretation, his egalitarianism and critique of English law, are particularly noteworthy. All statutes should be consistent with 'the moral attributes of God'; true law does not depend on kings, but on God, who instructs humanity by the law of nature and the positive law of scripture.[69] He attacked the oppression of judges and lawyers, echoed the Leveller belief that laymen could decide cases, and declared that 'legislators that make laws contrary to natural justice and the law of God may be guilty of rebellion.'[70]

The similarity to Gordon's ideas in the 1780s is striking, and as the Presbyterian head of the Protestant Association Gordon was in direct contact with Murray, who headed the Association in Newcastle.[71] Murray died in 1782, but his even more uncompromising pupil, Thomas Spence, moved to London from Newcastle in December 1787 or January 1788, shortly before Gordon was sentenced.[72] Biblical literalism, united with millenarian ideas, sustained his arguments and

68. Thomas R. Knox, 'Thomas Spence: the Trumpet of Jubilee', *Past & Present*, no.76 (August 1977), pp.79–82; Chase, p.42–3, 46–7; Hole, pp.220ff; James E. Bradley, *Religion, Revolution, and English Radicalism: Nonconformity in Eighteenth-Century Politics and Society* (Cambridge, 1990), chs.4, 5.

69. Quoted in Bradley, p.140 n.55; see also p.143 n.65, and, in general, ch.4 for a full exposition of Murray's thought. In an attack on corrupt kings, he remarked: 'though I would not wish to see a poor *Moabite* feed crows upon a gibbet, yet it would certainly be just that such as have swallowed more than their proper share of emoluments should be obliged to restitution;' quoted Bradley, p.153.

70. Bradley, pp.173, 155.

71. Eugene Black, *The Association: British Extraparliamentary Political Organization 1769–1793* (Cambridge, Mass., 1963), p.152; Kathleen Wilson, 'The Rejection of Deference: Urban Political Culture in England 1715–1785', Ph.D. thesis Yale University (1985), pp.358–360.

72. Chase, pp.21, 45–6.

inspired his rhetoric. Spence appropriated Milton and Bunyan's use of the idea of 'Jubilee' from Leviticus 25, using it as his image of revolution in property and society and human nature.[73] I have no evidence that Gordon met Spence, but it has been persuasively argued that minoritarian sectarian traditions, including Spencean ideas, had a much more extensive circulation than the absence of public notice, or a printed tradition, might suggest. Personal connection and sectarian continuities were the means of transmission.[74] I am not arguing that Gordon was a proto-Spencean, but their visions do overlap.

The apocalyptic vision of God's justice and man's injustice, and an intense commitment to biblical literalism, was well-established in the groups with which Gordon is likely to have become increasingly familiar as he moved from parliamentary to extra-parliamentary agitation, as he talked less to the King and ministers of state, and more to the poor. Spence himself, whose earlier writings did not emphasize biblical or millennial themes, turned in this direction after moving to the metropolis.[75] London from the 1780s abounded in prophetic and mystical sects, whose members were also often active in plebeian politics.[76] Spence, an important figure in that world, recognized Lord George Gordon as another. Spence issued at least seven commemorative tokens in his honour after his death in Newgate in 1793. They portrayed Gordon as a Jew. The reverse images were ones Spence often used, such as Cain

---

73. Malcolm Chase, 'The concept of jubilee in late eighteenth-and nineteenth-century England', *Past & Present*, no.129 (November 1990), esp.135–140; for an evocation of the much longer tradition of Jubilee see Peter Linebaugh, 'Jubilating; or, how the Atlantic working class used the Biblical Jubilee against capitalism, with some success', *Midnight Notes*, no.10 (Fall 1990), pp.84–98. On their arrival in Sierra Leone, the black emigrants and deportees (above, n.33) marched ashore singing, and celebrated their release from captivity, their return in freedom to the homeland where they had been enslaved: 'The day of Jubilee is come; Return ye ransomed sinners home'; Fyfe, *History of Sierra Leone*, p.37.

74. Harrison, p.24; Chase, *People's Farm*, p.18.

75. Chase, pp.46ff.

76. J.F.C. Harrison, *The Second Coming: Popular Millenarianism, 1780–1850* (London, 1979), pp.24–30; E.P. Thompson, *The Making of the English Working Class* (Harmondsworth, 1968), pp.51–5, 127–30.

and Abel with the motto 'The beginning of Oppression'; 'Honour', and an open hand with a heart in the palm and laurel branches (1793); and 'we were born free and will never die slaves.'[77] Appropriately, Spence was said to fling handfuls of his tokens, advertising his land plan and other reforms, at the crowds on their way to executions.[78]

The Quakers were another possible source of Gordon's ideas. According to Watson, 'he delighted in the society of the people commonly called Quakers.'[79] If he discussed the issue of capital punishment with Friends, or read their foundation texts, Gordon learned that George Fox considered Old Testament authority crucial on the issue of capital punishment. Fox had occasionally written the judges to advise them that death for theft was 'contrary to the law of God in the Old Time'. Specifically, he urged multiple restitution as in the Mosaic law.[80] At the end of the seventeenth century Fox's follower John Bellers called for complete abolition of the death penalty, and the scriptural evidence against punishment of theft by death continued to be voiced by Quakers.[81]

---

77. Spence also celebrated three 'noted advocates of the rights of man' on another token: More, Paine, and himself. R. Dalton and S.H. Hamer, *The Provincial Token-Coinage of the 18th Century* (repr., Lawrence, Mass., 1977), pp.165, 171; James Atkins, *The Tradesmen's Tokens of the Eighteenth Century* (London, 1892), pp.129–30.

78. Chase, pp.58–9. On Spencean millenarianism see also Iain McCalman, *Radical Underworld: Prophets, Revolutionaries and Pornographers in London, 1795–1840* (Cambridge, 1988), ch.3.

79. He thought their 'submission to arbitrary power, unnatural, and extremely improper in the present state of society', and according to his biographer, this is what prevented him becoming a Friend. But Watson is clear that Gordon 'always courted their society', and that they in turn visited him in prison, and in sickness. Watson, pp.58–9. John Coakley Lettsom, the Quaker physician, attended him in Newgate: *J.J. Lettsom: His Life, Times, Friends and Descendants* (London, 1933), pp.250–54. I owe this and other Quaker references to Malcolm Thomas.

80. George Fox, *Journal or Historical Account of his Life* . . . (Philadelphia, 1839), vol.1, pp.70–75; *An Instruction to Judges and Lawyers, that they may Act and Judge as did the Judges of Old* . . . (London, 1660).

81. 'Some Reasons Against Puting of Fellons to Death' in his *Essays about the Poor, Manufactures, Trade, Plantations, & Immorality* . . .

The images and themes and biblical literalism in Gordon's Botany Bay *Petition* could also be found in corners of the Church of England itself. J.F.C. Harrison has emphasised the extent of millennial debate in these decades, taking the form of reasoned disquisitions by Anglican and dissenting clergy on the relationship between the approaching end of the century and the prophetic passages of scripture. But there were some clergymen in the established church who went further. The Reverend William Whiston (1667–1752), the Lucasian Professor before he became a notorious Arminian, nonetheless enjoyed a royal pension even as he related natural phenomena to prophecies, started a society to promote Primitive Christianity, and announced the imminence of the millenium. He also believed that executions for theft and robbery were against God's law. The Reverend William Law (1686–1761), a high churchman, became a close student of the writings of the mystic Jacob Boehme, whose works had been published in the 1640s and 1650s (and attracted Fifth Monarchists); Boehme's works were reissued in four volumes between 1764 and 1781, in a 'William Law' edition, and became a source for millenarians.[82] Law emphasised God's benevolence, and the Reverend Martin Madan (1726–1790), the popular preacher who was Chaplain of the Lock Hospital, was appalled that Law's theology undercut respect for God's wrath.[83] Madan of course was the author, two decades later, of the celebrated work of 1785 demanding the enforcement of the capital statutes.[84] The significant irony is that Madan himself was a biblical literalist, who had done much to destroy his own career in 1780 by publishing a two-volume defence of polygamy, arguing that it was sanctioned – by the Mosaic law. Moreover, about the time Gordon was sentenced the contemporary controversy about the slave trade, always informed by biblical reference, erupted in a spate of pamphlets about

---

(London, 1699), reprinted in *John Bellers: His Life, Times, and Writings*, ed. George Clarke (London, 1987), p.103.

---

82. Harrison, pp.19ff; *Dictionary of National Biography*; Capp, pp.185–6.

83. McGowen, 'Religion and the Criminal Law', p.208; Martin Madan, *A Full and Complete Answer to the Capital Errors Contained in the Writings of the Late Rev. William Law* (London, 1763).

84. Above, n.7.

whether the Mosaic law sanctioned modern slavery. Among such controversialists, Gordon appears less strange a figure.[85]

In the eighteenth century, then, we can find continuing references to the Mosaic argument against the death penalty in published religious controversy.[86] Some Anglican clerics in the 1720s referred to it as an argument unfortunately still to be heard, and one to be opposed; it appeared in dissenting sermons, and in periodicals and pamphlets in the 1770s.[87] It was perhaps even more commonly heard in New England. Joel Barlow, for example, defending a dissertation on the criminal law on his admission to the bar of Connecticut in 1786, wrote:

> . . . The political institutions of Moses, which in general were as riged & sanguinary as those of any nation in the world, were in this particular hapily adapted to the passions of human nature. They applied the punishment of theft to those passions which were most likely to be wrought upon to prevent the commission of the crime. The fear of death does not necessarily counteract the love of ease & unlawful gain but the fear of the los[s] of our own property & a desire for that of others as likewise the terr[o]r of hard labour & the love of indolence, are opposites in nature & the greatest opposites in nature are found by the chymists to nutralize & convert each other.[88]

It would be misleading, however, to suggest that the argument from the Old Testament was only to be found among those radicals who read the political tracts of the seventeenth century, or who knew radical dissenters like John Murray, or

85. Madan's experience with prostitution through his position of chaplain at the Lock Hospital lay behind his book. Not all took the Mosaic law as seriously: Law, for example, considered it 'mere carnal ordinances', temporary arrangements suited to the Jews at that time. Kenneth Hylson-Smith, *Evangelicals in the Church of England 1734–1984* (1989), pp.30ff; *Dictionary of National Biography*; *Thelyphthora, or a Treatise on Female Ruin*. On the slave trade controversy, see Davis, *Problem of Slavery*, ch.11, esp. pp.541–51.

86. By the later eighteenth century, there is a significant shift: it became important for Quakers to attack the law of Moses. See below.

87. McGowen, 'The Changing Face of God's Justice', p.87, citing the *London Magazine* for 1772, and *Thoughts on Capital Punishments* (1770); McGowen does not note the specific scriptural basis of the arguments.

88. Theodore Albert Zunder, *The Early Days of Joel Barlow, A Connecticut Wit* (New Haven, 1934), p.192 [*sic*].

who came under the influence of Quakers or heterodox Anglican divines. It seems likely that we also have here an instance of a continuing popular tradition among the poor, one sustained by popular readings of the scriptures, especially the assertions in Genesis and Psalms that the world was God's gift to man and the promise in Revelations of the millenium. We know that the poor continued to recite the words of Genesis 1, that God made the creatures for the use of man, as an argument against the game laws. That had been a radical argument also in the seventeenth century.[89] It seems equally likely that the Leveller argument against capital punishment for property offences was also known to the poor, as well as to radical dissenters, democrats who drew sustenance from the literature of the Commonwealth, and all those who sought in the Christian Word a Law greater than the law of England. Its use by Gordon may be evidence that it was common among artisanal and plebeian radicals in London by the 1780s, men and women whom, by the middle of the decade, he wanted to represent. In that milieu millenarianism had a wide popular following by the early 1790s, and it seems likely that there were many currents of it in London in the 1780s also. Gordon explicitly refers to such beliefs in the *Petition*: 'this advanced period of the world' is a phrase that held immense meaning for those holding such beliefs.[90]

His conversion to Orthodox Judaism, and the way in which it occurred, suggests one last source for both his scriptural certitude and his democratic habits. To the titillation of the public and the delight of his enemies, he underwent circumcision, and adopted orthodox dress and beard and the name Israel Bar Abraham George Gordon. As early as 1783 Gordon had begun publicly addressing the Jewish communities of London, urging them to support the Protestant cause and beware what he believed to be Catholic treachery in the negotiations with America.[91] In August 1785 he wrote to Emperor Joseph II, protesting that the Austrian envoys to

---

89. Zaller, pp.135, 138.

90. Above, n.48.

91. *Copy of a letter from the Right Honourable Lord George Gordon to Elias Lindo, Esq. and the Portuguese; and Nathan Salomon, Esq. and the German Jews* (London, [1783]).

London insulted him 'because I loved the Jews' and inviting Joseph to escape Catholic tyranny and mend his ways.[92] There had been a press report of his intention of becoming a Jew as early as September 1785; by November that year *The Times* was gleefully calling him 'Lord Crop', and making jokes about the declining market for pork.[93] Apart from a few references in the paper in 1786 and early 1787[94], there was apparently little or no public discussion of his serious interest in Judaism until July 1787, when it was reported that he was worshipping with the Jews at Amsterdam (where he fled after conviction but before sentence).[95] He was sent back to England by the Dutch authorities, and from August to December 1787 lived in the Jewish community in Birmingham, learning Hebrew, until he was discovered.[96] The government sent a King's Messenger to secure his arrest, and Gordon was arrested on a charge of contempt of court, and imprisoned in London to await sentence.[97] He was said to be unrecogniz-

---

92. *Copy of a letter from the Right Honourable Lord George Gordon, President of the Protestant Association, to Joseph Benedict Augustus, Emperor of Germany and King of the Romans* [dated London, 10 Aug. 1785], reprinted in Solomons, p.11.

93. *The Times* 7 Sept., 11 Nov. 1785. Earlier that year he was reported to have stopped shaving until his friend Gershom Robertson's remonstrance for himself and 12,000 operatives was complied with, apparently a reference to the Glasgow weavers' strike: *The Times*, 10 Feb. 1785; above, n.21.

94. 31 Oct., 9 Nov. 1786; 7, 26 March and 5, 9 April 1787.

95. *The Times*, 23 July 1787; *Public Advertiser* 26 July 1787. Differing theories about the date of his conversion are given in Israel Solomons, pp.19–20. Watson argued that his conversion to Judaism gave the government the incentive to prosecute him without fear of repercussions: Watson, p.80. I have not made a full search of the press.

96. *Aris's Birmingham Gazette*, 10 Dec. 1787; Solomons, p.24; W.A. Beckett, *Universal Biography* (3 vols., 1836).

97. Watson, p.83; Solomons, pp.24ff. Watson suggests that Gordon was deliberately given bail at the time of his conviction because his popularity was not entirely ended by his conversion. The surviving drafts of the certificates for the warrants, and the warrants, include one for Gordon's arrest, 'Mr Justice Buller's warrant 20 June 1787. This warrant was improper – directing that the defdt should be bailed & accordingly a new one issued on the certificate of 8 December 1787'. PRO, KB 33/5/13.

able, orthodox in beard and dress. He received many Jewish visitors in Newgate while he waited to appear in King's Bench in January 1788.[98]

Watson tried to account for Gordon's conversion, which was disastrous for his more respectable political causes, as the product of extreme disappointment, a self-identification with an outcast group. But he also remarks that Gordon himself said that he was led to it in part because 'the Jews literally adhered to the laws of Moses.'[99] Gordon did his best to do so. He informed a prison visitor sent to him by John Wesley in 1789 that 'as our Lord was born in Judea, and conformed to Jewish customs, opinions, and manners, so we were bound to imitate his example in these things. For this reason, added he, I think it right to conform to his example in appearing as a *Jew* and in maintaining an external conformity to his life and manners.'[100] In this he followed and anticipated radical Protestants of other generations, particularly millenarians. The adoption of the customs and rites of the Jews by some English Christians occurred in both the sixteenth and seventeenth centuries; intense interest in the relationship of Jewish history to Christian eschatology encouraged such identifications. A

---

98. *The Times*, 17, 18, 19 Dec. 1787; *Gentleman's Magazine*, vol.62, pp.1120–21.

99. Watson, pp.77ff. If there is an emotional or cognitive connection between the executions of the 'Gordon' rioters, and Gordon's subsequent championing of those condemned to death for other crimes (above, n.46), he may have been affected greatly by the execution of the only Jew among the rioters, Samuel Solomons of Whitechapel, a pencil-maker, on 20 July 1780. Two stories are reported about him. An eyewitness wrote many years later, 'One was said to be a Jew, and a little incident respecting this man had dwelt upon my memory. His next-door neighbour on one side was crying out loudly from fear and the Jew nudged him, as a hint to show more fortitude, and he became silent.' Perhaps more significant, Solomons had attacked the house of a man whom he accused of being a thief-taker, one who had lived 'by the price of blood.' Solomon's view of the death penalty was also that of Gordon; and he died for it. Peter Linebaugh, *The London Hanged*, p.364; Israel Solomons, 'Lord George Gordon's Conversion,' p.6; George Rudé, *Paris and London in the Eighteenth Century: Studies in Popular Protest* (Collins: London, 1970), p.289; Old Bailey *Proceedings*, pp.418–20, no.312; *Aris's Birmingham Gazette*, 31 July 1780.

100. Joseph Benson, *Memoirs of the Life of the Rev. Peard Dickinson* (London, 1803), pp.65–6.

group of Fifth Monarchists, the sect that particularly favoured the laws of Moses in the seventeenth century, had followed one Tillam in East Anglia, who emigrated to the Palatinate after the Restoration. There they adopted all Jewish rites, including circumcision, sacrifices, and the ceremonial and dietary laws.[101] Richard Brothers, who was probably assuming his identity as a prophet about the time of Gordon's trial, believed (among other common millenarian tenets) that he was destined to lead the Jews back to the Holy Land and rebuild Jerusalem; he believed that many descendants of the ten lost tribes were living in England and would return with him. Gordon apparently held similar beliefs.[102] In the nineteenth century, too, millenarian as well as British Israel beliefs led other Englishmen to claim the identity of Jews (and sometimes to celebrate the justice of Mosaic law).[103]

Gordon's own identity as a Jew was cast in a millenarian mould, in both the content of his belief and his personal ties. Indeed, what is most notable about his conversion is that it marked a further stage in his practice of social equality. He had been refused admission by the Chief Rabbi in London (probably fearful of the consequences for his community of so notorious a convert) and Gordon sought and found what he wanted from Rabbi Jacob of Birmingham, in a community of the very poor.[104] When Gordon was found, he was reported to be living in 'one of the dirtiest houses in Dudley Street' because the woman who owned it, a caper and anchovy

---

101. Fifth Monarchists and similar sects advocated the judicial and governmental institutions of the ancient Jews, and after the Restoration many of them found refuge in Holland, as did Gordon. I do not know if there is any evidence that he encountered remnants of that tradition, as well as Judaism, while he was in Amsterdam. Capp, pp.155, 190ff, 201–2, 222, 236, 266.

102. Harrison, ch.4; Watson, p.79. The government was sufficiently alarmed by the political dangers of Brothers' prophecies that he was imprisoned as insane by order of the Privy Council in 1795.

103. Harrison, pp.137, 141, 155, 157.

104. *The Jewish Chronicle*, 25 Aug. 1905; James Picciotto, *Sketches of Anglo-Jewish History* (London: Trubner, 1875), p.185; Solomons, p.22; W. Hutton, *History of Birmingham* (1781), p.122, comments on their poverty.

hawker, had a son who was a man of 'much learning.'[105] One newspaper reported that those among whom he lived called him Moses, 'risen from the dead in order to instruct them and enlighten the world.'[106] This may be journalistic embroidery, but it suggests the possibility that Gordon came to his new faith in a Jewish community where biblical literalism and chiliasm was current, as it was among many poor Christian sectarians in the 1780s and 1790s.[107] After his reappearance in London in 1788 he quarrelled with Jews who did not observe Orthodox law and he came to identify those who shaved off their beards and transgressed other laws as the rich Jews, indulged by unprincipled rabbis.[108] His hopes of influencing international affairs by persuading Jews in finance to follow his principles in funding governments were short-lived, for although the press reported shortly after his return that he was esteemed by some of the wealthy, his followers were soon only the Polish and Turkish Jews, the very poorest.[109]

All the sources from which Gordon probably derived his biblical literalism, then, whether Christian or Jewish, were also sources heavily tainted, in the eyes of church and state, with the sedition of democracy. The fact that the brother of a peer could have such personal associations almost defied belief: that he gave legitimacy to their dangerous ideas was most alarming. It is evident that by the time of his imprisonment he aroused chiliastic expectations.[110] Certainly he had

---

105. *The Times*, 21 Dec. 1787.

106. *Felix Farley's Bristol Journal*, 15 Dec. 1787; Solomons, p.86.

107. The idea is repeated in a broadside entitled 'The Christian turned Jew', Solomons p.41. For the older and continuing links see Todd M. Endelman, *The Jews of Georgian England 1714–1830: Tradition and Change in a Liberal Society* (Philadelphia 5739–1979), ch.2.

108. Watson, p.89; Angel Lyon, *A Letter from Angel Lyon, to the Right Honourable Lord George Gordon, on wearing beards; with Lord George Gordon's answer, and a reply from Angel Lyon* (n.p., n.d.; dated in text as June 1789); also reprinted in Solomons, pp.31–6. The relevant passage is Leviticus 19:27. cf. Endelman, p.122.

109. *The Times*, 19 Dec. 1787; Watson, pp.75, 90.

110. Watson, p.127, reports one of a 'great variety' of eccentrics who visited Gordon, a woman claiming to have been made pregnant by the Holy Ghost, who had been comforted by the Angel Gabriel with the

gained a reputation, much earlier, for concern for the people and for equality in his personal dealings with the poor.[111]

It is not surprising that the *Petition*, addressed to the streets by a man with such a history and such friends, at a time of crisis in the criminal law, so disturbed the government and the judges. The Attorney General's argument to the jury, that if it went unpunished government could not subsist, was a credible claim to such an audience. The mob, with whom Gordon had repeatedly been complicit since 1780, might well in its ignorance and literal-mindedness listen to such a madman. The convicts, crammed into overcrowded jails from which escapes were common, might well rise. The bench now made the gravity of the offence abundantly clear. By the day his sentence was to be pronounced, 12 June 1787, Gordon had fled to Holland, but Mr Justice Ashhurst exercised his oratory on the printer, Thomas Wilkins. The 'gross and scandalous libel', 'calculated to excite discontent and sedition in the prisoners confined under sentence of death, or transportation', and to spread the idea that the criminal laws were 'arbitrary and tyrannical' and the judges unjust, was of the greatest seriousness:

> . . . it is indispensably necessary, that the dignity of the State be protected against the attempts of the wicked, who endeavour to depreciate the characters of those entrusted with the administration of the law, lest by degrees they come to despise the law itself, and sap the foundation of all Government.[112]

Wilkins was sentenced to two years in prison.[113] For the moment, in the absence of Gordon himself, the authorities (at

---

news that the end of the world was at hand, and that the child was 'destined to announce the glad tidings of universal redemption'; Gabriel instructed her to go to Gordon for advice.

---

111. See below for his democratic practices.

112. *Gentleman's Magazine*, vol.62, p.635.

113. The Law Officers recommended Wilkins's release the following year in response to his petition and because he had given the authorities information that might help them detect other offenders; he received a free pardon. PRO, HO48/1B, letter of A. Macdonald and J. Scott, 11 July 1788; *Annual Register* (1788), Chronicle, p.208. Wilkins was also investigated in December 1788 in connection with Gordon's libellous attack on the King: see below.

least as represented by the press) used his conversion as prima facie evidence of insanity, and some anti-semitic scurrility was published in *The Times*. Chapbooks and broadsides hawked in the streets carried the same message.[114] When Gordon himself finally appeared for sentencing in January 1788, after his arrest in Birmingham, Ashhurst repeated some of the language he had used on Wilkins, singled out 'the scurrilous language and low abuse' of the Botany Bay petition, and deplored Gordon's 'mean ambition of being popular among thieves and pickpockets, and to stand as the champion of mischief, anarchy, and confusion.' He had tried to instill 'a hatred, contempt, and abhorrence of the criminal laws of this country, of all others the most famed for lenity, and to traduce those who are entrusted with the administration of justice.'[115]

The Common Law and the Law of God

Those who were entrusted with the administration of justice, the twelve common law judges of England, no doubt felt grossly libelled by Gordon's charge in the *Petition* that they sat in 'whited halls' 'making a show of justice and religion' while they 'perverted judgements' under 'a nominal administration of justice'. But they also had good professional reasons for taking exception to his claim that they sat 'with their backs to the word of the living God. . . .'[116] For judges as well as clerics still justified the law of England by reference to biblical passages.

In the interregnum, appeals by defendants to a fundamental Christian law, or a questioning of judicial authority, were met from the bench of the Commonwealth with simple, robust assertions in reply. Thus Chief Justice Keble in *Lilburne's Case* (1649), when Lilburne pleaded his right to counsel on the basis of the Golden Rule:

> You say well: the law of God is the law of England; and you have heard no law else, but what is consonant to the law of reason, which is the best law of God; and here is none else urged against you.[117]

---

114. 18, 26 Dec. 87; Solomons, pp.39–42.

115. *The Times*, 30 Jan. 1788.

116. Above, at n.45.

117. 4 *State Trials* 1307.

According to the same judge in *Love's Case* (1651), 'We have no law practised in this land but is the law of God . . . all the laws of this nation are Christian, and stand with evangelical truth, as well as with natural reason, and they are founded upon it. . . .'[118] Mr Justice Garmond in *Streator's Case* (1653), after Captain Streator had provocatively quoted the Book of Job, retorted, 'God made man, and gave him a law to live by; and the laws of England are grounded on the laws of God. . . .'[119] For radicals who were partisans of a Commonwealth tradition, such dicta may have carried considerable weight into the eighteenth century. Moreover, they appeared at first sight to be congruent with a much longer tradition in English law, one that spanned the interregnum.

Thus, after the Restoration, Mr Justice Hyde declared, 'The second ground of the law of England is the law of God.'[120] He was making brief reference to a central tenet of the common law. In Coke's phrase, the law of nature was 'written with the finger of God in the heart of man'; by it 'were the people of God a long time governed, before the law was written by Moses, who was the first reporter or writer of law in the world.'[121] A corollary of this understanding, with deep roots in medieval law, was that the Mosaic law and other scriptural injunctions had a place within the professional literature of the common law. We can find lawyers and judges citing biblical passages in a variety of cases. One of the extended examples occurred in the year of Gordon's trial. Mr Justice Gould, the judge with whom Gordon consulted at the time of his offence, himself cited the law of Moses the following year in *Steel* v *Houghton et uxor*, the gleaning case. Gould made the relevant passages from Leviticus a central part of his argument. At the end of the century, Lord Kenyon, Chief Justice of King's Bench, buttressed his argument that forestalling, regrating and engrossing were still crimes with words from scripture.[122] Nor was this simply remarks *obiter*,

---

118. 5 *State Trials* 238.

119. 5 *State Trials* 383, 387.

120. *Manby* v *Scott* (1663) 1 Mod.126.

121. *Calvin's Case* (1608), 4 Coke 21.

122. Hay, 'The State and the Market: Lord Kenyon and Mr Waddington',

on a par with judicial recourse to Seneca or Ovid. For according to Coke's well-known maxim (at a time when maxims were held to embody the settled principles of the common law, and Coke the highest of authorities) *Summa ratio est quae religione facit.*[123] Noy explained, citing *Doctor and Student*: 'If an act be made directly contrary to the law of God, as for instance, if it be enacted that no one shall give alms to any object in never so necessitous a condition, such an act is void.' Where there was conflict, 'Man's laws [must yield] to God's laws.'[124]

Since scripture was God's express declaration of the law of nature (this is Blackstone's formulation, in the mid-eighteenth century),[125] and the common law the English version of natural law, it was understandable that judges would sometimes cite scripture as authority. Blackstone, it is true, wrote that *mala prohibita*, purely positive or municipal laws, had no moral force behind them: obeying them was simply a matter of prudence. His editor Edward Christian, the first professor of laws at Cambridge, emphatically disagreed, arguing in the 1790s that the burden of obedience to government meant that positive and natural law were intimately intermingled. He quoted *Doctor and Student*: 'In every law positive well-made, is somewhat of the law of reason and the law of God; and to discern the law of God and the law of Reason from the law positive, is very hard.'[126] All the examples he cites are statutes. The view that many statutes were

forthcoming, *Past & Present*; *Steele* v. *Houghton* (1788), 1 H. Blackstone 51 at 54; Peter King, 'Legal change, customary right, and social conflict in late eighteenth-century England: the origins of the great gleaning case of 1788,' *Law and History Review*, vol.10 no.1 (Spring 1992), pp.1–31. In *Smith* v. *Gould* (1706) the plaintiff cited Leviticus in defense of chattel slavery: 2 *Salk.* 666, 92 *English Reports* 338, cited in Davis, *Problem of Slavery*, p.474 n.9.

123. Coke on Littleton 341a.

124. William Noy, *The Grounds and Maxims of the English Laws* (6th ed., Dublin, 1792), pp.1, 19.

125. William Blackstone, *Commentaries on the Laws of England* (12 ed.,ed. Edward Christian, London, 1793–4), vol.1, p.42.

126. *Commentaries*, vol.1, p.58 n.7. Christian's reputation among the judges, it should be added, was not high.

simply declaratory of the common law helped sustain these interpretations.

The primacy of Christianity in any conflict with the laws of man continued to be asserted by judges well into the nineteenth century. One authority observed that although Coke's maxim should be understood 'in a somewhat qualified sense' (notably because the laws of man did not punish many wicked acts and breaches of social duties), nonetheless

> It may . . . safely be affirmed that, if ever the laws of God and man are at variance, the former are to be obeyed in derogation of the latter; that the law of God is, under all circumstances, superior in obligation to that of man and that, consequently, if any general custom were opposed to the divine law, or if any statute were passed directly contrary thereto . . . such a custom, or such an Act, would be void.[127]

The maxim of course had no absolute weight. If scripture contradicted the outcome sought by the bench, it was not difficult to make distinctions that qualified its application. Mr Justice Gould's use of Leviticus was rejected by his fellow judges, and Lord Kenyon's quotation of Proverbs 11:26 was thought to be as irrelevant by his successors as the other authorities he had cited.[128] But the invocation of scripture was still heard from the bench in the eighteenth century, it was believed by some judges to have some of the weight of law, and it was invoked in terms that made references to the law of God a significant part of the celebration of the sacral nature of the courts and of English justice. Arguably it was becoming more common at the end of the century, as men with strong Evangelical connections, like Lord Kenyon, were increasingly to be found on the bench, and as the legitimacy of

---

127. Herbert Broom *A Selection of Legal Maxims* (1882 ed.), p.19.

128. Hay, 'The State and the Market: Lord Kenyon and Mr Waddington'. By the nineteenth century, the sense of the claim that 'Christianity is part of the law of England' had changed: no longer did it denote the fundamental identity of the law of God and the law of man, but rather the different assertion that an offence against Christian institutions or practices was necessarily an offence also against English law: the issue arose in cases dealing with such issues as blasphemy, whether charitable trusts for anti-Christian purposes were valid, etc. Some of these cases are reviewed in *Bowman* v. *Secular Society*, L.R. (1917) Appeals Cases, 406.

the existing constitution came under attack.[129] Gordon's citation of scripture was as offensive as it was dangerous, a mis-
appropriation of judicial discourse that was also a libel on the
judges.[130] His offence grew greater as he went on to libel the
King.

Monarchy and the Pardon

The 'blaze of glory' around the courts, their 'lustre and
dignity', ultimately derived, according to the judges, from the
glory of the monarch: the judges were 'the Channels by which
the King's Justice is conveyed to the People.'[131] Christian
doctrine, judicial authority, kingly majesty were indivisible:
all were in part mysterious, awesome, powerful. They were,
in short, partly sacral in nature. Having attacked Christian
doctrine and judicial authority before his conviction, Lord
George Gordon, Israel Bar Abraham George Gordon, completed his political pilgrimage by attacking monarchy itself.
And here we return to the death penalty. For capital punishment, its mystery and its awe, was not something only of
importance to divines and judges: it was the sacral stuff of
kings. Kings, indeed, linked divine and human justice.

Even before his convictions in 1787, Gordon had shown
what to contemporary gentlemen was a shocking irreverence
for monarchy. Although George II had been Gordon's god-
father,[132] he was presuming on his rank when he badgered
George III in person, in 1783 and again in 1785, on the
subject of both religion and imprisoned debtors. He was
barred from the court of St. James as a consequence.[133] The

---

129. I am investigating the use of scriptural authority in judgements of this
period.

130. I am completing a study of libels on the judges and the courts in the
eighteenth and nineteenth centuries.

131. Mr Justice Wilmot's undelivered judgement in *R.* v. *Almon* (1765),
Wilmot, 255–6. On this case see Hay, 'Contempt by Scandalizing the
Court: A Political History of the First Hundred Years', *Osgoode Hall
Law Journal*, vol. 25 no.3 (Fall 1987), pp.431–84.

132. R. Chambers, *A Biographical Dictionary of Eminent Scotsmen* (new
ed., 1855).

133. *The Times*, 1 Sept. 1786. In December 1787, after Gordon had fled to

report that he tried to intervene on behalf of Margaret
Nicholson, who was incarcerated as mad after she made an
attempt on the life of the king in 1786, showed he was
dangerous. He then befriended Count Cagliostro, and libelled the Count's 'persecutor', the Queen of France, and her
English ambassador, for which the government successfully
prosecuted him concurrently with the case on the prisoner's
Petition. In that proceeding, he attempted to subpoena Mrs
Fitzherbert, the Roman Catholic 'married' mistress of the
Prince of Wales, whose exact relationship to the Prince was
the subject of Parliamentary controversy at the time; during
the trial Gordon impugned the sexual reputations of both the
French Queen and the Empress of Russia, until silenced by
the court. (The Attorney General declared he was 'a disgrace
to the name of a Briton.') After his conviction on that libel
(concurrently with the Botany Bay pamphlet) he proceeded
to compound his original libel on royalty by publishing outrageous reflections on the sexual reputations of not only the
Queen of France, but of Queen Elizabeth and Catherine the
Great, whose lust for her soldiery was carefully spelled out.[134]

Holland, it was discovered that one John Mitchell, an usher at St.
James, with direct access to the King, was corresponding with
Gordon. Mitchell was immediately dismissed, but investigation
showed that he was a former servant of the Duke of Gordon's family,
who used him as an intermediary for necessary correspondence with
Gordon; Lord Aylesford intervened with Lord Sydney on his behalf.
PRO, HO 42/12 fols. 416–421v.

---

134. The prosecution remarked at trial that the libel that Marie Antoinette
had persecuted Cagliostro (who had been imprisoned in connection
with the seditious scandal surrounding the affair of the diamond
necklace) 'had been known and felt in the capital of France.' After the
trials it was usually cited as the reason for Gordon's sentence,
although all the evidence suggests that the government had been more
concerned by the *Petition*. Whether this revision occurred because
attacks on the French monarchy came to be considered more
outrageous during the revolutionary wars, or because there was
sensitivity about capital punishment, or because of Burke, is unclear.
Burke, reflecting on the 1780 riots and Gordon's recent conviction,
wrote: 'We have rebuilt Newgate and tenanted the mansion. We have
prisons almost as strong as the Bastile, for those who libel the queens
of France.' A nearly contemporary biographer thought that Gordon's
imprisonment had been two years for the libel on the Queen of

The connections between his religious heterodoxy and his anti-monarchical beliefs were shown in other ways. After his excommunication in 1786 for contempt toward the courts of the Archbishop of Canterbury, other victims of the church courts appealed to him. A few months after his imprisonment he was encouraging an oppressed group of Nottingham dissenters in their rebellion against Anglican marriage (several of their wives having been incarcerated for nineteen months); they claimed the rights enjoyed by Jews and Quakers. Their minister thanked Gordon for his support in a letter which Gordon published, castigating 'The law of tyrannical or unjust power, by which poor helpless men are deprived, some of their lives, others of their liberty, some of their wives, and many, very many of their rights and property.' This was a clear indictment of both criminal and ecclesiastical law, and its political implications were not concealed: the writer predicted God's righteous wrath on persecutors and mentioned among other examples Henry VIII, Queen Mary, and Charles I.[135]

In judging the significance of Gordon's insults to royalty in the 1780s, it is useful to recall the public language of orthodoxy. It was precisely in these years, 1783–87, that Anglican clerics found it important to emphasise the sanctity of kingly authority. In earlier years the clerical defence of the House of Hanover had usually been expressed in general

France, and three years for a libel on the Empress of Russia. During the trial, Gordon was challenged by Walter Smythe, Sir Charles Bampfyld, and Henry Harvey Aston, partisans of Mrs Fitzherbert; he took out articles of the peace against them. Sarah Maza, 'The Diamond Necklace Affair Revisited (1785–1786)' in Lynn Hunt (ed.), *Eroticism and the Body Politic* (Baltimore, 1991), pp.63–89; *The Times*, 24 Sept., 21 Nov. 1785, 12 Aug. 1786, 25 Jan., 1, 3, 7, 9, 10, 11, 12, 16 May, 6, 8 June 1787, 29 Jan. 1788; 22 *State Trials* 213; *Gentleman's Magazine*, vol.61, pp.532–3; *A Letter from the Right Hon. Lord George Gordon to the Attorney General of England*; Edmund Burke, *Reflections on the Revolution in France*, intro. A.J. Grieve (London, 1964), p.81; *Eccentric Biography; or, Sketches of Remarkable Characters* (1801); PRO, KB 21/44, pp.328, 330, 332, 335.

135. 9, 28 March 1787, 24 Sept. 1788. Bradley, *Religion, Revolution, and English Radicalism*, p.56, mentions such a case 'as late as 1750'; clearly, there were others.

terms, the divine authority of constituted government, in which kingly power was constrained within the conventions of whig constitutionalism. But the royal martyr and monarchical authority were significantly rehabilitated in the 1780s. The sermons preached on Martyrdom Day, 30 January 1783 and 1787, to the House of Lords by the Bishop of Bristol and the Bishop of Oxford were unequivocal defences of Charles I and the sacredness of the person of the King.[136] The 1780s were marked, in religious writings on social theory, by a marked insecurity. Hole suggests some reasons: the American colonies lost, the King's policy in tatters, riots, dearth, radical reform.[137] But arguably one of the most immediate causes (although it was a consequence of all those mentioned) was that the criminal law was then at its most ferocious. And this directly implicated monarchy. The operation of the criminal law, including the royal pardon, called for the most unequivocal bolstering of the monarchical mystery in the mid-1780s.

The royal pardon was the prerogative of kings, the duty of kings, and in conventional wisdom the attribute which brought them closest to divinity. It generated reverence for monarchy year in, year out, in the administration of the law. The political significance of the pardon was believed to be very much bound up with the popularity of regimes. When Blackstone wrote in the 1760s that 'these repeated acts of goodness coming immediately from his own hand, endear the sovereign to his subjects, and contribute more than anything to root in their hearts that filial affection, and personal loyalty, which are the sure establishment of a prince', he was not simply inventing an argument with which to silence Beccaria.[138] He was also uttering the conventional wisdom of England's rulers, repeating a commonplace of ecclesiastical, constitutional, and legal discourse. What Blackstone did not spell out was the equally notorious fact that the effect of not granting a pardon could reflect very badly on the Crown.[139]

---

136. Hole, pp.52–3.

137. Hole, pp.84–6.

138. Blackstone, *Commentaries*, vol.4, p.397; Cesare Beccaria, *On Crimes and Punishments* (trans. Henry Paolucci, New York, 1963), ch.20.

139. Beccaria had made precisely this argument: that a pardon not

The anonymous author of *An Argument to Prove the Affections of the People of England to be the Best Security of Government* (1746)[140], whose object was mercy for the rebels of the '45, explained why. He began by summarizing the view of those who opposed pardons:

> Wholesome Severities, it may be urged, can do the King no Disservice with his People: He may still retain their Affection, and yet the Laws have their Course in punishing the Guilty. For, whilst he doth not interpose one Way or other, of what Consequence can it be to him, how many or how few are brought to the Scaffold? To which I reply, That tho' I do not know HOW? it is, or why it should be so; yet the Dead Warrant is always supposed to come from the *Crown*, and that when the *Crown* doth not interpose in Favour of *Sufferers*, it is taken for granted, that it is well-disposed to their Execution.

The belief that the King actually signed the death warrant was also reported by Daines Barrington in 1775, as a vulgar error, and by Voltaire (who believed it). In short, the prerogative of mercy could only contribute to 'the sure establishment of a prince' if it was administered with great care. This was particularly the case when the stability of the regime seemed threatened, either by revolt, as it was in 1745, or during the chancy business of a Hanoverian succession.[141] During the reigns of the first two Georges, the unpopularity of the monarchy with many subjects, the intermittent threat of Jacobitism, and the periodic absences of the King in Hanover (when the pardon fell largely into the hands of the Lords Justices) kept the issue sensitive into Blackstone's time. These were among the considerations that caused George III, on his accession, to show a particular interest in his prerogative power of mercy. The royal pardon was particularly important in sacral celebration because it joined the quasi-divinity of kings with the 'blaze of glory' about the courts.[142] Although reverence for George III was inculcated throughout the 1780s, the background of very high rates of hanging was a

---

granted, since a pardoning system aroused hopes, inevitably seemed an act of oppression. Loc.cit.

---

140. Copy in PRO, SP 36/87 fol.155.

141. See the full discussion in my forthcoming book.

142. Above, n.131.

constant reminder that the pardon was not often being exercised. After the execution of Phoebe Harris, burned at the stake in 1786, and in the middle of the legal proceedings against Gordon, even *The Times* called for a reformation of the laws, 'that the stream of mercy might flow with brightness and with energy; and that the reign of a sovereign, distinguished for personal clemency, might be adorned by judicial wisdom and humanity.'[143] The issue of the pardon became even more sensitive in 1788, for in October of that year the King fell apparently mad and became incapable of exercising his duties.

At this crucial juncture Gordon's contempt for monarchy led to a new outrage. Although in prison, he had distributed handbills reflecting on George III's condition in insulting terms borrowed from Deuteronomy and Kings: 'the effects palpably intended, were to alienate from his Majesty, the affections of his people, by the most scandalous perversion of the texts above mentioned.' When challenged, Gordon stroked his beard and calmly replied, 'Such are the words of the Old Testament.' He would not cite the 'flattering' portions of scripture on behalf of the crazed King, as so many other Jews and Christians recently had done. *The Times* recommended closer confinement in Newgate and a new prosecution in the ecclesiastical courts.[144] The government was said to be anxious to prosecute the printer on an *ex officio* information, but was unable to find sufficient evidence.[145]

Thus, having insulted the ecclesiastical and civil courts in 1786 and 1787, Gordon proceeded to attack George III. The progression is not surprising. Some of the sources of his apparent republicanism were probably the same as those of his biblical literalism: seventeenth-century sectarians, and perhaps the Reverend James Murray of Newcastle.[146] But

---

143. 13 Feb. 1787; the paper advised that in such an instance Parliament should make provision for those injured in their emoluments by such a reform. See also the review of the play, 'Such Things Are', same issue.

144. *The Times*, 26, 28 Nov. 1788.

145. *The Times*, 1 Dec. 1788.

146. Gordon probably used 1 Kings 12, a chapter about royal wickedness that was one of several often cited by the Reverend James Murray. In his published attacks on oppressive royal authority Murray also cited

THE LAWS OF GOD AND THE LAWS OF MAN 105

Gordon also had a unique perspective on royal oppression and royal justice. Incarcerated in the felons' side of Newgate, where the largest number of capital convicts in England awaited execution, he cannot have been unaware that the King's illness brought about a suspension of the normal operation of the capital statutes. From early November 1788 until late February 1789 the King was incapable of attending the 'hanging cabinet', which considered pardons for London and Middlesex, and it appears that condemned convicts were given repeated reprieves for the entire period until the King could deal with the recommendations of the bench and of petitioners. As a consequence, a large number of prisoners were under sentence of death but nursing desperate hopes.[147]

This unintended demonstration that the normal operation of the prerogative brought death rather than mercy led to governmental embarrassment on George III's recovery. When by March 1789 the King was again able to deal with death sentences, the Home Secretary strongly advised leniency rather than a clearing of the jails by mass hangings:

. . . the consideration of the great length of confinement of several of the unhappy persons, the number of them, *and the interruption which such a spectacle gives to the general joy and happiness of the present time*, has

---

King Eglon of Moab: 'I should beg the delicate reader's pardon, for making mention so often of dirt and nastiness; but as it is the excrement of kings and great men, I hope I shall be excused: This is not *common dirt*.' Quoted in Bradley, p.164.

---

147. The following table shows that prisoners in London and Middlesex were principally affected, as the King's madness fell after the summer assizes, and only a few late reprieves from the circuits would thus be affected. John Howard reported that by December 27, 1788 'there remain 34 convicts under sentence of death [for London and Middlesex], of whom no report hath been made, on account of his Majesty's indisposition'. (*An Account of the Principal Lazarettos*, p.258, note to Table XIII). He recovered before the beginning of Lent assizes of 1789.

Table 1: Percentage executed (and percentage change from previous year) in London, and on the Home, Western, and Norfolk circuits.

Jurisdiction	1785	1786	1787	1788	1789	1790	1791
London/Middx	54	53(−2)	58(+9)	26(−55)	25(−4)	33(+32)	40(+21)
Circuits	48	35(−27)	37(+6)	26(−30)	32(+23)	33(+3)	29(−12)

made a pretty general impression upon the minds of his Majesty's subjects.[148]

Evidently the King concurred. The hanging figures for 1789, like those in 1788, were the lowest in many years.

Revolution and the Law of God

Gordon's attempt to subvert the sacral nature of kingship in 1788, and his use of biblical texts to do so, suggests the increasingly revolutionary nature of his thought. After his conviction, his reputation as a friend of the poor and the criminal apparently had wide currency. Not long after his imprisonment he was reported to be 'exciting by his own evil example a spirit of turbulence, and riot, amongst the poor unfortunate women convicts in Newgate', through what *The Times* called 'frantic schemes of new fangling the laws of this country and shaping them down to the model of a *Chapter of Exodus*.'[149] The 'Mosaic Law Reformer' was removed from contact with these women, but his popularity among his fellow-prisoners, and the poor outside prison walls, continued to grow.[150] With the outbreak of the French revolution, he appears to have moved to a logical political conclusion: that is, Jacobinism, the revolutionary repudiation of aristocracy and monarchy. Gordon's Jacobinism was well known, to the people as well as to the press. In Newgate he held dinners, to which outside guests came: 'they were composed of all ranks, and ranged as chance directed; the jew and the Gentile, the legislator and the labouring mechanic, the officer and the soldier, all shared alike: liberty and equality were enjoyed in their full extent, as far as Newgate would allow.' Watson went on to claim that 'No man was more beloved by his fellow

---

148. *Later Correspondence of George III*, vol.1, p.402, my emphasis. See John Ehrman, *The Younger Pitt: the Years of Acclaim* (New York, 1969) pp.664–5 for the celebrations on the King's recovery.

149. 12 August 1788. This report may refer to Gordon's advising Isabella Stewart, on trial for theft, to cite the recent Royal Proclamation, which enjoined adherence to God's law, in an argument to the bench that she should not be hanged or transported for theft, but owed only double restitution. The startled judges sentenced her to death. Watson, pp.105–6.

150. *The Times.*, 13 Aug. 1788.

prisoners than Lord George; he divided his substance with those who had no money, and did every thing in his power to alleviate their distress. He clothed the naked, and fed the hungry; but his fortune was inadequate to relieve all their wants.'[151] Watson is anxious to claim Gordon for the Jacobin cause, but his account is consistent with Gordon's popular reputation and with what we know of his life by the mid-1780s. *The Times* reported with scorn as early as 1786 that he showed his writings to 'a waiter' for approval.[152] In 1791 the *Leeds Mercury* reported that a mob had appeared outside Newgate, demanding his release so that he could participate in the Bastille Day celebrations of 14 July. Soldiers were called in to prevent an attack on the prison, and the mob outside dispersed; but by then the prisoners inside were rioting. Troops were sent in, and others were despatched to deal with a similar mob outside the King's Bench prison.[153]

Such incidents, if accurately reported, made Gordon's release from prison highly undesirable for government, particularly after the declaration of war with revolutionary France in 1793. As the experience of Richard Brothers shows, the ministry was more anxious than ever to imprison prophets of democracy and the millenium.[154] At the time of his imprisonment, *The Times* had remarked that Gordon's sentence could amount to imprisonment for life, because Mr Justice Ashhurst sentenced him to a total of five years in Newgate, but also a £500 fine, and the enormous sum of £15,000 in bonds to keep the peace at the end of his sentence. It was highly unlikely that he would ever be able to guarantee such sums, and *The Times* suggested that royal mercy would not be inappropriate.[155] Mercy was not forthcoming in 1788; it was

---

151. Watson, pp.107–109.

152. 9 Nov. 1786.

153. 19 July 1791; I owe this reference to Nicholas Rogers. This may be the event described by Watson, p.134–5, in which he alleges that 'early in the summer' a group of sailors waited on Gordon, and proposed to liberate him from Newgate by force, to proceed to plant the tree of liberty in England, or, if the people were not yet ready, to take him to France. The plan, says Watson, was postponed.

154. Above, n.102.

155. 4 Feb. 1788. The sentence for the *Petition* was three years; the rest of

even less likely in 1793. In January that year Gordon petitioned King's bench to be released from Newgate, having
served five years. The scene in Court was both pathetic and
ridiculous: Gordon, bearded and unkempt, refused to remove his hat, which was taken from him in a struggle with the
officers of the court. He explained he meant no contempt, but
that his religion demanded that he keep his head covered; he
improvised a 'turban' with a nightcap and a handkerchief. He
offered to pay his fine (money given him by his brother the
Duke), but the two impoverished Polish Jews whom he
brought as sureties were dismissed as wholly insufficient. It
was said that rich Jews were too prudent to offer him help, and
his family would do no more for him.[156]

Gordon returned to Newgate and died there of jail fever in
November 1793, age 42. He died devoted to the French
revolution (which promised toleration for the Jews as well as
freedom for the world). By then, as we have seen, Israel Bar
Abraham George Gordon was a hero to Thomas Spence and
to many poorer Englishmen and women who hoped, if not for
the millenium, at least for a revolution.

God's Scriptures and Bentham's

The crisis of the 1780s passed without substantial damage to
the sacral nature of capital punishment, or to the state/legal
system which used it so lavishly in those years. The celebration of the quasi-divinity of monarchy, already noticeable in
the speeches of leading churchmen in the 1780s, was vastly
heightened by the official celebrations when George III
recovered from his illness in 1789. A host of pardons became
part of the celebration, as we have seen, and both sentences
and executions dropped to very low levels in 1788 and 1789.
There were even fewer after the outbreak of war with France

the terms were attributed by Ashhurst to the conviction on the second
libel, but the Attorney General expressed the opinion that the *Petition*
was the more serious offence. Gordon was required to post £10,000
and to find two sureties of £2500 each. According to Watson, pp.84–5,
the cabinet sent Gordon's brother with an offer of clemency, in return
for a recantation and silence in the future; it was rejected.

156. Solomons, p.45; *The Times* 6 Feb. 1788.

in 1793, a consequence of the common eighteenth-century pattern of low levels of prosecutions in wartime.

But by the 1790s, Gordon's central argument against the criminal law of England, that it contradicted the law of Moses, was being rapidly abandoned even by many of those who had earlier espoused it. We can find it being repudiated by critics of the criminal law on both sides of the Atlantic, probably first in America, then in England. Gordon had used the argument about the Mosaic law of theft at a particular juncture, the 1780s, when hundreds were being executed, overwhelmingly for property offences. By 1793, even in England, the proportion of thieves on the gallows was declining, and in states such as Pennsylvania, with a re-awakened Quaker heritage stimulated by republican ideals of a reformed criminal justice, it was already low.

In such circumstances the law of Moses, far from seeming merciful, seemed too vengeful. Benjamin Rush, who led the movement for the abolition of the death penalty in Pennsylvania in the 1790s, derided the Mosaic law as one designed by God to curb 'the ignorance, wickedness, and "hardness of heart" of the Jews.' It demanded capital punishment even for offences which had ceased to be capital in England itself. Rush constructed from other scriptural passages, notably from the New Testament, a case for the abolition of capital punishment entirely.[157] A similar argument was made by the radical George Dyer in England in 1793:

> In defence of capital punishments, I know, it is common to produce the authority of the jewish legislator: but whatever weight may be allowed the authority of Moses, as it respected the Jews, it has little, as it relates to modern nations. The jewish law, to say the most, was formed in barbarous times, and made conformable to barbarous manners. Idolatry and other crimes were punished with death. I may add, that David was full of severity, and Solomon was a despot. Shall we say to modern governments, *Go, and do likewise?* The laws of Him, whom christians profess to follow, give no sanction to the shedding of human blood.[158]

---

157. Benjamin Rush, *Considerations on the Injustice and Impolicy of Punishing Murder by Death* (Philadelphia, 1792), pp.4–6; see also Louis P. Masur, *Rites of Execution: Capital Punishment and the Transformation of American Culture, 1776–1865* (New York, 1989), p.68.

158. George Dyer, *The Complaints of the Poor People of England* (2nd ed.,

This was also Tom Paine's view of the law of Moses, and he provoked Bishop Watson to retort (using an unfortunate example), 'you may as reasonably attribute cruelty and murder to the judge of the land in condemning criminals to death, as butchery and massacre to Moses in executing the commands of God.'[159] In 1798 William Blake wrote in the margin of his copy of Watson,

> The laws of the Jews were (both ceremonial & real) the basest & most oppressive of human codes, & being like all other codes given under pretence of divine command were what Christ pronounced them, The Abomination that maketh desolate, i.e., State Religion, which is the source of all Cruelty.[160]

The Quakers, democrats, and visionaries most visible to us in the historical record thus abandoned an argument of four centuries. And so too, of course, had Bentham: 'those who believe in the Christian religion, believe also in the Jewish religion; and under the Jewish religion, abundant was the application made of death-punishment; and thus may be seen *authority-begotten prejudice* operating in support of it.'[161]

This was the epitaph of the public argument that God's law was more merciful than that of England. By the time Bentham's words were published, the punishment of death for theft had almost disappeared in England. Fewer than 20 persons, about 1% of those actually sentenced to death for property offences, were executed in 1830. That English law contravened 'the judicials of Moses' was irrelevant not only in the eyes of the utilitarian infidel, it had become largely irrelevant and would soon become entirely so to the law of England.

London, 1793), p.28..

---

159. Thomas Paine, *The Age of Reason* (1794–5); Richard Watson, *An Apology for the Bible in a Series of Letters addressed to Thomas Paine by R. Watson, D.D., F.R.S.* (London, 1797), p.25.

160. Geoffrey Keynes, ed., *The Complete Writings of William Blake* (London, 1966), p. 393. I owe this reference, like so much else, to Edward Thompson.

161. *Works* (Bowring), vol.1, p.531: 'Appendix on Death-Punishment' to *Principles of Penal Law* [Dec. 1830].

By 1830 there had been more than a generation of debate in which was forged the modern argument against capital punishment, one that finally prevailed over the resistance of the judges and their parliamentary supporters. It is the argument – emphasizing legal rationality, proportionality, humanity, moderation, deterrence, and the importance of public opinion – with which we are now familiar. In that debate the defenders of capital punishment also increasingly use the same language, often borrowed from Paley's pragmatic defence, first published in the 1780s. From both sides, the result was a de-sacralization of the death penalty as a central mystery of monarchy and state. Gordon's offence may have been significant in this development in its early years. He showed how necessary it was to control the religious interpretation of capital punishment, but also how difficult it might be to do so. The traditional monarchical-religious defence of capital punishment could too easily be inverted into its own critique. The links Gordon made – judicial terror: religion: monarchy: social inequality – mirrored the same links in orthodox thought, but in subversive terms.

Gordon's vision disappeared, so completely that later writers used it as evidence that he was mad. Yet it had convinced Sir Thomas More, and the Levellers, and George Fox, and it was continually renewed among those without power. The argument that pitted God's law against man's in the name of divine mercy spoke to the poor who hoped for the millenium, and to the men and women who waited in Newgate in the early months of 1787 for death or transportation to Botany Bay. Like them, Israel Bar Abraham George Gordon, prophet of the laws of God, was soon forgotten, as was his message. But for a critical few months it threatened to undermine the foundation of terror on which, according to the Attorney General and the judges, all government was erected.

Chapter Four

Trade Unions, The Government and the French Revolution, 1789–1802

John Rule

Interest in the relationship of trade unionism in Britain to the political agitation of the Jacobin era has largely concentrated on the circumstances in which the Combination Acts of 1799 and 1800 were passed, on their effects, intended and unintended, and on the closely related matter of the extent of trade union links with extreme radical politics. In respect of this last concern, the arguments of Edward Thompson advanced almost thirty years ago in *The Making of the English Working Class* have largely set the agenda in a debate in which the nature of the evidence on matters involving secret organisation, underground activity and revolutionary politics hardly permits firm and final conclusions. More recently wider issues have been raised over the role of trade unions in this period, which have implications for the context in which the act of 1799 was passed. Examining the economic role of trade unions in the last decades of the eighteenth century is as significant as considering the extent of their political involvement at revolutionary or unsurrectionary moments like 1799–1802, or the effect of the Combination Acts of 1799 and 1800 in politicising trade unions. It is also important to assess the extent to which jacobin ideology was congruent with the attitudes and assumptions of the organised artisan trades and whether in general trade unions were effective in protecting or advancing the interests of working men.

In revolutionary France trade unions were illegal. The Le Chapelier Law of 1791 was not only eight years in advance of the British general prohibition of 1799, but its opposition was more fundamental. It too had arisen from the petitioning of masters engaged in a particular industrial dispute – the Parisian carpenters playing the role of London's journeymen millwrights. However, it was more manifestly ideological in its premises – although it will be argued below that the English parliament too was acting in an ideological manner in a wider sense than opposing conservatism to radicalism. The Combination Acts of 1799 and 1800 were clearly intended both to prevent the spread of working-class organisation into the 'populous' newly industrialising areas and to offer employers in general the rapidly effective weapon of summary jurisdiction when faced with strikes. The Le Chapelier Law in a more clear-cut manner opposed trade unions in the name of the revolutionary constitution and in defence of the rights of man:

> If, against the principles of liberty and of the constitution, citizens attached to the same professions, arts and trades, should make agreements among themselves tending to refuse in concert, or to accord only at a determined price the aid of their industry or of their labours, the said deliberations and agreements . . . are declared unconstitutional and against the declaration of the rights of man. . . .[1]

Echoes of this are to be found in some British radical writings: the rights of man over-riding the rights of association. There was general agreement among radicals over the unfairness and oppressive nature of the existing laws which punished combinations of workers, 'the only means the poor could have of raising the price of their labour', as one Norwich radical put it. John Thelwall wondered why manufacturers and merchants could combine with impunity, while 'labourers and mechanics who enter into associations to appreciate their own labour are sentenced, like felons, to a gaol'. Tom Paine[2] condemned laws which disabled the workmen from bargaining freely over the price of their personal labour, which was 'all the property they had', but in praising the virtues of the French Constitution of 1791, he stressed its insistence that 'all trades shall be free and everyman free to follow any occupation by which he can procure an honest

---

1. For an important discussion of the Le Chapelier Law see: W.H. Sewell, *Work and Revolution in France. The Language of Labour from the Old regime to 1848*, (Cambridge, 1980), pp.88–91.

2. H.T. Dickinson, *Liberty and Property. Political Ideology in Eighteenth-Century Britain*, (1979), p.268; Thomas Paine, *The Rights of Man*, (Dolphin Books, New York, 1961), pp.493–4., 312–313.

livelihood'. An anonymous pamphlet of 1794 enumerates 24 benefits which would come about as a result of a 'reform of the representation'. The sixth is that 'Workmen might no longer be punished with imprisonment for uniting to obtain an increase in wages, whilst their masters are allowed to conspire against them with impunity', but the fifth had stated: 'A poor and industrious man might no longer be prevented from getting his living by the various franchises, privileges and charters of different trades and corporations shutting him out from exercising perhaps the only trade he is capable of. . . .'[3] In so far as there was an effective trade unionism among artisans and journeymen in the eighteenth century, its cornerstone was the ability to defend an exclusive property of skill, usually through maintaining apprenticeship. This was a frontier against 'over-stocking' the trade with 'unfair' workmen. It was in the language of special, not general rights, that in 1817 the journeymen watchmakers were still protesting to the Prime Minister that in allowing the ending of statutory apprenticeship, he had bowed 'to the pretensions to the allowance of universal uncontrolled freedom of action to every individual', which had fostered the French Revolution and which, if allowed to prevail, 'would hasten the destruction of the social system so happily established by the British Constitution'.[4]

Perhaps we should not over-labour the point. There is an evident ideological polarity, but there is little evidence to confirm that substantial numbers of British skilled-workers, already organised into more or less effective trade unions, ever considered and then rejected radical politics because they perceived a clear threat in Jacobin ideology to the principles and assumptions upon which their trade unions were based. Yet it should at least be recognised that whereas radical orators could sway trade unionists by attacking legislation designed to oppress them, they could not easily point

3. 'Revolutions without Bloodshed, or Reformation preferable to Revolt', Anon, 1794, reprinted in G.D.H. Cole and A.W. Filson, eds, *British Working Class Movements. Select Documents 1789–1895*, (1967), pp.48–52.

4. *BPP, Select Committee on the Petitions of Coventry Watchmakers*, 1817, VI, p.18.

across the Channel and claim that things went much better with workers' combinations over there.

The problem of selling jacobin ideology to some groups of organised manufacturing workers has recently been considered by Dr Randall in the context of workers in the woollen industry. He rightly insists that the reception of radicalism depended not just on an analysis of ills, but on the 'culture and customary context of the community into which it was being introduced'. Thus a group could be simultaneously feared for its proclivity towards industrial action, yet regarded as politically loyal. This was the case with the woollen workers of the west country. In this region, in contrast with the West Riding, where the small working-clothier was still a culturally dominant figure, the separation of labour and capital had long existed. It was a divorce which contemporaries well-recognised as the structural feature explaining the relatively high level of trade unionism and frequency of industrial disputes in the area.[5]

Yet as the influential Gloucestershire magistrate Sir George Paul put it in 1798, although there was 'no reason to fear the political principles of the people', 'the sore point of increasing machinery might encourage some to threaten the manufacturers'.[6] Randall suggests that the culture of the woollen workers amounted to a traditional 'industrial moral economy' which, although it embodied 'a strong sense of craft and class consciousness', did not amount to a challenge to the existing economic order. Rather it sought to maintain and defend 'rights' within it. These were not 'natural' rights but special ones legitimated by a strong sense of the regulation of the trade through custom and law. If capitalists sought to ignore these rights, then the first line of resistance was to appeal to local and national authorities, magistrates, courts and ultimately parliament. Until 1809, when parliament repealed the old statutes regulating the woollen manufacture through apprenticeship, wage assessment and restrictions on the use of machinery, the organised protests of the weavers and shearmen remained very largely within the parameters of

---

5. A. Randall, *Before the Luddites. Custom, community and machinery in the English woollen industry 1776–1809*, (Cambridge, 1991), p.280.

6. Randall, *Before the Luddites*, p.273.

a traditional political economy, even in their attacks on machinery.[7]

This traditional political economy was part of the old regime opposed by the new radicalism of the Jacobin and Painite kind. The irony was that by the end of the first decade of the nineteenth century, at what Thompson has called 'the crisis point in the abrogation of paternalist legislation and in the imposition of the political economy of laissez faire upon and against the will and conscience of the working people', it was becoming increasingly clear that government was relinquishing its traditional role.[8] But expectations were slow to change and until disillusionment set in many artisans were more inclined to petition for old style regulation than to embrace whole-heartedly the Jacobins' emphasis on diminished regulation and their faith in free markets for labour as well as commodities. Paine applied the test of reason to traditional institutions and customary expectations. To the weavers, especially of the west country, as Randall points out, 'Collective security could seem therefore to be threatened by such an ideology rather than augmented by it'.[9] These workers could not easily see their future in the democratic state of petty producers. What they sought, in the face of the encroachments of laissez-faire, was the continuance of reciprocal obligations and responsibilities and of a role for a traditional authority which regulated and arbitrated the balance of power between groups in the labour market. The west-country woollen workers were far from alone in this. As Randall has pointed out, even the 'domestic' system of woollen cloth production in the West Riding with its widely proclaimed social harmony was under pressure from the late-eighteenth century, as a polarisation grew between a number of large capitalists innovating in methods and organisation and the traditional small independent clothiers. Here too the master clothiers and the journeymen saw their interest as best served by the 'old legislative code', while the innovators saw theirs' as best served by its rescinding: 'It was thus to West-

---

7. Randall, *Before the Luddites*, pp.279–80.

8. E.P. Thompson, *The Making of the English Working Class*, (Penguin ed. 1969), p.594.

9. Randall, *Before the Luddites*, p.280.

minster that all sides were to look to settle the issue and before
Parliament that they were to lay their case'.[10] Similar expectations explain too why other groups like framework knitters,
calico printers and cotton weavers can be found as 'loyal
petitioners' of the very institutions which 'rational' jacobin
radicalism opposed. Professor Dickinson has remarked on
the failure of radical leaders to make use of the potential or
organised labour:

> Although trade unions had begun to appear in a number of violent
> disorders and effective strikes, most radicals had not yet grasped that
> labour's industrial strength might be a powerful weapon of political
> change[11]

But Professor Christie has seen the trade unionism of
skilled workers as something which actually worked against
the radical politicisation of organised workers:

> In whatever ways men combined, so as to attain some degree of security
> in their lives, if, and so far as these activities were successful, they took
> the sting out of human discontent and so contributed to social stability.
> They helped to achieve what was felt to be some sort of tolerable balance
> of interests between different sections of the community. Although
> workmen's organizations in the eighteenth century often encountered
> by failure, nevertheless they also secured a sufficient degree of success to
> have these effects.[12]

Christie's argument draws upon the recent demonstration
that trade unions and industrial action were more widespread
and more effective in the eighteenth century than traditional
labour historiography recognised.[13] As one of the historians
involved, I would be among the last to deny this. But it is a
relative re-assessment. Eighteenth-century trade unionism
was not *generally* and consistently effective. The Combination Act of 1799 originated in the efforts of London's master-
millwrights to secure a specific act against combining journeymen in their trade. They were backed by the city's large

---

10. Randall, *Before the Luddites*, p.277.

11. Dickinson, *Liberty and Property*, p.259.

12. I.R. Christie, *Stress and Stability in Late Eighteenth-Century Britain*,
    (Oxford, 1984) pp.124–5.

13. In particular he draws upon C.R. Dobson, *Masters and Journeymen: A
    prehistory of industrial Relations*, (1980) and John Rule, *The
    Experience of Labour in Eighteenth-Century Industry*, (1981).

machine-using, politically well-connected business interests, including the big brewers to whose operations the regular attention of the millwrights was essential. As such it was clearly an attempt to exorcise an established and effective trade union. In so far as it was high-jacked in the course of its parliamentary passage to be reshaped into a general proscription of trade unionism, it reflected both the wish to constrain the activities of existing combinations, which were judged to have become so powerful that they challenged the authority of masters over men, and also the anxiety to stop the further spread of trade unionism, especially into the industrialising midlands and north.[14]

To the extent that these were the main motivations, then the introduction and passing of the Act of 1799 in itself supports in part Christie's argument, for it shows at the highest level a recognition that trade unions could be effective and were an increasing presence. It does not, however, show that Government considered them to be a politically stabilising force. Indeed, in so far as it was motivated by political anxiety to enact a general prohibition, then Government believed the opposite. But to what extent were unions perceived as a present threat to the political system?

Writing on the rapid passage of the general ban on trade unions in 1799, the Webbs considered that 'The grounds for this drastic measure are nowhere clearly stated, but it appears to have been connected with the marked increase of Trade Unionism among the textile workers of Yorkshire and Lancashire'.[15] This connection is likely enough, but it leaves open the question of just what ministers feared from the spread of trade unionism, including the Prime Minister, for it was Pitt himself who brought in the Bill. Many historians have argued that the dominant fear was the spread of political subversion in the form of Jacobin and Painite radicalism. As the Webbs put it:

> Under the shadow of the French Revolution, the English governing classes regarded all associations of the common people with the utmost alarm. In this general terror lest insubordination should develop into

14. *Lords Journals*, XLII, July 1799.

15. S. & B. Webb, *The History of Trade Unionism*, (1911 ed.), p.62.

rebellion were merged both the capitalist's objection to high wages and the politician's dislike of democratic institutions.[16]

This is somewhat unclear as to whether 'capitalists' and 'politicians' are being viewed as separate interests brought together, or whether it was the case that government itself was increasingly accepting free-market capitalism as the 'natural way of things', and already beginning to adopt its particular political economy of laissez-faire. According to Edward Thompson:

> The Combination Acts were passed by a Parliament of anti-Jacobins and landowners whose first concern was to add to the existing legislation intimidating political reformers.

He continues to say that 'they were also intended' to give more effective power of legal action to employers in dispute with combined workers.[17] Possibly this 'second intent' was in fact the 'first concern'. This is not to deny the significance of the political moment. Without the apprehension deriving from the French Revolution, it does not seem likely that the Act of 1799, offending so blatantly against principles of equity and fair treatment, could have passed into law with so little opposition through a Parliament in which inheritors of the conservative paternalist tradition still sat in such numbers. It is this *abdication* on the part of the 'natural' rulers to the wishes of employers which is to be remarked, as it was both by Thompson and, even more emphatically, by the Hammonds who protested at: 'the most unqualified surrender of the State to the discretion of a class in the history of England'. They recognised that combination: 'As a political danger . . .' seemed [to the governing class] much more formidable since the French Revolution', but they did not see fear of a revolutionary popular radicalism as the prime motivation of the government. Rather they presented it as a move against a parallel danger of 'mutiny and insubordination':

> this was the danger from which the State ought to protect industry. Peace, order and progress all turned on discipline; the rough artisans ought not to be allowed to act or to think for themselves, but must be made to accept the rule of their masters without question: they must take what wages their masters, who were the best judges of the circumstances

---

16. Webbs, *History of Trade Unionism*, p.64.

17. Thompson, *The Making*, pp.550–1.

of the trade, chose to give them. The State, that is to say, was to abdicate in favour of the employers. The employers' law was to be the public law.[18]

In the only speech opposing the bill in the House of Lords, Lord Holland had argued on just these lines. The workmen, he said, laboured under the 'disadvantage arising from a certain degree of dread that pervaded all ranks of mankind lest the lower ranks should be seduced by subversive principles particularly afloat at this period', and the masters were seeking to maximise 'this temporary advantage' to 'enforce their views and render their workmen more dependent than they had hitherto been, and than in all fairness and equity they ought to be'.[19]

In asking leave to introduce the Workmen's Combination Bill on 17 June 1799, William Pitt stated an intention to remedy 'an evil of very considerable magnitude; he meant that of unlawful combination among workmen in general – a practice which had become much too general, and was likely, if not checked, to produce very serious mischief'.[20] He did not directly identify this potential for mischief with political subversion.

The petition from the millwrights' employers drew attention, not just to the existence of a combination of journeymen, but also to the effective and systematic way in which it had been for some time operating.

> . . . for enforcing a general increase of their wages, preventing the employment of such journeymen as refuse to join their Confederacy, and for other illegal purposes, and frequent conspiracies of this sort have been set on foot by the Journeymen, and the masters have been obliged to submit . . . in support of the said combination . . . the Journeymen have established a general fund and raised subscriptions, and so regular and connected is their system that their demands are made sometimes by all the Journeymen . . . at the same time, and at other times at some one particular shop, and in case of non-compliance, the different workshops (where their demands are resisted) are wholly deserted by the men, and other journeymen are prohibited from applying for work until the Master Millwrights are brought to Compliance, and the Journeymen,

---

18. J.L. & B. Hammond, *The Town Labourer*, (rep.1978 ed. J. Lovell), pp.79–80.

19. *Parliamentary Register*, IX, 1799, pp.65–6.

20. Hammonds, *Town Labourer*, p.83.

who have thus thrown themselves out of employ, receive support in the mean time from their general fund.[21]

The petitioners went on to complain that the only way of proceeding against the combination was the time-consuming and usually ineffective one of indictment before Sessions or Assizes. From this kind of representation, Parliament was being educated into seeing workers' combinations not as a short-term nuisance emerging from time to time in particular trades, but as a *systematic* abuse of power by journeymen which was spreading across the trades.

It has been reasonably suggested[22] that Pitt and his colleagues were influenced towards the need for a general act by a seven-page submission to the Privy Council entitled, *Observations respecting the Combinations of Workmen*. This seems probable, although the lack of any information over the authorship of this document makes it hard to be certain.[23] The *Observations* began by stating that combinations had both advanced in numbers and become more systematically effective in recent years. It instanced bricklayers, carpenters, cloth-dressers, weavers, tailors, shoemakers and cabinet makers as having strategies for strikes, delegate organisation and adequate funds, to win against employers resisting wage demands. It gave most space to a description of the organisation among the cloth-dressers, that is the skilled woollen-workers known as shearmen in the west country and as croppers in the West Riding. It remarked on links between the two districts and was very apprehensive about resistance to machinery. But at no point did it mention links between workmen's trade unions and political subversion. At very least, though, the report would have re-inforced the belief in the existence of a widespread, effective and growing trade unionism. It expressed a strong need for 'the timely aid of the Legislature', not least to prevent unionism spreading from the skilled workers among whom it was already assumed to be

---

21. Hammonds, *Town Labourer*, p.81.

22. For example by James Moher in the most recent account: 'From Suppression to Containment: Roots of Trade Union Law to 1825', in John Rule ed. *British Trade Unionism 1750–1850: The Formative Years* (1988), p.81.

23. PRO. PC 1/43/A. 152.

entrenched to the industrial workers of the midlands and the north. In such districts it would no longer be only a matter of small groups of skilled urban workers like the millwrights combining, but also of masses of rural textile workers, miners or even the new factory labour force of cotton-spinners. Pitt was known to have been especially concerned with the state of affairs in the populous manufacturing districts of the north.[24] Irrespective of any links with political subversion, trade union actions were being increasingly viewed as in themselves a form of subversion. In 1802, at a time when some voices were urging even tougher legislation against combinations, Earl Fitzwilliam, referring to a strike of croppers (shearmen) when Benjamin Gott, the prominent manufacturer, employed two men not recognised by their union at his Leeds factory, remarked:

> It is for the infringement of a law made by parties incompetent to make any law; a law (if I may so call it) subversive of the general rights of all his Majesty's subjects.

Concluding that the 'Journeymen are now masters', Fitzwilliam added, 'though masters cannot be vested with an unfitting authority over their servants, they may and ought to be protected in the full exercise of their own just rights'.[25]

It has been suggested that there was a strong link between disaffection, distress and the incidence of industrial disputes: that it was in the years of high food prices and most overt radical activity that trade unionists as well as political radicals and food rioters were most active. The food crisis of 1795/6 has been described by Roger Wells as the 'seminal period of union activity', but the link with distress is not that clear.[26] *The Times*, reporting at the end of 1800 that journeymen in several London trades had struck for higher wages, pointed out that these skilled men earned three times the wages of agricultural labourers and the 'lower mechanic': 'high prices did not fall severely' upon them. No mention was made of any

---

24. See *The Times*,. 18 June 1799.

25. The letter from Fitzwilliam is printed in full in: A. Aspinall ed. *The Early English Trade Unions Documents from the Home Office Papers*, (1949), pp.61–4.

26. R.A.E. Wells, *Insurrection. The British Experience 1795–1803*, (Gloucester, 1986), p.48.

political motivation, and *The Times* went on to make a general point:

> If every man who feels the burdens of these times is to revolt from his employment, and to discontinue his industry, society is disorganized at once.[27]

The evidence of incidence of industrial disputes, admittedly problematic, does not suggest a fit with distressed years. Professor Aspinall's collection of letters on trade unions drawn from the Home Office papers contains no documents for the years 1794 to 1798, while the count of industrial disputes made by Rodney Dobson suggests a very distinctive pattern. Sixty-two per cent of 103 disputes in the 1790s took place in the three years 1791–3: that is, in the years before there was a downturn in the earnings and expectations of skilled workers. Disputes in 1794–7 were well below the level of those taking place in the 'boom' of the early nineties, when there was a strike surge of similar dimensions to the better-known one which came with the repeal of the Combination acts in 1824.[28] Such a rhythm of disputes, with its evident peaks when the economy was doing well, suggests strongly that the context for trade union action was industrial rather than political. Reviving activity in 1798/9 after a nadir in 1796/7 probably played a part in convincing government that combinations presented a general problem, but nothing really suggests, neither the political situation nor the dimensions of revived industrial actions, that unless the millwrights' bill had been there to prompt events a general law would have been initiated at that particular moment. Quite possibly by 1801/2, when concern did exist that trade unions were linking with subversive radical politics, a proscription of some kind would have been implemented. However, by then the Combination Acts were already on the statute book, and this in itself was playing a role in the politicisation of the by then secret trade unions.

---

27. *The Times*, 23 December 1800.

28. Dobson's list is an appendix to *Masters and Journeymen*. Of course it cannot claim to be anything like a full count of the unknowable number of disputes taking place, only of those reported in the press; nevertheless, the pattern seems very clear.

Professor Christie' suggestion that established trade unions were serving their members' interests effectively by the 1790s is consistent with a plausible explanation of the passing of the Combination Act in 1799. Indeed it is perfectly congruent, as we have seen, with specific evidence fed directly to the ministry. The real question, however, is not whether some such trade unions existed, they clearly did, but whether success, measured in terms of protecting and advancing their members' interests, was *generally* true of trade unions.

To answer this question trade unions can be considered in different groups. The first best fits Christie's characterisation: well-established combinations of urban journeymen. They are best represented by London's skilled workers like tailors, printers and fellmongers. But they were not confined to the capital.[29] Against these unions it is generally accepted that the Combination Acts had little effect. Taken by surprise in 1799, they managed to mount a campaign before the amending act of 1800, with nearly identical petitions coming from ten provincial cities as well as from London. In fact they soon learned that with only a modicum of circumspection they could carry on as before. In 1812 a stockinger from Nottingham, in London to lobby for the framework-knitters' bill, was treated with derision by the London carpenters, when they learned that the knitters had no permanent trade union:

> What would our trade be, if we did not combine together? perhaps as poor as you are, at this day! Look at the other Trades! They all combine. . . . See the Tailors, Shoemakers, Bookbinders, Goldbeaters, Printers, Bricklayers, Coatmakers, Hatters, Curriers, Masons, Whitesmiths, none of these trades receive less than 30s a week, and from that to *five* guineas this is all done by Combination, without it their Trades would be as bad as yours.[30]

In 1818 Francis Place described the London tailors as having had for almost a century 'a more tremendous and perfect system of combination . . . than was ever by the greatest alarmist supposed to exist'. He demonstrated, using the tailors and the printworkers as examples, how strongly unionised trades were able to keep up their real incomes

---

29. On the incidence of trade unionism see the works of Rule, 1981 and Dobson, 1980 already cited.

30. Quoted in Thompson, *The Making*, pp.263–4.

despite wartime inflation and the existence of the Combination Acts.[31]

The situation of Birmingham's artisans seems to have been very similar. In that city between 1800 and 1810, shoemakers, tailors, brushmakers, cabinetmakers, and candlestickmakers are recorded as having formed combinations and struck. Combination is also known to have existed among metal platers, bone and ivory brushmakers, turners and toymakers, horn, button and spoon makers, bellows-pipe makers and steel grinders. A further 13 groups of workers are known to have secured increases of wages, some at least through combination.[32]

Of course, many skilled urban artisans did become involved in radical politics, but not in reaction to industrial pressures or from economic desperation; rather, like Francis Place himself, they did so from the same sense of dignity and worth which underpinned their trade societies. They deemed themselves as worthy of joining the political nation and capable of saving it from its present corrupt and parasitic regime. Francis Place was later to say of the London Corresponding Society: 'It induced men to read books, it taught them to respect themselves. . . . It elevated them in society'. In 1822, while attending an anniversary celebration of the acquittal of Thomas Hardy and the other LCS leaders from their treason charge, he recognised 24 people who had been division leaders with him in the 1790s, twenty of whom he remembered had then been, like himself, journeymen or shopmen. A quarter of a century on, they were all 'in business all flourishing men'.[33] Whatever the role of middle-class leaders in the radical movement, the contribution of such artisans was critical. Indeed, it was precisely this presence, as Edward Thompson discerned, which made the radicalism of the 1790s 'popular'.[34] There seems little point in reading

---

31. *Gorgon*, 3 & 10 October 1818 for the tailors and 28 November 1818 for the printworkers.

32. G.J. Barnsby, *Birmingham Working People*, (Wolverhampton, 1990), pp.39–40.

33. Francis Place, *Autobiography*, (ed. M. Thale, Cambridge), 1972, pp.198–9.

34. Thompson, *The Making*, pp.22–7.

through lists of names and occupations of journeymen radicals and wondering if they were also members of their respective trade societies. Most of them surely were.

So too were most of the 2500 members of the radical corresponding society at Sheffield in 1792. Joseph Mather, the radical filesmith and balladeer, was the author both of 'God save Great Thomas Paine' and of 'Watkinson and his Thirteens', one of the most bitter songs ever produced from an industrial dispute.[35] John Gales provided a radical mouthpiece with his *Sheffield Register*, and supported the cutlers' unions steadfastly through a period of industrial disputes from 1791 to 1797. The small workshop, semi-independent artisan structure of the cutlery manufacture was, as a Government agent recognised, unusually fertile ground for both trade unionism and Painite radicalism.[36] Only an extraordinary degree of pre-disposition could view the protest actions of Sheffield's cutlers and filesmiths as 'compartmentalised'.[37]

It seems reasonable to conclude that there were many groups of skilled workers in metropolitan and provincial England who gained a great deal from their trade societies, and who continued to do so despite the legislation of 1799 and 1800. Many from the ranks of these organised journeymen may have embraced radical politics, but they were not driven to this by economic impotency nor, once they realised how little had been changed *for them* by the Acts, by a perception that their trade unions were seriously threatened. But this group did not represent the whole picture. Another group of trade unions embraced those occupations and districts where combinations were more precarious, less entrenched, and in some cases still struggling into being. This was especially the case in some of the strongly expanding trades, like iron-

---

35. J. L Baxter and F.K. Donelly, 'The Revolutionary Underground in the West Riding. Myth or Reality?' *Past and Present*, 64, (1974), p.125. For Mather's bitter strike poem see: G.I.H. Lloyd, *The Cutlery Trades*, (1913), pp.241–2.

36. The report is reprinted in Aspinall ed. *Early Trade Unions*, pp.4–6.

37. For the label 'compartmentalist' applied to several of E.P. Thompson's critics see: F.K. Donelly, 'Ideology and early English Working-class history: Edward Thompson and his critics', *Social History*, 2, (May 1976), pp.219–38.

puddling, coal-mining, and cotton spinning, and in rural manufactures like weaving and framework-knitting: in other words it was especially the case in the increasingly populous industrial districts of the north, lowland Scotland and the midlands. Here there was less open trade unionism and larger and more scattered populations to organise. Here the Combination Acts presented a much more serious constraint and here, too, there was greater distress. Pitt's special fear of the spread of combination to the workers of the industrialising north certainly seems to suggest that pre-emption in this respect was one motive for the Act of 1799. The report to the Privy Council had been especially concerned with the organisation of the wool croppers, describing them as 'a very numerous body' with a fund exceeding £1000 and able to exercise through their links, not just between adjacent northern counties, but also with the west of England, a 'despotic power' which 'almost exceeds belief'. There were strong grounds for expecting trouble from the introduction of machinery into Yorkshire, for it had already happened in the west country.[38]

Pitt's misgivings, which were fed by Wilberforce, himself a Yorkshire member, were shared by others. Early in 1800, during a court case commenced before the passing of the 1799 act, involving the trial of two Hull shoemakers for combination, both counsels drew attention to the north. One described combinations as 'extremely common in the northern manufacturing parts of the kingdom'. The other said that 'this sort of combination prevailed in almost all the great towns in the north of England'. He went on to add that such associations were 'easily convertible into every sort of political mischief'.[39] This is congruent with other evidence, which suggests concern that political subversion had already struck roots among manufacturing workers was less evident than apprehension over the potential which workers' organisations seemed to offer radical agitators. Cotton weavers belonged to this category. In the early days of the manufacture they had some degree of effective unionism, but when machine-

---

38. PC 1/43/A 152 1799. The best account of the campaign against machinery in the west country is in Randall, *Before the Luddites*, Chap.3.

39. *The Times*, 28 January 1800.

spinning transformed the yarn supply, the number of hand-loom weavers hugely multiplied and posed very different problems of organisation as the balance of advantage in the labour market shifted dramatically against them. Probably the emergence in 1799 of a mass agitation among the cotton weavers to petition Parliament for a regulation of wages was a significant factor in convincing the Government of the need for a general ban on trade unions.[40]

Again there is little evidence that the Government felt that workers engaged in industrial disputes had already become generally politically disaffected. What concerned them and even more those in authority locally was the prospect that industrial discontent might be played upon by agitators who, given the existence of trade unionism, would have the opportunity not only of converting working-class individuals, but of politicising working-class organisations. Thus a Lancashire magistrate wrote to the Home Secretary on 11 April 1799 of an Association of Weavers, formed to petition Parliament, that it seemed to 'threaten harm', because 'their publications and the arrangement of the plan are able and great. . . . It is distributed into divisional committees and a central committee, and pains are taking to confederate the neighbouring towns'.[41]. But already on 9 April, Wilberforce had made his famous intervention into the debate on the Millwrights' bill, urging a general remedy for 'a general disease in our society'. The ball had then already been set rolling towards the proscription of trade unions when the government began to receive detailed intelligence from Lancashire. In May the Government was sent a printed paper addressed by the Association of Weavers to the public. Despite the strongly loyalist tone of parts of this paper, its sender warned of 'arts . . . used to disturb their peace and make them discontented'.[42] A return communication from the Home Office dated 2 August, by which time the Combination Act had been in force for only three weeks, strongly suggests that the course of events was being taken very seriously and that most

---

40. For an account of the weavers' agitation see J.L. and B. Hammond, *The Skilled Labourer*, (ed J. Rule, 1979), pp.45–54.

41. Aspinall, *Early Trade Unions*, p.20.

42. Aspinall, *Early Trade Unions*, pp.20–4.

probably it was the weavers' agitation, as well as the much-reported strength of the cloth-dressers' organisation which explains Pitt's special concern with events in the north. The Home Office had suggested placing spies 'that it may be known whether any other subjects are discussed there than those connected with the Petition to Parliament'. It further recommended that a general meeting of the district's magistrates be called:

> with a view first of manifesting to the weavers the readiness of the magistrates to take into consideration the difficulties under which they [the weavers] at present labour, and to explain to them the temporary causes to which these difficulties are only to be attributed; and secondly to guard against them being led away by ill-disposed and seditious persons who, without any intentions of assisting them, and without either the wish or ability to do so, endeavour to inveigle them into illegal proceedings and breaches of the public peace'.

The magistrates were also cautioned to be especially vigilant in the case of 'the emissaries from the Societies, who will be constantly on the watch to take every advantage of the present situation of the weavers. The apprehending any one of these emissaries will . . . tend more effectively than any other circumstances, to prevent any serious or regulated plan of operations from growing out of the temporary difficulties you have stated'. The Lancashire magistracy did as it was asked. A handbill was circulated which concluded by 'most affectionately' advising the distressed cotton weavers 'not to give ear to the evil suggestions and writings of a set of emissaries who . . . are now employed by certain unlawful and seditious societies, to poison their minds and excite them to disaffection and mischief'.[43]

Learning that 'the spirit of association has spread itself into many parts of Lancashire' had, the Home Secretary observed, 'great weight' with him. Although conceding that the weavers' purpose of petitioning parliament was not contrary to the Act of 1799, he considered that the existence of established associations of workmen with delegate meetings and capable of printing and circulating addresses to the public 'must lead to a conclusion that, if nothing injurious to the safety of the Government is actually in contemplation, Associations so formed contain within themselves the means of

43. Aspinall, *Early Trade Unions*, p.25–31.

being converted at any time into a most dangerous instrument to disturb the public tranquility'.[44] Letters of this kind, sent so soon after the Act's passing, certainly indicate a concern that combinations formed for industrial purposes were capable of being politicised by radical agitators, but just as quickly the first signs were appearing of an unintended but significant consequence of the new legislation. Information was being received from the cotton districts that cotton workers were organising 'under an idea that the late Act of Parliament for preventing unlawful combinations of workmen is oppressive to them'.[45]

The Lancashire magistrates issued a handbill which began with a reference to 'various and repeated attempts . . . by violent handbills and other inflammatory publications, to encourage an illegal oposition' to the Act of 1799. This raises a major question: if the Act was intended, in part at least, to be pre-emptive, how far was the outcome the opposite of what had been intended? Did its passing in fact foster an association between a now illegal and hence underground trade unionism and the equally proscribed radical organisations?[46] The argument that it did, at least so far as the industrial north was concerned, was an important step in the argument of *The Making of the English Working Class*, and a central one too in the more specific study of Oldham's cotton workers by John Foster. To Thompson, 'It was Pitt who, by passing the Combination Acts, unwittingly brought the Jacobin tradition into association with the illegal unions.'[47]

Illegal unions became, in Yorkshire and Lancashire, 'the stock upon which Jacobinism had been grafted'. Certainly the passing of the Acts created an issue which radical agitators might hope to turn to advantage. From Sheffield an informer wrote of a 'general spirit of disaffection created in every class of artisan and mechanics by the late Bill'. Even historians who have not been ready to accept Thompson's larger argument that the Acts created a 'widespread secret combination, half

---

44. Aspinall, *Early Trade Unions*, p.27.

45. Aspinall, *Early Trade Unions*, p.26 and see also the Home Office reply pp.28–9.

46. Aspinall, *Early Trade Unions*, pp.31–2.

47. Thompson, *The Making*, p.546.

political, half industrial, in emphasis' across the manufacturing districts of the two counties tend to agree that, however well London's well-established trade unions managed to live with the Combination Acts, unions in the manufacturing north and midlands were inevitably politicised to some degree by them.[48]

In his detailed study of Oldham, John Foster argued that a radical vanguard which had been forming from 1793 was enabled to take over the leadership of the local trade unions: 'In south-west Lancashire almost every labour organisation seems to have passed into their hands'. He quotes one informer as saying 'The republicans are drinking Mr Pitt's health'. Foster does however stress that Oldham's radicalism was the outcome of an unusual configuration of local circumstances. In his 'control' town, South Shields, a local trade union movement which was among the strongest in the country by 1790 did not come under radical control. Possibly this was because the years of the French Wars were ones of considerable prosperity for that town's ship-builders and seamen, throughout which they were able to maintain effective unionisation.[49]

Robert Glenn's recent study of Stockport presents the late-eighteenth and early nineteenth-century formation of trade unions as *paralleling* an increasing local interest in Jacobin ideologies and movements. Yet, despite the long decline in the living standards of cotton-weavers from the early 1790s and the appearance of their Association in 1799, he concludes that the Jacobins had limited success in their attempt 'to infuse the weavers' sectional movement with wider political goals'. Although Glenn accepts that some leaders were both political radicals and trade unionists, he still sees the political movement as essentially distinct from the industrial one. He concedes that there is evidence from Manchester that Jacobin agitators organised the campaign against the Combination Acts in order to gain adherents. Here they brought together at a single meeting of activists, representatives from the calico printers, shoemakers, fustian cutters and machine makers.

---

48. Thompson, *The Making*, p.546–7.

49. J. Foster, *Class Struggle and the Industrial Revolution. Early Industrial Capitalism in Three English Towns*,. (1977 edition), pp.34–8 105–7.

At a second meeting the cotton spinners were also represented and other evidence links the cotton weavers to the agitation. Glenn, however, considers it 'doubtful' whether at Stockport the Jacobins were able to gain a similar foothold in as many trades, while accepting that there was considerable concern over the local branch of the Weavers' Association.[50] It is true, as we have seen, that the Weavers' *Address* to the public was replete with expressions of loyalty:

> Are you afraid that we should approach the Government, and there tell the truth? – that ye use the mean artifice of stigmatising us with the name of Jacobins, that ye raise your rumours of plots . . . we are firmly attached to our King and country . . . having that confidence in Government which ought to be universal, we believe that when our real situation is laid before the Legislature, some method will be devised to ameliorate our condition.[51]

As the weavers were in the process of petitioning for a regulation of the manufacture, such language could be considered cause-serving rhetoric, but more likely it is representative enough of their general attitude in May 1799, two months before the passing of the first Combination Act. That act was passed in July and twelve months later the Government had turned down the regulation of wages and offered instead the unsatisfactory Arbitration Act. Any swing towards radicalism probably took place over 1800. This was certainly the opinion of the master manufacturer William Radcliffe, who thought that until then the weavers had 'as a body' been 'as faithful, moral and trustworthy as any corporate body among his Majesty's subjects'. The failure of their campaign, and the passing of the Combination Acts were by then being reinforced by anti-war feeling.[52]

Such a view is in line with Alan Booth's conclusions from his examination of the food riots in the north-west in 1795 and 1800–01. He concluded that in the latter the 'poor' were far more politically conscious than they had been in the former. By March 1801, with the suspending of the Habeas Corpus Amendment Act, there was a crop of meetings which 'were

50. R. Glenn, *Urban Workers in the Early Industrial Revolution*, (1984), pp.117, 129–33.

51. Aspinall, *Early Trade Unions*, p.22.

52. Glenn, *Urban Workers*, p.132.

neither simply economic nor political, but encompassed all levels of working-class activity'. Booth considers a meeting held in Manchester in 1801, at which were discussed the continuation of the war, the high price of provisions and the regulation of wage levels, as a representative moment 'marking an important change in popular protest within the North-West'. It was partly a culmination of the previously separate struggles of trade unionists, political radicals and food rioters, and it marked at least the ending of food rioting as a separate response: something which was to be confirmed in the intermeshing of protests which was characteristic of Lancashire Luddism in 1811–12.[53]

In concentrating on the hotly disputed issue of the extent of a revolutionary or extreme radical movement linking illegal trade unionism to the banned societies, there is a danger of missing the broader point: the large role which industrial discontent probably played in politicising more generally a considerable part of the manufacturing populations of Yorkshire and Lancashire. In such a situation it is hardly surprising that the Government feared that trade unions, even if manifestly formed for industrial purposes, could become dangerous for the state. If widespread and increasing disaffection fed mostly into a broadly based campaign for the protection of wages, lowering of food prices, and some measure of parliamentary reform, it was also bound to increase to some degree the support for those who were advocating more revolutionary solutions. As Dr Booth has suggested for Lancashire, 'the tide of popular sympathies' was turning away from the loyalism which had predominated before 1795. Dr Elliot too in her re-examination of the Despard Conspiracy has identified this moment of sentiment shift in both Lancashire and in the West Riding. The coming together of previously separate strands of protest was creating a wholly new opportunity for revolutionary activists of 'attaching to their movement a discontented and malleable proletariat'. She points to a 'temporary, but substantial accession of popular strength to an otherwise elitist conspiracy'.[54] It is surely correct, whatever emphasis

53. A. Booth, 'Food Riots in the North-West of England 1790–1801', *Past and Present*, 77, (1977), pp.101–04.

54. A. Booth, 'Popular Loyalism and Public Violence in the North-West of

historians have recently put on the strength of popular loyalism, to reject the view that the working people in the 'populous manufacturing districts' were so fundamentally loyal that only marginal possibilities were ever open to agitators. Even Professor Dickinson, in pointing out that popular radicalism never achieved the level of support which loyalism secured, accepts that it was 'occasionally in the ascendant'. 1800 to 1803 was one such period of radical ascendancy, until it was swamped by a resurgent loyalism in 1803–5.[55] If fundamental loyalty to King and Constitution is to be the main explanation of why there was no revolution, then perhaps it was the more consistent and deep loyalty of those higher up the social scale which mattered most?

Given that little in the way of new evidence is likely to emerge, and that protagonists will continue to put their preferred interpretations of the letters sent to the Home Office and value or de-value the evidence provided by spies and agents, there seems small point in debating again the 'Black Lamp' controversy over the extent and true purpose of nocturnal meetings taking place in the West Riding in 1801–2. I am not suggesting that revolutionary agitators were forming new organisations, or even placing special emphasis on permeating trade unions, but only that a situation was in being in which meetings of discontented industrial workers, notably the croppers, who were already in dispute, were being held. It is pointless to argue as to whether industrial or political matters were discussed at these meetings, for clearly both would have been. Which predominated and to what degree is the unresolved matter of the continuing debate.[56] Dr Randall has recently suggested several reasons to think that jacobin

England, 1790–1800', *Social History*, 8, no. 3, (1983), p.313; Marianne Elliot, 'The Despard Conspiracy Re-considered', *Past and Present*, 75, (1977), p.53. For the growth of patriotism see Linda Colley, *Britons: Forging the Nation 1707–1837* (1992).

55. H.T. Dickinson, 'Popular Conservatism and Militant Loyalism 1789–1815', in H.T. Dickinson ed. *Britain and the French Revolution 1789–1815*, (1989), p.124.

56. For the 'Black Lamp' episode see: Thompson, *The Making*, pp.520–2; Baxter and Donnelly, 'Revolutionary Underground in the West Riding' and J.R. Dinwiddy, 'The Black Lamp in Yorkshire 1801–2', *Past and Present*, 64, (1974), pp.113–23.

radicalism was more likely in the West Riding than in the west country woollen districts even though the woollen workers were facing similar problems in both districts. There were centres of urban radicalism in the former district, notably Sheffield and Leeds. The small independent clothiers were under increasing pressure from larger merchant capitalists and the economic ideology of the radicals that centred on small producers could well have had an appeal. Although the two best-informed and influential people on this matter, Earl Fitzwilliam, the Lord Lieutenant for the West Riding, and William Cookson, the mayor of Leeds, were initially disinclined to believe that there was a political dimension to the woollen workers' agitation, both came to accept it as a real possibility.[57] However, it seems most likely that if disillusionment with the political system became more widespread among woollen workers and independent clothiers, then it did so after the report of the Committee of 1806 led to the repeal in 1809 of all the protective legislation regulating the woollen manufacture. That report had been effectively the work of Wilberforce, and in it is clearly revealed that he at least had seen the cloth-dressers' union as a political threat: 'such institutions are in their ultimate tendencies still more alarming in a political than in a commercial view'. The 'baneful effects' in a Sister Kingdom were proof enough. The repeals of 1809 were the background to the direct action and more evident politicisation of the 1812 disturbances, for as 'Ned Ludd' put it, 'We petition no more, that won't do, fighting must'.[58]

If, as Edward Thompson has written, 'at any time before the 1840s it is a mistake to segregate in our minds political disaffection and industrial organisation'[59], some qualifications need to be made. The well-established craft trade unions, those that kept their standard of living up despite wartime inflation and had come to realise that the existence of the

---

57. Randall, *Before the Luddites*, pp.264–79, This is the best interpretation of the role of political radicalism in labour disputes in the West Riding. The changing attitudes of Cookson and Fitzwilliam can be seen from some of their letters reprinted in Aspinall, *Early Trade Unions*, pp.40–54, 59–62.

58. Randall, *Before the Luddites*, p.248.

59. Thompson, *The Making*, p.546.

Combination Acts hardly threatened their trade organisations, were obviously not politicised by industrial causes. There is a strong continuity between their effective bargaining in good years like 1792 and that which was characteristic of the first decade of the nineteenth century.[60] They, however, hardly represented the situation of most trade unionists, although they embraced a surprisingly large number of different trades. Some trade unionists able to survive and operate successfully in a specific economic orbit may have felt little inclination to challenge the political status quo, but many workers in much more populous trades fared differently.

Perhaps as well as the finishing date of the 1840s we need a starting date for Thompson's assertion. It seems to me that around 1800 would serve that purpose, for even if the government was not largely motivated by fear of political radicalism in securing the Combination Acts, it was very soon at least considering their value in this respect. It is true that it remained uncertain and hesitant in using them. In leaving prosecution up to employers, it had legislated in a form which severely reduced the Acts' effectiveness as a weapon against those who threatened mutiny against the state. Possibly if the legislation had been framed just a little later, it might have avoided this constraint.

Thompson's case for the Luddite years of 1811–12 lies beyond the scope of this paper. By then things seem clearer and it is easy to share his acceptance of the remark of the contemporary, Rev. J.T. Beecher, who blamed Luddism on 'Jacobinical principles . . . cherished until they have become intimately incorporated with the state of society'.[61] By then several groups of provincial manufacturing workmen were experiencing a growing disillusionment with Government, after they had organised to approach Parliament for a regulated amelioration of their deteriorating conditions. This, as we have seen, was what the cotton weavers were attempting from 1798. It was what the weavers and shearmen of the west-country were seeking in 1799–1800, and the calico printers in

---

60. For successful artisan unionism in London during the years of the Combination Laws see: I. Prothero, *Artisans and Politics in Early Nineteenth-Century London. John Gast and his Times*, (Folkestone, 1979), pp.22–62.

61. Thompson, *The Making*, p.545.

1804. What has to be noted is that in trades like these workers were not just facing, as Thompson put it, the intensification of two forms of pressure, economic exploitation and political oppression, but they were doing so in the context of a changing political economy. Slowly groups of workers were realising the increasing futility of following the paths which had offered hope so long as the paternalist ethos remained strong at Westminster. This was leading some at least to develop an interest in political change. It might have been capitalist employers who were oppressing them, but it was Government which was letting them down. It would have been surprising if such groups, some of whom, like the calico printers and framework knitters, had been in the recent past operating an effective industrial unionism, had not begun to wonder about the form of government. What this realisation would have suggested was not so much the use of industrial weapons like the strike to secure political change, for it was the failure of industrial action which was part of the problem: rather there was an increasing sense that political reform might be a preliminary for the restoration of economic strength.

Some of Thompson's more judicious critics have conceded that 'industrial militants must often have been politically militant as well'.[62] In fact the overlap of personnel is the simplest and strongest argument against compartmentalisation of working-class protest into separate spheres of action and organisation. As Thompson put it:

> In friendly societies which, while legal, were disbarred from forming regional or national links, the 'no politics' rule was often observed. Some of the old-established trades clubs had a similar tradition. But in most manufacturing communities the initiation of *any* organised movement is likely to have fallen on a small number of active spirits; and the men who had the courage to organise an illegal union, the ability to conduct its correspondence and finances, and the knowledge to petition Parliament or consult with attorneys, were likely also to have been no stranger to *The Rights of Man*.[63]

As Baxter and Donnelly have pointed out, trade unionism was not synonymous with radical politics even in the northern manufacturing districts, but the overlap was considerable and

---

62. Dinwiddy, 'Black Lamp', p.113.

63. Thompson, *The Making*, p.546.

complex.[64] No general industrial pressures were pushing all trade unions towards political activism, but for many workers economic weapons were becoming ineffective, and in some instances that in itself was partly attributable to legal proscription after 1799. There was nothing permanent about the mood of the manufacturing working-classes. In short, trade unionism between 1789 and 1802 cannot be generalised into either a conservative or a radical force. Different unions operated and struggled in different economic and social orbits. For some, once effective, there was the bitter experience of increasing impotency to the point of very survival. For others little changed. The widespread distress of the famine years apart, the experience of well-being in these years was extremely varied and so accordingly were the economic pressures for political radicalisation.

There is, then, little mystery over a general act against combinations galloping onto the statute book on the back of a petition from a particular trade. The millwrights provided an occasion, but Wilberforce's reference to a 'general disease' was directed towards receptive ears. Belief was already growing that trade unionism was becoming a 'system' threatening not only the authority of masters, but the commerce and prosperity of the nation. The political situation needed only to reinforce this. Government in 1799 was not forging a new weapon for the state. But it was not blind to the changes taking place in manufacturing, especially the introduction of machinery, and it accepted the need to assist the employers in the subordination of the workforce. Not without misgivings on the part of some paternalists, Government moved towards an extension of summary justice and came down clearly on the side of the masters.[65]

---

64. Baxter and Donnelly, 'Revolutionary Underground', p.126.

65. For the significance of the Acts of 1799 and 1800 as labour legislation see the important article by John Orth, 'The English Combination Laws Reconsidered', in F. Snyder and D. Hay eds. *Labour Law and Crime: An Historical Perspective*, (1987), pp.123–47.

Chapter Five

William Blake and the Great Eastcheap Orthodoxy

Alec Morley

Swedenborg! strongest of men, the Samson shorn by the Churches!
William Blake in *Milton*

I

In seeking the sources of inspiration of William Blake's poetry, historians and literary scholars have always had to deal with a great degree of uncertainty. Blake's engagement with the ideas of any thinker, like his social relationships with those around him, was never a calm, measured thing. An impulsive and independent artist, made more so by the popular failure of his art, Blake could praise someone of the stature of John Milton as a sublime poet and then, almost as an aside, insist that he had got the entire scheme of *Paradise Lost* and *Paradise Regained* back to front. In a similar way Blake could refer to Emanuel Swedenborg, the visionary theologian, as 'the strongest of men' and then satirize his theological conservatism by inverting it in *The Marriage of Heaven & Hell*.

In spite of these kinds of contradictions there has been a tendency in Blake scholarship to try to peg the poet-artist to one dominant influence and then read his entire body of poetry accordingly. Thus we have read about Blake the Romantic poet, Blake the neo-classicist, Blake the gnostic,

The author wishes to thank Harold Mah and Robert Malcolmson for reading and commenting on this essay.

Blake the frustrated Anglican, Blake the proto-Marxist revolutionary, and hope soon to get a glimpse of Blake the
antinomian Muggletonian.[1] Casting Blake as an ardent Swedenborgian has also been common. But the problem with
Blake the Swedenborgian, as with many of the other Blakes,
is that the iconoclastic mind of the poet has been reduced to a
more comprehensible and stable thing than it ever was.
Blake's Swedenborgianism, developed by a number of
scholars earlier in this century,[2] was presented as a mirror
reflection of Swedenborg's theology and Blake himself as a
devout follower of the sectarian movement. The reality was
very different, as David V. Erdman showed in his 1953 article
on 'Blake's Early Swedenborgianism: a Twentieth Century
Legend.'[3]

Blake's reading of Swedenborg, as his annotations have
shown, was seldom straightforward. It was a complex engagement with a complex, sometimes pedestrian, but uniquely
millennarian religious outlook that was especially appealing,
if only for the audacity of its vast prophetic scope, to a
religious revolutionary such as Blake. An understanding of

Quotations from Blake are taken from Geoffrey Keynes, ed., *Blake:
Complete Writings* (London: OUP, 1969) and given with the letter K and
the page numbers in brackets after the quote.

1. Marilyn Butler, *Romantics, Rebels, and Reactionaries: English
   Literature and its Background 1760-1830* (Oxford, 1982) finally begins to
   take Blake out of the Romantic canon after decades of awkward
   inclusion; Kathleen Raine, *Blake and Tradition* (Princeton, 1968)
   argues for the neo-classicist influence; see Desiree Hirst, *Hidden Riches:
   Traditional Symbolism from the Renaissance to Blake* (London, 1964)
   for Blake's other esoteric causes; J. Davies, *The Theology of William
   Blake* (London, 1966) presents the case for his frustrated Anglicanism;
   on Blake's suspected proto-Marxism see G. Sabri-Tabrizi, *The 'Heaven'
   and 'Hell' of William Blake* (New York, 1973); E. P. Thompson has for
   some time been preparing a manuscript on Blake the Muggletonian.

2. For one typical example, see H. N. Morris, *Flaxman, Blake, Coleridge
   and other men of genius influenced by Swedenborg* (London, 1915).
   Pierre Berger, Edwin Ellis, and the poet W. B. Yeats were also guilty of
   reducing Blake's religious background to orthodox Swedenborgianism.

3. David V. Erdman, 'Blake's Early Swedenborgianism: a Twentieth
   Century Legend', *Comparative Literature*, v (1953), pp. 247-57. While
   admitting influence in later years, Erdman shows that based on existing
   evidence the notion that Blake grew up a Swedenborgian must be
   regarded a wilfully contrived myth.

this particular millennarianism makes Blake's own outlook more comprehensible and gives even his very popular poetry new meaning. His famous lines, beginning

> And did those feet in ancient time
> Walk upon England's mountains green?
> And was the holy Lamb of God
> On England's pleasant pastures seen?(K480)

were put to music by Sir Hubert Parry (1848-1918) and are now so well loved and so often sung as to be considered England's unofficial anthem. But this rousing Victorian musical accompaniment runs roughshod over the verse. The question marks at the end of the first two stanzas are ignored, thus changing the strong sentiment of doubt or wonderment – in typical Victorian fashion – into an unqualified statement of faith. Freed from the music, the very moving final stanza reads more like a statement of revolutionary intent:

> I will not cease from Mental Fight
> Nor shall my sword sleep in my hand
> Till we have built Jerusalem
> In England's green and pleasant Land. (K481)

Here, in fact, is Blake's millennarianism; uniquely Swedenborgian in that there is an effort to be made to *build* Jerusalem – it is not just to happen at the sound of some trumpet blast – and that at least part of that effort is to be made internally or spiritually in the form of 'Mental Fight'.

With Blake's exposure to new and potentially revolutionary millennarian ideas in Swedenborg's writings, one must also consider his relationship to the sectarian Swedenborgian movement. For if Swedenborg had got Blake thinking of building a New Jerusalem in England's 'green and pleasant Land', then it followed that Swedenborg's disciples should have acted as fellow builders. But not all the other readers of Swedenborg interpreted the millennarianism of their prophet in the same way as Blake did. Disenchantment with the religious orthodoxy these people established may have caused Blake to alter his treatment of Swedenborg's ideas and to use his poetry both as an exposition of his own positions and as a critical commentary on the English Swedenborgian movement as well. A reading of some of Blake's most famous poetry, *The Songs of Innocence and Experience*, using the context of Blake's complex Swedenborgianism as a guide,

raises the possibility that his love-hate relationship with Swedenborg and the Swedenborgians played itself out in his
poetry: that the seemingly innocuous *Songs of Innocence*
have hidden in their pleasing words a religious and political
sub-text which is carried into the *Songs of Experience* and
provides, if not a comprehensive explanation for everything
Blake thought and did, some better understanding of the
evolution of his unorthodox methods.

II

Emanuel Swedenborg (1688-1772), like many of his learned
peers and predecessors of the seventeenth and eighteenth
centuries, took great interest in the prophecies of the Old and
New Testament and spent much time interpreting their specific revelations.[4] In the rational spirit of the age and according
to his scientific training, but with the claim that he was
recording what truths God and the Angels of heaven related
to him, he set out the 'spiritual sense' of the Sacred Scriptures.
He explicated this 'internal meaning' from the literal sense of
the Bible, doggedly working through Genesis and Exodus
and then the entire Book of Revelation. He continued until he
had filled more than eight-thousand pages of biblical explication, all in Latin and often in an abstruse style.[5]

Swedenborg, having been born into privilege as the son of
the Bishop of Upsala and in his early years travelled and
mixed with the intelligentsia of Enlightenment Europe, followed a life in pursuit of scientific understanding interspersed
with periods of service to his country as Chief Engineer of
Mines, which was then a top position in the Swedish government. In 1772, some fifteen years after moving into his
theological and overtly visionary phase, he passed away

4. According to Christopher Hill, 'both [John] Napier and Newton
   attached more importance to their researches into the *Apocalypse* than
   to logarithms or the law of gravitation.' *Intellectual Origins of the
   English Revolution* (Oxford, 1987), p. 7. Swedenborg certainly thought
   more of his *Apocalypse Revealed* and *Apocalypse Explained* than of his
   well-received *Principia* on the relationship of the planets.

5. For a good brief description of Swedenborg's theology, see the second
   chapter of Marguerite Beck Block's *The New Church in the New World:
   a Study of Swedenborgianism in America* (New York, 1932), pp. 19-51.

quietly in London, and little came of the bulk of his life's work until the 1780s when small but determined groups of London readers began to meet regularly and discuss the 'Divine Truths' found in his theological writings. More of his various works were translated into English and published, and word spread through the streets of London and later to Continental Europe and America. In the context of industrializing England and her revolutionary American colonies, these writings had an explanatory power which perhaps made up for Swedenborg's credulous claims of preternatural communications with the world of angels and wicked spirits. For though there were a great many ideas to be absorbed from his theological work, Swedenborg's unique millennarianism stood over them all, organizing and then infusing the entire theological scheme with a purpose. This crowning prophecy, as revealed to him by God and made more as a statement of historical fact than imminent event, was that the Last Judgement spoken of in Revelation and prophesied in the two Testaments had already been accomplished. He wrote that since the year 1757 the world had been living in the intra-millennial age, the thousand year reign of God in his Second Coming.[6]

In terms of natural events, the year 1757 did not at all live up to such a billing. The received biblical account of events leading to the Last Judgement called for more than one Lisbon earthquake. They spoke of Armageddon and the end of the natural world. But Swedenborg's explication, his reading of the 'internal meaning' or 'spiritual sense' of biblical prophecy, was that all these cataclysmic events took place in the other world, what he referred to as the 'Spiritual World'. In this spiritual world the hells, which had become too powerful and threatened to block out God from the souls of men and women as they walked on this earth, were conquered. Order was reestablished and an equilibrium between good and evil, heaven and hell, restored. The only influence on natural men and women in the natural world was that freer communication with God and the heavens had been initiated, and that people were now once more in freedom to choose for

---

6. Emanuel Swedenborg, *Concerning the Last Judgement and the Destruction of Babylon* (London, 1788).

themselves good ways over evil.[7] As well, the deeper truths
regarding God, humanity, and the universe were now available through the medium of Swedenborg's writings. Though
he claimed for himself nothing more than the role of God's
scribe – and initially published his books anonymously – he
maintained the truths contained in his writings to be the
Lord's Second Coming in manifest form for the further
salvation of His people.

This was the revolutionary news that initially bound the
little groups of readers together. And indeed they treated it as
such. Like the French revolutionaries, they double-dated all
publications (but with reference to 1757 rather than 1789),
and Blake later satirized this by opening his *Marriage of
Heaven & Hell* with a similar reference to that date. Swedenborg's readers spoke in the new language of his fresh revelations: of internal truths, natural and spiritual
correspondences, regenerating souls, and the 'Divine Humanity' of God. And at all times they considered themselves
to be living in the intra-millennial age. Through Swedenborg
these New Jersualemites, who came from nearly every class of
British society, had seen the 'new heaven' and now they
longed for the 'new earth', of which John had prophesied:

> And I saw a new heaven and a new earth,
> for the first heaven and the first earth
> were passed away. And there was no more sea.

They looked on the world – particularly in Europe and the
rebellious American colonies in the tumultuous late eighteenth century – as though it was in the throes of a Spiritual
Revolution and oriented themselves accordingly.

If a belief that the Last Judgement had already occurred
and the millennium begun was central to these early readers
of Swedenborg, there were other things about his writings
that appealed to them as well. No other theologian or Christian sect raised the Bible (and by extension the written word)
to a position of such importance; for Swedenborg the Word of
God *was* God, and the internal meaning of the Word, which
had been revealed to him, was the Lord in his Second Com-

---

7. Block, *New Church*, pp. 36-7.

ing.[8] Attaching a corresponding spiritual meaning to natural biblical symbols, Swedenborg provided this spiritual sense of the Bible, but he warned that a knowledge of these correspondences did not necessarily ensure a true spiritual understanding of the truths in the Word. The human intellect was not capable on its own of comprehending these truths; understanding came from the heavens as 'an influx into the interiors of the mind'. With these ideas Swedenborg invested the Bible with an authority beyond that of any Pope, Bishop, Saint, or even his own 'authoritative' writings on the subject. Although he claimed his revelations heralded the beginnings of a New Church which was to supercede the Christian one, it was in many ways just another manifestation of Christian protestantism and in keeping with this heritage contained frequent reference to the overthrow of the corrupt, established ecclesiastical institutions and their heretical theology. Above all, though, it appealed to Bible-loving people.

In eighteenth-century England, Swedenborg's 'spiritual sense' helped those university-educated clergymen who sought to reconcile religion and ascendant science. This was the Age of Reason and reason-bred thinkers were beginning to question the literal sense of the stories in the Bible and thus the authority of the Christian Church. For Blake's artisan community and the growing middle-classes, all of whom had been brought up on the Bible and Bunyan's *Pilgrim's Progress* and perhaps very little else, Swedenborg's writings empowered them to develop their own sense of morality. They needed only themselves and their Bible and the encouraging news of Swedenborg's revelation to find the true path through life. This revelation liberated them from the tyranny of priestcraft and opened new possibilities in deciding how they should live. Even though Swedenborg had provided the 'official' internal reading of Genesis, Exodus, the Prophets, Psalms, and Revelation, his warnings against using the doctrine of correspondences as a kind of dictionary to unlock the Bible's spiritual truths meant that each reader was still ultimately in control.[9] Besides this, Swedenborg had left many

---

8. See, for example, Emanuel Swedenborg, *True Christian Religion* (London: 1781), vol. 1, nos. 189, 192.

9. Block, *New Church*, p. 25.

parts of Scripture still to be mined. Blake and other creative minds took to this task with relish, and the result was often a radical new understanding of the world – quite different, perhaps, than even Swedenborg had intended.

A loyal core of people who had been exposed to Swedenborg's revelation kept reading what he wrote. Some did so because in his forty-odd volumes they found answers to the important theological issues of the day. Thorny issues like the Trinity – was there one God or three? – troubled many thinkers. Swedenborg went to great lengths to try to prove that there was one God alone. Elements of his rejection of the traditional doctrine of the Trinity appealed to a very different class of readers as well: to those attracted by the artistic and humane Christianity found buried amidst all the turgid theology. Unlike the Unitarians, Swedenborg did not reject the Trinity by rejecting the divinity of its third member, Jesus Christ. Instead, and more radically, he humanized all three parts of the Trinity to make one God: God-Man. The life, death, and resurrection of Christ were just the final stages of the process in which God took on the 'Divine Human'. For Swedenborg, Christ became the only God precisely because he had also become human.[10]

With the presence of the concept of the 'Human Form Divine' in 'The Divine Image' and other *Songs*, we have a suggestion that Blake was attracted to this radical humanism, which was at once absolutely anthropocentric and absolutely Christocentric. It was a fine balancing act, for it put Swedenborg and Blake (and the more daring New Jerusalemites) right on the sharp divide between Christian faith in the divinity of God and its anti-Christian denial – so cleverly stated by such eighteenth-century thinkers as Voltaire – of rejecting God's divinity as an affront to reason, humanity, and common sense. In the words of Czeslaw Milosz, Swedenborg met this rationalist challenge to Christianity by 'affirming that the divine is eternally human and the human is potentially divine.' More specifically, he did this by revealing the doctrine of correspondences which 'humanized or hominized God and the universe to such an extent that everything, from the smallest particle of matter to planets and stars, was given but

---

10. Czeslaw Milosz, *Emperor of the Earth: Eccentric Modes of Vision* (Berkeley, 1977), pp. 138-9; Block, *New Church*, pp. 40-1.

one goal: to serve as a fount of signs for human language. Man's imagination, expressing itself through language and identical in its highest attainments with the Holy ghost, was now to rule over and redeem all things by bringing about the era of the New Jerusalem.'[11] This, as few other theological systems could, appealed to Blake the poet, Blake the humanist, Blake the anti-intellectual intellectual, and Blake the radical Christian millennarianist.

III

On that Easter day in 1789 when William and Catherine Blake entered the rented Great Eastcheap chapel to attend the first General Conference of the New Jerusalem Church,[12] they noticed the sign that had been posted above the door. Taken from number 508 of Swedenborg's *Vera Christiana Religio* (True Christian Religion) and translated from the Latin *Nunc Licet*, it read: 'Now It Is Allowable'. One can imagine how Blake's antinomian sentiments, frequently expressed in his writing, would have been stirred by a statement such as this, and how he might well have taken it out of its limiting Swedenborgian context and placed it in the more permissive one of his soaring imagination. Perhaps he saw the members of the New Jerusalem Church as the first movement towards his longed-for brotherhood of a New Jerusalem on this earth, and the proceedings of the first Conference (not to mention the sign above the door) would have borne his hopes well.

Five hundred copies of a circular letter had been distributed with the news of the Conference 'to all Societies and individuals, that might be supposed interested in the establishment and prosperity of the New Jerusalem'. They were addressed to

Readers of the Theological Writings of Emanuel Swedenborg who are desirous of rejecting, and separating themselves from, the Old Church, or the present Established Churches, together with all their Sectaries,

---

11. Milosz, *Emperor*, p. 140.

12. This manifesto, signed by William and Catherine Blake, is now at the New Church College, Woodsford Green, Essex, England.

throughout Christendom, and of fully embracing the Heavenly Doctrines of the New Jerusalem.[13]

Given these rebellious terms and Blake's enthusiastic reading of a number of Swedenborg's works,[14] Blake's presence within a religious organization is comprehensible. And if one examines the surviving accounts of the Conference, one can conclude that he left it with the same positive feelings that had brought him there. Erdman notes that the resolutions to which William and Catherine Blake added their names 'expressed largely the humanitarian element of the New Doctrine' and resonate with Blake's own pronouncements on religion and its proper role in society,[15] as Resolutions XXVII and XXXI show:

> XXVII. Resolved Unanimously: that it is the opinion of this Conference, that men of every Religion and Persuasion throughout the whole world, even Pagans and Idolators, are saved, after receiving instruction in the Spiritual World, provided they have lived a life of Charity, according to the best of their knowledge . . .
> XXXI. Resolved Unanimously: That it is the opinion of this Conference, that the Writings of Emanuel Swedenborg are calculated to promote the Peace and Happiness of Mankind, by making them loyal subjects, Lovers of their Country, and useful Members to Society: and . . . to emancipate mankind from the mental Bondage and Slavery, whereby they have so long been held captive by the Leaders and Rulers in the Old Church.[16]

One of the leading organizers at Great Eastcheap was Robert Hindmarsh, and his first-hand account of the proceedings, though somewhat undependable for being a self-

---

13. Circular Letter advertising the First General Conference of the New Jerusalem Church, dated Great Eastcheap, London, 7 December 1788. Reprint in Swedenborg Library, Bryn Athyn, Pennsylvania.

14. Blake-annotated volumes of Swedenborg's theological writings: *A Treatise Concerning Heaven and Hell* (London: R. Hindmarsh, 1784); *The Wisdom of Angels Concerning Divine Love and Wisdom* (London: W. Chalken, 1788); *The Wisdom of Angels Concerning Divine Providence* (London, 1790). From his own sources we know that Blake also read an edition of Swedenborg's *True Christian Religion* and *The Earths in the Universe*, but his copies of these have never been found.

15. Erdman, 'Blake's Early Swedenborgianism,' p. 254.

16. Robert Hindmarsh, *Rise & Progress of the New Jerusalem Church, in England, America, and Other Parts*, ed. E. Madeley (London, 1861), p. 104.

conscious and highly selective recording of events considered to be monumentally important, does cast light on the environment Blake would have encountered there. 'It appeared,' wrote Hindmarsh, 'as if the times of Primitive Christianity were restored among us, when all things were held in common.'[17] But this strong sense of brotherhood did not last long, at least not for Blake. He may have read the full sentence from *Vera Christiana Religio*, only part of which had been quoted on the sign over the chapel door. 'Now it is allowable to enter intellectually into the mysteries of life,' is how it went, and we know from later comments he made that Blake considered Swedenborg's attempt to convey divine truths in a rational, intellectual form as madness. Swedenborg, Blake told Henry Crabb Robinson, 'was wrong in endeavouring to explain to the rational faculty what the reason cannot comprehend.'[18] As he advanced through Swedenborg's volumes, Blake found it more difficult to reconcile his god of 'Poetic Genius' with Swedenborg's reason-bred god, and it was perhaps this frustration that later burst forth in *Jerusalem*: 'I must Create a System or be enslav'd by another Man's./I will not Reason & Compare: my business is to Create.'[19] Whether the 'System' was that of Swedenborg, or Robert Hindmarsh, or the Rev Joseph Proud and the other conforming Swedenborgian sectarians, or simply systems in general, is a matter of speculation. What is certain is that the sectarian Swedenborgians, those involved in forming a specifically Swedenborgian church organization, 'began to put their Seer on a pedestal,' and came to rely completely upon the revelations of this one man for their religious inspiration.[20] The New Jerusalem Church was from April 1789 becoming increasingly orthodox in the traditional non-Conformist manner, and Blake, who had written in another annotation to Swedenborg's *Divine Love and Wisdom* that 'the Whole of the New Church is in the

17. Ibid., p. 107.

18. G. E. Bentley, Jr, *Blake Records* (Oxford, 1969), p. 312.

19. William Blake in Geoffrey Keynes, ed., *Complete Writings* (London: OUP, 1969), p. 629.

20. Peter Lineham, 'The English Swedenborgians, 1770-1840: a Study in the Social Dimensions of Religious Sectarianism' (University of Sussex, unpublished D.Phil. dissertation, 1978), p. 210.

Active Life & not in Ceremonies at all,' (K92) must have encountered these trends sometime soon after that first hopeful Conference.

It also seems that people like Hindmarsh, who had got the King's patronage for his successful printing venture and publicized the fact *ad nauseam*, turned to Church-building as though it was just another line of business, which promised not only material but social and spiritual returns as well. Hindmarsh's tale of the first ordinations of New Church clergy reads like a bad satire on Catholicism's belief in the apostolic succession. By his own account the first ordinations took place in July of 1787 at the home of Mr Thomas Wright, clockmaker, No. 6 Poultry Road in London. Twelve male members (for obvious symbolic reasons) were chosen by lot to take part in ordaining Mr Samuel Smith and Mr James Hindmarsh, Robert's father and formerly a minister in Wesley's methodist connexion. It had already been agreed that Robert, being secretary of the Society, would read the ordination service while each of the twelve placed his right hand on the head of the person ordained. But wanting divine sanction for his role of Reader, he apparently wrote the word 'ORDAIN' on one of the twelve lots used to pick the group and upon miraculously receiving this same lot claimed in his own history of the New Church to have been 'virtually ordained by the Divine auspices of Heaven.'[21] There are signs of mania here, not to mention credulity, and one suspects that Hindmarsh thought himself a kind of latter day Swedenborgian St Peter destined to sit at God's right hand.

The church historian James Hyde writes that from these first signs in 1788 Hindmarsh 'veered from the indefiniteness of his first perceptions of New Church truth, and, by the impetuosity of his fervent nature, became a pronounced ecclesiastic.'[22] By 1791 he had alienated the larger part of the

---

21. J. G. Dufty, 'Robert Hindmarsh and the first Ordinations in the New Church', New Church General Conference Library and Archives, Swedenborg House, Bloomsbury, London; cf. James Hyde, 'Some Notes Respecting Robert Hindmarsh: with a critique', *New Church Magazine*, March 1905, p. 118.

22. Hyde, 'Notes', pp. 118-9. One obvious reason for Hindmarsh's conservatism was the coming of the French revolution, which cast a general opprobrium on all English Dissenters.

Great Eastcheap Society over the degree to which the New Church priesthood was to control the affairs of the Church. By 1793 there was already a split which caused two separate annual Conferences to convene, the one favouring and the other rejecting an ecclesiastical hierarchy. In these circumstances it is not at all surprising that Blake should have been alienated before the others and that some of his *Songs of Innocence and Experience* should have been based first on his early hopes for the New Jerusalem Church and subsequently on the bitterness and disappointment of his 'experience' there; and that his satirical *Marriage of Heaven and Hell*, dated 1790, should employ 'Swedenborgian Angels' resembling the autocratic, theologically conservative priests who had suddenly begun to appear as leading figures in the Great Eastcheap Society.

Swedenborgianism in England developed in forms other than the orthodoxy at Great Eastcheap. Blake, as one example, represented a loose group of interested but independent readers who ranged from the artisan classes of London to the lower levels of the landed gentry in England and continental Europe.[23] The Rev John Clowes of St John's in Manchester and the Rev Jacob Duché of the Lambeth Asylum for Orphan Girls came from yet another grouping: members, and sometimes even clergymen, of the Established Church who read and believed what Swedenborg wrote but who firmly believed that ecclesiastical change was to be effected from within existing church organizations. Clowes, educated at Cambridge, not only expressed openly his Swedenborgian understanding of God, humanity, and the new spiritual age now dawning, but also took the New Dispensation outside Manchester to groups of enthusiastic Lancashire mill workers. Duché, also a Cambridge-educated Anglican clergyman, had been posted in Philadelphia in the 1770s and had come out in support of the Americans during the War of Independence but was forced into an English exile after changing his position to advocate pacifism in a letter to

---

23. For background on the English Swedenborgian movement, see Lineham, 'The English Swedenborgians'; also A. J. Morley, 'The Politics of Prophecy: William Blake's Early Swedenborgianism, 1757-1794' (Queen's University, unpublished M.A. thesis, 1991).

General George Washington. In England Duché found Swedenborg's revelations, and became a believer, but remained a
minister in the Church of England. Blake, suggests Erdman,
knew Duché and was familiar with the Swedenborgian teaching given at the Asylum in Lambeth.[24] It seems Blake had
some sort of contact with most of the various formations of
Swedenborgian activity in London, but ultimately settled on
an engagement with the ideas that set him apart from any of
the formal followers.

IV

For some time now a variety of scholars have noted Swedenborgian elements in some of Blake's *Songs of Innocence*.[25]
The renowned Blake scholar Kathleen Raine has more recently extended such claims in calling the collection of *Innocence* as a whole the 'Swedenborgian Songs'.[26] And more
recently still, Edward Thompson has suggested that Blake's
Songs of Innocence were compiled and expanded in response
to the call for a catechism for the instruction of children and a
hymn-book of praise and thanksgiving at the Great Eastcheap
Conference in 1789.[27] From these suggestions the possibility
arises that Blake's love-hate relationship with Swedenborgian
ideas and with certain Swedenborgians played a profound
role not only in the production of *Innocence* but in the entire
Songs of Innocence and Experience as well.

Past critics of the *Songs* have not missed the very obvious
expressions of humane concern Blake showed for the social
and economic victims of late eighteenth-century industrializing Britain. Among a number of the *Songs of Innocence* that
convey this sensitivity, 'Holy Thursday' and 'The Chimney
Sweeper' are concerned with the orphaned infant poor of
London. There may have been some Swedenborgian influ-

---

24. Erdman, 'Blake's Early Swedenborgianism', p. 257 n 27.

25. Mark Schorer, 'Swedenborg and Blake', *Modern Philology*, xxxvi,
    1938; John Howard, 'Swedenborg's *Heaven and Hell* and Blake's *Songs
    of Innocence*,' *Papers on Language and Literature*, iv, 1968.

26. Raine, *Blake and Tradition*, p. 3.

27. E. P. Thompson, 'William Blake and Which Tradition?' (Lectures
    given at Queen's University, Kingston, Canada, 1988).

ence behind these sentiments in Blake's mind, and both poems are more comprehensible if one considers the context of Blake's contact with the Swedenborgian Anglican Jacob Duché at the girls' orphanage in Lambeth, where Duché was chaplain and where Blake would have been exposed not only to Swedenborgian ideas but to those ideas put to work in the care of under-privileged children.

Here is 'Holy Thursday':

'Twas on a Holy Thursday, their innocent faces clean,
The children walking two & two, in red & blue & green
Grey-headed beadles walk'd before, with wands as white as snow,
Till into the high dome of Paul's they like Thames' waters flow.

O what a multitude they seem'd, these flowers of London town!
Seated in companies they sit with radiance all their own.
The hum of multitudes was there, but multitudes of lambs,
Thousands of little boys & girls raising their innocent hands.

Now like mighty wind they raise to heaven the voice of song,
Or like harmonious thunderings the seats of heaven among.
Beneath them sit the aged men, wise guardians of the poor;
Then cherish pity, lest you drive an angel from your door. (K121-2)

This was apparently something of an Anglican tradition, that one special Thursday of the year a procession of London's children – particularly the poor and orphaned from the various church orphanages – would make its way to St Paul's for a service of song.[28] The orphaned girls at Duché's Asylum would participate in this, and it is possible that among those 'aged men, wise guardians of the poor' that Blake praises in the second last line is the Rev Jacob Duché. What makes this more likely is the line that follows and completes the poem, for the notion of 'driving an angel' away from oneself – of having one close by in the first place – is unmistakably Swedenborgian. Swedenborg described the phenomenon of the constant presence of spirits in great detail – good angels and mischievous spirits in a balance maintained by God but constantly shifted by the quality of one's own thoughts and actions. Thus the possibility of chasing one's good angels away by failing to 'cherish pity'.

Geoffrey Keynes has supposed that Blake meant this poem to have an ironic message and be really a critique of how very

---

28. William Blake, *Songs of Innocence and Experience*, with an introduction and commentary by Geoffrey Keynes (Oxford, 1986), p. 139.

hypocritical such displays of charity were by an otherwise uncaring Established clergy.[29] But perhaps the *Songs of Innocence* were written with good will in the spirit of hope for what Swedenborg's prophesized new epoch of the New Jerusalem might bring. The sentiments are in keeping with Blake's positive marginalia written around this time in Swedenborg's *Divine Love and Wisdom*; the Rev Jacob Duché was one of those unlikely Anglicans whose political and religious interests so overlapped with Blake's own; and Blake was yet to encounter any of the Rev Proud or Robert Hindmarsh's Swedenborgian priestcraft. He has no reason to be ironic, and all manner of justification for what is one of his most sentimentally optimistic and overtly traditional Swedenborgian poems.

'The Chimney Sweeper' is, despite its realistic portrayal of the young sweeper's plight, also optimistic and even moralistic in a way that makes the poem appear to have been written as a form of religious instruction for children. This is most evident in the final stanza, but consider the entire poem:

When my mother died I was very young,
And my Father sold me while yet my tongue
Could scarcely cry ""weep! 'weep! 'weep! 'weep!"
So your chimneys I sweep, & in soot I sleep.

There's little Tom Dacre, who cried when his head,
That curl'd like a lamb's back, was shav'd: so I said
"Hush Tom! never mind it, for when your head's bare
"You know that the soot cannot spoil your white hair."

And so he was quiet, & that very night
As Tom was a-sleeping, he had such a sight!
That thousands of sweepers, Dick, Joe, Ned & Jack,
Were all of them locked up in coffins of black.

And by came an Angel who had a bright key,
And he open'd the coffins & set them all free;
Then down a green plain leaping, laughing, they run,
And wash in a river, and shine in the Sun.

Then naked & white, all their bags left behind,
They rise upon clouds and sport in the wind;
And the Angel told Tom, if he'd be a good boy,
He'd have God for his father, & never want joy.

And so Tom awoke; and we rose in the dark,
And got with our bags & our brushes to work.

---

29. Blake, *Songs*, commentary by G. Keynes, p. 139.

Tho' the morning was cold, Tom was happy & warm;
So if all do their duty they need not fear harm. (K117-8)

Here are the good Swedenborgian angels offering their comfort and wisdom, and here too in the final line is the Swedenborgian doctrine of divine providence, not altogether different from traditional Protestant notions, that all are cared for by God in ways unseen to humanity but particularly those who make themselves useful and are God-fearing. The sentiment belongs more to Wesley than Blake and was probably given a methodist gloss by the many former methodists who counted among the most ardent early sectarians of Swedenborg. Given Blake's later hatred of traditional Christianity one is once again tempted to explain 'The Chimney Sweeper' in ironic terms except that, as with 'Holy Thursday', it must be recalled that Blake was not yet hostile to these ideas in Swedenborg and to those who were promoting them.

In this case there is some hard evidence that sets 'The Chimney Sweeper' in a Swedenborgian context. We know from Blake's pencil annotations to Swedenborg's *Heaven & Hell* that he also read Swedenborg's bizarre collection of 'Memorable Relations', *The Earths in the Universe*. In those annotations Blake cites number 73 from *Earths* in support of the point he is trying to make. Just a few pages later, at number 79, there is a strange tale of Swedenborg's meeting spirits from the planet Jupiter who resembled chimney sweepers. Swedenborg describes these chimney sweepers as being covered black in soot and of evoking pity for their unfortunate state. The particular sweeper with whom he talks wants desperately to be let into heaven and Swedenborg eventually observes how this desire is finally gratified; upon news from an angel that the sweeper can now remove his clothes in preparation, he does so with amazing quickness. Angels then set him free in heaven to fly and romp about rather as the sweepers in Blake's poem are set free.

This is such a remarkable paragraph and relates so closely to the poem and to Blake's general interest in Swedenborg that it must be considered seminal to much else in Blake. It is written in the style of all the 'Memorable Relations', fable-like stories of Swedenborg's conversations with spirits in the spiritual world that are periodically interjected into the tomes of theological doctrine and that Blake later satirized as 'Memorable Fancies' in *The Marriage of Heaven & Hell*. Nonetheless, he was very interested in them as foundations for his artistic endeavours, as the lost painting of 'The Spiritual Precursor', listed in Blake's *Exhibition Catalogue* as having been drawn from Memorable Relation number 623 of Swedenborg's *True Christian Religion*, and this particular number show. Here is Swedenborg on the chimney sweepers:

> There are also spirits among those of Jupiter, whom they call chimney-sweepers, because they appear in such garments, and also with a sooty face . . . One such spirit came to me, and earnestly begged me to intercede for him that he might come into heaven . . . But I could only reply that I could bring him no help, and that this is of the Lord alone . . . he was then sent back among the upright spirits from his earth; but they said that he could not be in their company, because he was not such as they . . . He was of a black colour in the light of heaven, but he said that he was not of a black, but a brown colour. It was told me that they are such at first, who are afterward received among those that constitute the province of the seminal vesicles in the Greatest Man, or heaven . . . I was then permitted to tell him, that perhaps this was an indication that he would shortly be received. He was then told by angels to cast off his garment, which from his desire he rejected so quickly, that scarce anything could be quicker. By this was represented what are the desires of those who are in the province to which the seminal vesicles correspond. It was said that these spirits when prepared for heaven, put off their garments and are clothed with shining new ones, and become angels.[30]

This almost sounds like Blake, in his wild later poetry, though without the poetic forms. It contains the sexual themes that Blake emphasizes in the *Marriage* and the references to Swedenborg's Grand Man – his description of the spiritual world as corresponding in its different parts or societies to the parts of the human body. Blake makes repeated references to such a scheme: first quite innocently in 'The Divine Image'; then more boldly in the *Marriage* where his final 'Proverb of Hell' – in which the head represents the 'Sublime', the heart 'Pathos', the genitals 'Beauty' and the hands and feet 'Proportion' – describes an artistic Grand Man over Swedenborg's more scientific one. Raine has also spotted

---

30. Emanuel Swedenborg, *Concerning the Earths in the Universe* (London, 1787), paragraph 79. In Blake's annotations to Swedenborg's *Heaven and Hell* (this copy held in the Harvard College Library) he mentions paragraph 73 of *Earths*.

this number in Swedenborg and writes of it that 'there is nothing improbable in the suggestion that the figure of Orc-Eros has its beginning – or one of its beginnings – in this strange and uncouth fable of the erotic figure of the sweeper of chimneys.'[31] This is indeed possible, but with reference to Orc one is moving away from the *Songs* and into the prophetic poetry of Blake's later years.

V

If Blake first compiled the *Songs of Innocence* in response to the Conference call for new songs of praise for the fledgling New Church, as Edward Thompson has suggested, then his offering was not accepted: the following year, at the 1790 Conference, Robert Hindmarsh drew up a catechism for children and a collection of nearly three hundred hymns was chosen for the hymn-book, over one hundred of which had been rapidly composed by the Rev Joseph Proud, a former minister in the Baptist connexion.[32]

There is evidence which shows that writers other than Proud submitted 'songs of praise and thanksgiving' for the New Church hymnal and had their work rejected. In Proud's original bound manuscript containing his first drafts of the hymns which he composed for the Eastcheap chapel there are sums with notations written in pencil on the inside of the front board.[33] These appear to be a breakdown of the total number of hymns submitted and the number eventually chosen for the first New Church hymnal:

```
130   by Proud
146   by Others
 34   rejected
310
```

---

31. Raine quoted in David V. Erdman, *Prophet Against Empire: a Poet's Interpretation of the History of His Own Times* (Garden City, NJ, 1969), p. 132, n40.

32. Carl Odhner, *Annals of the New Church* (Bryn Athyn: General Church Press, 1905), p. 147.

33. Joseph Proud, 'MS. Hymns & Index', bound with annotations (held in the New Church General Conference Library and Archives, Swedenborg House, Bloomsbury, London).

The possibility exists that Blake submitted at least some of the nineteen *Songs of Innocence*, which we know were ready by the time he attended the Great Eastcheap conference in 1789; and that these submissions were among the thirty-four rejected in 1790. Why, one wonders in any case, would a natural poet such as Blake, so greatly taken at that moment by the idea of a New Jerusalem Church – or at least a New Jerusalem on earth – not submit his work in response to a call for new songs in praise of this Spiritual Revolution?

Hard evidence does not take the case much further. There is the orally-transmitted story, recorded many years later at the time of Blake's death, that Blake wrote the 'Divine Image' in *Innocence* whilst sitting in the Hatton Street New Church Chapel.[34] But this has been discredited by Erdman on the grounds that this specific chapel had not yet been built when Blake composed that song.[35] Apart from this one has to rely on the appearance of a handful of Blake's *Songs* in New Church periodicals published in the last two decades of his life;[36] any additional evidence must be drawn from a reading of the *Songs* that considers, above all else, the historical context of Swedenborg's London movement.

Presupposing for the moment that Blake did submit some of the *Songs of Innocence* to the New Church, his subsequent rejection could then be seen as another cause of his growing disenchantment with the sectarian Swedenborgians – though if it was, the source ran much deeper than mere umbrage at having had his work rejected. Set beside Proud's compositions, Blake's songs not only display far superior poetic quality but a radically different approach to religion. Compare Hymn CXXII by Proud, entitled 'The Divine Humanity of the Lord; the only object of Worship,' with Blake's 'The Divine Image'. First Proud:

---

34. G. E. Bentley, *Blake Records Supplement* (Oxford, 1988), p. 10; J. Spilling, 'Blake, Artist and Poet', *New Church Magazine*, vi, 1887, p. 254.

35. Erdman, 'Blake's Early Swedenborgianism', p. 251.

36. For a full list of bibliographical details, see Bentley, *Supplement*, p. 83. The two instances during Blake's lifetime are publication of 'The Divine Image' in *Dawn of Light* (April 1825) and 'On Anothers Sorrow', also in *Dawn of Light* (July 1825).

Darkness pervades the mind,
And clouds prevent the light,
That few Jehovah Jesus know,
Or worship Him aright.

But, Lord we come to thee,
And bow before thy throne;
In thy Divine Humanity,
Thou art our God alone.

Thy *esse* none can see,
That is beyond our sight
But thy Divine Humanity
Is seen in heav'nly light.

Thou art the only God,
The only Man art thou;
And only thee our souls adore,
At thy bless'd feet we bow.

In essence thou art one,
And one in person too;
Tho'in thy essence seen by none,
Thy person we may view.

The Human made Divine,
Our souls with joy adore;
And soon with angels we shall join,
To praise and love thee more.[37]

Proud is rather heavy-handed here, though the perceptive reader might have sensed what was coming from the length of the title alone. Now here is Blake's *Song*:

To Mercy, Pity, Peace, and Love
All pray in their distress;
And to these virtues of delight
Return their thankfulness.

For Mercy, Pity, Peace, and Love,
Is God our father dear,
And Mercy, Pity, Peace, and Love,
Is Man, his child and care.

For Mercy has a human heart,
Pity a human face,
And Love, the human form divine,
And Peace, the human dress.

Then every man, of every clime,
That prays in his distress,

---

37. *Hymns and Spiritual Songs for the Use of the Lord's New Church* (London, 1790), p. 142.

Prays to the human form divine,
Love, Mercy, Pity, Peace.

And all must love the human form,
In heathen, turk or jew;
Where Mercy, Love & Pity dwell,
There God is dwelling too. (K117).

Kathleen Raine writes that there could be no more simple, or beautiful, statement of the divine humanity of God, the central doctrine of Swedenborg's theology.[38] Thompson thinks the song a heretical version of the 'orthodox' doctrine established by the leaders of the young New Jerusalem Church.[39] There is no doubt in either case that this is a Swedenborgian song. The theme of the divine human and the lyrical form are found both in Proud's hymn and Blake's poetical song. But what a striking difference in tone! Whereas 'The Divine Image' conveys a sense of equality, as among 'heathen, turk or jew' and between God and Man, Proud's poem is laden with deference, and his main focus is upon the Lord. In Hymn CXCVII, entitled 'Our God in Human Form', Proud has included a footnote to the second line of the second stanza – 'Our God is man alone' – for the sake of doctrinal clarification:

> By man alone, understand that God is the only man, strictly speaking, as all mankind are men from him, and not in themselves. See E.S.[40]

This stern and somewhat anomalous pronouncement in the midst of three hundred hymns suggests that the Swedenborgian doctrine of the Divine Human was proving a contentious one within the fledgling Church. And judging from songs such as the 'Divine Image', Blake might easily be supposed to have been one of the contenders. In any case, the footnote is a further, more explicit example of what one already feels in Proud's verse to be a profound uneasiness with Swedenborg's radical equation of God-Man. He does his best to smother it with extreme deference to 'Our Lord and King' and repeated emphasis on the essential depravity of humanity.

---

38. Raine, *Blake and Tradition*, p. 20.

39. Thompson, 'Blake and Which Tradition?', Lectures.

40. *Hymns*, p. 221.

There is a beautifully sad little poem in the *Songs of Experience* that should be understood in the context of Blake's increasing divergence from sectarian Swedenborgians such as Proud. 'The Clod & the Pebble' reads:

> "Love seeketh not Itself to please,
> "Nor for itself hath any care,
> "But for another gives its ease,
> "And builds a Heaven in Hell's despair."

> So sang a little Clod of Clay
> Trodden with the cattles feet,
> But a Pebble of the brook
> Warbled out these metres meet:

> "Love seeketh only Self to please,
> "To bind another to Its delight,
> "Joys in another's loss of ease,
> "And builds a Hell in Heaven's despite." (K211)

Both Morton Paley and Kathleen Raine have commented upon the markedly Swedenborgian structure of the poem: they refer to the two diametrically opposed loves, the one selfless and the other selfish, as a central doctrine of the New Dispensation.[41] But this poem is not an endorsement of Swedenborgian theology. There is a personal sense of sadness, perhaps even bitterness, that infuses it and makes a wholly positive Swedenborgian reading impossible. Given what we know of Blake's antinomian attitudes about love, it seems likely that he is casting the Pebble's brand of love in an unfavourable light; and if so, this is a poem that is as much about his relations with other Swedenborgians as anything else.

One wonders whether Blake intended the 'Pebble of the brook' to be the Rev Joseph Proud. No conclusive evidence has been found to support this. All we know is that the two had become acquainted by 1798 when Proud invited Blake to join the Hatton Garden New Church society.[42] But another look at some of Proud's original hymns does bear it out. In his

41. Raine, *Blake and Tradition*, pp. 27-8; Morton D. Paley, '"A New Heaven is Begun": Blake and Swedenborgianism', in *Blake and Swedenborg: Opposition is True Friendship*, ed. H. Bellin and D. Ruhl (New York: Swedenborg Foundation, 1985), pp. 18-9.

42. Bentley, *Blake Records*, pp. 440-1.

Hymn CXXI, or 'Self Love condemned', the first two stanzas read:

> What fondness sinners ever prove,
> For that which is their own!
> Their little selves they dearly love,
> And love themselves alone.
>
> But what is self? a mass of sin,
> Corruption, filth, and dust;
> Pollution all without, within,
> And nigh to be accurs'd.[43]

Proud certainly sounds like the Pebble carrying on about love seeking 'only Self to please'. And the historical accounts of Proud seem to fit him to the role of the Pebble in an even more exacting manner. He was a fine orator and perhaps, as his very name suggests, something of an elitist.[44] We might imagine him as one highly skilled in 'warbling', who spoke in measured 'metres' and with the smoothness of a pebble. Proud used these skills to draw considerable numbers on Sundays, and it is thus not surprising that his hymns would be selected over those of lesser participants in the New Jerusalem Church. Compare the marginalized poet Blake: the 'little Clod of Clay' who sings his songs in offering them to the Church and is rejected and 'trodden' upon by Proud's herds of followers. As a song of uplift, of building a 'Heaven in Hell's despair', his is the song of the dispossessed in any land at any time, but it was of particular relevance to Blake in Swedenborg's intra-millennial age, when it and the other *Songs* were to help build Jerusalem 'in England's green and pleasant Land'.

VI

Despite all the hope and promise that Blake may have felt at the prospect of a new spiritual epoch full of imaginative liberty and a matching New Church that posted signs over its chapel doors saying that now all was allowable, one can imagine his despair upon realizing that this group of New

---

43. *Hymns*, p. 141.

44. David George Goyder, *The Autobiography of a Phrenologist* (London, 1857), pp. 85-90.

Jerusalemites was so very much like all the other established sects of the other established churches. The conservatism of the new sect was most obvious in the way it adopted many of the Old Church forms. The hymns are one example, but there are others. Robert Hindmarsh's catechism for children, written sometime between 1789 and the Second General Conference in April of 1790, has the old style theological forms with an added touch of Swedenborgian pedestrianism. It begins –

Quest. What are you?
Ans.   A human creature.
Q.   What is a human creature?
A.   A form receptive of love and wisdom, and thus capable of becoming an image and likeness of Almighty God.[45]

– and carries on thus for eight pages, all of which was to be memorized under the close supervision of a Hindmarshian priest. One is reminded of Blake's 'Little Boy Lost' who wonders aloud:

And Father, how can I love you,
Or any of my brothers more?
I love you like the little bird
That picks up crumbs around the door.

The Priest sat by and heard the child,
In trembling zeal he siez'd his hair:
He led him by his little coat:
And all admir'd the Priestly care.

And standing on the altar high,
Lo what a fiend is here! said he:
One who sets reason up for judge
Of our most holy Mystery.

The weeping child could not be heard,
The weeping parents wept in vain:
They strip'd him to his little shirt,
And bound him in an iron chain. (K218).

And perhaps made the little boy memorize the entire eight-page New Church catechism.

The Minutes to the Second Conference in 1790 reveal a preoccupation with the outward forms of worship which the

---

45. Robert Hindmarsh, ed., *Catechism for the use of Children agreeable to the Heavenly Doctrines of the New Jerusalem*. 2nd Edition (London: T. Goyder, 1821–65), p. 3.

New Church is to adopt, and by 1791 the 4th edition of the *Liturgy of the New Church* includes a 'Prayer for the King and Royal Family, both Houses of Parliament, and all Magistrates' in every order of service, a tradition lifted straight from the Church of England's *Book of Common Prayer*.[46] There is as well a movement, led by Hindmarsh, to establish a New Church priesthood meant to preserve the purity of the New Dispensation and enforce a conservative interpretation that might win the young church respectability and growth among the respectable classes.[47] There were, after all, a number of non-sectarian Swedenborgians about London advocating suspect and possibly even seditious readings of Swedenborg's writings,[48] and others, such as the Unitarian Joseph Priestley, were publishing critiques of the New Church that demanded a cogent, unified response.[49] This too was the time of Church and King mobs, and any newish-looking organization was in danger. In Birmingham in 1790 Priestley's laboratory and library were destroyed. Close by, the recently ordained Rev Joseph Proud bought off another such mob on the threshold of burning the city's New Church chapel by meeting them on the door step, throwing out coins, and shouting 'God Save the King'. He evidently told them that the doctrines of the New Jerusalem Church were in no way antithetical to the monarchy or connected to the Unitarians or Dr Priestley, and the mob moved away shouting 'Huzza, huzza to the New Jerusalem forever!'[50] For political reasons, the New Church shed much of its newness very early on.

'The Clod & the Pebble' and 'The Little Boy Lost' are not the only *Songs of Experience* that need to be placed in this context of zealous church-building. 'The Garden of Love',

---

46. Robert Hindmarsh, ed., *Liturgy of the New Church*. 4th Edition (London: Hindmarsh, 1791), pp. 55-6.

47. Odhner, *Annals*, pp. 167-8.

48. See Morley, 'Politics of Prophecy', pp. 95-110.

49. Joseph Priestley, *Letters to the Members of the New Jerusalem Church formed by Baron Swedenborg* (Birmingham, 1791); Robert Hindmarsh, *Letters to Dr Priestley* (London, 1792).

50. Joseph Proud, 'MS Memoirs', handwritten in 1822 (held in the New Church General Conference Library and Archives, Swedenborg House, Bloomsbury, London).

written sometime before 1794 during the period of Blake's growing disenchantment with the form of the New Church, is unmistakably directed at the rapid transformation that took place at Great Eastcheap: from a progressive theosophical group to a traditional Protestant sect with a dogmatic, conservative, and authoritarian priesthood. The poem is concerned with the repression of natural, instinctive religion – as represented by a 'Garden of Love', Blake's eighteenth-century version of the Garden of Eden – by the forces of traditional organized religion.

> I went to the Garden of Love,
> And saw what I never had seen:
> A chapel was built in the midst,
> Where I used to play on the green.
>
> And the gates of this Chapel were shut,
> And "Thou shalt not" writ over the door:
> So I turn'd to the Garden of Love,
> That so many sweet flowers bore,
>
> And I saw it was filled with graves,
> And tomb-stones where flowers should be;
> And Priests in black gowns were walking their rounds,
> And binding with briars my joys & desires. (K215)

This particular Chapel is without doubt the Swedenborgian chapel at Great Eastcheap, but instead of the inspiring, potentially antinomian intra-millennial phrase *Nunc Licet*, 'Now it is allowable', Blake now finds '"Thou shalt not" writ over the door'. And there, where previously flowers of Blake's antinomian garden had grown, 'Priests in black gowns were walking their rounds/And binding with briars my joys and desires.' This is a first-hand account of Blake's 'experience' with the sectarian Swedenborgians, though of course the poetry gives voice to principles larger than his dissent from Great Eastcheap. This dissent echoed his initial dissent from the established churches but is all the more poignant for revealing the personal disillusionment of his hopes for the New Jerusalemites and their promises to loose the 'mind-forged manacles' put in place by the tyrannical priestcraft of the Old Church.

There are other *Songs of Experience* that were set against Blake's experiences with the New Jerusalem Church, or that were adjusted to relate to it sometime in the years after 1789 and before *Experience* was printed in 1794. One likely example is a poem in Blake's *Notebook* called 'Christian Forebearance', which was included without alteration in *Experience* as 'Poison Tree'. It reads as though it has reference to Blake's immediate surroundings and personal arguments:

I was angry with my friend:
I told my wrath, my wrath did end.
I was angry with my foe:
I told it not, my wrath did grow.

And I watered it in fears,
Night & morning with my tears:
And I sunned it with smiles,
And with soft deceitful wiles.

And it grew both day and night,
Till it bore an apple bright.
And my foe beheld it shine,
And he knew that it was mine.

And into my garden stole,
When the night had veiled the pole:
In the morning glad I see,
My foe outstretch'd beneath the tree. (K218)

The Swedenborgian reference in this case has to do with an article, extended through a number of issues, in Robert Hindmarsh's New Church periodical, *The New Magazine of Knowledge of Heaven and Hell*.[51] The article is called 'The Poison Tree' and is about a certain tree in Java that bears poisonous fruit. The tone of the article is scientific, in the late eighteenth-century manner of reporting and examining oddities in the physical world for curious gentlemen readers, and in this particular piece there is no overt mention of Swedenborg or his ideas even though the magazine is a medium for the dissemination of his theological notions. What seems to have happened is that Blake wrote the poem at some point late in the 1780s, when we know that the part of his *Notebook* containing 'Christian Forebearance' was written, and then changed the title as he was preparing the *Songs of Experience* in the years immediately preceding 1794. He got the title from

---

51. *The New Magazine of Knowledge concerning Heaven and Hell*, ed. R. Hindmarsh (London, vol. 1, 1790), pp. 36-8; copies in the British Library; Swedenborg House, London; and Swedenborg Library, Bryn Athyn, Pennsylvania. I am grateful to E. P. Thompson for leading me to these early Swedenborgian periodicals.

Hindmarsh's magazine and with memories of his bitter experience at the New Jerusalem Church (and possibly with the ringleader Hindmarsh himself) used it here for its satirical value.

The new title does happen to suit the story of the poem, but there is something more than just convenience about this new arrangement. The real satirical thrust is thematic. Blake hated literalism. He hated the limiting, dogmatising tendency of reason. He believed passionately in the power of the individual imagination to gain a superior sense of truth. And we can ascertain from his annotations to Swedenborg's *Divine Love and Wisdom* and from *The Marriage of Heaven & Hell* (which may itself have been another satirical strike against Hindmarsh's presumptuously named *New Magazine of Knowledge of Heaven and Hell*[52]) that Blake faulted the sectarian Swedenborgians for dispensing with imagination in favour of a dogmatised, literal treatment of Swedenborg's writings. Blake's own vision of things was that 'the Last Judgement will be when all those are Cast away who trouble Religion with Questions concerning Good & Evil or Eating of the Tree of those Knowledges or Reasonings which hinder the Vision of God.'[53] This, one thinks, was what Blake hoped for the intra-millennial world; and he may have expected the self-declared intra-millennial vanguard of Swedenborg and the early Swedenborgians to have set an appropriate example.

But an exceptionally detailed knowledge of good and evil, heaven and hell, God and humanity, is, in fact, precisely what Swedenborg delivered in his two dozen tomes of academic Latin and exactly what he promised them to be. This much in Swedenborg Blake abhorred, and it was perhaps the context of Swedenborg's sectarian followers proclaiming loudly to the world that it was now within their grasp to understand all the mysteries of this world and the next that gave 'A Poison Tree' its satirical potency. Blake may have thought that the sectarians, by permitting Hindmarsh's literal approach to Swedenborg's revelations, were guilty of having eaten the

---

52. *The Marriage* was certainly written with a Swedenborgian audience in mind. See John Howard, 'An Audience for *The Marriage of Heaven and Hell*', in *Blake Studies*, III, 1970, pp. 19-52.

53. Geoffrey Keynes, ed., *The Notebook of William Blake* (New York: Cooper Square, 1970), pp. 114-5.

spiritually poisonous fruit of the 'Tree of the Knowledge of Good and Evil' that had previously ruined Eve and her partner Adam. It would follow that Hindmarsh's *New Magazine of Knowledge of Heaven and Hell*, and his own literal approach to the Bible and to Swedenborg's writings, constitute in Blake's poem that very 'Poison Tree' of literal religious knowledge. Not surprisingly, Blake finds its editor dead, or perhaps just spiritually ill, beneath it. By 1794, when this poem was first printed as part of the *Songs of Experience*, Hindmarsh's work with the New Church had reached a kind of dead-end: he had been expelled by the sect, which itself had become moribund (temporarily), and his *New Magazine* had gone under. 'Dead' would thus have been a cruel but telling metaphor to describe Hindmarsh at this moment, and everyone in that small community of believers would know exactly what Blake was getting at.

VII

There is a plate at the very end of an original copy of Blake's *Songs of Innocence and Experience* that contains no poetical text but is listed in the British Library's General Catalogue as 'The Regenerate Soul'.[54] The plate is a picture of a human form being raised by angels into Heaven. That the soul on its way to heaven should have been portrayed by Blake as a worldly human body is another indication of Swedenborgian influence on the *Songs* and yet another example of Blake's ongoing interest in Swedenborg's ideas.

Swedenborg's notion that a person took on a spiritual body after death very much resembling the natural body was new to the period. He wrote in one of his 'Memorable Relations' with characteristic nonchalance:

> In spirit I was once whisked up into the angelic heaven and into one of its communities, and then some of the wise people there came up to me and said, "What news from the earth?"
>   . . . I went on to say: "At this day the Lord has revealed facts about life after death."

---

54. Copy BB of the 'Songs of Innocence and Experience' is in the Department of Prints and Manuscripts at the British Museum, Great Russell Street, Bloomsbury, London.

The angels said, "What about life after death? Who does not know that a person lives after death?"

"They know," I said, "and they do not know. They say it is not the person but his soul, and that it lives as a spirit, and they foster a notion of a spirit like a wind or atmosphere, and that the person does not live until after the Last Judgement Day. And they think that then the parts of the body left behind in the world will be gathered again and put back together into a body, even though eaten by worms, mice, and fish, and that this is the way people are resurrected."

The angels said, "What is this? Who does not know that a person lives after death as a person, with the only difference that he lives as a spiritual person, and that a spiritual person sees a spiritual person just the way a material person sees a material person? And that they know not one difference, except that they are in a more perfect condition?"[55]

It seems that Blake and a few of his fellow artists knew about fully-formed spiritual bodies, and that they had gained this insight from Swedenborg. The engraver William Sharp, a friend of Blake's who had dabbled in Swedenborg before leaving him for the more sensational promises of the millennarian prophetess Joanna Southcott, designed a picture which was executed by the artist Benjamin West of two 'regenerating souls', the one male and the other a fully-formed female. It appeared on the frontispiece of a book of sermons by the Swedenborgian Anglican, the Rev Jacob Duché, and 'was the subject of much remark at the time' for its human representation of angels.[56]

The very concept of regeneration, or of a 'regenerating soul', is also important to Swedenborg. In his theological writings it describes the final and highest form of a human's spiritual transformation from being a receptacle of inherited evils – a modified version of original sin – to a self-determined receptacle of the Lord's divine love and wisdom. Swedenborg presents life as a dynamic and open-ended process. From protected childhood innocence one would begin to engage in self-directed, though divinely-supervised, struggles to reform inherited evil tendencies. If one was successful, these struggles culminated in a state of spiritual 'regeneration' and the reception into heaven with a perfected spiritual body after the

---

55. Emanuel Swedenborg, *De Amore Conjugali*, no. 532 (translated in *New Church Life*, vol. CXII, August 1992, pp. 364-5).

56. Charles Higham, 'The Rev Jacob Duche, M.A.', in *The New Church Review* (July, 1915), pp. 404-5.

death of the natural one. Placed at the end of the combined *Songs of Innocence and Experience*, which taken together recreate a kind of Swedenborgian life-struggle between opposing human emotions, this plate of 'The Regenerate Soul' shows Blake coming back to the Swedenborgian system.

On this one level of reading Blake's *Songs*, the chronology of their development can be seen to illustrate the nature and evolution of Blake's own difficult Swedenborgianism. Some of the *Songs of Innocence*, as Kathleen Raine has shown, express Blake's early and hopeful interest in Swedenborg's writings and in his call for a new and humane church whose distinguishing features would have nothing to do with new chapels but would show themselves through its people – the honest, humane, and brotherly 'prophets' of the new spiritual epoch begun, according to Swedenborg, in the spiritual world in 1757. *The Songs of Experience* document Blake's disappointment following the moment of great expectation in 1789 when, even as all the world seemed to be throwing off the old chains and violently rejecting the oppression of Kings and Priests, Swedenborg's sectarian followers not only failed to keep pace but actually tried to shore up the *status quo*. The rejection of Blake, of his poetical songs and prophetic principles, by the young sectarians epitomized the widespread rejection of new and humane principles in reaction to the initial successes of the French revolution. These were the years when Blake attacked Swedenborg and his traditional followers in the satirical *Marriage of Heaven & Hell* – not only because he disliked their orthodox approach to Swedenborg's radical theology but also because they had become a convenient symbol for all that was going wrong around him. In England, this was the time when Jacobins and republicans suffered the reactionary vengeance of Prime Minister William Pitt's treason trials, from which Blake's fellow-engraver William Sharp narrowly escaped and which Blake himself had to confront when he was arrested at Felpham, Sussex for forcibly marching a soldier out of his garden. The soldier accused Blake of sedition, and in the paranoid atmosphere which then prevailed, Blake had to defend his life in court.

But by joining both sets of *Songs*, the hopeful and the bitter, into one complete work 'shewing the contrary states of the human soul', as Blake did in 1794, one senses a degree of

reconciliation. The visionary theologian and the imaginative
poet could agree that states of mind and soul, often contrary
states, are more real than what meets the human eye. Likewise, Blake was preoccupied with the same millennarian
concerns of a new spiritual epoch that so exercised Swedenborg. But he did not get on with the sectarians and their
particular brand of Swedenborgianism. He chastened them in
Experience and lampooned them in the *Marriage*. He attacked them where they were most sensitive, which is to say he
attacked Swedenborg in the demagogic form they had made
of him. His real anger was not that they read and believed
what Swedenborg wrote but that they dogmatised the theology and dispensed with the visionary, imaginative approach
to spiritual understanding.

Blake said of Swedenborg in 1809 that

> the works of this visionary are well worthy the attention of Painters and
> Poets; they are foundations for grand things; the reason they have not
> been more attended to is because corporeal demons have gained a
> predominance; who the leaders of these are, will be shewn below.
> Unworthy Men who gain fame among Men, continue to govern man-
> kind after death, and in their spiritual bodies oppose the spirits of those
> who worthily are famous; and, as Swedenborg observes, by entering into
> disease and excrement, drunkenness and concupiscence, they possess
> themselves of bodies of mortal men, and shut the doors of mind and of
> thought by placing Learning above Inspiration. (K581-2)

At least some of these 'corporeal demons', those 'Unworthy
Men', were to be found among the ranks of the sectarian
Swedenborgians, the Hindmarshes and the Prouds. Here was
confirmation of Blake's continuing interest in Swedenborg
despite his fierce opposition to certain Swedenborgians. Swedenborg, in Blake's openly expressed opinion, had with his
prophecies established 'foundations for grand things', but he
had been 'shorn by the Churches', by the organizing, dogmatising zeal of a small group of professional church-builders.

Marguerite Block has written of Swedenborg's theology
that

> the main point to be grasped is that in *Heaven and Hell* Swedenborg is
> not describing merely the "future life", or "life after death", but the
> spiritual life which every one, "dead and alive", is living every moment
> . . . [and] that for a correct understanding of this spiritual world the

ordinary concepts of time and space must be eliminated. In place of them there are states, and changes of state only.[57]

Here is Blake's own system expressed in his *Songs* and 'shewing the contrary states of the human soul' – a system that, though independent, had as one of its foundations the visionary tales and theology of Swedenborg and was shaped by Blake's participation in the successes and failures of Swedenborg's London followers. We know this because of the historical record linking Blake and the early Swedenborgians; because of the Swedenborgian components of many of the *Songs*; and because the final plate of 'The Regenerate Soul' provides such a definitively Swedenborgian resolution to Blake's system of contraries. Even this system of contraries can be traced back to Swedenborg, for he had stated in his *Spiritual Diary* that 'where there is enlightenment there must be a view of contraries',[58] and he repeated this doctrine in one form or another a great many times. But if the *Songs* do indeed represent a Blakean system of Swedenborgian truths, this should not be taken too formally, for these truths were expressed by Blake as poetry. Poetry is not dogmatic, it is not mechanistic, and it cannot (or most certainly should not) be used to produce laws which limit and oppress humanity. The last thing Blake would have wanted for his poetics is a set of formalistic followers like the sectarian ones who had clasped Swedenborg.

In the poem *Milton*, immediately following the famous verses on Jerusalem, Blake exclaims: 'Would to God that all the Lord's people were prophets.' We can gather from this the nature of the internal transformation he hoped would take place in the minds of his peers. Swedenborg had laid the foundations for Jerusalem, and now he, Blake, as a fellow visionary, was trying to continue the work with his poetry:

In my Exchanges every Land
Shall walk, & mine in every Land,
Mutual shall build Jerusalem,
Both heart in heart & hand in hand. (K652).

---

57. Block, *New Church*, p. 31.

58. Emanuel Swedenborg, *The Spiritual Diary*, vol. 4, no. 4772 (London, 1889), pp. 196-7. Excerpts of the original Latin MS were published in English in the early New Church periodicals which Blake is presumed to have read.

It was to be a world of brotherhood and love. But unlike Swedenborg and himself, most of the Lord's people were not prophets. Blake wrote in annotations to the Bishop of Llandaff that 'Prophets, in the modern sense of the word have never existed. Jonah was no prophet in the modern sense, for his prophecy of Nineveh failed. Every honest man is a Prophet; he utters his opinion both of private & public matters . . . A Prophet is not a Seer, not an Arbitrary Dictator.' (K392) Swedenborg, who had not feared to speak of his visions even though such open talk would (and did) draw ridicule and cost him his privileged standing among intellectuals and elites, was most certainly a prophet in Blake's opinion. The sectarian Swedenborgians, so intent upon respectability and church growth, were most certainly not. After his great hopes for the New Jerusalem Church in 1789 had been disappointed, Blake turned to satire, recorded the bitterness of his experience, and lost himself in wild, ranting poetry.

Disappointment over the New Jerusalem Church was not the only thing that moved him into his prophetic phase. As Jacob Bronowski has written, 'William Blake lived in the most violent age of English history,' and he is right to insist that we try to understand Blake in this context of the 'age of revolution'.[59] But we should remember that spiritual revolution was for Blake inextricably tied to the other revolutionary developments of his unruly age and perhaps crowned it. Whether in the form of Swedenborg's 'spiritual sense' of the Word or Blake's artistic and visionary imagination, this was an age in which, as Raymond Williams expressed it, 'a new idea of a superior reality, even of a superior power,'[60] was perceived, developed, and acted upon.

---

59. Jacob Bronowski, *Blake and the Age of Revolution* (London, 1972), p. 15.

60. Raymond Williams, *Culture and Society: 1780-1950* (New York, 1985), p. 38.

Chapter Six

A Little Jubilee? The Literacy of Robert Wedderburn in 1817

Peter Linebaugh

> 'Tremble, O tyrants of the world
> And you . . . O fallen slaves, arise.'
> > Alexander Pushkin, 'Ode to Freedom' (1817)

> . . . and I often sat for hours motionless and speechless, wishing for
> some mighty revolution that might bury me and my destroyer in its ruins.
> > Mary Shelley, *Frankenstein; Or, the Modern Prometheus* (1817)

In this essay I wish to make three points about Robert Wedderburn who was born the son of a Jamaican slave in 1762 and died in London after the First of August Jubilee of 1834.[1]

First, I seek to understand the literacy of this man. Despite the publication of two books indisputably written by him and several issues of two different newspapers, he has been called illiterate. Literacy is a political category containing assumptions about the values, norms and institutions of society, and this was never as true as in the year 1817 when a deliberate reaction against demotic writing reached an apogee. I am especially concerned with three letters first published in *The Axe Laid to the Root, or a Fatal Blow to Oppressors, Being an Address to The Planters and Negroes of the Island of Jamaica*, a newspaper written and edited by Robert Wedderburn in London in October 1817. Six issues of this newspaper were

---

1. In the preparation of this essay I would like to thank Professor Robert Malcolmson, Professor Mavis Campbell, Professor Marcus Rediker, Professor Will Keach, Professor James Holstun, Ms. Brenda Coughlin, Miss Sarah Jean Thomas of the Spanish Town National Archive, Dr Kenneth Ingram of the Jamaican National Library, and Michaela Brennan my co-worker.

published. The correspondence was published in the last three of them, providing more than half the prose in the fourth and the sixth numbers. Thus, Wedderburn gave them supreme importance in his newspaper. The letters between Wedderburn and Elizabeth Campbell, his half-sister in Jamaica, give us a unique source of knowledge of the Atlantic working class. Iain McCalman, an authority on Wedderburn's writing, is inclined to accept the letters as authentic. Such correspondence is plausible considering that the free coloured people of Jamaica actively began organizing for civil rights in 1792 when reference was several times made to their 'secret societies' and 'secret correspondence.'[2] The correspondence crossed a race divide, a class divide, an imperial divide, and a geographic divide. Like Legba, the letters are at a cross roads.

The discussion of literacy leads to my other points. Rather than place Wedderburn on the margins or fringes of the London 'underground' where he is conceived as a criminal, a fool, or a fraud, I see him as a revolutionary who is able to bring to England experiences from the other side of the Atlantic. This is a matter certainly of geography, but just as influential is the proletarian experience of slavery and of sailoring. This is the second point.

Third, the project of communism against private property, drawing on the tradition of jubilee and associated with Thomas Spence, was not lunatic as claimed at the time, nor utopian as claimed afterwards, but it was an earnest attempt to solve the problems of poverty, slavery, factory and the plantation, and this is what Wedderburn set out to show in these letters, published in the year before Karl Marx was born.

'An illiterate mulatto seaman' is how Iain McCalman characterized Wedderburn. He emphasizes that the followers of Thomas Spence in London were in 'dishonourable,' casualized, or 'low status trades.' 'The economic marginality of such men' and illiteracy seem to be associated.[3] Describing his

---

2. Mavis Campbell, *The Dynamics of Change in a Slave Society: A Sociopolitical History of the Free Coloureds of Jamaica, 1800-1865* (1976), p. 71.

3. Iain McCalman, *The Radical Underground: Prophets, Revolutionaries*

language as 'coarse, violent and colloquial' at one point, at another he explained that 'Spence's parish land-reform plan also seemed to offer degraded artisans a chance to recover lost rights, status and self-respect, and his skilful use of plebeian propaganda forms might also have proved attractive to someone of Wedderburn's limited literacy.' In approaching the subject we need to be sensitive to the mentality that permitted Gardner, for example, to write of the African Baptists of Jamaica, 'they were generally slaves and therefore illiterate.'[4]

McCalman has written for several years about Robert Wedderburn, and his ideas have developed, yet his notion of literacy remains problematical. Recently he has published a selection of Wedderburn's writings, making it possible for many more readers to enter the discussion. 'By their nature, the writings . . . are characterized by numerous misspellings, examples of eccentric grammar, errors of syntax, and the like.' Coleridge noted that the literati who scorned those who could not write orthographically, or make smooth periods, could not conceive a new or vital truth.[5] In his more recent work McCalman is coming to a similar understanding. He writes that 'Wedderburn's breathless, hortatory style, erratic punctuation and vernacular language do not make for easy comprehension.' The introduction of the term 'comprehension' opens up the problem to the historical setting of 1817.

There is another problem. What is at issue is not language but discourse, language being a matter of syntax and lexicon, whereas discourse is a matter of values, norms, and institutions – a culture, in short. To the extent that language and discourse are separable, Wedderburn had no problem. He spoke another language, creole. This is how he rendered it in

and Pornographers in London, 1795-1840 (Cambridge, 1988), p. 43; 'Robert Wedderburn,' Dictionary of Labour Biography, Joyce M. Bellamy, et al, eds., volume VIII (1987), pp. 265-273; 'Anti-Slavery and Ultra-Radicalism in Early Nineteenth-Century England: The Case of Robert Wedderburn,' in Slavery and Abolition volume VII (1986), pp. 99-117; The Horrors of Slavery and Other Writings by Robert Wedderburn (Princeton, 1991), pp. viii, 18, 23.

4. W. J. Gardner, A History of Jamaica (1873), p. 360.

5. Biographia Literaria, chapter 9.

print. 'Top Tife, top tife, top tife! dat England man, dat white man, de Christian buckera tiffey my pickenninney, he hungry, he go yam 'im! Oh! der go noder, he tiffey my mamma, he be Cotolic Christian, he rosse my mamma in de fire, for yam, what me do for my mamma? Oh! me belly ache, me die!'[6] It might be translated as: 'Stop thief, stop thief, stop thief! The Englishman, the white man, the Christian is stealing my child. He's hungry, so he's going to eat him. Oh! there goes another, he is stealing my mother. He is a Catholic. He'll roast my mother on the fire for food. What can I do for my mother? Oh, my gut hurts; I could die.'

Those in a printed tradition are inclined to find illiteracy and ignorance synonymous. Wedderburn belonged to an oral culture where knowledge was preserved by word of mouth. His leap into print was a process of enculturation into new discourses. 'Literacy always comes with a perspective on interpretation that is ultimately political,' says James Paul Gee.[7] Wedderburn had to enter a hermeneutical circle with shared structures of meaning determined by the powerful. Hence understanding him is not so much a matter of defending him, though that may need to be done, as it is, on the one hand, exploring the increasingly reactionary meaning of literacy in 1817 and, on the other, pursuing the powerful and tricky theme suggested by Kamau Brathwaite that 'It was in language that the slave was perhaps most successfully imprisoned by his master, and it was in his (mis)-use of it that he most effectively rebelled.'[8]

Wedderburn's mother was named Rosanna. She was an enslaved cook and maid to Lady Douglas who was tricked into selling Rosanna to James Wedderburn, a doctor and 'man-midwife.' He had estates in Westmoreland (Mint, Paradise, Retreat, Endeavour, Inverness, Spring Garden, Moreland, and Mt. Edgcombe) which at his death were worth

---

6. Quotations unless otherwise noted are taken directly from *The Axe Laid to the Root*, and when possible from those selections appearing in McCalman's anthology.

7. 'What is Literacy?' Technical Report No. 2 (October 1989), Literacies Institute (Newton, Mass.), p. 162.

8. *The Development of Creole Society in Jamaica, 1770-1820* (Oxford, 1971).

£302,628 14s. 8d.[9] Rosanna had to bear him two or three children: James, a slave millwright, and John, referred to in the first letter, as well as Robert, who was born in 1762. Dr. James Wedderburn 'insulted, abused and abandoned' Rosanna. In his autobiography Wedderburn wrote in flagrant typography: "I HAVE SEEN MY POOR MOTHER STRETCHED ON THE GROUND, TIED HANDS AND FEET, AND FLOGGED IN THE MOST INDECENT MANNER, THOUGH PREGNANT AT THE SAME TIME her *fault* being the not acquainting the mistress that her master had *given her leave to go to see her mother in town!*' Although we do not know Wedderburn's age at this whipping, it is known that such trauma may permanently injure a child. That Wedderburn was not dumb struck, as was Billy Budd, is owing perhaps to the fact that he also witnessed his mother and his grandmother fight against such cruelty.

When Lady Douglas died in 1766, Rosanna was sold to Dr. Campbell, while Wedderburn, age four was sent to Kingston and the care of his grandmother who sold cheese, checks, chintz, milk, and gingerbread for Joseph Payne, her owner. 'No woman was perhaps better known in Kingston than my grandmother, by the name of "*Talkee Amy*", signifying a chattering old woman. Though a slave, such was the confidence the merchants of Kingston had in her honesty, that she could be trusted to any amount; in fact she was the regular agent for selling smuggled goods.' Her orality was multilingual.

When Wedderburn was eleven, his grandmother was seventy years old. Her master died at sea, and one of his ships, smuggling mahogany, was lost. His nephew succeeded to the property and was convinced by a malicious woman-slave that Talkee Amy had bewitched the vessel in revenge for his not having included her among five slaves he liberated before sailing away. Thus, the orality of Talkee Amy was magical with the power to cross seas, sink ships, subvert slavery. The nephew had her flogged, almost to death. The woman's malice despited herself, for her only child soon died and she sought Talkee Amy's assistance at the burial. 'I can forgive you, but I can never forget the flogging,' she said before setting about to help at the funeral. 'It being,' Wedderburn

---

9. National Archives (Spanish Town), *Inventory Book*, 1B/11/3, vol. 135.

comments, 'as great an object to have a decent burial with the blacks in Jamaica, as with the lower classes in Ireland.' The woman made a public confession of her guilt in the Kingston market-place.[10] Wedderburn tells these stories in his autobiography without much comment. The mother-tongue provided Wedderburn an example of redemption and a magical association of language and liberation. These are themes that arise many years later in his correspondence with Elizabeth Campbell.

She was Wedderburn's half sister and a Jamaican maroon. Indeed several Campbells are among those Trelawny Maroons who after the defeat in the Trelawny Town War were tricked into deportation to Nova Scotia, though I am not sure how she was related to them.[11] Some maroons lived outside their communities without giving up their maroon status. The Feurtado MS, notices the death of an Elizabeth Campbell aged 33 in 1825, a matron in the Public Hospital in Kingston.[12] We learn from the *Jamaica Almanac* of 1818 that in the parish of Trelawny Elizabeth Campbell owned Amity Hall and fifteen slaves. This is as near as I have been able to come to finding independent corroboration of the letters.

The first letter is the longest. Robert Wedderburn responds to the news that Elizabeth Campbell has set free his 'aged mother' as well as his brother from slavery. This action inspires Wedderburn to an enthusiastic denunciation of slavery and an exhortation to free her remaining slaves. He reminds her of the history of the maroons. By means of indirect quotation Wedderburn shows how Campbell manumitted her remaining slaves. The influences of early Christianity, the Exodic narrative, and Thomas Spence are clear. The letter concludes with a warning of vigilance against priests whether Protestant or Papist.

The second letter, conveyed across the Atlantic by a ship's cook, is the response of Elizabeth Campbell to Wedderburn.

---

10. *The Horrors of Slavery* (1824).

11. See Mavis C. Campbell, *Nova Scotia and the Fighting Maroons: A Documentary History*, No. 41 (January 1990) *Studies in Third World Societies*, pp. 196, 207, 211, 238.

12. National Archive (Spanish Town). See the *Inventory Book* volume 130, p. 236 (20 August 1818); see *Index to Manumissions* volume 1, number 47; National Library (Kingston).

Having set her slaves free and restituted to them the land, she seeks to have the deed recorded by the governor's secretary. He brings it to the governor's attention, and a dialogue between them ensues. He dismisses her with mutterings about St. Domingo. She then directly addresses Wedderburn asking him questions that have arisen as a result of reading the English newspapers.

The third letter is also from Campbell, who according to her promise at the end of the previous letter sends Wedderburn particulars, gained from her 'sweetheart,' about the meetings of the Jamaican Assembly where the Governor announced Campbell's extraordinary actions. One Macpherson arose to speak against the doctrines of Spence. He recommended revolt against the authority of the Crown unless the licenses to Dissenters were revoked. He moved that Campbell be treated as a lunatic and that the government confiscate her slaves and lands. He recommended that the Assembly begin to import English servants whose distresses in England would make them compliant tools 'against the Blacks' in Jamaica. He concluded by saying that the slaves will not be so easily bought off as the maroons. This is the last letter in the correspondence; it is the last story in the newspaper; and this is the last newspaper issued. It ends with 'To be continued.'

The correspondence begins with contrasts between writing and talking. 'How was I struck with wonder and astonishment, when John, our brother, described to me your manner and action when you went to your drawer and took the record and presented it to him, saying, here, John, take your freedom.' (96) Wedderburn has thus *heard* of the liberation. In the structure of the paragraph, speech is immediately contrasted with writing. The act of manumission, we learn, is an act of writing, a recording, a thing that may be kept in a drawer, handed over, &c. Freedom is inert and notarized while speech is free and dynamic. The point is emphasized at the end of the correspondence when the Governor's secretary reminds Miss Campbell that her actions mean nothing until 'their freedom is recorded' and then each former slave will be fined.

'The unexpected sound, you are no longer slaves, deprived [the slaves] of speech.' An old man was the first to speak, 'Lord help us! Missy, Missy, you sall sit on de same seat wid de Virgin Mary; may God make dee his servant. I will go toder country in peace.' Self-consciousness enters the expression of Miss Campbell who says of the old man, 'He then dropped, like Palmer, on the stage,' referring to John Palmer (1742-1798), actor, bill sticker, and door-keeper at the Drury Lane theatre. In alluding to Palmer, Wedderburn plays with his London audience's theatrical understanding. It knew that Palmer died on stage in Liverpool supposedly saying, 'There is another and a better world.' However, to the old man speaking to Campbell 'toder country' was Africa. Thus, the suggestion is that liberation is dramatic, that is, an 'audience' may be instructed by it, and paradise is an earthly reality.

'Reading the world always precedes reading the word.' 'Human beings first changed the world, secondly proclaimed the world, and then wrote the words.'[13] These are the postulates of Paulo Freire. From them a meaning of coherence is derived. Coherence approaches as the distance between discourse and practice is narrowed. Wedderburn's language does not 'cohere' in this sense. The discourses he appropriated, evangelical and democratic, he fractured and recombined to encompass experience in England and in Jamaica.

'Yes, the slaves shall be free, for a multiplied combination of ideas, which amount to prophetic inspiration and the greatness of the work that I am to perform has influenced my mind with an enthusiasm, I cannot support: I must give vent, I have commenced my career, the press is the engine of destruction.' (96) At the age of fifty-five Wedderburn commenced a new career, radical journalist. He had been a sailor (enlisting in the Royal Navy got him out of Kingston); he may have been an associate of Benjamin Bowsey or John Glover who led the opening of the Newgate prison during the Gordon Riots; he may have been associated with the great mutiny at the Nore.[14] He had been a tailor, and a 'flint' tailor too who had come

13. Paulo Freire, *Literacy: Reading the World and the Word* (Massachusetts, 1987), p. 35.

14. Peter Linebaugh, *The London Hanged* (London, 1991), p. 348-56.

upon hard times. He had been a preacher. He had been to prison. The paper he produced shows this; it is without the fluency of Wooler's *Black Dwarf* or the command of Cobbett's *Political Register*. Instead, it shows the intellectuality of migrants and their celerity of ideas. We can identify three sources: 1) the Legba-trickster which in an English setting appears as theatre; 2) the religious millenarianism partly arising from his association with a fellow American sailor, Richard Brothers; and 3) the Painite radicalism which Wedderburn developed in his relationship with Thomas Spence. We find these influences in the title, *The Axe Laid to the Root*.

As a phrase, 'the axe laid to the root' is more or less than a figure of speech alike to agricultural workers in England and to sugar estate workers in Jamaica. J. J. Thomas of Trinidad, the first grammarian of creole who elucidated its logic and syntax in 1869, knew that to understand speech he had to understand action. The plantation workers 'converted waste tracts of earth into fertile regions of agricultural bountifulness,' and the agricultural workers in England did that rooting necessary to 'improvement' and whose struggle against threshing machine was lively in 1816-1817.[15]

The phrase lay deep within the soil of radical protestantism. The combination of the power of the written word in association with the prophetic power of the Messiah had revolutionary meanings dating from the English Revolution. In 1651 Abiezer Coppe, having been imprisoned for several months for publications considered seditious and blasphemous (*A Second Fiery Flying Roule*, two years earlier, commanded the great ones to deliver their riches to the poor or otherwise have their throats cut!), decided to answer his critics by laying 'the Axe to the root of the Tree.'[16] As a phrase, 'the axe laid to the root' appears in Luke and Matthew where it forms part of the curse that John the Baptist lays against the Pharisees and Sadducees for their ethnic pride ('you viper's brood,' Luke 3:7); and it forms part of his annunciation of the Messiah and the coming baptism by fire ('the wheat he will gather into his granary, but he will burn the chaff on a fire that can never go

---

15. J. J. Thomas, *The Theory and Practice of Creole Grammar* (1869), p. 181.

16. See *Copp's Return* in Andrew Hopton (ed.), *Abiezer Coppe Selected Writings* (London, 1987), p. 72.

out,' Luke 3:17). It is thus associated with class war both as denunciation and redemption.

In African Christianity Christ was a secondary figure to John the Baptist.[17] Myalism was the name of the slaves' religion in Jamaica. 'It was the first Jamaican religion known to have addressed itself to the affairs of the entire hetero-geneous slave society,' writes Monica Schuler.[18] In 1791 under Moses Baker's leadership, it began to absorb aspects of the Baptist version of Christianity, particularly the inspiration of the Holy Spirit and attention to John the Baptist which were congenial to Akan and Yoruba practices of spirit mediumship and riverine spirits. Mervyn Alleyne writes that 'Myal organ-ization became a hotbed of slave rebellion.' As religion it could hold the memory of resistance (Tacky's rebellion, for example) when it had been lost otherwise, as Erna Brodber suggests. 'Ole African had been there and yes, the spirit had gone and yes, if he had said "the half has never been told," it probably meant that there are other things to come.'[19]

John the Baptist and his promise of 'the axe laid to the root' appeared at a decisive point in the life of the New York oysterman, shoemaker, and itinerant Methodist, the former Virginia slave, George White. He ran away from slavery to Philadelphia, and then to New York, where at the Bowery Church in 1791 he heard Rev. Mr. Stebbings preach from 'the axe is laid to the root of the trees' White fell prostrate on the floor, slain by the law and redeemed by Jesus. He began to have night visions of the torments to befall the rich. His daughter taught him to read and write. 'She could learn me nothing from the common spelling book; no, not so much as the alphabet; for my mind was so perfectly taken up with the notion of reading the Bible, that I could think of nothing else:-

---

17. Mervyn C. Alleyne, *Roots of Jamaican Culture* (1989), pp. 83-96. See also John Thornton, *Africa and Africans in the Making of the Atlantic World, 1400-1680* (Cambridge, 1992).

18. Edward Long, *History of Jamaica* (1774), and *'Alas, Alas, Kongo,' A Social History of Indentured African Immigration into Jamaica, 1841-1865* (Baltimore, 1980), p. 33-36.

19. Erna Brodber, *Myal, A Novel* (1988), p. 41.

therefore, from this sacred volume she had to instruct me, word for word.'[20]

These passages were central to African Christianity. 'Pinkster,' named after the German word for Pentecost or Whitsuntide, was a carnival for servants that by the mid-18th century was appropriated by Blacks and was widespread in mainland America. It is here that 'your sons and your daughters shall prophesy, and your young men shall see visions, and your old men shall dream dreams.' (Acts 2:17) Speaking of the black Baptists whom he had met, the Baptist missionary, John Clarke, wrote, 'Some of them thought the old men were to dream dreams, and their young men were to see visions.'[21] The reference is to the second book in Acts and to pentecostalism. Two themes must be stressed. First, following the big wind and the speaking in tongues, those of different languages understand each other, despite their multinationality. It will have been practically pertinent to the problems of an international proletariat. Second, the chapter expresses the communism of the early Christians: 'all that believed were together, and had all things common.' This is what got John Jea in trouble with his Dutch master in New York: 'the earth is the Lord's and the fulness thereof.'[22] George White dreamed dreams and saw visions. Pentecostal glossalalia was part of his message too, with the rich made low.

John the Baptist was crucial to Wedderburn. On 29 November 1819 a spy attended Wedderburn's chapel: '. . . there were about 200 young men who kept their hats on and applauded everything that he said most violent.'[23] On this occasion Wedderburn preached from Luke 1:68-79. This is the prophecy uttered by Zechariah on the birth of his son, John the Baptist. The kinfolk and neighbours were surprised

---

20. *A Brief Account of the Life, Experience, Travels and Gospel Labours of George White, An African Written by Himself and Revised by a Friend* (New York, 1810).

21. John Clarke, *Memorials of Baptist Missionaries in Jamaica* (London 1869), p. 9.

22. *The Life, History, and Unparalled Sufferings of John Jea, the African Preacher* (Portsea, 1817).

23. P.R.O., HO 42/199 (29 November 1819).

that the parents did not name him Zechariah, after his father. 'John,' the name proposed by his mother, was not a name in the patrilinear family. Zechariah called for a writing tablet on which he wrote, 'His name is John.' The matrinymic action gave to the people the gift of speech. Talk filled the hills, and the deliverance from enemies was prophecized. Wedderburn may have identified in several ways with these scriptural passages in the life of John the Baptist.

In 1812 Daniel Eaton published Tom Paine's *Age of Reason*, which tried to 'lay the axe to the root of religion.'[24] Written in prison in 1794, Paine attacked the three pillars of religion, mystery, miracle, and prophecy ('they are the means by which so many *Lo, heres!* and *Lo, theres!* have been spread about the world, and religion been made into a trade'). Mystery he hated most, being diametrically antithetical to reason; miracle he disdained as a showman's legerdemain. And once it was understood that prophet and prophesying originally meant poet and poetry, rather than knowledge of the future, then 'the axe goes at once to the root.'[25] This line of reasoning can be reversed: poetry may be treated as prophecy giving to the poet the power of the prophet. This is perhaps what Shelly did in his most revolutionary poem, *Queen Mab*, in which he converts the eschatological prophecy of Luke into revolutionary poetry.[26]

> From kings, and priests, and statesmen, war arose,
> Whose safety is man's deep unbettered woe,
> Whose grandeur his debasement. Let the axe
> Strike at the root, the poison tree will fall;
> And where its venomed exhalations spread
> Ruin, and death, and woe, where millions lay
> Quenching the serpent's famine, and their bones
> Bleaching unburied in the putrid blast,
> A garden shall arise in loveliness
> Surpassing fabled Eden. (IV, 79-88).

24. J. Ann Hone, *For the Cause of Truth: Radicalism in London, 1796-1821* (London, 1982), p. 225.

25. *The Age of Reason*, Part One, reprinted in *The Thomas Paine Reader*, Michael Foot and Isaac Kramnick, eds. (London, 1987), p. 413.

26. Thomas Hutchinson (ed.), *The Complete Poetical Works of Percy Bysshe Shelley* (Oxford, 1925), p. 767.

No book influenced Wedderburn more than the Bible. After coming to England in 1778, he began to study the scriptures himself in order to avoid becoming prey to corrupted preachers or false teaching. His attitude towards the Bible swung between grandiose respect and sarcastic criticism. He was as familiar with its passages of liberation and millenarianism as he was of its drolleries and contradictions. 'Their method of fighting is to be found in the scriptures, which they are now learning to read,' Wedderburn wrote of the slaves in *The Axe*.[27]

To Miss Campbell he vowed, 'Fast bound by eternal truth, I have hold of the God of Israel, like a Jacob, and will not let him go. I will be made a prince by prevailing, though a halter be about my neck,' and to the man who bought his older brother's birthright for a mess of pottage, who saw the angels go up and down the ladder, who became rich and migrated to Egypt where his sons sired the twelve tribes of Israel, Wedderburn vowed, 'Jacob, I will excel you in proportion to the present improved state of society.' (97). Denied his own patrimony, scorned by his 'legitimate' brother, Andrew Colville, Wedderburn must fool around in his attitude to Jacob.[28] J. J. Thomas wrote a tremendous rebuttal of the complacent racism of the Victorian historian J. A. Froude called *Froudacity* (1889). It ended with an invocation of Jacob who on returning from captivity had to labour with a working tool in one hand and a sword for defence in the other. This was the analogy for the plight of pan-Africanism after emancipation. Both men hold fast with Jacob, Wedderburn even 'though a halter be about my neck.'

The hangman's noose hung loosely around the necks of many militants. Wedderburn remembers three on whom it tightened: Cashman, hanged for his part in the Spa Fields riots; John Bellingham, the assassin of Spencer Perceval, the Prime Minister; and Edward Despard who died the death of a

---

27. *The Axe Laid to the Root*, no. 1, p. 12.

28. A. Colville was Wedderburn's brother. They exchanged acrimonious letters in a Sunday paper, *Bell's Life in London*, 29 Feb., 17 March 1824, reprinted in his autobiography, *The Horrors of Slavery* (1824), pp. 13-23.

traitor in 1803.[29] Miss Campbell was reminded by the Governor that 'There is a law made by the assembly to hang a slave. One has been hung for preaching, teaching, or exhorting, another has been hung for throwing up his hoe and blessing the name of King George, through mistaking the abolition of the slave trade for the abolition of slavery.' (106). 'Monk' Lewis attended slave court in Feb. 1816 to hear the hanging sentence against a 15 year old girl who attempted to poison her master. Wedderburn expressed his fear of hanging at the end of his autobiography: 'I should have gone back to Jamaica, had I not been fearful of the planters; for such is their hatred of any one having black blood in his veins, and who dares to think and act as a free man, that they would most certainly have trumped up some charge against me, and hung me.'

The limit of hanging had been reached in Jamaica, according to Miss Campbell's sweetheart, who told her the planters 'can do little, for the leaven is laid too long in the dough, and as the slaves are their bread, they must not hang them all.' (108) MacPherson in the Assembly said, 'it is in vain . . . to inflict death on the slaves for preaching, or exhorting their fellow slaves.' British policy was murderous, and it was prepared to contemplate murder on a large scale. A previous governor, Sir George Nugent (1801-1806), had received the following private and confidential message from Downing Street in 1804: 'The influence of a Free Black Government in Saint Domingo may be always dangerous, the extinction therefore of that class of slaves in whose fidelity there is no reason to rely, and the propagation of those alone who by the habits of infancy, childhood and education are susceptible of the attachment, appear to be the securest system.' Its internal clauses separating subject and object and the mere comma conjoining the danger of Haiti and the extinction of Jamaican slaves provide a grammar and punctuation of homicidal population policy.[30]

---

29. Old Bailey *Proceedings*, 15 January 1817; *The Political Register*, No. 21; O. Nigel Bolland, 'The Social Structure and Social Relations of the Settlement in the Bay of Honduras (Belize) in the 18th Century,' *Journal of Caribbean History*, volume 6 (May 1973).

30. National Library (Kingston), *Nugent Papers*, MS 72, Box 3

With these state murders came the counter-theme, vengeance. The failure to free the slaves, Wedderburn believed, was 'the cause of God Almighty smiting the Princess Charlotte and the babe.' Princess Charlotte expired giving birth to a still-born son on 6 November 1817. The Pentridge Uprising ('one of the first attempts in history to mount a wholly proletarian insurrection') took place in the summer of 1817.[31] November 7, the day after Princess Charlotte expired, Brandreth, the Baptist and former Luddite, Turner, the stonemason and veteran of the Egyptian campaign, and Ludlam, a quarryman and Methodist preacher, were hanged and quartered in a government frame-up. Wedderburn compared Brandreth to Moses. The discordance between the public reactions to their deaths and that of Princess Charlotte provoked Shelley to his best political pamphlet in which he calls for class justice as well as political reform, 'Many and various are the mischiefs flowing from oppression, but this is the representative of them all; namely, that one man is forced to labour for another . . .'[32]

The pedagogy of Bible study is an essential topic for understanding its usefulness to the workers in Jamaica. In the 1790s George Liele had introduced the class-leader system. The black ministers washed the feet of their disciples.[33] 'Slaves who could read the Bible . . . had thrust into their hands the sanction and inspiration of English protest movements from Wycliffe to the Levellers, and some found lessons there the missionaries did not teach'.[34] Scriptures were often taught aloud, by means of hymn singing and lining out. Methodist hymnody was rich with references of jubilee. Wedderburn wrote and published hymns of his own in his early pamphlet.

(1804-1806), fol. 279.

---

31. Thompson, *The Making*, p. 733.

32. *An Address to the People on the Death of the Princess Charlotte* (1817).

33. Violet Smythe, 'Liberators of the Oppressed: Baptist Mission in Jamaica 1814-1845,' B.A. Thesis, University of the West Indies (Mona), 1983. See also, Albert J. Raboteau, *Slave Religion: The 'Invisible Institution' in the Antebellum South* (1978).

34. Mary Turner, *Slaves and Missionaries: The Disintegration of Jamaican Slave Society 1787–1834* (Urbana, Illinois, 1982), p. 86.

John Jea wrote a book of hymns in 1817.[35] Of course, many Spencean publications included his songs, and always to popular tunes such as 'Salley in the Alley' or 'God Save the King.' The first generation of African American Baptists taught with hymns; indeed, Moses Baker, the Baptist, was arrested on a charge of sedition in 1796 for including in his sermon the hymn,

> We will be slaves no more,
> Since Christ has made us free,
> Has nailed our tyrants to the cross,
> And bought our liberty.

One Jamaican black Baptist was hanged and another transported for formenting rebellion in 1816. A Jamaican King of the Ibos was elected and a song sung:

> O me good friend, Mr. Wilberforce, make we free!
> God Almighty thank ye! God Almighty thank ye!
> God Almighty make we free!
> Buckra in this country no make we free:
> What Negroe for to do? What Negroe for to do?
> Take force by force! Take force by force!

The singer of the song explained that 'He had sung no songs but such as his brown priest had assured him were approved of by John the Baptist . . . [who] was a friend to the negroes, and had got his head in a pan.'[36]

Wedderburn summarized an interpretation of early Christianity presented by Thomas Evans in *Christian Policy, the Salvation of the Empire* (1816) which stressed the communism of the early Christians and the betrayal of the Church. Following Evans, Wedderburn writes that 'The Christians of old, attempted this happy mode of living in fellowship or brotherhood, but, after the death of Christ and the apostles, the national priests persuaded their emperor to establish the Christian religion, and they also embraced, in hypocrisy, the Christian faith. They took possession of the Church property, and call it theirs, which remains in their hands to this day; but they have taken care to hedge it about with laws which punish with death all those who dare attempt to take it away.' (99)

---

35. Gates, *The Signifying Monkey: A Theory of African-American Literary Criticism* (Oxford: New York, 1988), p. 158.

36. Lewis, *op. cit.*, p. 187.

The last of the letters contains an argument about the Methodists. Miss Campbell is arguing with the Governor's secretary. He accuses her of listening to the Methodists. The fear of the Methodists at this time is difficult to over-estimate. Secret and nightly meetings were held by brown Methodists on estates in St. Thomas-in-the-East at Christmas 1815 in the belief that the Regent and Wilberforce wanted the slaves free.[37] Between 1807 and 1814 the Wesleyan chapel in Kingston was closed.[38] Hence, it was with some courage that Miss Campbell replied, 'I say, God bless the Methodists, they teach us to read the bible.' In 1804 the British and Foreign Bible Society was formed, and in 1812 its branch in Jamaica was established. Bitter as the struggle between the missionaries and the anti-mission party was, one thing was clear: in Brathwaite's words, 'Only one missionary (a Baptist) within the period of this study [1780-1820] ever dared to challenge his own Mission's decision of local political silence,' and he was dismissed in 1817, a month before *The Axe* began publication.[39]

Two events are important to our understanding of the background to these letters, because each raised the question of literacy and its relationship to the struggle for freedom. The first is Bussa's Rebellion among the slaves of Barbados that took place on Easter 1816. The second is the Spa Fields meetings in London in November and December 1816. The first was a continuation of the liberation begun by the Haitian revolution and war of independence. The second was a development of the Luddite revolt against the employment of machinery.

In the 19th century the abolitionist movement in England began to interfere directly between masters and slaves. Three abolitionist initiatives of registration, amelioration, and emancipation were followed by massive slave uprisings in Barbados (1816), Demerara (1823), and Jamaica (1831).

---

37. Lewis, p. 173-4.

38. Donald G. Mathews, *Slavery and Methodism 1780-1845* (Princeton, 1965); John Wesley, *Thoughts Upon Slavery* (1774); Mary Turner, *op. cit.*

39. Brathwaite, op. cit., p. 259.

Such reciprocal mobilization on either side of the Atlantic began with the slaves most in touch with British culture. Barbados was the oldest sugar colony, and it was the most creolized of the British West Indies. This is the significance of Bussa's Rebellion. Literacy was of decisive importance.

In June *The Times* correspondent referred to 'the principal instigators of this insurrection, who are negroes of the worst dispositions, but of superior understanding, and some of whom can read and write . . .' Horace Campbell writes that 'The widespread nature of the revolt and the organizational skills which went into the planning was the result of a new kind of leadership; this was the leadership of the religious preacher, literate in the English language and in the African religious practises, who combined the ideas of deliverance and resistance. It was a leadership which could read the newspapers and interpret debates to fellow slaves.'[40] Nanny Grigg, a domestic worker on the Simmons plantation, frequently read English and local papers and she informed the other slaves of news from Haiti and England. It was widely rumoured that the Imperial Registry Bill of 1815 was actually an Act of Emancipation.[41] Rumour was a strategy of resistance.[42] The goal of the Parliamentary proponents of registration had been to prevent the smuggling of slaves into British colonies and to establish a data base for slave demography. Joseph Marryat led the attack on the Parliamentary abolitionists with his *Thoughts on the Abolition of the Slave Trade*. In this he warned against the growth of a mulatto population whom the abolitionists had seen as a source of stability. In Grenada the mulattos played a prominent role in the rebellion of 1795.

Fear of the south American revolution and the emancipation of slaves (Miranda was a man of colour) was present in the thoughts of the planters. In Haiti Pétion presided over the distribution of land to former plantation slaves. Simon Bolivar asked in his famous 'Letter from Jamaica' (1815), 'is

---

40. Horace Campbell, *Rasta and Resistance from Marcus Garvey to Walter Rodney* (New Jersey, 1987), p. 28.

41. Seymour Drescher, *Capitalism and Antislavery: British Mobilization in Comparative Perspective* (New York, 1987), p. 107; Robin Blackburn, *The Overthrow of Colonial Slavery, 1776-1848* (1988), p. 323-5.

42. Mary Turner, *op. cit.*

not the entire New World in motion?' In 1816 he invaded
Venezuela and decreed the freedom of the slaves. In Pernam-
buco in 1817 a sizeable revolt of slaves was suppressed. In
January 1817 San Martin took the Spanish forces in Chile
completely by surprise after a heroic trek across the mountain
passes. Artigas led the anti-colonial poor in Argentina: 'in the
shade of his speech poor people find refuge: but this brown
man, illiterate, courageous, perhaps fierce, will never be a
statute.'[43]

In Barbados propaganda of insurrection was conveyed by
literate, free coloured people. The outbreak of Bussa's Rebellion engulfed half the island. A quarter of the sugar crop
was burnt, and scores of people were hanged, despite which,
another insurrection was attempted in September 1816.[44] The
Parliamentary abolitionists withdrew the plan for a central
register, and Wilberforce sponsored an address to the Prince
Regent formally declaring there was no plan for introducing
emancipation into the West Indies. Among the blacks of
Jamaica, however, the feeling was different. When 'Monk'
Lewis arrived in Jamaica in 1816 the coxswain of his canoe
gave him some important intelligence. 'Blacks must not be
treated now, massa, as they used to be; they can think, and
hear, and see, as well as white people; blacks are wiser, massa,
than they were, and will soon be still wiser.'[45]

In addition to the mulatto population, Marryat expressed
determined opposition to the Methodist missionaries. The
Kingston Corporation passed an Ordinance saying that
nothing brought religion into more disrepute than preaching
Holy Scriptures 'by uneducated, illiterate, and ignorant persons and false enthusiasts,' so henceforth a license was required to preach. The secretary of the Wesleyan Methodist
missions found it necessary to write a defence in consequence
of the alarm produced among the planters by Bussa's Re-

43. Eduardo Galeano, *Faces and Masks*, translated by Cedric Belfrage
    (1987), p. 117.

44. Hilary Beckles, *Black Rebellion in Barbados: The Struggle Against
    Slavery, 1627-1838* (Barbados, 1987), pp. 95-113.

45. Matthew Gregory Lewis, *Journal of a West Indian Proprietor (1834)*, p.
    165.

bellion.[46] In 1816 there were 39 Methodist missionaries in the British West Indies.

'The free Mulattoes are reading Cobbett's Register, and talking about St. Domingo,' Miss Campbell wrote Wedderburn. The coloured people had become an independent political force in Jamaica by 1817. Coloured women on committees controlled the Methodist church; schools in Kingston were dominated by them; while protesting their loyalty to the Empire, they had become a vociferous voice in newspaper and petition, and an activist presence in the streets of Kingston. Troops were called out to disperse their picket protesting the colour bar at the theatre in 1815. They won concessions, such as the removal of legal disabilities to inheriting property and giving evidence.[47]

Writing had become dangerous to the planters. One Strafford, a merchant with business in Haiti, brought pamphlets to the attention of the Assembly 'in which were found doctrines destructive of the tranquility of this island, containing direct incitement to the imitation of the conduct of the slaves of St. Domingo, and loading the proprietors of slaves with every odious epithet.' The Committee on the Present State of the Colony warned against any sudden changes to the 'religious, moral and civil state' of the slaves. Here the political nature of literacy becomes clear. The meeting of the Assembly was not published 'fearing it should fall into the hands of the slaves.' The Assembly was prorogued.[48] Print no longer provided a secret code of communication reserved for the plantocracy. Miss Campbell learned of its particulars from her lover. *The Axe Laid to the Root, or a Fatal Blow to Oppressors, addressed to the Planters and Negroes of this Island* had come to the attention of the Jamaican Assembly. A reward was offered for copies of the tract – slaves bringing it forward were to be rewarded with freedom, and free men bringing it were to be awarded a slave from the estate of Miss Campbell. The actions of the Assembly were even more

---

46. Richard Watson, *A Defence of the Wesleyan Methodist Mission in the West Indies* (London 1817), p. 10.

47. Edward Brathwaite, *op. cit.*, pp. 193-6, 209; Turner, *op. cit.,* p. 82.

48. National Library of Jamaica, *Votes of the Honourable House of Assembly* (28 October-16 December 1817), p. 127.

serious, as they nullified Miss Campbell's manumission:
'slaves and lands set free by an Spencean enthusiast should
not be entered on the records.'

Prejudice against the Methodists was as great as prejudice
against obeah, judging at least by the causes cited for Jamaican mortality, some dying of 'a rank methodist fever,' others
'a miserable victim to obeah machination.'[49] The censorship
of print and the licensing of preaching could not extinguish
such fevers. The slave in the Caribbean had to learn to 'play
fool to catch wise.' Liable to lie, inclined to misunderstand,
the slave played Quashee. The divine trickster of Yoruba
mythology is Esu-Elegbara, the guardian of the cross roads
and the divine, pentecostal-like messenger who knows all
languages. Dr. Henry Louis Gates, Jr., has established the
relationship of Legba to the signifying monkey of African
American tradition whose indirection, satire, parody, and
irony has taken myriad of forms.[50] Not the least of these is the
double-voiced text of print that oscillates between the first
and third person, as does the Campbell-Wedderburn correspondence. Gates refers to it as 'the speakerly text.' In the
Caribbean, he shows, this trickster is characterized by dark
colour and tiny size.[51] We can see such signs in London.
Wedderburn's partner in London debate was a black dwarf
named Samuel Waddington, a shoemaker and printer, who
played the radical buffoon, often in drag. T. J. Wooler was
tried for seditious libel in 1817 for publishing *The Black
Dwarf*, the radical paper that vied with Cobbett's.

'The Spa Fields meetings of 15 November and 2 December
1816 were of sensational importance.'[52] On 2 December Dr.
Watson's son, a sailor, stood up on a wagon, surrounded by
the red, white and green flags of the future British republic,

49. B. W. Higman, *Slave Population and Economy in Jamaica, 1807-1834*
    (1976), p. 109.

50. Gates, *op. cit.*

51. Orlando Patterson, *The Sociology of Slavery: An Analysis of the
    Origins, Development, and Structure of Negro Slave Society in Jamaica*
    (1969); and Gates, op. cit., and Houston A. Baker, Jr., *Workings of the
    Spirit: The Poetics of Afro-American Women's Writing* (Chicago,
    1990).

52. I. J. Prothero, *Artisans and Politics in Early Nineteenth Century
    London: John Gast and His Times* (1979), p. 73.

and asked the 10,000 present, 'If they will not give us what we want, shall we not take it?' The riot led to the suspension of habeas corpus in March, and to the Seditious Meeting Act which explicitly singled out Spenceans as having 'for their object the confiscation and division of the land, and the extinction of the funded property of the kingdom.' The riots gave a severe fright to the middle class which as a result more easily acquiesced in the repression of what could be said, printed, and thought.[53]

In the autumn of 1816 a committee was formed, called the Society of Spencean Philanthropists, which called the meetings. Thomas Preston was the secretary. Preston had sailed to St. Kitts as a store-keeper. He thought of himself as a 'Jack Tar.' He joined the Spencean Philanthropists in 1814, the year that Spence died. Of his role in the Spa Fields meeting, he wrote: 'I was accidentally introduced to a body of men who had contemplated a petition to the Prince Regent for the abolition and regulation of machinery . . . I grew in favor with these anti-machinists, and they elected me their secretary.' We thus must see the Spa Fields riots as an extension or continuation of the Luddite disturbances. Castle, the spy, later said in court: 'he told me . . . they were meeting for the express purpose of doing away with machinery . . .' The organizers of the meeting appealed to the proletarian parts of the London working class, not to its skilled artisans. They went to Paddington 'amongst the navigators,' or labourers digging the Prince Regent's Canal. They appealed to porters, coal and ballast heavers; to the factory workers in Petty-France; to the soldiers in the theatre district; to the smiths around London Bridge; to London Dock workers. The soldiers were reminded of the mutinous temper in Ireland; and factory labourers at Maudsley's machine-tool work in St. George's Fields were canvassed. Distressed weavers helped with the banners which were brought from Bethnal Green.[54]

The existing historiography of the Spa Fields riots does not stress the opposition to machinery. The references to slavery

53. Malcolm Chase, 'Thomas Preston,' Joyce M. Bellamy, John Saville, David Martin (eds.), *Dictionary of Labour Biography*, vol. VIII (1987).

54. *A Correct Report of the Trial of James Watson, Senior, for High Treason* (1817).

likewise tend to be omitted. Slavery was on Thomas Preston's mind. In 1817 in his autobiography he summarized his life before meeting Spence: 'I was, to toil and trouble, an unregistered slave.' Young Watson in the weeks before the riot was heard arguing with a servant wearing the livery of Chancellor Leach. 'He was like a negro,' said Watson, 'that had run away, and had a mark of disrespect; and that very soon the time would come, when his master might lose his estate, and that he might be as good a man as his master.' And at Spa Fields he asked, 'Will Englishman any longer suffer themselves to be trod upon, like the poor African slaves in the West Indies, or like clods or stones?'[55]

While the insurrection was easily suppressed, it seems the pace of the introduction of machinery was slowed. In 1817 David Ricardo published his *Principles of Political Economy and Taxation*. Clearly the distress of 1816 and the Luddite struggle deeply influenced this treatise on political economy, the first since 1776, for he changed his mind about machinery. 'The opinion entertained by the labouring class that the employment of machinery is frequently detrimental to their interests . . . is comfortable to the correct principles of political economy.' He meant not to discourage employment of machinery, but to support its *gradual* introduction.[56] 1817 was also the year of the notorious fifth edition of Thomas Malthus, *Essay on Population*, which was revised to refute 'systems of equality,' and particularly the Spenceans.[57] It is remarkably like the prosecutor's voice. The Attorney-General in his opening statement against Watson implied as much in explaining the Spencean principle: 'that no man ought to be a private proprietor of land, but that it ought to be common, as it were for the public. I will enter into no discussion of the folly or absurdity of such a principle, which is

---

55. *The Life and Opinions of Thomas Preston* (1817), and *The Trial of James Watson* (1817), volume 1, p. 72.

56. *Principles of Political Economy and Taxation*, R. M. Hartwell (ed.) (Penguin, 1971), p. 384.

57. T. R. Malthus, *An Essay on the Principle of Population* (1817), vol. 2, pp. 274-284.

absolutely destructive of every right of property, and must go to the annihilation of every comfort.'[58]

A debate runs through history among elites who are divided in their policy to the literacy of the working class. Some say literacy should not be encouraged because it will make workers unhappy with their lot. Others say that, if delivered in the right moral framework, literacy can be a powerful mode of forming obedient citizens.[59] The Quaker, Joseph Lancaster, opened a school in Borough Road in 1801 that used monitors, strict discipline, and pupil-teachers. Dr. Andrew Bell used the same system in Madras, and he brought it back to England where it was preferred since he was an orthodox Anglican. 'Utopian schemes,' he wrote, '. . . for the diffusion of general knowledge would soon confuse that distinction of ranks and classes of society, upon which the general welfare hinges. There is a risk of elevating by an indiscriminate education the minds of those doomed to the drudgery of daily labour above their condition.'

The upper class wished to restrict printed publication and literacy to only a narrow part of the population. Coleridge's writings of 1815-1817 grew increasingly arcane. *Biographia Literaria* was written for an hour of peril; never had revolution seemed so near in England as in 1817. He sought to wean the student from 'the vocabulary of common life.' The diffusion of literature and multitude of books had lamentable effects. *Biographia Literaria* was a 'masterpiece of counter revolution.'[60] In 1817 he wrote two Lay Sermons, addressed to the higher classes of society. The style is difficult, abstruse and lofty. He advocates a turn to religion, hierarchy, and the constitution. The debate over schooling and the rise of the Lancastrian movement in education ('the moral steam engine,' said Coleridge) reflected a need to produce a segment within the urban population which could meet the clerical needs of expanding commerce.

---

58. *The Trial of James Watson* (1817), volume 1, p. 46.

59. James Paul Gee, 'The Legacies of Literacy: From Plato to Freire Through Harvey Graff,' *The Journal of Education*, vol. 171, No. 1 (1989), p. 164.

60. Marilyn Butler, *Romantics, Rebels, and Reactionaries: English Literature and its Background, 1760-1830* (Oxford, 1981), p. 165.

In October 1816 William Cobbett began to sell the *Political Register* for 2d. and that weekly paper became the voice of a new part of the reading public, anti-ministerial and reformist. Yet it was also against insurrection and revolution. It advised the journeymen and labourers not to attack the bakers, butchers, and brewers when the price of life's necessities rose, nor should they fly on their employers when their wages were reduced.[61] After the Spa Fields Riots he fled the country. In the U.S. he began work on *A Grammar of the English Language in a Series of Letters; Intended for the Use of Schools and of Young Persons in General*, which was published in 1818. Having taught the labourers not to insurrect, he was now going to instruct them how to write. He reappropriated the vehemence of the rhetoric of the 1790s. Olivia Smith writes: 'In little over two years Cobbett had reactivated the audience, extended its boundaries, and enabled it to learn how to write.'[62] What were those boundaries?

Much proletarian experience was ignored. One thinks of labourers, prisoners, and slaves whose language, to the extent that it was noticed at all, was reflected condescendingly as slang, cant, profanity, or foreign. Cobbett was not well positioned to hear such variety. In 1817 he was deriving more than ten thousand pounds from his writings.[63] In exile in Long Island, he found that the paternalist mode of class diction that had worked for him in England, only gave offence: 'his people (it is said) could not bear the opprobrious name of servant and, with the exception of one person, left him.' In New York 'master' has ceased to be acceptable to hired people – it was regarded as synonymous with slave keeper – and was replaced by boss. This was the year that the N.Y. legislature passed a slave emancipation law.[64]

The crisis of readership as well as the urgency of communication is reflected by the number of 'Addresses' that are offered in the revolutionary year, 1816-17. Unlike the essay or the treatise which appealed to a silent noetics, and retained the assurance of power and cultivated the vatic quality ('on

---

61. *Political Register*, January 1817.

62. *The Politics of Language, 1791-1819* (Oxford, 1984), p. 231.

63. *A History of the Last Hundred Days of English Freedom*, p. 15.

64. James Flint, *Letters from America, 1818-1820* (1822), p. 12.

high') of print, Coleridge's addresses, Robert Owen's addresses at the City of London Tavern in August 1817, or Cobbett's Address to the Journeymen and Labourers of England, Wales, Scotland and Ireland (Nov. 1816), or Shelley's Address to the People on the Death of the Princess Charlotte in November 1817, or, in the same month, Wedderburn's Address to the Planters and Negroes of Jamaica, all implied that they arose from speech with a well-defined political audience. These forms too are removed from the oralities of ship, shop, estate, commons, public house, prison, or plantation. Yet they are closer to orality than the genteel intimacies in the non-rhetoric style of Jane Austen, or the ideological theorizing of Ricardo or Malthus.

While Wedderburn was a Spencean and played a prominent, indeed decisive, role in the post-war Spencean community, he did not present himself in his correspondence with Elizabeth Campbell as doctrinaire: on the contrary, he wished to recollect Miss Campbell to her own history, and in doing this to remind his London readers of theirs. Wedderburn begins his letter to Miss Campbell by appealing to her ancestors who struggled for freedom: 'you have fallen from the purity of the Maroons, your original, who fought for twenty years against the Christians, who wanted to reduce them again to slavery, after they had fled into the woods from the Spaniards.' (97) Wedderburn refers to the first Maroon War. The maroons 'can be seen as the first Americans' because they were the first in the New World to strike a blow for freedom.[65] Wedderburn conceives their early history as an extension of the freedom that Cromwell had defeated in the English Revolution when the Diggers and the Levellers were suppressed. 'While they were asserting the rights of man at home, they were destroying your ancestors then fighting for their liberty.' (97) The maroon history began with the conquest by Cromwell; indeed, his defeat of the Levellers and Diggers permitted the conquest. Wedderburn also intends us to see in maroon history the garden Shelly prophecized.

---

65. Orlando Patterson, 'Slavery and Slave Revolt: A Sociological Analysis of the First Maroon War 1655-1740,' *Social and Economic Studies* (1970) and Mavis C. Campbell, *The Maroons of Jamaica, 1655-1796: A History of Resistance, Collaboration & Betrayal* (Trenton, New Jersey, 1990).

The recounting of this story provides in almost ritual form the acts of manumission that Miss Campbell is to perform: 'then call your slaves together, let them form the half circle of a new moon, tell them to sit and listen to the voice of truth, say unto them, you who were slaves to the cruel Spaniards stolen from your country, and brought here, by Cromwell, the great, who humbled kings at his feet, and brought one to the scaffold, sent a fleet out, whose admiral dared not return without performing something to please his master, came here and drove the Spaniards out; the slaves, my people, then fled to the woods for refuge, the invaders called to them to return to bondage, they refused; they contended for twenty years, and upwards; bondage was more terrific than death.' (98) Admiral William Penn (1621-1670) led 40 ships into the Spanish Main in 1655, being defeated at San Domingo but capturing Jamaica. His reputation has been clouded by rushing home just as supplies were becoming scarce and by dealing with the Prince of Wales behind Cromwell's back. After a spell in the Tower, he waited on his Irish estates for favourable political circumstances.[66] Thus, the knowledge and the telling of history is the prelude to freedom.

'The Maroons were not barbarous, nor voracious; this was provided by a bold flag of truce, whose name, I am sorry to say, I cannot recollect.' (97) That memory fails Wedderburn at this point recollects us to his orality, the comprehensive memory being one of the possibilities of print, and its infallibility one of its illusions.[67] It is unclear which truce Wedderburn refers to. The historiography provides several possibilities. For example, Tate, a surgeon, carried a white flag when he went to bring in Parkinson, 3 March 1796, the last of the Trelawny Town maroon leaders. Or it may have referred to Dr. Russell when he advanced on behalf of Col. Guthrie to make peace with Cudjoe in March 1738 ('At last Russell offered to change hats with him as a token of friendship'). Or, he may have referred to Mr. Werge who in December 1795 threw down his arms and approached the maroons to announce the end of war. 'On this, Fowler, the

---

66. Granville Penn, *Memorials of Sir William Penn*, 2 vols. (1833).

67. See Walter J. Ong, *Orality and Literacy: The Technologizing of the Word* (New York, 1982).

Maroon, advanced and took him by the hand, and at Mr. Werge's proposal changed hats and jackets with him.'[68] The presence of the benevolent or courageous Englishman appears in the telling of the maroon story right down to Edward Kamau Brathwaite's authoritative study.[69] The printed tradition is not necessarily better or more accurate; indeed, it relies on oral evidence too, as Dallas depends on one of the English soldiers for his account.

The point is that Wedderburn and Campbell belong to a tradition in which the memory of struggle and liberation is maintained. It revolves around individual anecdotes, but simple as such history may appear to professional historians, it is mnemonic knowledge maintained by strict canons of secrecy. Wedderburn brought this knowledge into the context of print and radical discussion in London, which was familiar certainly with some parts of the tale such as the Cuban bloodhounds imported to hunt the Trelawny Town maroons. But Wedderburn showed how incidents of the story compare with similar incidents in the popular tradition of English history: the mediator was not assassinated, unlike Wat Tyler. The comparison between British medieval history and the Trelawny Town Wars may seem far-fetched, and yet it was very much alive in 1817.

Wat Tyler, leader of the Peasant's Revolt of 1381, who had opened the prisons and negotiated with the King to abolish serfdom, was invoked by the younger Watson during his speech at the 2 December 1816 Spa Fields meeting. He said (as recorded by a police short-hand writer), 'My friend has been described by the treasury journals as a second Wat Tyler: no bad title, for be it recollected, that Wat Tyler rose for the purpose of putting down an oppressive tax, and would have succeeded, had he not been basely murdered by William Walworth, then Lord Mayor of London.'[70]

---

68. R. C. Dallas, *The History of the Maroons* (1803), vol. 1, p. 55 and vol. 2, p. 135.

69. *The Development of Creole Society in Jamaica, 1770-1820* (Oxford, 1971).

70. *The Trial of James Watson* (1817), vol. 1, p.72.

Nowhere did the contrast between orality and literacy have such dire consequences as in diplomatic relations. Wedderburn refers to the maroon treaty, one 'without a written document, which exists to this day, by verbal tradition.' In these contests of power, literacy was employed against the weaker party. The first charter for the Jamaican maroons, of 1663, granted freedom, 30 acres per adult, and an independent judiciary in exchange for loyalty and bringing children up in 'the English tongue.' In addition to its written form, Cudjoe's Treaty of March 1739 was solemnized by an Ashanti oath and a cup of blood. The treaty ending the Trelawny Town War had three written provisions, and an oral understanding '. . . that they should not be sent off the island.'[71] This provision was violated, as a spokesman of the planters reminded the Jamaican Assembly in 1817, in a speech which Miss Campbell recounted in her last letter to Wedderburn. The story actually concludes the printed correspondence. The precipitating cause of the Trelawny Town War (1795-1796) was the fact that two maroons, having been found guilty on the evidence of two white men of killing tame hogs, were whipped by a slave in the Mo' Bay workhouse in violation of a central principle of every maroon treaty allowing a separate maroon magistracy for trial and punishment. In June 1796, 568 of the defeated Trelawny Town maroons were placed on transport ships and sailed for Nova Scotia. Kenneth Bilby shows how British perfidy during the Trelawny Town peace negotiations is preserved in oral tradition to this day.[72]

'I, who am a weak woman, of the Maroon tribe, understood the Spencean doctrine directly: I heard of it, and obey, and the slaves felt the force directly.' (107) Miss Campbell refers to herself as 'a weak woman.' It may be that she was ill, or it may be she was ironic, malingering, signifying. It is a pose she may have had to assume with the Governor. 'Well, child, I will hear you on this head at a more convenient time.' Let it not be supposed from Campbell's apparent acquiescence to the Governor's ridiculous tone that the women workers of Jamaica

---

71. Campbell, *The Maroons*, pp. 23, 126-135, 230.

72. 'The Treacherous Feast: A Jamaican Maroon Historical Myth,' *Bijdragen: Tot de Taal, Land, en Volkenkunde*, vol. 140 (1984). See also, Richard Price, *First-Time: The Historical Vision of an Afro-American People* (Baltimore, 1983).

submitted without fight. On 26 January 1816 'the women, one and all, refused to carry away the *trash*.' The mill stopped, the driver drove, and 'a little fierce young devil of a Miss Whaunica flew at his throat and endeavoured to strangle him: the agent was obliged to be called in, and, at length, this petticoat rebellion was subdued.'[73]

Why does a weak woman of the Maroon tribe understand the Spencean doctrine directly? This is a crucial question of the correspondence because it indicates an assumption common to maroons, Spenceans, and the readers of *The Axe*. The answer may be the emphasis upon provisioning, or agricultural production for immediate use, that is common to both the Spenceans and the maroons. The maroons were the first domestic-oriented agriculturists of the island. 'Fruit and vegetables were to be found in every band, for the first thing every Maroon group did, as a prerequisite of survival, was to plant provision grounds,' with plantains, cocoa, bananas, pineapples, sweet corn, and cassava.[74] Or the answer may be the fact that strict impediments to individual accumulation were collectively set both in Spencean writing and in maroon practice, where cattle were grazed in communal pastures and the allotted lands were held in common. In any case, Robert Wedderburn was showing a commonality of interests between the working class in Jamaica and in England, a commonality that began a century and a half earlier in a common history.[75]

If we agree with Edward Thompson that the working class in England was made in 1817, we may also agree with Michael Ventura who argues that the origin of rock 'n' roll may be found in that year. In 1817 dancing and music were forbidden in New Orleans except on Sundays at Congo Square. Michael Ventura writes: 'Every history of jazz goes back to the slave celebrations in a field that came to be called Congo Square in what was then the center of New Orleans . . . On Sundays slaves from all over the city arrived, watched over by white police and an encircling throng of white spectators.' As a later witness wrote, at Congo Square 'labor the dancers, male and

---

73. Lewis, *op. cit.*, pp. 139, 179.

74. Campbell, *The Maroons*, p. 6.

75. As I argued in 'All the Atlantic Mountains Shook,' *Labour/Le Travailleur*, No. 10 (Autumn 1982).

female, under an inspiration of possession, which takes from their limbs all sense of weariness, and gives to them a rapidity and a duration of motion that will hardly be found elsewhere outside of mere machinery.'[76] Thus, jazz and the 'English working class' were made at the same time.

Black and white workers interfaced on the docks. James Kelly wrote of Jamaica in 1838, 'Sailors and Negroes are ever on the most amicable terms . . . There is a feeling of independence in their intercourse with the sailor . . . In the presence of the sailor, the Negro feels as a man.' And in the demography of the period, 'Coloured births were most common amongst slaves employed on wharves.'[77] In London the black community was spied upon by Tom and Jerry who went slumming in the East End to All Max: 'every *cove* that put in his appearance was quite welcome: colour or country considered no obstacle. . . . All was *happiness* – everybody free and easy, and freedom of expression allowed to the very echo. The group motley indeed;- Lascars, blacks, jack tars, coal-heavers, dustmen, women of colour, old and young, and a sprinkling of the remnants of once fine girls, &c., were all *jigging* together.'[78]

How were the two sides of the Atlantic connected? The process of conquest itself made some connections. Miss Campbell reminded Wedderburn of the Duke of Bedford's real estate interests in South America and his 'swallowing up the property of others.' In addition to the Duke, John, his brother and his three sons were all Members of Parliament. 'The years in which he was responsible for the management of the Russell estates were made notable by the final and highly successful assault on the remaining commons and wastes.' Wedderburn noted 'that many of our countrymen . . . have gone to join the insurgents in South America,' doing so 'to

---

76. *Shadow Dancing in the U.S.A.* (St. Martins: Los Angeles, 1985), pp. 122-3.

77. *Voyage to Jamaica*, 2nd edition (Belfast, 1838), pp. 29-30; and Higman (1976), p. 147.

78. Pierce Egan, *Life in London* (1821), pp. 320-1.

satisfy the cupidity of desperate adventurers.' In December 1817 five regiments sailed for South America.[79]

Some answers are found in the isothermal lines of the Wedderburn-Campbell correspondence. The Governor's Secretary in Jamaica tried to dissuade Miss Campbell from freeing her slaves. She could do nothing, she told him, her former slaves were already talking on market days. 'I told them not to speak of it, but they talked of it the more. The news is gone to Old Arbore and St. Anns, to the Blue Mountains, to North Side, and the plantain boats have carried the news to Port Morant, and Morant Bay.' Thomas Thistlewood provides a more closely observed description of coastal communication. 'The way to go was by water, along the trenches, canals and rivers, and along the coastline, from one estate's barcadier or jetty to another, in all manner of small craft, manned by slaves who heard and carried news.' Professor Turner calculates that the time it took for news arriving on the English mail packet to reach the inland markets was less than three days.[80] So much for talk.

The Governor was aware that the Spencean doctrine circulated via the newspapers. *The Courier* claimed that the Spenceans had 300,000 people ready for insurrection. This paper as well as the *Political Register* published Spence's Plan. But the Plan had appeared much earlier, before the Spa Field riots. Robert Southey was hired by the Government to answer the Reformers and he published Spence's Plan ('the Scalping Philanthropist,' he called Spence) in *The Quarterly Review*, October 1816. It may have reached Jamaica in this form. Southey respected Spence, but regretted that he had not been transported at his trial in 1801.

---

79. Christopher Trent, *The Russells* (Muller: London, 1966), p. 219, *The Forlorn Hope* (October 18, 1817), and Alfred Hasbrouck, *Foreign Legionaries in the Liberation of Spanish South America* (Columbia: N.Y., 1928).

80. Douglas Hall, *In Miserable Slavery: Thomas Thistlewood in Jamaica, 1750-86*, Warwick University Caribbean Studies (London, 1989), p. 26; Turner, p. 47; Julius Scott, 'Afro-American Sailors and the International Communication Network: The Case of Newport Bowers,' Colin Howell and Richard J. Twomey (eds.), *Jack Tar in History: Essays in the History of Maritime Life and Labour* (New Brunswick, 1991).

From reading the newspaper accounts, Miss Campbell 'was quite surprised to find that the good people of England were so much against the Spenceans: I thought the Blacks were the only objects of slavery and oppression. You will send me word what Sir Francis Burdett things of it.' This leading Parliamentary Reformer, married to the Coutts banking family, was hostile to it, advocating that the proprietors of the country arm themselves. Miss Campbell was shocked that Coke of Norfolk confessed ignorance of the Spencean doctrine, and she wished Wedderburn to tell her more about him. Coke's estates of 43,000 acres were unenclosed when he inherited them in 1776. With enclosures he increased their rental value from £2,200 to £20,000. 'Let us seize the villain and before night we will have his heart on a gridiron,' said the angry poor when they learned that he supported the Corn Law of 1815. He escaped their wrath with a bruising, while the Hussars dispersed the crowd.[81]

Talk, newspapers, and letters. Miss Campbell wrote, 'I send this letter by a black cook: I dare not trust it to the Post, for they open people's letters.' (108) The black ship's cook was a common figure in the Navy and merchant marine. John Jea was ship's cook aboard the *Iscet* of Liverpool when it was captured by the French in 1810. Jea was born in Calabar. He was enslaved to a New Yorker. He had an Indian wife, then an Irish wife. He had sailed the seven seas, and travelled extensively in England.[82] The black ship's cook had become a stereotype in nautical fiction reaching its apogee in Frederick Marryat's *Mr Midshipman Easy* (1836). The black cook remained as important to pan-African communication as the sleeping car porter did during the era of rail.

Ira Dye has determined that the proportion of blacks and mulattoes in the English navy at the end of the Napoleonic

---

81. M. W. Patterson, *Sir Francis Burdett and His Times*, 2 volumes, (Macmillan: London, 1931), and A. M. W. Stirling, *Coke of Norfolk* (London, 1907).

82. Graham Hodges, *Black Itinerants of the Gospel: The Narratives of John Jea and George White* (Madison, Wisconsin: 1993). Two black stowaways aboard the ship 'Hayward' from Jamaica stole the watch of the second mate as the ship lay moored off Blackwell on 6 July 1816. Apprehended in Shadwell, tried at Old Bailey, they were transported for seven years. See, *Proceedings*, 10 July 1816.

Wars was 25%.[83] By war's end the policy was adopted to reduce this proportion by ceasing to recruit blacks and by discharging those already in service. It is not surprising then to find the black demobilized sailor was a significant figure in London. He was closely observed by John Thomas Smith, the keeper of the Prints in the British Museum, whose sketches of Joseph Johnson ('Black Joe'), who was severely wounded in the merchant service, and of Charles M'Gee, an ancient one-eyed native of Ribon, Jamaica, and chaunter of patriotic ballards at a busy begging stand on Ludgate Hill, were published in December 1815.[84] The mode of observation was condescending ('Black men are extremely cunning and often witty') and quite without respect of the collective force of former plantation workers. Rather the aim appeared to be to individualize a mass experience, and to demean or trivialize a different cultural experience.

During the crisis of the autumn and winter of 1816 the municipal authorities took active steps to control the independent mobilization of the urban proletariat. These steps indicate to us the political composition, as it were, of the internal structure of the crowd. For one thing, householders were instructed to prevent their servants, apprentices, and children from going to Spa Fields – in effect, a curfew was imposed, to be enforced by property owners. For another thing, the City authorities arrested strangers and detained 'foreign and black sailors,' in effect preventive detention.[85] While scholars or antiquaries might present the African-American as a benign figure of compassion, a 'street character,' those responsible for the established order of the City of London understood the danger of a nautical proletariat joining London's idle apprentice in insurrectionary alliance. We do not know for a fact that Robert Wedderburn was part of the Spa Fields riot, nor that he was not. It is known that another black American sailor, Richard Simmonds, prominently flourished his cutlass ('Were his actions such as to create terror to those in the

---

83. 'Physical and Social Profiles of Early American Seafarers, 1812-1815,' in Colin Howell and Richard J. Twomey (eds.), *Jack Tar in History*.

84. *Vagabondiana; Or, Anecdotes of Mendicant Wanderers Through the Streets of London* (1916).

85. Stanley Palmer, *Police and Protest in England and Ireland, 1780-1850* (Cambridge, 1988), p. 169.

house?') at a gunmaker's shop in the Minories. 'I saw him harranguing the mob for half an hour; during the whole time he was the most active man among them,' said a City constable. A week later he was apprehended on an outward bound East Indiaman. He claimed several blacks and mulattoes were involved.[86]

Perhaps the most profound book of 1817 was *Frankenstein; Or, the Modern Prometheus*, completed in May by Mary Shelley. Dr. Frankenstein, it will be recalled, creates a monster by modern methods and modern materials. He applies science to the production of a new kind of 'person.' The body parts have been stolen from grave-yards, just as Burk and Hare robbed graves to supply the anatomists with carcasses, or as the slave traders created zombies. Then the breath of life was supplied by electricity. In an argument like that of the machinery promoters, Dr. Frankenstein hoped that by creating a new species he would be blessed for ever, but he found the opposite: the slave that he created became obsessed by revenge. 'I was benevolent and good; misery made me a fiend.' This is the story of the proletariat in the era of the Luddites. 'The strange system of human society was explained to me. I heard of the division of property, of immense wealth and squalid poverty . . .' It is a Spencean, communist monster. Educated on Milton, Volney, and *The Sorrow of Werter*, the monster learned that unless he had wealth or nobility, 'he was considered as a vagabond and a slave, doomed to waste his powers for the profits of the chosen few.' Mary Shelley captured a feeling of the new proletarian forces – inarticulate, imprisoned, and repressed.

This proletariat was nautical and international. In 1817 Shelley wrote *The Revolt of Islam*, a long poem whose heroine is carried away in a slave ship; she is rescued by a ship; she urges the sailors to mutiny, and transforms the vessel into a beacon leading a revolutionary fleet against tyranny. The vision has plenty of experience to back it up, from the sailors strike in Liverpool in 1778 to the mutinies of Spithead and the Nore in 1798 to the Tyneside seamen's strike of 1815.[87] This

---

86. Old Bailey *Proceedings*, 15 January 1817, and Iain McCalman (1991), p. 15.

87. Norman McCord, 'The Seamen's Strike of 1815 in North-East Eng-

maritime proletariat was by no means illiterate as we can see from the memoirs of those prisoners of war incarcerated at Dartmoor. They read the newspapers, or had them read to them, and were as familiar with Joanna Southcott, the millennarian, as with Molyneux, the black boxing champion. Books, pens, ink, and paper were available, and schools were established among the prisoners. They were anything if not social critics; this included the prison surgeon, who said that 'the capitalists ruled and turned the wheels of the government at their will and pleasure.'[88] Dartmoor was a microcosm of Atlantic intellectual currents. Methodist preachers exhorted the men, a Jacobin free-thinker scoffed at all religion. Irish guards, veterans of Spain, organized theatricals. Indeed, theatre was the activity that brought people together on their own terms perhaps more than anything. Twice a week plays were produced. Waterhouse, a Massachusetts prisoner, waxes eloquent in describing a production he saw of *Othello* in Prison House Number Four where the African-American prisoners (450 in number) were held.[89]

The question of literacy was at the centre of a theological power struggle in Prison House Number Four. Simon, the priest, was a powerful orator. John, who could read and write, challenged Simon's spiritual authority. John had served the Duke of Kent (3rd son of George III) and explained that it was proper to *read* prayers. Simon replied that 'prayers ought to spring at once, warm from the heart, and that *reading* prayers was too cold a piece of work for him or his church.' John explained that all the noble families of England read prayers, and furthermore religious exercises aboard his Britannic majesty's ships of war, where John had once served as a captain's steward, were also read. Simon replied that whoever could not pray without a book was damned! With the aid of a Methodist, a compromise was reached. Simon continued to preach and John sat at an honoured position next to the Bible.

1816-17 was crucial in the science and institution of repression. The treatment of the insane was closely tied to political

England,' *The Economic History Review*, 2nd series, XXI (1), April 1968.

88. Benjamin Waterhouse, *A Journal of a Young Man of Massachusetts* (Boston 1816) reprinted in *The Magazine of History*, No. 18 (1911).

89. *Ibid.*

suppression. In 1816, when the ward for the criminally insane was opened in Bedlam, one of its first inmates was James Hadfield, a veteran, a spoonmaker, a supporter of *The Rights of Man*, and a follower of the Islington cobbler, Bannister Truelock, the radical millennarian. He had shot at George III. Parliament passed the Criminal Lunatics Act of 1800, the origin of the insanity plea, which enabled the government to detain Hadfield for the rest of his life.[90] George Turner, a follower of Richard Brothers and then of Joanna Southcott, was locked up in a mental hospital for proclaiming in January 1817: 'I am ordered on the 28th to go to the Palace Yard and declare the Word of the Lord against the Treasury. Horse Guards, Carlton House, the Playhouses, Churches, and Chapels, the Tower, Somerset House, and other public places . . . Those who are not worth a penny now must be lords of the land. No rents must be paid. No postage for letters. No turnpikes. No taxes. Porter a gallon for one half-penny. Ale the same.'[91]

Millbank, the prison inspired by Bentham's panopticon, received its first inmates, 36 female convicts 'under considerable fear and alarm,' in June 1816. Also in 1816 the Society for the Improvement of Prison Discipline (SIPD) was formed by three anti-slave abolitionists. It favoured work, seclusion, and central authority. It believed that terror would deter and that reflection would reform, if communication among prisoners could be prevented. Acoustics was a new science; the problem was to convert information into noise. The suspension of loose canvas between broken brick cavities in the walls mangled intelligibility. Michael Faraday was part of these experiments at Millbank. Indeed a year earlier Faraday was appointed Superintendent of the Apparatus of the Laboratory at the Royal Society. In 1817 William Cubitt, the civil engineer, invented the tread mill so that prisoners could 'grind the wind.' By 1824 54 of them had been installed in

90. Richard Watson, 'The Origin of Insanity as a Special Verdict: The Trial for Treason of James Hadfield (1800),' *Law & Society Review*, volume 19, No. 3 (1985).

91. G. R. Balleine, *Past Finding Out: The Tragic Story of Joanna Southcott and her Successors* (New York, 1956), p. 77.

England. Prisoners called it 'the wheel of life' or 'the everlasting staircase.'[92]

Repression brings resistance. In March 1816 a government spy collected a letter from 'the Tri-Coloured Committee' to 'Our Fellow Countrymen suffering Incarceration.' It announced that 'the prison doors will be opened . . . [and] your lofty Bastiles be reduced to Ashes.'[93] 1817 saw the first strike at the prison, led by Judith Lacy who went into 'fits.'[94] The Evans', father and son, were jailed in Horsemonger Lane prison. Wedderburn published *The Forlorn Hope* largely to aid them. A few weeks later in *The Axe Laid to the Root* he warned the slaves: 'have no prisons, they are only schools for vice, and depots for the victims of tyranny.' He compared the prison and the slave experience, like Henry Mayhew was later to do.[95] Wedderburn wrote Miss Campbell that, 'I will inform you for your present safety, and for the future good of your offspring, to let the slaves go free immediately, for in their prison house a voice is heard, loose him and let him go.' (97)

Whitworth Russell became the chaplain at Millbank. He told a new inmate who could not read or write that he now had 'every cause to be thankful at the opportunities afforded you here.' 'Not at all,' Fleming the inmate replied, 'I have reason to curse the Penitentiary and everybody belonging to it.' 'Be silent,' said the chaplain, 'I shall not stand by and listen to such reprehensible language.' 'I'll not be gagged, I shall speak the truth,' continued Fleming, until he was physically removed and transferred to the dark.[96] In this way superior force was allied with literacy, an attribute of authority in the arsenal of punishment. It took an extraordinary man to challenge this. George Anderson, 'an unorthodox black man' who had

92. J. W. Horsley, *Jottings from Jail* (1887), p. 5.

93. E. P. Thompson, *The Making of the English Working Class* (1968), p. 692.

94. Arthur Griffiths, *Memorials of Millbank, and Chapters in Prison History* (London 1875), volume I, p. 60.

95. Henry Mayhew and John Binny, *The Criminal Prisons of London* (London, 1867), p. 592; and H. Bruce Franklin, *Prison Literature in America* (N.Y. 1978).

96. *Ibid.*, vol. I, pp. 198-9.

been educated at a missionary college, sowed seeds of dis-
belief in the minds of the prison population.[97] 'He had turned
the chaplain and his sacred office into ridicule, asserting that
the services of the Church of England were nonsense, from
beginning to end, that the prayers contained false doctrine,
that the Athanasian Creed was all rubbish, and that the
church "went with a lie in her right hand."' Whitworth Russell
was no match for him. Once in the heat of chapel debate over
a passage of scripture, the chaplain jumped up to reach his
Bible and struck his leg against the table. 'Oh, my leg,' he
exclaimed. Later Anderson drew a caricature of the scene
writing underneath, 'Oh, my leg!' and thenceforth, the prisoners knew Russell, tripped by his own literacy, as 'Oh My
Leg.'

We also must be careful not to trip. Jubilee was a literate
tradition to Wedderburn, and it was also a practical matter
which Wedderburn had some experience of. This perhaps is
the most important thing about his correspondence with
Elizabeth Campbell. Jubilee is an Old Testament legal practice of land redistribution, debt cancellation, slave manumission, and year-long sabbath. In the New Testament the
jubilee text is part of the fulfillment of a prophecy in Isaiah,
the voice crying aloud in the wilderness to level mountains, to
straighten the corners, and smooth the rugged way for deliverance. And deliverance happens on earth in open jails, in
recovered sight, and healed wounds. In the Book of Luke this
jubilee (4:18) lies close to the axe laid to the root (3:9).

In modern history the notion has provided a powerful
constellation of ideas for those opposing enclosure of common or waste land into private property in Britain and for
those opposing slavery on the plantations in the America and
the Caribbean. The oral tradition of jubilee is largely
African-American and anonymous. As James Cone has written, 'It matters little to the oppressed who authored scripture;
what is important is whether it can serve as a weapon against
oppressors.'[98] The literate, scholarly tradition is British and it
is associated with particular authors, such as John Bunyan

---

97. Griffiths, *Memorials of Millbank*, p. 60.

98. *A Black Theology of Liberation*, 2nd edition (1986), p. 31.

and James Harrington.[99] The Methodists brought these traditions together in the Americas. The itinerant founder of
American Methodism, Francis Asbury, preached on jubilee
texts in 1776, 1790, 1800 and 1801.[100]

'Do people ever act contrary to any divine law, when they
resume their rights, and recover their property out of the
hands of those who have unnaturally invaded it?' and 'Was
the jewish jubilee a levelling scheme?' asked Dr. James
Murray in *Sermons to Asses* (1768) and republished in 1817.
In England in the 1790s discussion of jubilee was joined by
Coleridge who lectured on 'the essentially *socialistic* Character of the Law of Moses,' especially of jubilee. He did so in
uncharacteristically direct sentences: 'The Lands were restored. Property is Power and equal Property equal Power. A
Poor Man is necessarily more or less a Slave. Poverty is the
Death of public Freedom – it virtually enslaves Individuals
. . .'[101] Thomas Spence was inspired by the notion in the 1770s.
His 'Jubilee Hymn; Or, A Song to be sung at the Commence-
ment of the Millennium, If Not Sooner' (1782) was sung to the
tune of the national anthem. In the 1790s it had entered the
discussion of African-Americans as a subject of preaching
and as a theme in song. Spence seems to have been aware of
this.[102]

> For who can tell but the Millennium
> May take its rise from my poor Cranium?
> And who knows but it God may please
> It should come by the West Indies?

---

99. Peter Linebaugh, 'Jubilating; Or, How the Atlantic Working Class
    Used the Biblical Jubilee against Capitalism, with Some Success,' *The
    Radical History Review*, No. 50 (1991), pp. 143-180; James Harrington,
    The Art of Lawgiving (1659), and John Bunyan, *The Advocateship of
    Jesus Christ* (1688).

100. *The Journal and Letters of Francis Asbury*, 3 vols (1958), ii, 222, 312,
     and 498.

101. Patton and Mann (ed.), *The Collected Works of Samuel Taylor
     Coleridge*, vol. i, *Lectures 1795* (New York, 1971), p. 122 ff. See also
     The Universalists Miscellancy, or Philanthropists Museum, vol. i
     (1797), pp. 140-143.

102. In his last published writing, *The Giant Killer*, Spence wrote about
     slavery. See, P. M. Ashraf, *the Life and Times of Thomas Spence*
     (Newcastle, 1983).

The government was well aware of the power of jubilee. In 1809, the 50th anniversary of the reign of George III, it put on a jubilee of its own. Cobbett believed that jubilee will 'have the effect of reconciling the minds of the labouring people to a state of dependence and beggary.' Malcolm Chase seems to agree; he calls the royal jubilee 'politically anodyne,' yet debtors were released, amnesty declared for deserters, extra rations allowed for soldiers and sailors, and prisoners of war were freed.[103]

Wedderburn distinguished the jubilee from Spence's Plan. True, there was considerable overlap. 'Spence's Plan' had many forms of presentation: it appeared in song, on the coinage, in wall-chalkings, and, particularly in 1816 and 1817, in the newspapers like this:

SPENCE'S PLAN
For Parochial Partnerships in the Land,
Is the only effectual Remedy for the
Distresses and Oppressions of the People.
The Landholders are not Proprietors in Chief, they are but the
Stewards of the Public;
For the LAND is the PEOPLE'S FARM.
The Expenses of the Government do not cause the Misery that
Surrounds us, but the enormous exactions of these
'Unjust Stewards'
Landed Monopoly is indeed equally contrary to the benign
Spirit of Christianity and destructive of
The Independence and Morality of all Mankind.
'The Profit of the Earth is for all,'
Yet how deplorable destitute are the great Mass of the People!
Nor is it possible for their situations to be radically amended, but
By the establishment of a system,
Founded on the immutable basis of Nature and Justice.
Experience demonstrates its necessity; and the Rights of Mankind
Require it for their preservation.

Wedderburn argued the superiority of this plan: 'it admits no mortgages; it needs no jubilee,' he wrote. His approach to jubilee may be contrasted with that of Coleridge for whom jubilee was an anti-accumulation device – accumulation being responsible for 'nine-tenths of our Vices and Miseries.' Jubi-

---

103. *The Political Register* October 1809, and Malcolm Chase 'From Millennium to Anniversary: The Concept of Jubilee in Late Eighteenth and Nineteenth Century England,' *Past & Present*, No. 129 (November 1990), pp. 132-47.

lee allowed Coleridge to defend revealed religion during revolutionary times, whereas to Wedderburn jubilee was a practice of revolutionary liberation. His approach may also be contrasted with that of Charles Hall whose 1805 treatise, *The Effects of Civilization on the People in European States*, with its headings and subheadings, was a logical, ponderous exposition in which private property and poverty are attacked and shown as essential to 'civilization.' The Mosaic Law, and jubilee in particular, are examined as part of human history. Wedderburn's approach is essentially oral; Hall's is essentially bookish. Like Coleridge, Hall refers to Jewish history and to Sparta. Spence differs in that his examples came from America and Africa.

As a student of scriptures Wedderburn was quite aware of the complexities of the Mosaic jubilee. 'And there it is written, that the slave which would not accept his liberty at the end of the seven years jubilee, must have his ears cut off, because he loved his master and mistress, and despised the law of liberty; he was never to have the benefit of another jubilee while he lived.' 'The slaves begin to talk that if their masters were Christians they would not hold them in slavery any longer than seven years, for that is the extent of the law of Moses,' quoting Leviticus 24:39-40. Servants to America indentured themselves for a period of 7 years. Manumitted coloured people were issued Certificates of Freedom which were valid for only seven years.[104] Hence, as Wedderburn shows, some of the Mosaic law of jubilee was already part of trans-Atlantic labour policy.

Miss Campbell assures Wedderburn that the freed slaves 'are singing all day at work about Thomas Spence, and the two Evans' in Horsemonger Lane prison.' Having freed her slaves, Elizabeth Campbell then redistributed her land. Her motivation is complex and contradictory to the tidy minded. It is reported, on one hand, that 'Miss Campbell then cried, the land is yours, not because Wedderburn, the Spencean says so, for I have read the word of God, and it says, the Lord gave the earth to the children of men.' Her action is not ideological; it is sacred. On the other hand, she says, 'I am now instructed by a child of nature, to resign to you your natural right in the soil on which you stand, agreeable to Spence's

---

104. Brathwaite, *op. cit.*, p. 170 quoting 1 Geo. III c.22 (1760).

plan.' Her action complies with the instructions of a Spencean
'child of nature.' Doubtless, the motivation is mixed. She
wishes to stress, though, that her deed is not unique, rather it
is neighbourly. '. . . I will manage it myself, as your steward,
my brother will assist us, we shall live happy, like the family of
the Shariers in the parish of St. Mary's, who have all things
common.' (99)

Who were the Shariers of St. Mary's? Dr Kenneth Ingram
speculated that it might refer simply to 'sharers,' people who
shared.[105] The *1818 Almanac for Jamaica* gives no 'Shariers'
for St. Mary's though it does list three estates, Mt. Resolution, Mt. Regale, and Tremolesworth owned by Alex, John
and Samuel Shreyer. 281 slaves worked Tremolesworth, and
ten each the two other estates. Prof. Campbell suggested
(conversation, 8 May 1991) that it is a family name. In 1817
'Monk' Lewis employed a kind of jubilee on his sugar estates
in Westmoreland to prevent 'inequitable' accumulation of
property among his slaves: 'I made it public, that from
henceforth no negro should possess more than one house with
a sufficient portion of ground for his family, and on the
following Sunday the overseer by my order, took from those
who had too much to give to those who had too little, and
made an entire new distribution according to the most strict
Agrarian law.'[106]

It is well to remember that 1790-1820 was a period of social
engineering in the internal organization of villages and provisions grounds by the Jamaican big planters. The actions of
Elizabeth Campbell are consistent with identified themes of
Jamaican agrarian history in this period. A survey of maps
and plans of estates shows that the proportion of houses in
villages with regular linear layout peaked around 1810; thereafter the surveyor less confidently depicted the provision
grounds. Higman describes competing conceptions of spatial
order held by slaves and planters.[107] Wedderburn anticipates
the post-emancipation transformation of agriculture to small

---

105. In private conversation at the National Library (Kingston, Jamaica,
     1990).

106. Matthew Gregory Lewis, *Journal of a West India Proprietor* (1834), p.
     405.

107. Barry Higman, *Jamaica Surveyed: Plantation Maps and Plans of the
     Eighteenth and Nineteenth Centuries* (Kingston, 1988), p. 261.

holding settlements in 'free villages' founded by missionaries within the north coast estate zone, or formed by squatters on abandoned estates or on underutilized back lands. Higman writes, 'the planters continued to be disinclined to measure out precise areas [for renters of provision grounds] and the shifting character of land use persisted.' Some of these free villages predated emancipation, and they may have established customary practices that have lasted into the 20th century as 'family land.' That jubilee should not be excluded from an influence in this development is stressed in Claud McKay's novel *Banana Bottom* about one such village, named Jubilee.[108]

I have tried to show that we may 'comprehend' the letters Wedderburn published in *The Axe Laid to the Root* if we understand the experiences of African American slavery and the London working class, linked experiences that rarely found their way into print, at least by those who had them. Having thus read his world, it is possible to 'read' his writing. But to read that world, we needed to use his writing as a source. Once this process is underway, it ceases to be so useful to describe Robert Wedderburn in terms of literacy. It is significant that MacCalman associates the literacy of Robert Wedderburn with what he calls the 'shadowy tavern underworld,' or the 'black underground.' James Walvin uses this metaphor as well when he writes of 'the subterranean mass of rootless poor blacks.'[109]

The metaphor of 'underground' is misleading. In fact, it was a contemporary metaphor. Coleridge wrote: 'Whether the spirit of Jacobinism, which the writings of Burke exorcised from the higher and from the literary classes, may not like the ghost in Hamlet be heard moving and mining in the underground chambers with an activity the more dangerous because less noisy, may admit of a question.'[110] The connota-

---

108. *Jamaica Surveyed*, p. 262. See Sidney W. Mintz, 'The Historical Sociology of Jamaican Villages,' in Charles V. Carnegie (ed.), *Afro-Caribbean Villages in Historical Perspective*, African-Caribbean Institute of Jamaica (Kingston, 1987).

109. James Walvin, *Black and White*, p. 12.

110. Samuel Taylor Coleridge, *Biographia Literaria: Or Biographical*

tions are interesting. Thriving underground, like Hamlet's ghost, the spirit of democracy is thus nocturnal, spiritual, and frightening. Moreover, in choosing 'exorcise' as the verb describing Burke's criticism, the suggestion is made that democracy is diabolical. Finally, it is 'writing' that rids the literate classes of Jacobinism; orality and talk presumably belong underground. The hierarchy of learning parallels the hierarchy of the social structure; literacy is 'high' and orality is 'low'. Assumed by these metaphors is a link between light and print. Once again, illiteracy and ignorance are combined, and both with darkness underground.

Wedderburn was a poor man and he had served time in more than one jail. But he was not shadowy. He did not hide. On the contrary, it was the spies who wrote down his speeches who hid. And is not this true more generally? Is not our knowledge really the opposite? The London African-Americans were quite in the daylight of action. Benjamin Bowsey and John Glover were leaders of the Gordon Riots; Simmonds was a leader in the Spa Fields Riots; Davidson of Jamaica was prominent in the Cato Street conspiracy. As for being 'rootless,' this too is misleading. I have tried to argue that Wedderburn's roots were widespread. They were both proletarian and international. The discourse expressing that experience is not going to be easily understood by a literacy defined by private property and refined propriety.

Let us consider Jane Austen, who died in 1817. A subtle technician of counter-revolution, the topical, anti-Jacobin references remained with her to the last. Jane Austen revised her novel, *Northanger Abbey*, early in 1817 to include a reference to the Spa Fields riots of 2 December 1816. Her characters, Catherine, Eleanor, and Henry, are walking above Bath on Beechen Cliff. They converse, correct one another's diction, assess novels, evaluate landscape paintings, and complain about history: 'the quarrels of popes and kings, with wars or pestilences, on every page; the men all so good for nothing, and hardly any women at all.' Henry agrees that little boys and girls ought to be taught history though it is a torture. 'You would allow,' he says, summing up penal and pedagogical policy, 'that to torment and to instruct might

---

Sketches of My Literary Life and Opinions (1817), Everyman's Library, 1965, p. 106.

sometimes be used as synonymous words.' Henry descants upon the visual aesthetic of an oak and from that 'to oaks in general, to forests, the inclosure of them, waste lands, crown lands and government, he shortly found himself arrived at politics; and from politics, it was an easy step to silence.' This pause is filled by Catherine's solemn news that something uncommonly dreadful was about to happen in London, 'murder and every thing of the kind.' It is left to Henry to explain that it is insurrection that is plotted, 'the Bank attacked, the Tower threatened, the streets of London flowing with blood.' The reference, added in 1817, is to Spa Fields.[111] Thus, Jane Austen deals with revolution at first by silence, and then by letting the male character instruct in a diction of alarmed gentility.

This sort of diction was remarked on by Thomas Preston, who in 1817 published his own account of the Spa Fields meetings. He commented on literacy: 'There were many people, who, though conversant with their dictionary, would have it, that Reform meant Deform, and that Revolution was a compound of Blood and Madness.'[112] Censorship of language extended from underwear – 'unexpressibles,' 'unspeakables,' and 'don't mentions' were new words in 1817 – to the suppressed volume of the Board of Agriculture of 1816 whose eighth question, 'what is the state of the labouring poor?' contained the answer 'the state of the Labouring Poor is very bad.'[113]

Paul Johnson claims that Wedderburn was 'an early instance of the belief that clerical status offered some protection to law-breaking radicals in their battle with authority . . . Such clerico-progressives were to become commonplace in the 20th century.'[114] Perhaps he refers to the downfall of the

---

111. Marilyn Butler, *Jane Austen and the War of Ideas* (Oxford, 1975), p. 181. Jane Austen died in June 1817. Igor Webb, *From Custom to Capital; The English Novel and the Industrial Revolution* (Ithaca, 1981).

112. *The Life and Opinions of Thomas Preston, Patriot and Shoemaker* (1817), p. 13.

113. Peter Fryer, *Mrs Grundy: Studies in English Prudery* (1963) and *The Agricultural State of the Kingdom* (1816).

114. Paul Johnson, *The Birth of the Modern: World Society 1815-1830*

Duvalier regime in Haiti. The Monday before Easter Sunday 1985 Jean Bertrand Aristide preached at the Cathedral of Port-au-Prince, the capital of the island whence began the African American revolution two hundred years ago when Boukman, believed to be an ex-slave from Jamaica, beat the drum of revolt. The forces of opposition were beginning to coalesce against the tyrant. The youthful slum dwellers of the capital were the most cynical and the last to join. Aristide appealed to them by preaching on jubilee – 'thus we who are slaves must one day share the land – we can feel it in our gut. Because the land is not for a little fistful of gluttons, but for us all.' 'In the year of grace,' he said, 'we do not close our eyes. In the year of grace, we do not fold our arms and wait.'[115]

(New York, 1991), p. 384.

115. Jean-Bertrand Aristide, *In the Parish of the Poor; Writings from Haiti* (Maryknoll, 1990), p. 78.

Chapter Seven

The Fabrication of Deviance: 'Dangerous Classes' and 'Criminal Classes' in Victorian England

Victor Bailey

The Scarman Report on the Brixton riots of 10-12 April 1981 opens with a graphic description of the weekend's events.* Television viewers, it says, 'watched with horror and incredulity . . . scenes of violence and disorder in their capital city, the like of which had not previously been seen in this century in Britain'.[1] The national press had sketched more luridly the image of a 'hooligan criminal element', directed by political extremists, the apocryphal 'Four Horsemen of the Apocalypse', hooded motorcyclists with citizens' band radios.[2] The imagery was always far-fetched. The disorders broke out in response largely to the methods used by the police to diminish street crime in Brixton: the exercise of the

* I am grateful to the Hall Center for the Humanities, for the research fellowship which made it possible to complete this essay, and to the Department of Special Collections, Kenneth Spencer Research Library, University of Kansas. I would also like to thank the editors of this volume, plus Ann Fidler (U.C. Berkeley), Martin Wiener (Rice), Ben Sax and Ann Schofield (Kansas) for their valuable comments on the initial draft of the essay.

1. Lord Leslie George Scarman, *The Scarman Report. The Brixton Disorders 10-12 April 1981* (Harmondsworth, 1982), p. 14.

2. See, e.g., *Daily Mail*, 8 July 1981; *Daily Express*, 8 July 1981. See also Clive Unsworth, 'The Riots of 1981: Popular Violence and the Politics of Law and Order', *Journal of Law and Society*, vol. 9, Summer 1982, p. 77; Graham Murdock, 'Reporting the riots: images and impact' in John Benyon (ed.), *Scarman and After* (Oxford, 1984), pp. 74-78.

power to 'stop and search', the use of the 'sus' law to net 'suspected persons and reputed thieves', and the appropriately named 'Swamp '81', the saturation policing operation that was applied in the days immediately preceding the disorders.[3] Accordingly, the rioters' limited objective was to evict the police from the streets of Brixton. Yet the imagery died hard. It coloured reactions to the riots, a few months later, in Liverpool and Manchester; and to the 1985 disturbances in Handsworth (Birmingham) and in the Broadwater Farm Estate (Tottenham, North London), where a policeman was brutally stabbed to death, the first metropolitan constable to be killed in a riot since 1833.[4] The problems of crime, riot and policing were aggregated into a disturbing portrait of what is now fashionably dubbed the 'underclass', what the Victorians labelled the 'dangerous classes'.[5]

These events provide my entrance to the early Victorian era, when the imagery of the 'dangerous classes' – a threatening amalgamation of poverty, vagrancy and crime, aroused to rebellion by radical rhetoric – was first deployed, and when many of the attitudes to crime and criminals which we hold today were set in place. If I was one of the early cartographers of this terrain, under the incomparable guidance of the historian honoured by this Festschrift, my footprints have long since been obliterated, and more mapping has been done in the intervening years. The aim in returning to this ground is to incorporate the additional evidence into a new chart of how and why this dramatic definition of the Victorian outcast appeared, and how and why the collective construct of the 'dangerous classes' was gradually reduced by social classification and by police and penal routines to the slimmer notion of the 'criminal classes', no longer associated with political subversion and social breakdown.

Above all, the essay is a challenge to the 'political' interpretation of criminal policy as a direct response to burgeoning fears of revolution, and thus as having more to do with class

---

3. *Scarman Report*, pp. 94 & 176-77; John Clare, 'Eyewitness in Brixton' in Benyon (ed.), *Scarman and After*, p. 51.

4. See 6 *Hansard* 84, 23 October 1985, cols. 348-88; Brian Robson, *Those Inner Cities* (Oxford, 1988), pp. 37-38.

5. See Robert Reiner, 'Crime and Policing' in S. Macgregor & B. Pimlott (eds.), *Tackling the Inner Cities* (Oxford, 1990), p. 45.

war than with 'crime' per se. The centrepiece of this argument is the limited purchase the threatening image of the 'dangerous (and labouring) classes' ever gained in England, compared to the continent, and the fairly rapid shift to the more limited and manageable image of 'criminal classes', distinct from the labouring classes. These two points – Victorian England's 'exceptionalism' and the brief life there of ruling class panic – are, I would contend, neglected truths due for restatement.

As such, the essay is concerned with the discourse of crime: with the terminology used by middle-class Victorians to express the fears and obsessions of their world, and with the way these words, and their meanings, changed over time. It is not only concerned, however, with the discourse of reformers, jurists, and administrators who spoke and wrote about crime. For many of these people not only defined the boundaries of the 'respectable' and the 'dangerous', but also helped to create laws and institutions for dealing with the outcast, which were instrumental in enclosing the dominant meanings within the administrative practice of criminal justice. Over and above the interplay between dominant discourse and law enforcement strategies, the essay seeks to link particular stereotypes of deviance, and the manner in which they were applied, to the wider political project of establishing and reinforcing the moral boundaries between different sections of the vast body of the working population. The emergence and evolution of the discourse of the 'criminal and dangerous classes' is related, in short, to the crucial political and cultural debate on the emerging proletarian 'order'.[6]

---

6. My approach to the subject has been influenced by Martin Wiener's important cultural interpretation of Victorian crime and criminal justice, *Reconstructing the Criminal. Culture, Law, and Policy in England, 1830-1914* (Cambridge, 1990). The book relies too exclusively, in my view, on an individualist, as distinct from a collectivist, reading of crime, and explores only the single cultural image of the wilful, undisciplined and unmoralised criminal. Nonetheless, it reveals how much moral values and distinctions mattered to the Victorian discussion of criminality. For a similar decipherment of the nineteenth-century debate on poverty, see Gertrude Himmelfarb, *The Idea of Poverty. England in the Early Industrial Age* (New York, 1985).

I

Two features of eighteenth-century society warrant immediate attention, as a way of establishing the base line from which we can measure the change in attitudes to crime wrought by the transition to an urban, industrial society. The first is the 'picturesque' description of the underworld of rogues and vagabonds. From Elizabethan times on, the 'rogue literature' conjured up a criminal subculture with its corporative structures and craft subdivisions, its distinct locales and haunts, and its own cant (or dialect), rites and values: a portrait of an anti-society of professional villains, cheats and thieves; one standing in juxtaposition to the world of honest labour. Whether such a 'deviant' underworld existed outside the pamphlet literature is, for present purposes, beside the point. What counts is that perceptions of a bounded netherworld were deeply etched by this traditional 'ethnography' of crime.[7] The second feature is an elite tolerance of crime and riot, displayed both in 'the margin of [minor] illegality', conceded to, and demanded by, the poor (the obverse being the pivotal role accorded the awe-inspiring ritual of public execution), and in the doings of the 'city mob', whether out to force justices to increase wages or to root for Church and King.[8]

Both features of early-modern society were subverted by such long-term 'civilizing' processes as a growing demand for security of daily life and a rising standard of personal self-discipline, and, more specifically, by the change in attitudes caused by the events of the 1780s and 1790s. The portrait of a circumscribed underworld was challenged by a sense of crisis about the levels of violent and property crime, first voiced in Martin Madan's *Thoughts on Executive Justice* (1785), made

---

7. See T. C. Curtis & F. M. Hale, 'English Thinking About Crime, 1530-1620' in L. A. Knafla (ed.), *Crime and Criminal Justice in Europe and Canada* (Ontario, 1981), p. 117; Peter Linebaugh, *The London Hanged. Crime and Civil Society in the Eighteenth Century* (London, 1991), pp. 71-72.

8. See Michael Ignatieff, 'State, Civil Society, and Total Institutions: A Critique of Recent Social Histories of Punishment' in M. Tonry & N. Morris (eds.), *Crime and Justice: An Annual Review of Research* (Chicago, 1981), vol. 3, pp. 166-67; E. Hobsbawm, 'The City Mob' in idem, *Primitive Rebels* (New York, 1965), pp. 111-20.

shrill by the end of transportation and the demobilization of thousands of soldiers and sailors in 1786, and barely muted by the outbreak of war in 1793.[9] The licence granted the city mob was severely curtailed once the Gordon and Priestley riots exemplified the threat that popular turbulence posed to property, and once the French Revolution frightened the elite into viewing the poor as a race of potential revolutionaries.[10]

The person who more than anyone expressed this new perception of crime was Patrick Colquhoun. A Glasgow merchant, Colquhoun had moved to London in 1791 looking for government employment, which he found the following year as a stipendiary magistrate under the Middlesex Justice Act 1792.[11] His reputation rests, however, on his several treatises on crime, police and indigence, written in the nervous aftermath of the French Revolution.[12] At first blush, Colquhoun's description of the state of crime in the metropolis recalls that of 'picaresque' literature. Crime is a trade, with an infrastructure of receivers and lodging houses; the more daring of 'the Criminal Phalanx' form themselves into gangs or societies to plan and execute robberies.[13] This eighteenth-century image of crime pales into insignificance, however, at

9. Martin Madan, *Thoughts on Executive Justice, with respect to our criminal laws* (London, 1785), pp. 4-5 & 79. See also J. M. Beattie, *Crime and the Courts in England 1660-1800* (Oxford, 1986), p. 225; Elaine Reynolds, 'The Night Watch and Police Reform in Metropolitan London, 1720-1830', Ph.D. thesis, Cornell University, 1991, pp. 228-32.

10. Allan Silver, 'The Demand for Order in Civil Society: A Review of Some Themes in the History of Urban Crime, Police, and Riot' in D. Bordua (ed.), *The Police* (New York, 1967), pp. 3-4; M. Ignatieff, *A Just Measure of Pain* (London, 1989), p. 89.

11. On Colquhoun, see Sir Leon Radzinowicz, *A History of English Criminal Law and its Administration from 1750* (London, 1956), vol. 3, pp. 211-19; D. Philips, '"A New Engine of Power and Authority". The Institutionalization of Law-Enforcement in England 1780-1830' in V. A. C. Gatrell, B. Lenman & G. Parker (eds.), *Crime and the Law* (London, 1980), p. 175; Reynolds, 'The Night Watch', p. 357.

12. Patrick Colquhoun, *A Treatise on the Police of the Metropolis* (London, 1800, 6th. ed; first pub. 1795); idem, *A Treatise on the Commerce and Police of the River Thames* (London, 1800); idem, *A Treatise on Indigence* (London, 1806).

13. Colquhoun, *Treatise on Police*, p. 101.

the side of Colquhoun's estimates of the size and composition of metropolitan crime.

In a memorandum of 1793, Colquhoun estimated that '[t]he property stolen and pilfered in and about this Metropolis by means of a Systematic plan of Depredation (exclusive of those Thefts Robberys and Burglarys which are committed by common and *professed Thieves*)' came to £800,000 per annum. 'This System,' he continued,

> is Carried on through the medium of *menial Servants & Domestics, – Journeymen, Apprentices, Labourers, Porters and others who are employed* in *private Houses, Shops, Warehouses, Work shops, Manufactorys* . . . and also in the Dockyards.[14]

It is evident also from his more detailed description of those implicated in riverside delinquency, that as much as ninety per cent of all crimes were committed by those employed in loading and discharging the ships and vessels in the River Thames: watermen, lightermen, lumpers and coal heavers; and that almost one-third of the total number of port workers was delinquent.[15] In the *Treatise on Indigence*, the full breadth of Colquhoun's vision is revealed in estimates of those in Great Britain 'presumed to live chiefly or wholly upon the labours of others'. Over 1,320,000 people, or 1 in 8 of the entire population, was indigent (in receipt of parish relief), vagrant, living by prostitution, or criminal.[16] Colquhoun's figures must be taken with a bag of salt, if accurate social observation is the quest.[17] As a reflection of an attitude of mind, however, they are invaluable.

Clearly, Colquhoun found difficulty in distinguishing and demarcating the active delinquent from the poor who were indigent through 'culpable causes'. To meet the threat from

---

14. The 1793 memorandum is reproduced in Radzinowicz, *History*, vol. 3, Appendix 5, p. 507.

15. Colquhoun, *Treatise on Police*, pp. 217-43; idem, *Treatise on the Commerce*, pp. 50-80. See also L. Radzinowicz, *A History of English Criminal Law* (New York, 1957), vol. 2, p. 359; E. P. Thompson, *The Making of the English Working Class* (Harmondsworth, 1982), p. 59.

16. See Radzinowicz, *History*, vol. 3, pp. 239-40 and 513-18 (Appendix 5).

17. By estimating the number of women who supported themselves by prostitution at 50,000, Colquhoun condemned every fourth female in London, irrespective of age, to prostitution!

the criminal and indigent poor, he proposed a regular system of police, whose tasks included regulating those institutions of the urban poor (such as lodging houses) which encouraged crime, and a Pauper Police Institution.[18] With counter-revolutionary zeal, moreover, Colquhoun advised keeping close track of the thousands of 'miscreants' in London, for they, 'upon any fatal emergency, (which GOD forbid!) would be equally ready as their brethren in iniquity were, in Paris, to repeat the same atrocities.'[19] Thus were the 'dangerous classes' linked in this discourse to revolutionary violence. With the exception of the Thames River Police Act 1800, however, Colquhoun made little headway with his vast scheme to invigilate the poorer sections of society. Not even this practised self-publicist was able to gain governmental attention. His conservative critics, moreover, repeatedly attacked his 'disposition to think ill' of what Sir Richard Phillips described as 'the two large classes of poor shop-keepers and labourers'.[20] Yet Colquhoun's vision contrasted markedly with the previous image of a criminal underworld, isolated by its customs, speech and mode of life, and distinguishable from the labouring poor. His alarmist campaign, his strategy of exaggeration, which became a model for other 'moral entrepreneurs' in the cause of police and prison reform, prepared the ground, moreover, for a vocabulary of 'the dangerous classes'.

It is at this point, in my view, that historians of crime and criminal justice go to excess. They have the strong tendency to write the history of the first half of the nineteenth century in terms of the threat of 'the dangerous and labouring classes',

18. See *28th Report from the Select Committee on Finance*, House of Commons Sessional Papers, vol. 112, 1798, Appendix C, pp. 47-53; *Report from the Committee on the State of the Police of the Metropolis*, Parliamentary Papers (P.P.), 1816, V (510), pp. 32-33. See also N. Rogers, 'Policing the Poor in Eighteenth-Century London: The Vagrancy Laws and Their Administration', *Histoire Sociale-Social History*, vol. XXIV, May 1991, pp. 144-45.

19. Colquhoun, *Treatise on Police*, p. 532.

20. Richard Phillips, *Modern London: being the History and Present State of the British Metropolis* (London, 1804), p. 146. See also Ruth Paley, '"An Imperfect, Inadequate and Wretched System?" Policing London Before Peel', *Criminal Justice History*, vol. X, 1989, p. 98.

and the associated introduction of new instruments of policing and punishment.[21] The logic of the argument is seductive. The first decades of the nineteenth century were ones of extraordinarily rapid population increase. Towns were magnets; England, and a fair bit of Ireland, went to London.[22] Young men between 16 and 25 years of age, the chief protagonists in crime and disorder, formed up to one-third of the adult male population of these towns. While industry summoned these migrants, it could not keep them all in continuous work. Economic crises, unemployment, and a divisive urban structure ripped apart the traditional web of interdependence between elites and the labouring classes. Cities became breeding grounds of crime and disorder. Elites felt insecure in an urban situation characterised by a growing ungovernability of the poor.[23]

Enter acute political conflict. The popular radical movement recurrently challenged the rule of the governing classes. The position became more volatile still when, in the 1840s, radicalism coincided with Irish discontent and revolution abroad.[24] For many of the propertied classes, we are told, the

---

21. The most important texts, from which the summary in the next two paragraphs is drawn, are Silver, 'The Demand for Order', pp. 3-4; Ignatieff, *A Just Measure*, p. 210; R. D. Storch, 'The Plague of the Blue Locusts. Police Reform and Popular Resistance in Northern England, 1840-57', *International Review of Social History*, vol. 20, 1975, p. 62; idem, 'Policing Rural Southern England before the Police' in D. Hay and F. Snyder (eds.), *Policing and Prosecution in Britain 1750-1850* (Oxford, 1989), pp. 262-63; D. Philips, '"A Just Measure of Crime, Authority, Hunters and Blue Locusts." The "Revisionist" Social History of Crime and the Law in Britain, 1780-1850' in S. Cohen & A. Scull (eds.), *Social Control and the State* (Oxford, 1986), pp. 63-65; C. Emsley, *Crime and Society in England 1750-1900* (London, 1987), pp. 58-59; V. A. C. Gatrell, 'The Decline of Theft and Violence in Victorian and Edwardian England' in Gatrell et al, *Crime and the Law*, p. 272; idem, 'Crime, authority and the policeman-state' in F. M. L. Thompson (ed.), *The Cambridge Social History of Britain 1750-1950* (Cambridge, 1990), vol. 3, pp. 249-51.

22. The population of London rose as follows: 1801, 1 million; 1830, 1.5 million; 1846, 2.25 million.

23. Cf. Stuart Woolf (ed.), *Domestic strategies: work and family in France and Italy 1600-1800* (Cambridge, 1991), pp. 198-99.

24. See J. Saville, *1848. The British State and the Chartist Movement*

decay of order not only presaged a rising incidence of crime, but also threatened political catastrophe. In their obsession with the 'dangerous and labouring classes', the propertied amalgamated different kinds of dread – depredation and confiscation, robbery and revolution – and different social strata. Practically the whole of the non-respectable poor was 'criminalised' and collectivised. Finally, the imminent collapse of civilisation at the hands of the 'dangerous and labouring classes' was exploited to great effect by police and prison reformers to scare the ruling classes into abandoning the inadequate police and penal strategies of old.

An undoubted influence on the interpretation of the early nineteenth century in terms of the threat of social revolution has been Louis Chevalier's history of change in the perceptions of crime and disorder in Paris. Chevalier argued that the human invasion of Paris led to acute overcrowding, disease, poverty and starvation. Large swathes of the urban workforce turned to crime or revolution to express an alienation that was rooted in these fundamental biological realities. The result was that Paris became a city in which crime no longer existed on the margins of society, but permeated the mass of the poor. The 'classes laborieuses' rubbed shoulders with the criminals of the 'classes dangereuses'; indeed they became virtually indistinguishable. Vice and poverty, the underworld and the world of labour, were utterly confused.[25] If historians have contested Chevalier's linkage of criminal and revolutionary violence – holding rather that the combatants of 1830 or 1848 were skilled artisans, not the uprooted 'dangerous classes'[26] – they generally accept that bourgeois Parisians obsessively feared the 'dangerous and labouring classes'. Michel Foucault, most notably, confirmed that an increased overlap of politics and crime served

---

(Cambridge, 1987), p. 33.

---

25. Louis Chevalier, *Labouring Classes and Dangerous Classes in Paris During the First Half of the Nineteenth Century* (London, 1973), pp. 80-120 & 141-42.

26. See, e.g., George Rudé, *The Face of the Crowd. Studies in Revolution, Ideology and Popular Protest*, ed. by Harvey Kaye (Atlantic Highlands, 1988), pp. 233-38.

as a support for the 'great fear' of a people who were believed to be criminal and seditious as a whole, for the myth of a barbaric, immoral and outlaw class which, from the empire to the July Monarchy, haunted the discourse of legislators, philanthropists and investigators into working-class life.[27]

Historians of the British scene have too readily assumed that what was feared in Paris was also feared in London and the northern industrial towns. But was it like this? In the following section, I shall suggest (no more) that while the perceived need to re-constitute a stable and orderly society unquestionably underlay police and prison reform, the role of class fear has been exaggerated; that while it is possible to find statements which compare closely with those of Chevalier's informants, and of which historians of criminal justice have made the most, these are distinguished by their rarity. Few English observers saw a close connection between the 'dangerous' and labouring classes; few depicted a 'dangerous class' of subversive significance. Fears of an alliance between the criminal and working classes were neither as potent nor as pervasive as most British historians contend; by implication, class fear was less influential than commonly claimed in creating paid constabularies and the prison system. The evidence suggests, rather, that the Victorians saw in the marginal people among the urban poor – the vagrants, streetfolk, prostitutes, and thieves – the main danger to the social and moral order. Considered a problem less of collective social breakdown, however, than of deficient moral restraint, the pre-eminent response of the social and political thinkers of the early- to mid-nineteenth century was to fashion those distinctions for which the Victorians are justly renowned – the ragged, the pauper, the criminal – and to protect the honest and independent poor from the moral infection of these groups.

---

27. Michel Foucault, *Discipline and Punish. The Birth of the Prison* (London, 1977), p. 275. See also J. Merriman, *The Margins of City Life. Explorations on the French Urban Frontier, 1815-1851* (New York, 1991), pp. 14-15.

II

Colquhoun expected his dire warnings to be taken more seriously once the war against France was over, and when, he predicted, the 'phalanx of delinquents' would be supplemented by discharged soldiers and sailors.[28] His forecast came true after 1815, to judge from the published figures of those committed to trial for indictable offences; data which doubtless fuelled the post-war anxiety about a steep increase in crime.[29] Moreover, crime advanced in tandem with political unrest. Once the restraint of war-time patriotism was removed, a working-class Reform movement arose, and assumed revolutionary proportions before the 'Peterloo Massacre' of 1819 led to its abatement.[30] In such times of popular agitation and political turmoil, Colquhoun's alarum also found its seconders. William L. Bowles, chaplain to the Prince Regent and a Wiltshire magistrate, traced 'the dreadful Increase of Crime' to the expansion of the 'pauper population', and to 'the alteration in the reasonings, feelings, and habits of mind, particularly in fermenting populous districts, in consequence of the French Revolution!'[31] Ten years later, the conservative poet and historian, Robert Southey, had the ghost of Sir Thomas More (representing tradition against the evils of modern life) warn that the defective state of 'police and order' would exact a high political price:

> [Y]ou have spirits among you who are labouring day and night to stir up a *bellum servile*, an insurrection like that of Wat Tyler, of the Jacquerie, and of the peasants in Germany . . . Imagine the infatuated and infuriated wretches, whom not Spitalfields, St. Giles's, and Pimlico alone, but all the lanes and alleys and cellars of the metropolis would pour out; . . . the lava floods from a volcano would be less destructive

---

28. Colquhoun, *Treatise on Police*, p. 563.

29. See Gatrell, 'Decline of Theft', p. 239; idem, 'Crime, authority and the policeman-state', pp. 250-51; Ignatieff, *A Just Measure*, pp. 153-58.

30. Harold Perkin, *The Origins of Modern English Society 1780-1880* (London, 1969), pp. 208-13. For the coincidence of 'normal' crime and political unrest, see D. Philips, *Crime and Authority in Victorian England. The Black Country 1835-1860* (London, 1977), p. 83.

31. William L. Bowles, *Thoughts on the Increase of Crimes, the Education of the Poor, and the National Schools* (London, 1819), pp. 6 & 12.

than the hordes whom your great cities and manufacturing districts
would vomit forth.[32]

Yet despite Southey's apocalyptic statement, the post-
Peterloo years were not ones in which the propertied classes,
even in London, seemed to worry much about a supposed
amorphous 'dangerous class', allied with sections of the labouring poor, and incited by political radicals. Rather, these
years were characterised by the emergence of the notion
(though not yet the phrase) of a 'criminal class', an hereditary
'race', distinct from those who worked for a living, impelled
by profligacy not unemployment, and to combat which a
permanent police was recommended. If the 1816 Committee
on Police could ask about 'that class of persons who ordinarily
commit crimes, meaning the poor and indigent', the 1828
Committee, in contrast, asked the Chief Magistrate, Sir
Richard Birnie, whether thieves were 'low artizans employed
in any trade or business' or 'a class distinct by themselves, who
do nothing but thieve', to which Birnie replied that they were
'trained up from what I may call juvenile delinquents', and
hence followed no trade.[33] Other magistrates concurred, as
did leaders of the radical movement. Francis Place's opinion
that thieves formed a separate class of the community is well
known; but John Wade also claimed that thieves 'are born
such, and it is their inheritance: they form a *caste* of themselves, having their peculiar slang, mode of thinking, habits,
and arts of living'.[34] This evidence is in keeping, finally, with
the view that the Metropolitan Police Act 1829 was passed in

---

32. Robert Southey, *Sir Thomas More: Or, Colloquies on the Progress and
    Prospects of Society* (London, 1829), vol. 1, p. 114.

33. *Report from the Committee on the State of the Police of the Metropolis*,
    P.P. 1816, V, p. 226 (evidence of John Gifford, senior magistrate,
    Worship St. Division); *Report from the Select Committee on the Police
    of the Metropolis*, P.P. 1828, VI (533), p. 45. See also George B.
    Mainwaring, *Observations on the Present State of the Police of the
    Metropolis* (London, 1821), p. 59; Randle Jackson, *Considerations on
    the Increase of Crime, and the degree of its extent* (London, 1828), p. 23.

34. John Wade, *A Treatise on the Police and Crimes of the Metropolis*
    (London, 1829), p. 158. For Place, see Brian Harrison, 'Traditions of
    Respectability in British Labour History', in idem, *Peaceable Kingdom*
    (Oxford, 1982), p. 191.

response to rising crime, as distinct from the fear of riot and the 'dangerous classes'.[35]

From 1829, an interpretation in terms of the threat of a subversive 'dangerous class' has a more convincing ring to it. In the next two years, the concurrent though separate movements of rural incendiarism ('Swing'), unemployment and the growth of trade unions, and an extra-parliamentary agitation demanding reform under threat of armed resistance, coming in the wake of revolution in France, and in conjunction with an outbreak of cholera, could not but refresh the imagery of an anarchic alliance of workmen and criminals.[36] The climax came with the reform riots of October 1831. Consider, for example, the reformer E. G. Wakefield's pamphlet, *Householders in Danger from the Populace*. Exploiting the fears aroused by the Bristol riots, Wakefield declared that London could be thrown into revolution by a conjunction between the 30,000 'common thieves', ever ready to sack the capital, 'the Rabble' – (some 60,000 poor and semi-criminal costers, drovers, brickmakers, scavengers, and low prostitutes), and the 'Desperadoes', or Owenite socialists, who would lead this 'populace' against the propertied.[37] Wakefield was probably recognized for what he was – a scaremonger out to frighten

---

35. Historians disagree on this issue. Some emphasize the role of riot and class fear (see Paley, 'Policing London Before Peel', p. 113; Hay & Snyder, *Policing and Prosecution*, p. 10), some the perception of increasing crime (Reynolds, 'The Night Watch', p. 16), while some hedge their bets and stress both (Philips, 'A New Engine', p. 182). See note 37 below for the role of riot in provincial police reform.

36. See G. Rudé, 'Why was there no Revolution in England in 1830 or 1848?' in idem, *The Face of the Crowd*, p. 150; Thompson, *Making*, p. 898; D. J. V. Jones, *Crime, protest, community and police in nineteenth-century Britain* (London, 1982), p. 17.

37. Edward Gibbon Wakefield, *Householders in Danger from the Populace* (London, n.d. Oct. 1831?), pp. 3-5. Cf. Thompson, *Making*, pp. 894-95. For the Bristol riots, see Joseph Hamburger, *James Mill and the Art of Revolution* (New Haven, 1963), p. 176; George Rudé, 'English Rural and Urban Disturbances on the Eve of the First Reform Bill, 1830-1831', *Past and Present*, no. 37, July 1967, p. 98; Mark Harrison, *Crowds and History. Mass Phenomena in English Towns, 1790-1835* (Cambridge, 1988), p. 303. Harrison also suggests (pp. 309-11) that the reform riots convinced many outside (if not within) Bristol of the case for provincial police reform, which the 1835 Municipal Reform Act introduced.

the landed elite into conceding reform; his 'dangerous class', moreover, was drawn from the marginal sections of London society, and never ascends beyond the street-folk.[38] But his minatory language doubtless fed alarm concerning what radicals, criminals and the under-employed might jointly do.

Against the fears of an overlap between the labouring and dangerous classes during the Reform crisis must be set the 1834 Poor Law, the conclusions of the statistical societies, and the *Constabulary Report* of 1839: the first contributed to the project of dividing the labouring from the 'dangerous classes', the latter two reinforced the portrayal of a distinct criminal class. The Poor Law Commission grew out of the long-standing debate on how best to halt the 'pauperism' (the state of dependence upon public authorities) of the labouring classes, a pauperism that, it was felt, led to crime. The *Poor Law Report* and subsequent Poor Law Amendment Act aimed to diminish the pauperisation of the labouring classes by fencing off the 'independent poor' from the workhouse pauper, thus promoting 'moral restraint' among the former. If the law had the side effect of making paupers feel like criminals (workhouses were not known as 'bastilles' for nothing), and hence of unintentionally shaping a 'dangerous class' of paupers and criminals, it also withdrew a significant section of the labouring poor from the taint of pauperism and crime and facilitated their eventual integration into the 'moral consensus'.[39]

In their surveys of the social ills of industrialization, the statistical societies increasingly absolved the factory system, placing the blame instead on moral degeneracy and the growth of cities. Crime was ascribed to the moral condition of individuals (idleness, intemperance), not to economic want; and it was linked to the existence of an hereditary criminal class.[40] Edwin Chadwick was equally convinced that crimes

---

38. Joseph Hamburger, *James Mill and the Art of Revolution*, pp. 70-73.

39. See Himmelfarb, *Idea of Poverty*, ch. VI.

40. See E. Yeo, 'Social Science and Social Change: A Social History of Some Aspects of Social Science and Social Investigation in Britain, 1830-1890', Ph.D. thesis, Sussex University, 1972, pp. 88-102; Randall E. McGowen, 'Rethinking Crime: Changing Attitudes Towards Law-Breakers in Eighteenth and Nineteenth-Century England', Ph.D.

against property were not primarily caused by 'blameless poverty or destitution', but by the criminal's rational estimate of the profitability of 'a career of depredation'. Most crime, he thought, was committed by a class of 'habitual depredators', migratory in habit.[41] Accordingly, the *Constabulary Report* called for a rural police force to assist in making a life of crime less profitable than honest labour. Chadwick was well-versed in the ways of alarming his readers, but unlike Colquhoun (whose inflated estimates of 'malefactors' Chadwick tried to correct), he rarely if ever attempted to construct an image of a 'dangerous class' of indigent and criminal, or to link 'habitual depredators' with the trade union or Chartist movements, despite his concern to catalogue the strikes and violence of organized operatives.[42] One is left with the feeling that Chadwick's reforming vision was shaped by a determination to ensure that crime did not undermine the motive to industry on the part of the labouring poor, not by fear of a subversive dangerous class. And, again, this evidence corresponds with the generally accepted view that the Rural Police Act 1839 owed its origin to the grudging recognition on the part of the rural gentry that a new police would better maintain the daily peace, not to the fear of an alliance between criminals and 'physical force' Chartists.[43]

thesis, Illinois University, 1979, pp. 202-03; Lawrence Goldman, 'The Origins of British "Social Science". Political Economy, Natural Science and Statistics, 1830-1835', *Historical Journal*, vol. 26, 1983, pp. 589-90.

41. *First Report of the Commissioners appointed to inquire as to the best Means of establishing an efficient Constabulary Force in the Counties of England and Wales*, P.P. 1839, XIX (169), p. 73. Chadwick's associate, W. A. Miles, did much to promote the image of criminals as 'a Race "sui generis", different from the rest of Society': *Second Report from the Select Committee of the House of Lords appointed to inquire into the Present State of the Several Gaols and Houses of Correction in England and Wales*, P.P. 1835, XI (439), p. 583. See also PRO, HO 73/16, papers of W. A. Miles.

42. Cf. Himmelfarb, *Idea of Poverty*, pp. 383-4 & 397. See also A. P. Donajgrodzki, '"Social Police" and the Bureaucratic Elite: A Vision of Order in the Age of Reform' in idem, *Social Control in Nineteenth Century Britain* (London, 1977), pp. 65-67.

43. Cf. A. Brundage, 'Ministers, Magistrates and Reformers: The Genesis

Belief in 'the existence of a class of persons who pursue crime as a calling', expressed by Matthew Davenport Hill, Recorder of Birmingham, in his July 1839 charge to the grand jury, was, it is clear, firmly rooted in middle-class discourse before the vocabulary of 'les classes dangereuses' arrived.[44] How, then, was the French formulation received in England? In the early 1840s, Honore Frégier's *Des classes dangereuses* was reviewed, although not widely, in the quarterly press.[45] Henry Milton in the *Quarterly Review* emphasised Frégier's assumption that 'it is from the poor and vicious of the *operative classes* that the criminal portion of the community is chiefly recruited', while the reviewer for the *Athenaeum* was struck by how in cities, 'poverty and crime, which should have no necessary connexion, are so inextricably intermingled as to be perpetually mistaken the one for the other'.[46] French example had the greatest impact on the historian, staunch tory, and sheriff of Lanarkshire, Archibald Alison. His articles in *Blackwood's Edinburgh Magazine* in 1844 represent the high water mark of British attention to the political consequences of what Alison called 'this prodigious and unrestrained increase of crime and depravity among the working classes in the manufacturing districts', which, he alleged, would so multiply '"les classes dangereuses" as they have been well denominated by the French, as, on the first serious political convulsion, may come to endanger the

---

of the Rural Constabulary Act of 1839', *Parliamentary History*, vol. 5, 1986, p. 62. Charles Dickens' *Oliver Twist* (1837-38) probably reinforced the image of a criminal milieu, separate from that inhabited by the labouring poor, separate even from that of the workhouse pauper.

---

44. M. D. Hill, *Suggestions for the Repression of Crime contained in Charges delivered to Grand Juries of Birmingham* (London, 1857), p. 7.

45. The full title of Frégier's social survey was *Des Classes dangereuses de la Population dans les Grandes Villes, et des Moyens de les rendre meilleures* (Paris, 1840), 2 vols. Frégier was a bureau chief in the headquarters of the Paris police. In a study which had the dangerous classes as its brief, Frégier found himself unable to delineate clearly the labouring from the dangerous classes. See Chevalier, *Labouring Classes*, pp. 141-42.

46. *Quarterly Review*, vol. LXX, June 1842, pp. 1-44; *Athenaeum*, 4 April 1840, pp. 267-91.

state.'[47] Urban and mining populations were especially de-moralized, in Alison's opinion, by strikes that kept the la-bouring poor idle. He had in mind the Plug riots in England and the strikes in Scotland in 1842, the latter requiring Alison's personal intervention at the head of a band of soldiers and police.[48] He was particularly pained by the fact that nothing was being done to remedy the evils:

> Meanwhile, destitution, profligacy, sensuality, and crime, advance with unheard-of rapidity in the manufacturing districts, and the dangerous classes there massed together combine every three or four years in some general strike or alarming insurrection.[49]

These statements have been used by historians to suggest that the forties witnessed a 'criminalization' of the entire body of non-respectable urban poor, and to argue that the Vic-torians lumped together the 'criminal class', the 'pauper', and the 'labouring poor'. The times were certainly ripe for such an amalgam, particularly in London. Migrants flooded into the capital in the 1840s, one in six from Ireland, many of whom fetched up in unskilled labouring jobs. In 1848, London was hit by depression, cholera paid another grim visit, Ireland and the Continent were turbulent, and metropolitan Chartism was at its most insurrectionary.[50] Predictably, Alison's fears found an echo of sorts in the capital. In 1847, Captain William John Williams, a prison inspector, told a House of Lords Committee that had transportation been stopped some years

47. *Blackwood's Edinburgh Magazine*, vol. LV, May 1844, pp. 544-45.

48. See Sir Archibald Alison, 1792-1867, *D.N.B.*, vol. 1 (London, 1968), p. 288.

49. *Blackwood's Edinburgh Magazine*, vol. LVI, July 1844, p. 2. The first example of 'dangerous classes' in the Oxford English Dictionary (O.E.D.) is from Sir Arthur Helps, *Friends in Council*, ser. II (London, 1859), vol. 1, p. 131: 'I admit that in most of the European nations there are dangerous classes, dangerous because uncared for and uneducated; but surely there is no state in Europe in which an army of one hundred thousand soldiers could not keep down the dangerous classes, if the bulk of the people were reasonably well affected to the government.'

50. See Lynn Lees, 'Metropolitan Types. London and Paris compared' in H. J. Dyos and M. Wolff (eds.), *The Victorian City* (London, 1973), vol. 1, pp. 414-15; D. Goodway, *London Chartism, 1838-1848* (Cambridge, 1982), pp. 68-69; Saville, *1848*, pp. 93 & 96-99.

back, the condition of London 'would have been similar to Paris; for we know that a criminal Population collected together in Hordes are always ready Instruments of popular Violence'.[51] Edmund Antrobus warned that London Chartists, 'whose ranks are always swelled by a vast proportion of the 30,000 idlers and thieves which infest the town', were said to be arming.[52] For some, clearly, the Chartist, rioter and petty criminal were indivisible.

Yet even in the forties, and even in London, where a huge concentration of urban poverty stood adjacent to the largest concentration of wealth and property of any European city, the imagery of an Archibald Alison was more than offset by the beginnings of a debate on juvenile delinquency, and by statements that cautioned against an indiscriminate amalgamation of different social strata. Sir Charles Shaw, for example, the Manchester police chief, insisted in 1843 that the classes which figured in the criminal statistics 'must not be confounded with the Working Classes, for the former consist of what the French call "Les Classes Dangereuses."'[53] Even Alison took comfort from the fact that 'nine-tenths of the crime, and nearly all the professional crime' came from the lowest class – 'this dismal substratum, this hideous *black band of society*'.[54] His view was unchanged when rioting broke out in Glasgow in March 1848. The disturbances left 'the most respectable of the working people' untouched; they were caused, he informed the Home Office, by 'Chartist oratory working on the passions of the unemployed', but no subversive intent was evident, 'except in the very lowest and most depraved class in which it is synonymous with the wish for

51. *Second Report from the Select Committee of the House of Lords appointed to inquire into the Execution of the Criminal Law, especially respecting Juvenile Offenders and Transportation*, PP. 1847, VII (534), q. 2720, p. 300.

52. Edmund Edward Antrobus, *London, Its Danger and Its Safety* (London, 1848), p. 16.

53. *Manufacturing Districts. Replies of Sir Charles Shaw to Lord Ashley M.P. regarding the Education, and Moral and Physical Condition of the Labouring Classes* (London, 1843), pp. 20 & 23.

54. *Blackwood's*, vol. LVI, July 1844, p. 12.

Plunder'.[55] Here we seem closer to the saturnalia of crime portrayed by Dickens in *Barnaby Rudge* (1841) or to the brutalized, degraded outcasts of Disraeli's *Sybil* (1845) and Reynolds' *The Mysteries of London* (1845-48) than to political revolution. There are important distinctions, then, which historians need to respect, between Alison's 'dangerous classes . . . [who] combine every three or four years in some general strike or alarming insurrection' and Dickens' 'scum and refuse of London, whose growth was fostered by bad criminal laws, bad prison regulations, and the worst conceivable police'.[56] Dickens' fear of urban revolt essentially came down to a criminal class, a species apart, living in isolated 'rookeries', overshadowed by the new police and the new penitentiaries. In this matter, Charles Dickens' vision was in accord with the dominant contemporary discourse.

III

In the aftermath of Chartism, and in an era of greater economic and political stability, the 'dangerous classes' were subjected to further classification. They were no longer endowed with any subversive potential; nor were they seen, except very intermittently, to pose a problem of disorder at all. Lawyers, charity workers, and social investigators turned their attention instead to the presentation of an increasingly detailed taxonomy of what was now called the 'criminal classes', and to its embodiment in institutional and legislative forms. In the minds of many mid-Victorians, the 'dangerous classes' became practically synonymous with the 'criminal classes', a body supposedly separated by a deep moral and social gulf from the honest labouring poor, and needing to be ever-more constrained by the instruments of criminal justice.

The vocabulary of the 'dangerous classes' did not, of course, disappear overnight. The slum life literature of the 1850s continued to take readers on tours of the 'swamps' and 'wilds' of London, where felons, prostitutes, tramps, and 'the

---

55. Cited in Saville, *1848*, pp. 254-55, note 30.

56. Charles Dickens, *Barnaby Rudge* (London, 1991), p. 441; G. W. M. Reynolds, *The Mysteries of London* (London, 1846), vol. II, pp. 187-89. For Disraeli, see L. Cazamian, *The Social Novel in England 1830-1850* (London, 1973), pp. 203-5.

hordes of Irish' lurked, ready to issue forth at times of popular
rebellion; and where 'the honest and the hard-working labourer' was compelled to live among and be infected by these
'dangerous classes'.[57] Even that quintessential text of mid-
century optimism, *Meliora*, contained a description of the
'substratum of society', composed of paupers and criminals,
'the throes and the heavings' of which might one day occasion
society's overthrow.[58] Nor were more sober analysts of the
crime problem yet exempt from using the terminology in its
widest sense. Thomas Beggs, whose *idée fixe* was the evil
influence of intemperance, opened his 1849 enquiry into
'juvenile depravity' with an estimate of the numbers of the
'dangerous class' – 'comprising thieves, paupers, vagrants,
prostitutes, imposters, and mendicants'.[59] Such statements,
however, were eye-catching prefaces to studies which, like
many others between 1846 and 1852, identified what Mary
Carpenter called the 'perishing and dangerous classes' (or
incipient and actual delinquents), a group roaming the streets
like 'city arabs' and, claimed Lord Ashley, 'distinct from the
ordinary poor'.[60]

It was through this coterie of specialists, and particularly
their first conference in Birmingham in late 1851, which met
to consider the question of preventive and reformatory
schools, that the actual term 'criminal class' entered 'crimi-
nological' parlance.[61] The accolade of 'semantic' forerunner,

---

57. See, e.g., Thomas Beames, *The Rookeries of London* (London, 1850),
    pp. 119-20 & 209-14.

58. Viscount Ingestre (ed.), *Meliora: Or Better Times to Come* (London,
    1853), p. 21.

59. Thomas Beggs, *An Inquiry into the Extent and Causes of Juvenile
    Depravity* (London, 1849), p. 26. Cf. Jelinger C. Symons, *Tactics for the
    Times: as regards the Condition and Treatment of the Dangerous Classes*
    (London, 1849), p. 1.

60. Mary Carpenter, *Reformatory Schools, for the Children of the Perishing
    and Dangerous Classes and for Juvenile Offenders* (London, 1851);
    Report from the Select Committee on Criminal and Destitute Juveniles,
    P.P. 1852, VII (515), p. 98; 3 *Hansard* XCIX, 6 June 1848, col. 431
    (Ashley).

61. See S. J. Stevenson, 'The "criminal class" in the mid-Victorian city: a
    study of policy conducted with special reference to those made subject
    to the Provisions of 34 & 35 Vict., c. 112 (1871) in Birmingham and East

however, probably belongs to Leeds reformer, Thomas Plint. Over one-third of the crime of large towns, said Plint in 1851, could be traced to the 'criminal class', whose origin and natural history urgently needed investigation. A number of fallacies had to be abandoned. The 'criminal class' was not a product of the factory system; it was not recruited from the ranks of industrial workers.

> May it not be said of the class that it is *in* the community, but neither *of* it, nor *from* it? Is it not the fact that a large majority of the class is so by descent, and stands as completely isolated from the other classes, in blood, in sympathies, in its domestic and social organization . . . as it is hostile to them in the whole '*ways and means*' of its temporal existence?[62]

The 'criminal class', said Plint, was a '*pariah* and exotic tribe', morally distinct from the 'operative classes':

> No exact analysis of crime can be obtained, until the exact proportion of this class to the indigenous and really working population . . . which is separate and distinct from what must be considered a foreign, or, . . . a non-indigenous body – is ascertained.[63]

Plint was intent to concentrate crime within a clearly demarcated section of the urban community: the 'criminal or dangerous classes'.

Plint reminds anyone familiar with the *Communist Manifesto* (1848) of the 'dangerous class', the 'ragged proletariat' or 'lumpenproletariat' of Marx and Engels. The comments made by these two political thinkers on the lowest stratum of urban society had little or no influence on the mid-Victorian mind, since they only became available in translation years later. But it surely enhances the credibility of bourgeois social attitudes and categorization to recognise that Marx and Engels followed them closely. Engels' view of crime as a primitive form of insurrection, the earliest phase of the 'social war', inscribed in his study of the English working class in the mid-forties, quickly gave way to the view that criminals, vagrants

London in the early years of registration and supervision', D. Phil. thesis, 1983, p. 1.

---

62. Thomas Plint, *Crime in England. Its Relation, Character, and Extent as developed from 1801 to 1848* (London, 1851), p. 153.

63. Ibid., p. 122. Cf. Rev. J. Edgar, *The Dangerous and Perishing Classes* (Belfast, 1852).

and prostitutes formed a 'dangerous class', 'which in all big
towns forms a mass sharply differentiated from the industrial
proletariat', indeed even from the lowest pauper classes, and
which was a danger to the working-class struggle since it could
be 'bought' by counter-revolutionary forces.[64] The contempt
displayed by Marx and Engels for the 'lumpenproletariat'
stemmed partly, of course, from their theoretical commitment to the 'working proletariat'.[65] But their description of
the 'lumpen', depicting it even as a nomadic tribe or race,
bears a striking resemblance to the bourgeois depiction of a
foreign and exotic world within urban society.[66] As such, the
Marxist concept of the 'lumpenproletariat' paralleled contemporary social categorization, and likewise, albeit for different reasons, drew a strict line of demarcation between the
working and dangerous classes.

It was Henry Mayhew, much more than Marx, who fashioned the mid-Victorian image of the 'dangerous classes'. In
London Labour and the London Poor (1861-2), Mayhew
concentrated on the street-folk, mostly street sellers or tot-
ters, who were an atavistic 'wandering tribe', with their own
physiognomy, moral conventions and mode of life. The first
three volumes of *London Labour* dealt with those who
earned an honest livelihood; the final volume examined those
'which are in reality the dangerous classes, the idle, the
profligate, and the criminal'.[67] In this volume, and in *The
Criminal Prisons of London* (1862), Mayhew offered 'a scien-

---

64. F. Engels, *The Condition of the Working Class in England*
(Harmondsworth, 1987), pp. 156 & 224; *The Communist Manifesto*
(Harmondsworth, 1987), p. 92; K. Marx, *Capital* (London, 1928), p.
711. See also H. Draper, 'The Concept of the "Lumpenproletariat" in
Marx and Engels', *Economies et societes*, vol. 6, 1972, p. 2294.

65. See P. Q. Hirst, 'Marx and Engels on law, crime and morality',
Economy and Society, vol. 1, 1972, pp. 40-41.

66. See R. L. Bussard, 'The "Dangerous Class" of Marx and Engels: The
Rise of the Idea of the "Lumpenproletariat"', *History of European
Ideas*, vol. 8, 1987, p. 687; P. Stallybras, 'Marx and Heterogeneity:
Thinking the Lumpenproletariat', *Representations*, no. 31, 1990, pp.
70-72.

67. H. Mayhew & J. Binny, *The Criminal Prisons of London* (London,
1862), opening advertisement. See also K. Williams, *From pauperism
to poverty* (London, 1981), pp. 260-62.

tific classification of the criminal classes'. Criminals were divisible, he said, into two classes, the habitual and the casual; habituals committed burglary, robbery, and larceny from the person, all of which were 'regular crafts requiring almost the same apprenticeships as any other mode of life.'[68] As for causes, Mayhew rejected the ones commonly advanced – drink, ignorance, poverty and vagrancy – and instead echoed the *Constabulary Report*, in thinking that crime was due 'to that innate love of a life of ease, and aversion to hard work'. Thus, Mayhew built on the base of Chadwick's 1839 Report, which he considered still 'the most trustworthy and practical treatise on the criminal classes'[69], to construct an image of

> a large class, so to speak, which belongs to a criminal race, living in particular districts of society . . . these people have bred, until at last you have persons who come into the world as criminals, and go out as criminals, and they know nothing else.[70]

This was an image of the criminal problem that reached its apogee in the 1860s.

In the sixties, periodical articles dealing with crime and punishment were crop-full of references to the 'criminal classes'. One reason for this was that the end of the system of transportation, and the new task, as an essayist put it, 'of washing our foul linen at home', forced a major re-appraisal of the 'convict question'.[71] Another factor was that from 1857 the judicial statistics included tables on the numbers of 'known thieves and depredators, receivers of stolen goods, prostitutes, vagrants, etc.', in each police district; these data lent credibility to the notion of an identifiable class of criminals.[72] Thirdly, the public panic caused by a rash of violent robberies in London in 1862, which the press and parliament blamed on convicts released on licence (or tickets-of-leave),

---

68. Ibid., pp. 45 & 87.

69. Ibid., pp. 84 & 386.

70. *Second Report from the Select Committee on Transportation*, P.P. 1856, XVII (296), q. 3531, p. 343. Cf. *Criminal Prisons*, pp. 89 & 413.

71. 'How to deal with the Dangerous Classes', *Leisure Hour*, 1 January 1869, p. 54.

72. See V. A. C. Gatrell & T. B. Hadden, 'Criminal Statistics and their interpretation' in E. A. Wrigley (ed.)), *Nineteenth Century Society* (Cambridge, 1972), p. 348.

magnified the image of a separate 'criminal class'.[73] And finally, the Punishment and Reformation section of the newly-founded Social Science Association, made up of lawyers, prison administrators, and penologists, fixed its investigative gaze on the study and treatment of the 'criminal class'.[74]

Two different, not to say contradictory, images of the 'criminal class' are present in this literature. The first is of a group of rational, calculating, 'habitual criminals', whose organization, according to William Pare, 'is as complete . . . as that of any other class in society, both in their business and social arrangements'. The practices of this business were governed 'by the selfsame economic principles that govern ordinary trading operations'. There were operatives (the thieves) trained to the craft from an early age, there was a division of labour ('mobsmen', 'shofulmen'), and there were capitalists (landlords, receivers) whose money was the 'lifeblood of the system'.[75]

The second image of the 'criminal class' was of an irrational, degenerate 'race', marked by distinct physical and mental traits. While Mayhew described 'a criminal race', James Greenwood evoked 'a wily, cunning man-wolf', and Mary Carpenter discovered 'a peculiar low expression, unlike that of the labouring portion of society'.[76] The view that the

---

73. See J. Davis, 'The London Garotting Panic of 1862: A Moral Panic and the Creation of a Criminal Class in mid-Victorian England' in Gatrell et al, *Crime and the Law*, pp. 190-91 & 212; R. Sindall, *Street Violence in the Nineteenth Century: Media Panic or Real Danger?* (Leicester, 1990), passim.

74. See L. Goldman, 'The Social Science Association, 1857-1886: a context for mid-Victorian Liberalism', *English Historical Review*, vol. CI, 1986, p. 99. L. Radzinowicz and R. Hood in *A History of English Criminal Law* (London, 1986), vol. 5, pp. 73-84, examine the 'criminal classes', but their account relies substantially on Kellow Chesney's *The Victorian Underworld* (Harmondsworth, 1976), which in turn drew heavily on Henry Mayhew.

75. William Pare, 'A Plan for the Suppression of the Predatory Classes', *Transactions of the National Association for the Promotion of Social Science*, 1862, p. 474; Edwin Hill, *Criminal Capitalists* (London, 1872).

76. *Second Report from S.C. on Transportation*, p. 343; J. Greenwood, *The Seven Curses of London* (London, 1869), p. 86; H. Martineau, 'Life in

'criminal class' was 'as distinctly marked off from the honest industrial operative as "black-faced sheep are from the Cheviot breed"', was firmly endorsed in the 1870s by many prison officials. Dr. Bruce Thomson, resident surgeon at Perth prison in Scotland, described 'a set of demi-civilized savages, who in hordes prey upon society . . . and, only connecting themselves with those of their own nature and habits, . . . must beget a depraved and criminal class hereditarily disposed to crime'.[77] Lieut.-Col. Edmund Du Cane, the man in charge of the convict prison system, pondered the suggestion of Dr. Gover, surgeon of Millbank prison, that habitual criminals and vagrants 'are examples of the race reverting to some inferior type . . . the type of what Professor Darwin calls "our arboreal ancestors"', a view that the use of photography in penal administration seemed to authenticate.[78] This medical and biological discourse came to fruition in Cesare Lombroso's theory of 'l'uomo delinquente' or the 'born criminal'. The theory *qua* theory gained few adherents in Britain, but the language of degeneration prevailed, thereby buttressing assumptions about the existence of a 'criminal class'.[79]

IV

As befitted practical workers in the realm of criminal justice, the authors of much of this literature proposed taking what they saw as the 'war against crime' to the enemy. 'Criminals may be considered like a hostile army which is engaged in carrying on war against society', said Du Cane in his 1875 address to the Social Science Association, 'and the law lays

the Criminal Class', *Edinburgh Review*, vol. 122, October 1865, p. 342 (quoting Carpenter).

77. James Bruce Thomson, 'The Hereditary Nature of Crime', *Journal of Mental Science*, vol. XV, January 1870, pp. 489-90.

78. E.F. Du Cane, 'Address on the Repression of Crime', *Trans. NAPSS*, 1875, pp. 302-3.

79. See Daniel Pick, *Faces of Degeneration. A European Disorder, c.1848-c.1918* (Cambridge, 1989), pp. 182-83. See also W. D. Morrison, *Crime and its Causes* (London, 1891), p. 198.

down the plan of the campaign against them'.[80] In the treatment of habitual criminals, he continued,

> very great advances have been made of late years; we have in principle recognised the existence of a criminal class, and directed the operations of the law towards checking the development of that class, or bringing those who belong to it under special control.[81]

Already in 1868, in discussion of Sir Walter Crofton's address on the 'criminal classes' to the S.S.A., Lord Houghton had posed the rhetorical question:

> Was it possible for any person to go about with the police through the criminal portions of London without saying that these dangerous classes were as completely in the hands of the police – as completely watched every hour of their life as they could be in any way whatever?

The very residential concentration of these 'dangerous classes', Houghton observed, 'gave the police absolute power over them'.[82] These statements alert us to the need to examine the degree to which the law and its administration assisted the creation of both the stereotype of the 'criminal class' and the life histories or criminal careers that exemplified the stereotype.

It is apparent from the research of the past fifteen years that, whatever Victorians thought, very few Victorian criminals were full-time 'professionals'. Most crimes were committed by ordinary working people who supplemented their meagre income with thefts of food, fuel or clothing. Nor were most offenders different in social and cultural stamp from the bulk of the 'honest poor'.[83] Yet this research also reveals how public perceptions and attitudes interacted with law enforcement strategies to reinforce the notion of a 'criminal class'. An axiom of policing history is that the day-time patrolling of the Victorian police sought to impose a new standard of social discipline. More strictly, the police used their discretionary powers under the Vagrancy Act 1824 and the Metropolitan

---

80. Du Cane, 'Address', p. 272. See also McGowen, 'Rethinking Crime', p. 285.

81. Ibid., p. 275. See also M. D. Hill, *Suggestions*, pp. 155-56; W. Crofton, *The Present Aspect of the Convict Question* (London, 1864), pp. 15-20.

82. See discussion of W. Crofton, 'Address on the Criminal Classes and their Control', *Trans. NAPSS*, 1868, p. 306.

83. See Philips, *Crime and Authority*, chs. 6-8; Jones, *Crime, protest*, ch. 4.

Police Act 1839 to intensify the supervision of members of marginal street economies (costers, hawkers, prostitutes), ragged children and juveniles, and vagrants. Most of those arrested or summoned for non-indictable crimes throughout the entire nineteenth century were deemed to be drunks, prostitutes or vagrants.[84] Historians are beginning to question whether the police had the manpower or willpower to attack working-class street life so vigorously, and to uncover judicial opposition to police campaigns against barrow-boys or prostitutes.[85] Yet it does seem that urban policing responded to the stereotype of the 'criminal and dangerous classes' by targeting the economically marginal elements, whose lives were lived in the street, and the 'rookeries' of crime and vice.[86] Studies of juvenile crime and of prostitution reveal how the police assisted in the transformation of delinquents and street-walkers into identifiable outcast groups.[87] The notion of a distinct 'criminal area' provided a map for the police to locate the crime problem. The more the police focused on these communities, the more the detection and hence the apparent incidence of crime increased, thus confirming the emerging perception of these areas and their inhabitants. In

84. See Storch, 'The Plague of the Blue Locusts', p. 84; Goodway, *London Chartism*, pp. 103-4; C. Steedman, *Policing the Victorian Community* (London, 1984), pp. 56-59.

85. J. Davis, 'A Poor Man's System of Justice: The London Police Courts in the Second Half of the Nineteenth Century', *Historical Journal*, vol. 27, 1984, p. 328; S. Inwood, 'Policing London's Morals: The Metropolitan Police and Popular Culture, 1829-1850', *London Journal*, vol. 15, 1990, pp. 129-44.

86. See J. Davis, 'From "Rookeries" to "Communities": Race, Poverty and Policing in London, 1850-1985', *History Workshop*, issue 27, 1989, pp. 68-70; idem, 'Jennings' Buildings and the Royal Borough. The construction of the underclass in mid-Victorian England' in D. Feldman & G. Stedman Jones (eds.), *Metropolis. London* (London, 1989), pp. 11-31; idem, 'Urban Policing and its Objects: Comparative Themes in England and France in the Second Half of the Nineteenth Century' in C. Emsley and B. Weinberger (eds.), *Policing Western Europe* (New York, 1991), pp. 9-14.

87. S. Margarey, 'The Invention of Juvenile Delinquency in Early Nineteenth-Century England', *Labour History*, no. 34, 1978, pp. 17-24; J. Walkowitz, *Prostitution and Victorian Society* (Cambridge, 1980), ch. 10.

these ways, the police played a part in 'making' a criminal or outcast class, which public ideology had first fashioned.[88]

Did mass imprisonment likewise create an identified 'delinquent' group? Michel Foucault would have said that it did. Prison, he argued, manufactures delinquents, both by the study of the criminal type, whose pathological character and habitat distinguishes him from the non-delinquent, and by converting offenders into recidivists or career criminals (the subsequent object of police surveillance). This served the crucial political purpose, Foucault maintained, of driving a wedge between the criminal and working classes. Foucault argued, indeed, that the prison's only true success was in constructing a 'criminal class', with a monopoly on crime, and one distinct from and shunned by the working-class community.[89] The evidence for all this is not overwhelming. Repeated imprisonment, with restrictions on visits, letters and other forms of outside contact, may well have served to isolate the criminal from his family, neighbourhood and class. The penal regimes of the time, moreover, in undermining the physical and mental health of prisoners and in releasing them ill-equipped to find work, consigned them to the 'lumpenproletariat'. But these are more the *un*intended consequences of imprisonment. It seems unlikely that the creation of a 'criminal class' was a deliberate ploy in a strategy of 'divide and conquer'. A more plausible thesis is that the prisoner identified with the 'inmate subculture', emerging from incarceration as a confirmed 'ex-convict', condemned to membership of the social 'residuum'.[90]

But what of the policy to punish and supervise the habitual criminal, a policy encouraged by the violent robbery or 'garotting' panic of 1862? The Royal Commission on Penal

---

88. The weight of policing continues to bear more heavily on the social 'residuum' or 'underclass', whom the police invidiously term the 'slag' or 'scum', and whom they persist in seeing as their main clientele: D. J. Smith & J. Gray, *Police and People in London* (Aldershot, 1985), pp. 120 & 434-36.

89. Foucault, *Discipline and Punish*, part 4, chs. 1-2. Cf. Ignatieff, 'A Critique', pp. 172-73.

90. See D. Garland, *Punishment and Welfare. A history of penal strategies* (Aldershot, 1985), p. 39; idem, *Punishment and Modern Society. A Study in Social Theory* (Chicago, 1990), p. 173.

Servitude of 1863 identified 'a class of persons who are so inveterately addicted to dishonesty, and so averse to labour', that there was no chance of their abstaining from a life of crime.[91] Hence, the Penal Servitude Act of 1864 provided for mandatory, monthly reporting to the police by ticket-of-leave men, and gave the police power to arrest any licence holder suspected of having committed a crime, or having broken a condition of his licence. The next step was to extend such surveillance to the larger number of habituals released from local prisons. Under the 1869 Act (as amended by the Prevention of Crimes Act 1871), any person twice convicted of a felony and sentenced to imprisonment (as distinct from penal servitude) could be subject to police supervision for seven years. This legislation also inaugurated a system of registration and identification of a 'criminal class' of habituals.[92]

Enforcement of these Acts was decidedly spotty. In London the law was null and void, since the stipendiary magistrates called upon the Commissioner of Police in person to inform the court each time a licence holder failed to report to the police. The metropolitan police had a difficult time supervising criminals who were, claimed the Police Commissioner, 'a most migratory class'.[93] The register of every person convicted of felony – and by 1876 there were almost 180,000 persons in it – was so bulky as to be beyond monitoring. Even the slimmer Register of Habitual Criminals, with some 7-8,000 names in twelve volumes, was 'perfectly useless', according to a London detective superintendent.[94] It is safe to

91. *Report of the Commissioners appointed to inquire into the operation of the Acts relating to Transportation and Penal Servitude*, P.P. 1863, XXI (6457), p. 25 (para 36).

92. See M. W. Melling, 'Cleaning House in a Suddenly Closed Society: the Genesis, Brief Life and Untimely Death of the "Habitual Criminals Act, 1869"', *Osgoode Hall Law Journal*, vol. 21, 1983, p. 326; Radzinowicz & Hood, *History*, vol. 5, pp. 254-56.

93. PRO, HO 45/9442/66692, 'Report of the Departmental Commission to inquire into the Detective Force of the Metropolitan Police', January 1878, q. 5183, p. 208 (E. Henderson). See also S. J. Stevenson, 'The "habitual criminal" in nineteenth-century England: some observations on the figures', *Urban History Yearbook*, 1986, p. 48.

94. Ibid., q. 1860, p. 66 (J. Thomson). See also PRO, PRI. COM 2/404, Register of Habitual Criminals, 1869-76.

conclude only that the habitual criminals legislation strengthened the public perception that a 'criminal class' existed, and that by inhibiting the re-integration of the hardened criminal into working-class life (doing for habitual criminals what the Contagious Diseases Acts of the 1860s did for the common prostitute), it gave some substance to this perception.[95]

V

In the mid-Victorian years, the 'dangerous classes', which had only rarely been prominently profiled, were pared down further to a problem of an habitual 'criminal class', or, at most, to a 'residuum' of criminals, vagrants and 'roughs'.[96] The confidence in being able so to classify, subdivide and diminish the size and threat of the 'dangerous classes' was challenged, however, on two separate occasions (1866-67 and the mid-1880s) by a metropolitan-based fear that, in circumstances of renewed political turmoil, the dangerous and labouring classes were closing ranks. Yet both sets of events, in their own way, revealed the immutability of boundaries drawn over a longer period.

In a setting of trade depression, unemployment, the return of cholera, and bread riots (blamed on 'roughs and juvenile thieves from Kent-street and the Mint'), the reform bills of 1866-67 raised the political temperature once more.[97] Not

95. Cf. Stevenson, 'The criminal class', p. 375; Melling, 'Cleaning House', p. 355. The legislation also perhaps contributed to a late-century prison population which was older than the population at large, and more hardened by previous prison sentences: Gatrell & Hadden, 'Criminal statistics', pp. 378-85. For discussion of the important possibility that popular value-systems, themselves, recognised and reinforced the demarcation between the working and dangerous classes, see Ignatieff, 'A Critique', pp. 173-74.

96. The O.E.D. defined 'rough' as 'a man or lad belonging to the lower classes and inclined to commit acts of violence or disorder.' The first example of 'rough' in the O.E.D. is dated 1837; ten years later, the *Illustrated London News* rendered 'rough' as 'an electioneering name for ruffians.' The mid-Victorian gloss was of men who worked at particular unskilled and casual occupations (navvies, bricklayers' labourers, dockers); they were not necessarily criminal, though amateur thieves were thought to be among their number.

97. *Times*, 26 January 1867, p. 5.

since the 1840s had there been so much nervousness about political change and expectation of political violence. The worst fears of the alarmists were confirmed by the events of July 1866, when Reform League demonstrators, having been forbidden access to Hyde Park, forced an entry. This symbolic violation of boundaries, and the subsequent days of disorder, led Matthew Arnold to complain bitterly that the erosion of authority had emboldened the 'residuum' into 'marching where it likes, meeting where it likes, bawling what it likes, breaking what it likes'.[98] Such incidents, however, impelled politicians, radical and conservative alike, to emphasise that the vote would not be given to 'the residuum . . . of almost hopeless poverty and dependence'.[99] Only the 'respectable working class' had the moral qualities and civic virtue to deserve incorporation into the constitution. These arguments gave political blessing, then, to the social construct, 'respectable artisan', and to its moral antithesis, the 'residuum' or 'dangerous class'.[100] As such, the crisis helped to narrow the definition of the 'dangerous class', confining it largely to a residue of 'roughs' and the 'criminal classes'.[101]

The second metropolitan challenge to mid-Victorian certainties came in the 1880s. Once again, economic depression and unemployment, exacerbated by a new crisis in the provision of working-class housing, aroused fears of an insurrectionary alliance between the 'residuum' and the 'respectable working class'. The residential mixing of the criminal and working classes, of which witnesses informed the Royal Commission on the Housing of the Working Classes in 1884,

---

98. M. Arnold, *Culture and Anarchy* (Cambridge, 1950), p. 105.

99. 3 *Hansard* 186, 26 March 1867, cols. 636-37 (John Bright). The O.E.D. cites this reference to the 'residuum', a term 'applied to persons of the lowest class.'

100. See E. P. Hennock, 'Poverty and social theory in England: the experience of the eighteen eighties', *Social History*, vol. 1, 1976, pp. 78-79; G. Crossick, 'From gentlemen to the residuum: languages of social description in Victorian Britain' in P. J. Corfield (ed.), *Language, History and Class* (Oxford, 1991), pp. 161-63.

101. For the contemporaneous attempt to distinguish between the unemployed (in casual jobs and decaying trades) and the semi-criminal 'incompetent class', see Alsager Hill, *Our Unemployed* (London, 1868), pp. 8-10.

especially endangered the social and moral boundaries drawn in the 1860s.[102] Once again, an outbreak of disorder in central London brought mounting middle-class fears to the surface. The Trafalgar Square riot of 8 February 1886 provoked the journalist, Alexis Krausse, to fear the conjunction of the 'vast criminal population' of London (a section of which 'sacked the West-end a few weeks ago'), the 'unprincipled individuals' who preached revolution and riot, and the large number of 'hungry men . . . with honest hearts and of respectable antecedents, their stomachs empty, their children sickly, their future a blank'.[103] But these fears were not widely shared. As I have argued elsewhere,[104] the standard interpretation of the riots affirmed the established distinction between the 'real working class', including those who were unemployed, and the 'residuum', what Engels called 'the masses of the Lumpenproletariat whom Hyndman [leader of the Social Democratic Federation] had taken for the unemployed'.[105] The social differentiation inscribed in the 1867 Reform Act held fast, even in the face of the Trafalgar Square riot.

At the end of the 1880s, moreover, the 'residuum' or 'dangerous class' was further reduced in size and menace by the initial volume of that leviathan social survey, orchestrated by Charles Booth, *Life and Labour of the People in London*, and by the London dock strike. Booth's first category of social classification, Class A, was described as '[t]he lowest class, which consists of some occasional labourers, street-sellers, loafers, criminals and semi-criminals'. From this largely hereditary, 'savage semi-criminal class of people', including the inmates of common lodging houses, whose children were the street arabs, came

---

102. See G. Stedman Jones, *Outcast London* (London, 1971), ch. 11.

103. A. S. Krausse, *Starving London* (London, 1886), pp. 163-64. Cf. H. Solly, 'Our Vagrant and Criminal Classes', *Leisure Hour*, 1887, pp. 761-67.

104. V. Bailey, 'The Metropolitan Police, the Home Office and the Threat of Outcast London' in idem (ed.), *Policing and Punishment in Nineteenth Century Britain* (London, 1981).

105. Engels to Bebel, 15 February 1886, *Correspondence of Marx and Engels* (1934), p. 447.

the battered figures who slouch through the streets, and play the beggar or the bully, or help to foul the record of the unemployed . . . [these are] the ready materials for disorder when occasion serves.[106]

Booth put their numbers at roughly 11,000 or 1.2 per cent of the East End population. These figures were the foundation of his legendary statement that

> The hordes of barbarians of whom we have heard, who, issuing from their slums, will one day overwhelm modern civilization, do not exist. There are barbarians, but they are a handful, a small and decreasing percentage: a disgrace but not a danger.[107]

This paragraph seized the imagination of reviewers. The *Spectator* extrapolated from Booth's figures an estimate for the entire city: 'most assuredly it does not amount to more than 1 per cent of the total population of London – or only fifty thousand in five millions'.[108] As the reviewer noted, Booth would leave the police to harry the 'residuum' or 'criminal scum' out of existence.

In the summer of 1889, the strike of 100,000 dock workers, by running its course (including a mass demonstration through the West End) without disorder, served to show that the London dockers, and by extension the casual labour force, were not the demoralised, semi-criminals of middle-class imagination. It proved, too, according to one contemporary evaluation of the strike,

> that the hordes of East End ruffians who have been supposed (did they but know their power) to hold the West in the hollow of their hands,

106. Charles Booth, *Life and Labour of the People in London* (London, 1892), pp. 37-38 & 174.

107. Ibid., p. 39. Here Booth was pointedly replying to Henry George's *Progress and Poverty* (New York, 1898 ed. 1st. pub. 1879), vol. II, p. 535. Cf. what Sir William Harcourt, the prominent Liberal M.P. told the House of Commons: 'I do not share the opinion of those who hold that, apart from the criminal classes, there is a large floating population of what is called 'the dangerous classes.' I do not believe in the existence of the dangerous classes to any very great extent in the Metropolis.' 3 *Hansard* 330, 14 November 1888, col. 1165.

108. *Spectator*, 20 April 1889, pp. 535-36. In fact, the figures for Class A that Booth's survey eventually submitted were: 37,610 or 0.9 per cent of London's population. See G. Himmelfarb, *Poverty and Compassion* (New York, 1991), p. 108.

were a fantastic myth: for this Great Strike would have been their opportunity.[109]

The few small-scale disturbances that did occur were invariably attributed by the metropolitan police to the 'roughs', not striking dockers.[110] The dock strike had the undoubted effect, therefore, of promoting a large number of casual workers – those in Booth's Class 'B' – to the ranks of the working class proper, and thus of detaching them from 'the gutter proletariat,' in Engels' evocative phrase.[111] The problem of the 'residuum', said Hubert Llewellyn Smith, one of Booth's assistants, would become 'essentially one of the treatment of social disease', and could be safely left to the social administrator.[112]

VI

The image of deviance embodied in the language of the 'criminal and dangerous classes' overshadowed the Victorian debate on crime and punishment. Crime was thought to be embedded in the lowest sectors of the social order; it was seen as a product of an alien, almost an outcast, group. Encoded in this language was a set of values which verified the tenets of political economy; criminals were masterless men without gainful employment, attracted by the ease of a life of crime. By denying that crime was an integral feature of working-class life, induced by poverty or unemployment, the discourse exonerated the process of economic production and the inequitable distribution of wealth, incriminating instead urban dislocation and moral in-discipline. Instrumental in the elaboration of this discourse were the 'urban gentry', who in government reports, Social Science Association addresses, and the periodical press, defined the boundaries between the 'dangerous' and working classes, whittled down the collective

---

109. H. Llewellyn Smith & Vaughan Nash, *The Story of the Dockers' Strike Told by Two East Londoners* (London, 1889), p. 6. Cf. H. H. Champion, *The Great Dock Strike in London* (London, 1890), p. 6.

110. Joan Ballhatchet, 'The Police and the London Dock Strike of 1889', *History Workshop*, issue 32, Autumn 1991, p. 57.

111. Quoted in Himmelfarb, *Poverty and Compassion*, p. 53.

112. Llewellyn Smith and Nash, *The Story of the Dockers' Strike*, p. 165.

construct of the 'dangerous classes' to that of an encircled 'criminal class', and contributed 'solutions' to the very problem their language framed. Their formulations shaped the content of policing and punishment, and thus law enforcement reinforced the concept of the social 'residuum'.

More significantly, however, the Victorian fabrication of deviance took place as an integral feature of the structural and moral differentiation of the working classes. The early stages of industrialization and mass urbanisation, in conjunction with some serious challenges from political radicals, led middle-class observers to discern the emergence of a 'dangerous class' and, occasionally, even links between the dangerous and labouring classes. Their fears of an insurrectionary alliance were never, in my view, as strong or as widespread as many historians of police and prisons have maintained. But the idea of a marginal group of paupers, prostitutes, beggars and thieves gave point to the task of separating the labouring poor from the dependent paupers, the honest poor from the habitual criminal. The elite perception of the 'dangerous classes' in the first half of the nineteenth century is intelligible only in relation to this larger project of partitioning the working population, the better to forestall the moral contagion of pauperism and criminality.

After 1850, economic stabilisation, the demise of radical possibilities, and the 'disciplines' of moral reform, factory labour, and 'self-help', led middle-class observers to postulate the existence of a 'respectable working class' that was segregated from its economic and moral antithesis, the urban 'residuum', of which an habitual criminal class was the cornerstone. This 'dangerous class' was seen less as a threat to public order and more as evidence of the moral boundary between those who could be granted full citizenship and those deemed unfit for membership of the 'political nation'. The incorporation of the 'respectable working class' reduced the 'residuum' to a politically insignificant stratum, a problem amenable to policing and social administration. This, then, is the broader political and cultural context in which the language of the 'criminal and dangerous classes' must be set. Only by constructing an historically-thick account of the way Victorian society's language of social description assisted the invention of deviance can one appreciate the full significance of social distinctions that have shaped beliefs and behaviour from that day to this. It remains to be seen whether the growth of a semi-permanent, increasingly black 'underclass' in our present inner cities[113], representing the 'de-incorporation' of sections of the working class and from which the riots of the 1980s drew their force, will undermine the set of social distinctions constructed by the Victorians.

---

113. See R. Dahrendorf, *Law and Order* (London, 1985), pp. 106-08; J. K. Galbraith, *The Culture of Contentment* (New York, 1992), ch. 3.

Chapter Eight

'Our Party is the People': Edward Carpenter and Radicalism in Sheffield

Sheila Rowbotham

I was never formally a student of Edward Thompson's. However, he sent me off to read the Carpenter papers in Sheffield when I was in my early twenties, and the collection of books and pamphlets in the Thompsons' house introduced me to several of Edward Carpenter's friends in Leeds, including Isabella Ford, Tom Maguire, and Alf Mattison. From them, and from Edward Thompson, I acquired a scepticism about received versions of the socialist past which focused on the official fronts of organisations, such as national conferences and leading theorists. The tantalising quest to enter the interior world of politics, engaging with the passions and feuds of people long ago, can be elusive and frustrating for it means becoming entangled in the ways people lived and acted and the confusions of their lives rather than neatly summarising concepts. It is, however, a means by which assumptions which have become overlaid and insights which have been lost can be made to resurface. Such an approach provides a vital opening for understanding groups whose needs and views have often been dismissed within labour movements and labour history. It is also a starting point for rethinking the past of both popular movements and socialism, by reconstructing as sympathetically as possible what people themselves believed they were doing.

Edward Thompson's work contains a tension: the passionate entanglement with the past has been accompanied by a powerful pull towards contemporary political and social problems. The struggle to look backwards and forwards at the same time is evident in his writing. The connecting theme has been an endeavour, important for socialists and feminists alike, to shake free the aspiration for human liberation: the yearning to which Marx sought to give substance and ended by welding tragically to economic production. The theoretical course taken by Edward Thompson points to a new synthesis of material life and culture, of social existence and social being, of individuality and communality. A more complex and dynamic approach to class relationships and to people's consciousness of their class has been a continuing process which has driven him to make new furrows through the past, turning over the retrospective tracks of socialist tradition to uncover again and again the untouched grounds of assumption.

So many taken-for-granted meanings of socialism have been undermined in present times that memories which have slipped out of mind begin to assume a new significance. It seems thus appropriate to muse upon another time of flux, before modern socialism was first cast. This essay explores the terms of protest within radicalism during the 1870s and early 1880s just before the Sheffield Socialist Club was formed.

When Edward Carpenter arrived in Sheffield in 1877 his initial reaction was horror at the sooty air. In 1874 he had left a safe and privileged existence as a Cambridge curate for the peripatetic life of a lecturer in the University Extension Movement. Influenced by Walt Whitman and troubled by the French Commune, he was questing for a more natural and democratic way of life. He fretted for a few years among the northern middle-class supporters of University Extension, but was eventually to discover more congenial company among groups of radicals and rebels in the North.

Edward Carpenter was not alone in his unhappiness with the world of privilege. Indeed, guilt and a mild social cons-cience were coming to be quite an asset to any new young liberal courting the working-class radical vote. 'The condition of the people' might be a subject for earnest debate at university, or the inspiration for a lecture in a working men's club. But for most of these young social reformers it was to remain a matter of changes from above without bringing their own positions within the social order or their own attitudes and responses into question.

With Carpenter it was different. His preoccupation with socialism as an alternative way of living, his commitment to sexual liberation, his pioneer writing on sex psychology, his ethical concern with making a new, non-religious morality, all involved subjectivity and an inward commitment. The social change he wanted was intended to free himself as well as the working class. He saw the personal sense of isolation which many of the more sensitive young Victorians expressed as part of the same distorted system of social relationships which forced workers to labour long and hard to increase capital which they did not own or control.

Both Carpenter's conscience and a psychological yearning for deeper self-expression carried him beyond social reform to socialism. He was not content to survey the poor from a distance or devise abstract schemes for their improvement. His prose-poem 'Towards Democracy' (1883) demanded complete identification with those who were suffering. He was preoccupied with the tragedy of alienation: the social separation between people of different classes and between the sexes, and the separation of 'civilised' human beings from their own natures. His antagonism to the capitalist system was not just because of inequality, poverty, and material hardship, but because the private ownership of capital made direct relationships between people impossible. It was no use to try and change capitalism merely as an external system; Carpenter wanted a transformation of social relationships. Coming as he did from a religious background, he thought this implied not merely an outer change in capitalism's structure but also an immediate call to begin to live differently. An ethical concern to live according to an ideal found a response in many middle class men and women who, while breaking with Christianity, retained a religious framework for their thinking. It also struck a chord of utopianism, which was strong in those radical and communtarian traditions which were to pass into the early socialist movements in Britain.

Carpenter's presence in Sheffield meant that a record exists of people whose activities would otherwise have been largely unrecorded. It is consequently possible to sketch a picture of a radical milieu during the 1870s which reveals threads going back to the early nineteenth-century movements as well as forward to the socialist movements of the 1880s. Echoes of the Owenites and Chartists were carried through the lives of individuals and families. Institutions like the Hall of Science and movements like secularism point to more shadowy networks. These informal links were shifting and elusive, for in this period individuals did not settle down in national organisations but moved between national and even international activism before returning to local self-help groups when the political going got rough. They also oscillated intellectually between strands of extreme radical individualism and advocacy of nationalisation of the land and public services, and between secularism and heterodox forms of spirituality. There was a stress on freedom but also a belief in the need for discipline. Their politics combined a vision of a new moral world through communal cooperation with a transformation in human relationships. They were concerned not only about a change in the ownership of production and a redistribution of wealth, but also about living differently with others and with nature. The group Carpenter gravitated towards included ornery rebels who disapproved of respectable, middle-class Victorian attitudes along with earnest, pragmatic radicals pressing for single-issue reforms.

Among this latter group was Jonathan Taylor, an activist on the extreme fringes of municipal radical politics. Taylor was from a Chartist family in Holmfirth. He had come to Sheffield in 1863 and been prominent as a young man in open-air radical propaganda at the old Pump West Bar, a tradition he was to uphold with the socialists on the same pitch. Before becoming a socialist he had supported the radical politician, Samuel Plimsoll, and helped the municipal reformers, A. J. Mundella and Joseph Chamberlain, to organise radicals in the Liberal Party. Taylor served on the School Board from 1879, campaigning for free education and free dinners; he also supported a school and farm for truant boys who came up before the magistrates. The boys in his view were 'very much more sinned against than sinning'.[1] In 1885, when he had served six years on the School Board, he reminded his supporters how, 'at an open air meeting on the range of hills dividing the two counties of Lancashire and Yorkshire in the month of August 1857 now 28 years ago, I first raised my voice in favour

---

1. Jonathan Taylor, *Truant's School and Farm*, pamphlet, no date (Sheffield Public Library).

of a national system of education which should be compulsory and free.'[2] Carpenter described Taylor in *My Days and Dreams* (1916) as a man who was 'tall, lean, logical and conclusive to the last degree; who with a kind of homely unconquerable humour, compelled his hearers from finger to finger, and from point to point, of his argument, and somehow always succeeded in holding the most restive crowd, and for any purpose.'[3] Taylor's experience of municipal politics and knowledge of the locality were to prove extremely useful to the socialists.

Secularism provided another link between earlier radical traditions and the socialism of the 1880s. In the mid 1870s the Sheffield secularists still met in the Hall of Science, which had been founded by Isaac Ironside with support from the Owenites. There they would sit listening to famous speakers from London like Charles Bradlaugh or Annie Besant or local figures like W. H. Lill, a bootmaker, lecturing on 'What will Mrs. Grundy say?' Lill was later to join the Sheffield socialists and teach Carpenter to make sandals.[4] The Owenite and Chartist stress on the importance of social and cultural events as well as debate persisted among the Sheffield secularists in the 1870s. At the end of 1876, for example, they held a Christmas party for the children. Memory and tradition were also part of their politics. Early in 1877 the *Secular Chronicle* announced, 'On Monday January 29th we celebrated the Birthday of Tom Paine and although the rain poured down in torrents the evening was passed in a most agreeable manner'.[5] When they elected their committee in 1877, they chose, besides W. H. Lill, W. Pearson, a radical, and Wallace Nelson, a land nationaliser, both of whom were to be associated with the socialists later.[6]

---

2. *Sheffield Weekly Echo*, 31 October 1885.

3. Edward Carpenter, *My Days and Dreams* (1916), p. 132.

4. See the *Secular Chronicle*, 5 November 1876, 14 January 1877, 11 February 1877, 25 March 1877; and Carpenter, *My Days and Dreams*, p. 124.

5. *Secular Chronicle*, 11 February 1877.

6. See *Secular Chronicle*, 14 January 1877. On Pearson and Nelson see *Sheffield Weekly Echo*, 31 October 1885 and 18 September 1886.

Sheffield also had a history of schemes for home colonisation. These ranged from seizing cultivated land to Isaac Ironside's more moderate plan to reclaim the moorlands. This return to the land was partly seen as a remedy for poverty, but it also retained the utopian hope of prefiguring a different way of life to that of competitive capitalism.

During the 1870s the diverse impulses of radicalism cannot be located in any single organisation or movement; nonetheless, connections existed through small overlapping networks. Thus in August 1877, after a particularly successful talk by W. H. Neale on 'An Analysis of the Doctrine of Free Will', the audience was keen to carry on. A summer outing seemed a pleasant way to pursue theological controversy. The *Secular Chronicle* announced that 'the lecturer has agreed to continue the discussion at the communists' home at Totley four and a half miles from Sheffield on Sunday August 5th – Train at 2:30 Midland Station, J.W.'[7] The Totley 'communists' had been members of a mutual improvement class which had met in the Hall of Science in the early 1870s. Each member used to give a talk or a paper to the group to start off a discussion. If it was judged good enough this would then form the basis for an evening public meeting. While some of the members of the class were secularists, they also included some Unitarians and a Quaker. The Hall served as a centre for dissent of various kinds.

In the summer of 1875 debate had stimulated a communal experiment. A bootmaker, possibly W. H. Lill, had given a talk advocating 'communism'. The topic had caused controversy but he had gained a small band of supporters. This group had decided to establish communism by living communally and farming. Among them was M. A. Maloy, later to join the Sheffield socialists. In 1889 he wrote an account of this Totley experiment in *Commonweal*, the paper of the Socialist League: 'A few of us formed a society to propagate Communistic views, our ultimate object being to live the lives of Communists.'[8] Political conviction was entwined closely with a vision of living differently. But utopia was deferred for

7. *Secular Chronicle*, 5 August 1877.

8. M. A. Maloy, 'St. George's Farm', *Commonweal*, 25 May 1889. See also *Sheffield Evening Star and Daily Times*, 23 August 1875.

a while and the orderly habits of self-help were applied to the long-term project of buying land for a farm. Maloy describes how the 'communists' started to subscribe one penny a week for current propaganda expenses, patiently banking a total of from one to five shillings a week.

The Totley communists knew something about politics but were without experience in farming. Apart from the boot-maker who had inspired the attempt, there were ironworkers and an optician; the women are simply described as 'wives'.[9] One of the Totley 'communists', Joseph Sharpe, became a frriend of Carpenter's. His life reveals something of the man-ner in which utopian ideas were sustained through the years when there seemed to be little hope of social transformation.

Joseph Sharpe had been born at Mount Sorrell, near Leicester, and had been active in the Chartist movement. Carpenter says that 'he had often drilled with his comrades in the deserted granite quarries of Mount Sorrell; they had muskets and other weapons hidden away in their houses.'[10] Sharpe had been a butcher, a policeman, a factory worker, and a singer and harpist. When he came to Sheffield initially his music had been a great hit in the pubs and at village feasts. Later he started a shop which his wife ran. Carpenter de-scribed him as a man stubbornly holding onto his views regardless of the opinions of the world, 'convinced that his theories are the right oones.'[11] His politics were driven by his ideals; he was a great debater who liked to provoke parsons on such topics as free will and predestination. His spiritual vision was as heterodox as his politics; he worshipped the stars and believed in the 'harmonies of the spheres' but also maintained that 'discipline was very necessary to create harmony.'[12] He was a scholar and a dreamer as well as a politician and a theologian. He was able to forget his troubles and absorb himself in Shelley's poems, Humboldt's *Cosmos*, or Pick-ering's *Races of Man*. In his old age he became fascinated by

9. Maloy, 'St. George's Farm', *Commonweal*, 25 May 1889.

10. Edward Carpenter, 'A Minstrel Communist', *Commonweal*, 9 March 1889.

11. Ibid.

12. Ibid.

Dante, buying a translation of the *Inferno* and getting Carpenter to translate other works of Dante for him.

Joseph Sharpe lived to see socialism revive from the mid 1880s and joined in the early propaganda, presumably more at home as a wandering speaker than as a farmer or a shopkeeper. Totley, however, proved to be a failure; it collapsed, bristling with acrimony and disappointed hopes. The disputes about what went wrong were still painful after more than a decade. Sharpe was in no doubt at all that the communist farm had failed because the other members had not followed his ideas sufficiently closely. It seems that Totley attracted supporters who were all equally set in their conviction of their own rectitude. Carpenter observed that 'they were great talkers . . . knew next to nothing of agriculture . . . and were ready to dogmatise in proportion to their ignorance; and in a very short time they were hurling anathemas at each others heads; peace and fraternity were turned into missiles and malice; the wives entered the fray'.[13] He was inclined to be sceptical about their whole approach. In his view, grouping together in small communities either exploded into conflict or forced everyone to think the same, like the sects in the United States.

> Personally, I would not like to belong to a community of under a million people. I think with that number one might feel safe, but with less there would be a great danger of being watched. If one uses the common funds, for instance to have a glass of beer on the sly, and the majority were blue ribbonites, or to have a good dinner, and they were vegetarians; or if one wanted to use bad language, and the rest of the community was highly aesthetic [sic]; how one would be made to feel it.[14]

Whatever the relations among the Totley communists themselves, the intervention of a formidable autocrat, John Ruskin, certainly contributed to friction. Ruskin had formed the St. George's Guild to buy and settle land which would otherwise be uncultivated, with money contributed by the rich. Worker members were to be 'Life Guards of a New Life', cooperating in a system of strict discipline governed by

---

13. Ibid. See also Edward Carpenter, 'A Couple of Communists', in his *Sketches from Life in Town and Country* (London, 1908), p. 198.

14. Edward Carpenter, 'Correspondence: St. George's Farm, A Suggestion', *Commonweal*, 4 May 1889.

a 'simple and orderly tyrant'.[15] Ruskin's initial approach was made through Henry Swan, a student of his from the London Working Men's College, who had attended the early debates about communism. Maloy maintained they were suspicious of this intervention from the start:

> We knew that Mr. Ruskin believed that one man should rule absolutely, and all others should unquestioningly obey. We did not believe this, nor did we believe in taking the vow which was required in order to become a member of St. George's Guild, for our society was at this time composed of Secularists, Unitarians and one Quaker.[16]

Henry Swan, who had been installed by Ruskin as a curator in his museum at Walkley, Sheffield, came up with a compromise. Ruskin would lend the money to buy the land and leave them free to manage their own affairs. Tempted by this short-cut to communal ownership, they met Ruskin and some of the group chose the land, 13 to 14 acres at Dore and Totley, which Ruskin bought for £2,025. Every male member was in due course to pay back the sum and in seven years they would own the land collectively. Maloy, in retrospect, said that he was suspicious because Ruskin gave them no legal guarantee, but he was over-ruled by the others. They employed a working manager at 24s. per week, for they continued to work at their own trades, and a woman member prepared tea and sold farm produce to earn money for the farm.

Trouble broke out when it was discovered that the boot-maker who had first proposed the commune had been paid £100 by Ruskin. He was censured by the committee and told to return the money. Ruskin refused to receive it. The boot-maker then wanted to go and work on the farm and asked the society to run his boot shop, which they said they would not do. Feelings grew worse and worse until the bootmaker consulted secretly with William Harrison Riley,[17] a radical brought in by Ruskin to keep an eye on the Totley communists. Riley had not been in the mutual improvement class

---

15. *Fors Clavigera*, quoted in W. H. G. Armytage, *Heavens Below* (1961), p. 293.

16. Maloy, 'St. George's Farm', *Commonweal*, 25 May 1889.

17. Ibid.

which had initiated the Totley scheme;[18] though familiar with such groups, he had been involved in more cosmopolitan radical organising. He had worked as a cloth printer, engraver, and commercial traveller, not only in Britain but also in the United States, where he had met Walt Whitman. Through his participation in the First International, Riley had come into contact with Karl Marx and his theories, but he did not regard the employer of labour as the enemy, only monopolists of land and money. Active in the National Reform League, from March 1872 he had edited a radical journal, the *International Herald*, advocating republicanism, currency reform, producers' cooperatives, and nationalisation of the land and public services as well the 'Mutual Producers' Cooperative Land Emigration and Colonisation Company', which aimed to set up a commune in the United States.[19]

An admirer of the theories of the Chartist, Bronterre O'Brien, Riley was another link between Chartism and the Sheffield radicalism of the 1870s. After the collapse of the First International and republican organising, he had been forced to turn from large-scale politics to local projects and had initially been busy in Bristol, setting up a mutual help club. The club had aimed at cooperative distribution and established a centre for education and social meetings. A dispute arose over the sale of alcohol, whereupon Riley and his wife withdrew with some other members, who included John Sharland and his family, later to be among the founder members of socialism in Bristol. They started a new Social Improvement Institute which did not sell alcohol and was open to both sexes. It was not a financial success and closed after eighteen months.[20]

After the setback of his practical schemes, Riley had turned again to propaganda and moved to Sheffield in 1877 where, from July to December, he published *The Socialist*. Casting his net wide, in the first copy he told both Christians and atheists that they were all socialists, if they were honest. Since

---

18. William Harrison Riley, 'St. George's Farm, A Correction', *Commonweal*, 20 April 1889.

19. See Armytage, *Heavens Below*, pp. 294-298.

20. See Samson Bryher, *An Account of the Labour and Socialist Movement in Bristol* (Bristol, 1929-1931), pp. 13-14 and 18-19.

he defined a socialist as 'a person who endeavours to improve society [so] as to have it based and regulated on the most equitable and economical principles',[21] they had plenty of scope for agreement. In the last issue he suggested a radical British constitution in which he was more explicit about his politics. Article One of the constitution stated that 'The association of the people as a Commonwealth is for the purpose of increasing the happiness of the people.'[22] Later articles developed this proposition. It was the duty of everyone to labour; land was the inheritance of the Commonwealth; food, clothing, and other basic necessities should be distributed according to need from public stores. Article 19 asserted that 'All citizens have a right to do as they please, providing they do not threaten or interfere with the right of other people.'[23]

By the end of 1877 Riley, by this time a Christian Socialist, was isolated, taking consolation in his convictions despite the scorn of the 'orthodox'. 'I am glad to know that I am, to some extent, a visionary – a seer', prepared 'to endeavour to enlarge and improve the sight of mankind and to oppose the champions of darkness – the revilers and destroyers of sight.'[24] It was in this frame of mind that he came into close association with Ruskin and was accepted as a Retainer of the St. George's Guild early in 1878. He had already read Ruskin's work and mentioned him favourably in his *International Herald* in 1873. Ruskin might be 'a Tory', declaring that Riley and 'pretty nearly everybody else are blockheads',[25] but he was just as opposed to commercialism as the communists. From the mid 1870s Riley had cherished a dream of a cooperative village and was in correspondence with Ruskin about his ideas. Ruskin wrote from Coniston, 'Don't be in a

---

21. Ibid., p. 15.

22. Armytage, *Heavens Below*, p. 296.

23. Ibid.

24. Ibid.

25. Edward Carpenter, 'A Couple of Communists', *Sketches of Life in Town and Country*, p. 210.

hurry about your model village – I don't myself believe such a thing possible with our present means.'[26]

Despite the differences in their political views, Riley sided with Ruskin in his dispute with the Totley communists and behaved towards them in a high-handed fashion. Riley's intervention at Totley was still resented by Maloy in 1889. Acting for Ruskin, Riley had taken possession of the farm, 'telling our manager that he was master'.[27] A deputation from the original committee went to the farm 'to seek an explanation'.[28] According to Maloy, 'Mr. Riley coolly informed them that he was master there, and that they had no power. He met their remonstrances with sneers and in one case with threats of personal violence.'[29] Carpenter said Ruskin sent his servant, Downs, to evict the communists with a pitchfork.[30] The committee's two letters to Ruskin received no reply. They finally wrote declining all further responsibility. Relations between Riley and Ruskin were to decline between 1878 and 1880, and Riley himself was to be in his turn evicted. In the late 1880s and early 1890s he corresponded with another Guildsman with a grievance against Ruskin, William Graham, whom he had met at the Museum in Sheffield in 1878. Graham wanted to make public Ruskin's treatment of other settlers. Riley's response was to insist that while Ruskin's deceit and injustice had left him depressed, he did not want to publish his own account of the events. Even in the late 1880s and 1890s, he still hoped for a hearing within the Guild.[31] Ruskin felt the collapse of Totley along with the general failure of the Guild as keenly as Riley and the Sheffield communitarians. In 1878 he had a nervous break-

---

26. John Ruskin to W. H. Riley, undated (Riley papers, Beinecke Library, Yale University).

27. M. A. Maloy, 'St. George's Farm', *Commonweal*, 25 May 1889.

28. Ibid.

29. Ibid.

30. Edward Carpenter, 'A Minstrel Communist', *Commonweal*, 9 March 1889.

31. See W. Graham to W. H. Riley, 23 July 1888; W. H. Riley to W. Graham, 23 October 1888; W. Graham to W. H. Riley, 19 October 1888; W. H. to W. Graham, 2 February 1891; and W. H. Riley to W. Graham, undated Spring c.1891 (Riley papers, Yale University).

down, which had occurred partly, he said, because 'nothing came of my work'.[32]

Despite his gloom and the bad feeling which his behaviour at Totley had created, Riley's propagandising in the 1870s did have an impact, not only on the socialist movement in Bristol, but also in Sheffield. He left a political heritage intellectually; two converts, the Bingham brothers, were to become members of the Sheffield Socialist Society, later moving towards the anarchist-communists. Like most of the Sheffield radicals and early socialists, the Bingham brothers were far from being stereotypical proletarians, being provision merchants. Their sister, Louisa Usher, was one of the minority of women who became involved in the socialist group despite the opposition of her husband.

Exactly when Carpenter met Riley is not clear but he certainly was in contact with him by the summer of 1879.[33] In May 1880 he tried to intercede with Ruskin on Riley's behalf but Ruskin was adamant: 'I fear there's more to it than you think . . . he liked smoking better than digging – and I know of no texts in favour of any sort of smoke – tobacco least of all. But I entirely decline managing that kind of person.'[34] Soon after this interchange Riley and his family emigrated to Massachusetts; there he tried unsuccessfully to join other communities and struggled to support himself by journalism. His friendship with Carpenter was important to him and communications were maintained into the early 1890s. He followed the growth of the socialist movement in England, writing in 1894 to the *Manchester Labour Press* to complain that anarchists were being pursued by the authorities and that younger socialists forgot the men of the 1870s like himself 'who stood in the gap'.[35] Then, he contended, all socialists had

---

32. John Ruskin, *Fors Clavigera*, quoted in D. K. Baruah, *Edward Carpenter and the Early Sheffield Socialists* (Transactions of the Hunter Archaeological Society, vol. 10, 1971), p. 56.

33. See Charles Fox to Edward Carpenter, 23 July 1879 (Carpenter Collection, Sheffield Public Library).

34. John Ruskin to Edward Carpenter, 16 May 1880 (Carpenter Collection).

35. W. H. Riley, 'A Letter from America', *Manchester Labour Press*, 29 September 1894 (newspaper cutting in the Riley papers, Yale

been popularly regarded as rogues or fools and 'socialism was as unpopular in England as anarchism is now'.[36] He was lonely in old age and politically in exile. But he was still thinking of old friends from Bristol and Sheffield, like the Binghams. 'We are scattered widely – perhaps for good, as some seed is scattered by the unfeeling winds.'[37]

Edward Carpenter was unusual in the variety of intellectual strands which combined in his person. Apart from the local radical milieu in Sheffield, other influences included Shelley, Whitman, Thoreau, Buddha and Ruskin. Later he assimilated Engels, Olive Schreiner, William Morris, and Hyndman, along with the sex psychologists Havelock Ellis, Ulrichs, Krafft-Ebing and Moll – a motley crew, some of whom would have been disconcerted to find themselves in the same company. Carpenter challenged many aspects of Victorian orthodoxy. He questioned the benefit of 'civilisation' over other cultures, the superiority of Christianity over Eastern religions, and the mechanical basis of scientific thinking and Darwinism. Believing that capitalism made natural feeling impossible, he sought a way of life which would release spontaneous emotion. In 1879 he made friends with two independent spirits living in the countryside who knew Riley. They were to help him escape from the social conventions which he found increasingly oppressive. Albert Fearnehough, a scythemaker, and Charles Fox, a small farmer, had been students at Carpenter's Extension lectures. Fearnehough had approached Carpenter after a lecture to invite him to visit him and his friend, Fox, at the latter's farm at Bradway. It was to be the start of a long friendship across the class barrier.

Fearnehough had pushed a handcart about the Sheffield streets since he was nine. He was a big strong man, whose ideal, according to Carpenter, 'was the rude life of the backwoods'.[38] Fearnehough 'hated the shams of commercialism'[39] and 'was always getting into coils with his employers because

University).

36. Ibid.
37. W. H. Riley to W. Graham, 6 February 1891 (Riley papers).
38. Carpenter, *My Days and Dreams*, pp. 102.
39. Ibid., pp. 102-3.

he would not scamp and hurry over his work . . . and with his workmates because he would not countenance their doing so.'[40] He and his wife lived in a little cottage on Fox's farm and were to live with Carpenter at his home in Millthorpe. Carpenter has left a graphic sketch of Charles Fox as 'Martin Turner'. He was

> Derbyshire born and bred . . . of sturdy medium stature, solid, tough as oak . . . He wore . . . an ancestral green coat with brass buttons, which suited him well, and when he looked at you it was with that rustic no-how [sic] sort of look . . . Yet behind the impenetrable face, and hidden by those almost simpleton manners, lay an acute philosophic mind and a sense of humour.[41]

Fox, Carpenter records, had read widely, taught himself mathematics, liked children, protected animals, had a romantic fondness for young girls, and occasionally drank too much. His odd slow manner made his own people think he was lazy, but it was in fact a useful cover for his scepticism and impatience with humbug. Carpenter describes in eloquent detail Fox's encounter with a Methodist fundamentalist preacher, whom he challenged on the historical accuracy of 'Genesis', sardonically tying him up in theoretical knots. Charles Fox had his own philosophical resistance to any form of asceticism and to the competitive values of capitalism. He was committed to life on his own terms: 'People go about fussing to get on', he said,

> . . . toiling away, and taking no rest at nights – but it comes to nowt, it comes to nowt. I knew a man who gave up smoking. He was very fond of smoking, but he thought he would give it up and save the money; and so he did – for two or three years – and bought a cow. And then the cow died! Oh how sorry that man was for all the smoke he had lost – how he lay awake o'night thinking of all the good times he might have had with his pipe – all gone not to be recovered. He took to his baccy, and swore he'd never leave it again . . . Yes, some men toil, and it comes to nowt, and others can't help getting rich, they just swim into it. Best take it quietly and make the most of the days as they come. They'll never come back again.[42]

---

40. Ibid., p. 102.

41. Edward Carpenter, 'Martin Turner', *Sketches From Life in Town and Country*, p. 2.

42. Ibid., p. 14.

Fox and Fearnehough were important to Carpenter, who was exhausted from his Extension lecturing and frustrated by the isolation which accompanied the realization of his homosexuality. Their lives seemed to indicate to him that an alternative was possible: 'They represented, if nothing more,' said Carpenter, 'a life close to Nature and actual materials, shrewd, strong, manly, independent, not the least polite or proper, thoroughly human and kindly, and spent for the most part in the fields and under the open sky.'[43] Carpenter's visits to Bradway became more and more frequent and he joined in the farmwork. He began to plan going to live with them, travelling in to Sheffield for his lectures. In July 1879 he went back to Brighton to see his family; the contrast must have been stark. Charles Fox wrote to him saying that he was 'sorry for the squeamish people in high boots. Do you think that walking about on Brighton Pier in high soal'd and low heel'd boots and high collars to hold the chin up a good thing for health?'[44] He said he would not be 'exactly sorry'[45] if Carpenter stopped lecturing at Sheffield: 'Don't think there is great pleasure in lecturing to a lot of ignorant people having corns.'[46] Fox told him they had been visited several times by Riley, who was still in nearby Totley. Riley, an indefatigable propagandist, had lent Fox and Fearnehough 'some papers called *The Socialist* and the *Yankee Letters*'.[47] Carpenter moved first to Bradway and then, in May 1880, to neighbouring Totley. He lived there for nearly a year with Fearnehough and his family and continued his Extension lectures on the 'History of Music' before returning to Bradway when a cottage near Fox's became empty in March 1881.

Ruskin's troubles with the St. George's farm did not end when Riley emigrated. In 1882 he appealed to the public for funds to maintain it. He declared that he wanted to put the land under glass and grow tropical plants for botanical study

---

43. Edward Carpenter, *My Days and Dreams*, p. 104.

44. Charles Fox to Edward Carpenter, 23 July 1879 (Carpenter Collection, Sheffield Public Library).

45. Ibid.

46. Ibid.

47. Ibid.

as well as fruit, strawberries, gooseberries, and currants.[48] But the appeal was unsuccessful and around 1886 the faithful Downs and his son were ousted from Totley. In 1888 Graham wrote to tell Riley that Ruskin had 'let the place to a company of Communists whose head-quarters is another farm with quarry not far distant. You may know of this Community? It's founder John Furniss is a remarkable and noble kind of man.'[49]

It is not clear whether Riley had ever known Furniss but Carpenter had become friendly with him by the early 1880s and introduced Ruskin to Furniss' friend, George Pearson, who leased the farm. Carpenter left a description of John Furniss in *My Days and Dreams*:

> . . . he was a remarkable man, and perhaps the very first to preach the modern Socialism in the streets of Sheffield. A quarryman by trade, keen and wiry both in body and in mind, a thorough going *Christian* Socialist, and originally I believe a bit of a local preacher; he had somehow at an early date got hold of the main ideas of the movement, and in the early eighties used to stride in – he and his companion George Pearson – five or six miles over the Moors to Sheffield in order to speak at the Pump or the Monolith – and then stride out again in the middle of the night.[50]

Charles Ashbee, a friend of Carpenter's from King's College, Cambridge, met Furniss in the summer of 1886 and recorded the meeting in his journal. He said Furniss had been a methodist preacher who took the ideas of Christian communalism seriously. When he first arrived in Sheffield he had very little money but found a beggar who needed it more and shared it with him. After passing through 'the Valley of Darkness', Furniss began to preach Christ in the streets, somehow coming to socialism. The community in which he lived at Totley consisted of two men and three women. Ashbee said there was no private property and that they lived like the early Christians. He was deeply impressed by his

---

48. See Armytage, *Heavens Below*, p. 299.

49. W. Graham to W. H. Riley, 19 October 1888 (Riley papers, Yale University).

50. Edward Carpenter, *My Days and Dreams*, p. 133.

encounter with Furniss, writing about it to his friend Roger Fry, who was wary of Ashbee's social enthusiasms.[51]

The oscillation between community building and radical political campaigning, which had been a feature of the 1870s, was still evident in the early 1880s. Not only was John Furniss a utopian community dweller, in 1884 he was also treasurer of the Sheffield Working Man's Radical Association, an organisation with about two hundred members that was allied to the Social Democratic Federation. By 1885 he and Jonathan Taylor were involved in a minority faction within local radicalism which had decided not to support the liberal, Samuel Plimsoll, and instead were campaigning for a 'labour' candidate of their own, Mervyn Hawkes. They wanted the caucus to move Plimsoll to another constituency and adopt Hawkes.[52] Jonathan Taylor had been an old supporter of Plimsoll, as had N. Billamy, a working-class Extension student from Hull, but they both felt old loyalties had to be disregarded. Billamy's letter was read out to a radical meeting in Sheffield in October. With much reference to Cromwell and military metaphors, he reminded them of their radical heritage:

> The land is before us; our duty is to go up and possess it. If in the storming we are beaten back, we will reform again and with sturdy leaders, who will battle for right because it is right, we will again and again storm until wealth and privilege cry peccavii [sic]. Their standard fallen and the citadel in our hands, we can then show them an example of magnanimity, they cannot now conceive.[53]

Mervyn Hawkes was an opponent of the caucus (the Whigs, he called them) that controlled Sheffield liberalism. He declared himself proud of the Chartist heritage and for the reform of Parliament, Irish Home Rule, free education, 'root and branch land reform',[54] religious equality, temperance reform, and a strong navy. He was against taxes and the House of Lords. When asked to comment on the arrest of some London socialists in 1885, he denounced the action of

---

51. Charles Ashbee, Journal, 4 September 1886, in Charles Ashbee, MSS. Memoirs, p. 29 (Victoria and Albert Museum).

52. See *Sheffield Evening Star and Daily Times*, 27 August 1875.

53. *Sheffield Weekly Echo*, 24 October 1885.

54. Ibid, and *Sheffield Weekly Echo*, 31 October 1885.

the police and Government as 'infamous and brutal. (Cheers) I believe that the class of officials who do these things would have arrested Jesus Christ for preaching the Sermon on the Mount. (Cheers)'[55] (However, he could not contribute to their legal expenses because of the costs of his radical campaign.) Among his supporters, besides Jonathan Taylor and John Furniss, were Wallace Nelson, S. W. Drury, W. Pearson, W. H. Lill, C. H. Fox, E. Carpenter, and Louisa Usher (sister to the Bingham brothers).[56]

These people tended to be to the left of Hawkes and were all soon to be in or connected with the socialist movement in Sheffield. They had their meetings at the Wentworth Café, Holly Street, or the Temperance Hall, both haunts later of the Sheffield socialists. The *Sheffield Weekly Echo*, first subtitled *An Anti-Whig Journal* and later *Yorkshire Free Press*, put forward their views. It was an eclectic publication, carrying local news, articles by the anarchist, Kropotkin, and Jessica's 'Words for Women' which urged radical women to remember that their domain was not just the kitchen and to take radicalism seriously rather than meekly giggling and angling for compliments while the men talked politics. The campaign against the Contagious Diseases Act was reported; so too was the Sheffield Vigilante Association proposed by Mr. S. Hoyland as part of the Social Purity Movement. Articles on Radicalism in the past appeared; their heroes were an assorted lot – Caedmon, Bede, More, Drake, Raleigh, the Pilgrim Fathers, Cromwell, Milton, Marvell, Sidney, Russell, Fox, Cobbett, Burns, and Wordsworth.[57] Although Hawkes' candidature was unsuccessful,[58] the conviction took shape among these people that workers should manage their own affairs, that the land should be held in common, that labour created wealth, and that the Liberal Party was not a truly popular party but belonged to the landed aristocracy and the 'moneyocracy'.

---

55. Ibid.

56. See *Sheffield Weekly Echo*, 31 October 1885.

57. See *Sheffield Weekly Echo*, 13 February 1886, 17 April 1886, 8 May 1886, and 13 May 1886.

58. *Sheffield Weekly Echo*, 3 June 1886.

At a meeting in support of Hawkes in November 1885, John Furniss spoke passionately to an audience which included Taylor, Carpenter, Drury, Lill, Shaw, and Mrs. Usher. He was greeted enthusiastically by the audience and was evidently known to them. He reminded them of the years in which he had struggled to get working men into Parliament. Hawkes, he said, was not a working man like himself but he hadn't had 'his bread buttered for him':

> he has to earn both bread and butter for himself. Working men cannot live on the wind, and are already too much oppressed by the landlords and capitalists to be able to support even one working man representative out of a great town like Sheffield. Is ours a people's Parliament? We are told the Liberals are friends of the people. I don't want friends of the people. I want the people. (Cheers) Working men manage to create wealth and can therefore manage Parliamentary affairs. (Hear hear and applause) I hope the necessary educated class will be our own. I do not want to entrust my interests to the hands of a party whose whole education has been to rob me. I have no confidence in any capitalists. The whole association of their lives are counter to the workers' interests . . . I don't want 'Liberal parties'. I want justice not liberality. I want to manage my own affairs. If the workers only get the same idea neither party will be able to dislodge it . . . My party is the people . . . When the day of humanity shall dawn we shall know how to deal with them [the landed aristocracy, the moneyocracy]. The right of every man is to dwell on this earth which we have not made and which we ought to possess in common.[59]

He went on to assert that the land should be the inheritance of all the people and that all value created by the labour of the people should belong to its creators. The people, said Furniss, had to take up the present foundation of society and lay it anew.

There existed in Sheffield in the mid 1880s a radical political consciousness which had been formed by many intricate and interweaving strands. Inhabiting an intense nether world in relation to official liberalism, it was straining against the existing framework of politics. Locally these radicals had seen the failure of a vision of creating communism as a way of life, and their radical organising within the Liberal Party in support of Hawkes had been defeated. Both experiences, however, were carried into the origins of modern socialism in Sheffield. Edward Carpenter wrote the manifesto of the

---

59. *Sheffield Weekly Echo*, 14 November 1885.

Sheffield Socialists, which was signed by forty-one men and three women in 1886. The manifesto declared an intention 'to abolish the present state of society'.[60] In place of a society founded on the landlord and capitalist system which enabled one man to live on the labour of another, these radicals advocated a community in which everyone who could work would be employed, while those who could not would be provided for by the rest of the community. They believed in nationalisation of the land and gradual nationalisation of the large industries, a progressive income tax, and labour repres-entation in parliament and on councils, boards of guardians, and school boards. The old vision of transforming personal relations also persisted. In the summer of 1886 S. W. Drury declared that socialists wanted a society based 'on the teach-ing of Christ, "Thou shalt love thy neighbour as thyself", in opposition to the false society of today, whose motto is "Each for himself and the devil take the hindmost."'[61] Traditions of free speech were upheld as well. When the police began to interfere with the socialists' open air meetings, Jonathan Taylor came to their defence.[62]

The Ruskinian concept of community transcending class and atomistic individualism entered Sheffield socialism from the start. When John Furniss spoke at the opening of the socialists' Commonwealth café in Scotland Street, he defined the commonwealth as 'the common well being of the common people. By common people he did not mean one class. He held that they were all common flesh and blood and their necessities were common.'[63] He attacked the values of com-petitive self-help and getting-on; for every man who suc-ceeded, a thousand suffered. 'But he had learned from a grand old book that there was another idea of man, that was something that ministers didn't preach about at all. That book told him if he wanted to be happy he must not do it by making others miserable'.[64] Furniss was followed by a radical uni-tarian minister, Charles Peach, who had been involved in the

60. Sheffield Socialist Society (Mattison Collection, Leeds University).

61. *Commonweal*, 28 August 1886.

62. *Commonweal*, 25 September 1886.

63. *Sheffield Weekly Echo*, 26 February 1887.

64. Ibid.

campaign for Hawkes. Peach commended Furniss' community at Totley and argued that socialism was not merely the expression of the interests of a class but the natural outcome of human nature craving a freer and truer existence. Carpenter, who accompanied on a harmonium the songs which interspersed the speeches, also spoke on the meaning of socialism, which, he said, 'was not merely a movement for the industrial emancipation of men; it meant the entire regeneration of society in art, in science, in religion and in literature and the building up of a new life in which industrial socialism was the foundation.'[65]

These dreams of wellbeing nurtured qualitatively different values and relationships which might inform a common culture and replace those upon which capitalism thrived. Shaped from momentary insights, these aspirations transcended the attitudes, habits, and constraints of everyday life, offering alternative visions of how the world might be. The tiny band that gathered in the converted debtors' jail on Scotland Street to envisage the new life of communal happiness were soon to be swept into demonstrations against unemployment and police coercion. Some of them were to become embroiled in the debates and disputes which were the tumultuous reality of socialism and anarchism in the late 1880s and 1890s. Events moved rapidly. Not only political assumptions but the very structure of working class life in the city was shifting as large factories replaced small, scattered craft workshops. Labour representation would soon be achieved and public welfare services gradually emerged. Yet somehow in the bustle and manoeuvering of the modern socialist movement, the vision of a new way of life slipped away, though Edward Carpenter continued to affirm its significance and recorded the faith of his early friends in Sheffield. One of these friends, Joseph Sharpe, had died in poverty in 1889, still unconfirmed and worshipping the stars. Not long before his death he had told Carpenter that 'to belong to a Communistic society has always been the dream of my life and I don't despair of it now. Peace and goodwill and true fraternity – that's what we want.'[66]

---

65. Ibid.

66. Edward Carpenter, 'A Minstrel Communist', *Commonweal*, 9 March 1884.

Chapter Nine

The Forward March of Labour Started? Building a Politicized Class Culture in West Ham, 1898-1900

Leon Fink

Over the past two decades the loss of both programme and power by the British Labour Party has led historians to look back rather more darkly through the glass of working-class politics. Whereas some commentators see the problem in terms of historical *declension* – thus Eric Hobsbawm's 'forward march of Labour halted' – others are inclined to question the entire framework of a 'class'-based politics, the assumption, as Stuart Hall puts it, that 'economic facts transmit themselves directly into working-class heads.' Hall doubts that 'the culture of the working class is [necessarily] the culture of Labour.' Such 'political automatism,' he argues, 'is certainly at an end – if it ever existed.'[1]

---

1. For extended analysis of the recent problems of the Labour Party, see e.g. Eric Hobsbawm, 'The Forward March of Labour Halted?' in Martin Jacques and Francis Mulhern, eds., *The Forward March of Labour Halted?* (1981), pp. 1-19; David Howell, *British Social Democracy: A Study in Development and Decay* (New York, 1976); Andrew Taylor, *The Trade Unions and the Labour Party* (London, 1987); Leo Panitch, *Working Class Politics in Crisis: Essays on Labour and the State* (London, 1986); James E. Cronin, *Labour and Society in Britain, 1918-1979* (1984), esp. pp. 1-15; Stuart Hall, *The Hard Road to Renewal: Thatcherism and the Crisis of the Left* (London, 1988), quotation, p. 208. The general historiographical move away from 'class' as a defining concept of workers' political culture is neatly elaborated in James Epstein, 'The Populist Turn', *Journal of British Studies*, 32 (April 1993), pp. 177-89.

Gareth Stedman Jones is perhaps most sceptical of all about the 'whole idea of a "forward march of Labour."' Rather than a juggernaut of class solidarity, Labour's political successes rested from the beginning, he suggests, on a discontinuous 'social alliance between the organized section of the working class and the professional middle class broadly defined.' Once in power, the intellectual capital in Labour regimes was fashioned from 'Victorian liberal philanthropy' or a kind of middle-class service ethnic maintaining a 'separateness of caste' between workers and their middle-class allies. For Jones, moreover, the essentially 'conservative phenomenon' of Labour politics is less a betrayal than an accurate representation of dominant features of British turn-of-the-century working-class culture. Gareth Stedman Jones thus refers generally to a 'culture of consolation,' a class 'articulating its position within an apparently permanent social hierarchy.' He issues a particularly disconsolate verdict on the founding of the Labour Party as a merely 'defensive' apparatus, confirming an ideological shift in the popular movement 'from power to welfare.'

> If it sang Jerusalem it was not as a battle-cry but as a hymn. It accepted *de facto*, not only capitalism, but monarchy, Empire, aristocracy and established religion as well. With the foundation of the Labour Party, the now enclosed and defensive world of the working-class culture had in effect achieved its apotheosis.[2]

For all its search for sober, clear-headed retrospection, the disillusionment so apparent of late in the treatment of 'the Labour tradition' risks creation of its own illusions. In ascribing to past generations an unholy combination of rigid doctrine, pinched vision, and mostly hollow victories, latter-day historians may mistakenly play the 'ancients' for irrelevant fools. Such dismissal not only misses the enduring legacy of the past but also the rich record of choices and lessons, taken or not taken, learned or ignored. As early as the 1890s, British Labour pioneers grappled with variations on some of

---

2. Gareth Stedman Jones, *Languages of Class: Studies in English Working Class History, 1832-1982* (Cambridge, 1985), pp. 236-38, 243, 246-47. For a reinforcing, but more structural, explanation of Labour's inevitably 'vapid' ideological posture, see Ross McKibbin, 'Why Was There No Marxism in Great Britain?' in *The Ideologies of Class: Social Relations in Britain, 1880-1950* (Oxford 1990), pp. 1-41.

the same questions still affecting the Labour Party. 'Working-class politics' was for them less an historical given than an intricate construction project. The building materials, more-over, might conceivably have fashioned other structures or fallen into even earlier disrepair. Limited by time and place, class politics, sustained initially by a vanguard of socialist militants, had nothing 'automatic' about it. Indeed, it is perhaps the very fragility of the project that may, in a period of Labour's secular political decline and uncertain future prospects, most excite renewed historical interest.

Such, at least, is the spirit of my own re-examination of one of the famous starting points of Labour's 'forward march,' the brief initial victory of a socialist-led municipal government in the industrial London suburb of West Ham in 1898-1900.[3] Combining strong ties to the new unions with a broad appeal to the disaffected middle class, the West Ham Labour Group embarked on an ambitious programme of economic and social reforms. Yet, within a year the governing collection had already lost their majority; by 1900 they would be swept from electoral power and not for another decade would they reassemble a local majority. Even this first, brief taste of office, however, confronted the local labour pioneer legislators with political realities and strategic dilemmas that their followers would face throughout the coming century.

3. Research was originally accomplished during an independent year of study, 1968-1969, under the Comparative Labour History Programme directed by Edward Thompson at the University of Warwick. The work was first drafted as an undergraduate thesis under the direction of Professor Harold Hanham at Harvard University where it was awarded the Philip Washburn Prize. It was subsequently revised in 1971 as a seminar thesis for the late Professor Wilson Coates at the University of Rochester. Acknowledgement for help in the creation of the early manuscript is gratefully extended to Edward Thompson, David Montgomery, Fred Reid, and James Hinton at Warwick University; Mrs. Ellen Taylor and Mr. Kenneth Lewington at the Stratford Reference Library; Patricia Sylvester at Harvard; and Christopher Lasch, Herbert Gutman, Scott Ware, and Gregory Kealey at Rochester. For keeping me posted on debates within the British literature, I am most grateful to Anna Clark, James Epstein, and Neville Kirk. For final editorial guidance, I thank Susan Levine, Robert Malcolmson, and Edward Thompson. I also express appreciation to the Rockefeller Foundation for a fellowship year, 1990-1991, at the National Humanities Center.

The industrial suburb of West Ham, a parliamentary borough bordering Greater London to the north-east, was, in many respects, a classic site of Hobsbawm's manual working class, and consequently a prototypic setting for the rise of Labour politics. Composed of low-lying land given to frequent flooding, the district had supported little more than an agricultural village until the mid-nineteenth century, when it fell victim to unregulated industrialization. As early as 1857 Charles Dickens talked of the area

> as a place of refuge for offensive trade establishments turned out of town – those of oil-boilers, gut spinners, varnish-makers, printers, ink-makers and the like . . . No wonder that the stench of the marsh in Hallsville and Canning Town of nights is horrible. Disease comes upon human bodies saturated with the influence of such air as this breathed day and night, as a spark upon touchwood.[4]

Arthur Copping's 1905 description of 'that great city of the poor, lying like a flat, unlovely wilderness of mean streets,' confirmed the trajectory Dickens identified even if the community he had described was no longer recognizable.[5] Its population had risen from 38,000 in 1861 to 267,000 forty years later, making it one of the four fastest growing communities in England. While the construction of cheap, workmen's trains around 1880 allowed many of its labouring and black-coated workers to commute daily from their West Ham dormitories to London, a large part of the district's growth was due to its becoming an industrial centre in its own right as well as a home for many unemployed and uprooted. Within its southern borders lay the mammoth Victoria docks, a portion of the Royal Albert docks (together employing between 2500 and 5000 men a day), and the Thames Iron Works and Ship Building Company (3,000 employees); and to the north sprawled the locomotive and carriage works of the Great Eastern Railway in Stratford (5000 employees). A multitude of smaller factories proliferated in Canning Town including food, textiles, and gas works. Engineering and metal manufacturing employed more than ten percent of resident West

4. 'Londoners Across the Border,' *Household Words* (Sept. 12, 1857), pp. 241-42.

5. Arthur Copping, *Pictures of Poverty: Studies of Distress in West Ham*, (London: Daily News, 1905), quoted in Giles and Lisanne Radice, *Will Thorne: Constructive Militant* (London, 1974), p. 50.

Ham males. The noxious trades noted by Dickens had been augmented by soap works, bone-boilers, vitriol manufacturers, chemical manure works, and naphtha makers.[6]

The social composition of West Ham is suggested by the fact that 33,000 out of 38,000 homes in 1896 were cottages with a rateable value of twenty pounds of less. In general the best houses in the borough were found in North West Ham, and as poorer newcomers to the borough moved in, the older residents drifted northward. Among the poorest were some six thousand Irish-Catholics, most densely clustered near the docks at Canning Town.[7] About half the West Ham death rate claimed infant victims. In the worst wards of South West Ham, more than a fifth of the children did not reach the age of two. Still 'the excessive number of children of elementary school age' (the highest concentration in any London metropolitan or extra-metropolitan area) made education a particularly heavy burden on the ratepayers.[8] Unemployment in West Ham reached a crisis stage each winter. Casual labour associated with the docks and seasonal labour of the local gas works and brick yards contributed to skyrocketing rates of both indoor and outdoor pauperism in the 1890's. Father Andrew, who lived humbly with the Plaistow Society of Divine Compassion, noted in his dairy in December, 1894, 'I have found families without even the light of a candle sitting silently and starving in the dark.'[9]

Municipal government in the borough was a patchwork of new bodies piled upon old. In 1886 West Ham was given a charter of incorporation as a borough, supplanting some of the functions of older local boards (which continued in operation) with a town council of forty-eight councillors and

6. Asa Briggs, *Victorian Cities* (New York, 1965) p. 80; *Times*, Sept. 6, 1902; E. G. Howarth and M. Wilson, *West Ham: A Study in Social and Industrial Problems, Report of the London Inquiry Committee* (London, 1907), p. 20.

7. G. Haw, 'The Problem of Greater London,' in R. Mudie-Smith, ed., *The Religious Life of London* (London, 1904), pp. 340-42, 352-56.

8. S. Barnett, 'University Settlements,' in Will Reason, ed., *University and Social Settlements* (London, 1898), p. 23.

9. E. J. Hobsbawm, 'British Gas-Workers,' *Labouring Men* (London 1968), pp. 158-73; Howarth and Wilson, pp. 225, 339; K. E. Burne, ed., *The Life and Letters of Father Andrew* (London 1961), p. 32.

aldermen including the mayor who presided over each bi-weekly meeting. The municipal constituency of West Ham in 1898 was broken down into four wards: Canning Town and Plaistow (comprising together the West Ham South parliamentary division); Forest Gate and Stratford (comprising together the West Ham North division). Each ward was represented by nine councillors with staggered three year terms, three of whom came up for election each year in each ward on November 1. The six-year terms of the twelve aldermen were similarly arranged so that groups of four were replaced every three years by an election among the council members.

The voting power of the labouring population in the borough was limited in spite of its numerical preponderance. The British franchise itself remained severely restricted through 1918. Poverty, mobility, and illiteracy all militated nationally against access to the ballot: as late as 1910 as a result of outright franchise disqualifications and the capricious working of the registration machinery, 'some 40% of adult males were not on the electoral register.' In such circumstances, many apparently working-class districts retained an electoral complexion disproportionately middle-class. While across the country municipal elections rarely drew more than one third of those registered to the polls, in West Ham the typical turnout was lower still, closer to 25 percent. And the number of those who were eligible (and registered) fell below fifteen percent of the town's population (indeed in South West Ham the registration figure for 1900 was a mere 11 percent of the population).[10]

The rise of independent labour politics in West Ham was catalyzed by the new unionist crusades of the gasworkers and London dockers in 1889. The very difficulty of maintaining union membership and union recognition in industries of casual labour accentuated the importance of gaining pockets

10. Neal Blewett, 'The Franchise in the United Kingdom, 1885-1918,' *Past & Present*,32 (1965), pp. 27-56, quotation p. 27; *The Times*, Sept. 6, 1902; Paul Thompson, *Socialists, Liberals, and Labour: The Struggle for London, 1885-1914* (London, 1967), p. 134; Brian Keith-Lucas, *The English Local Government Franchise* (Oxford, 1952), appendix A, pp. 226-36; West Ham *Citizen*, June 24, 1899; G. W. Jones, *Borough Politics* (London 1969), pp. 33, 39; *Justice*, Nov. 3, 1900; and generally, local newspaper election statistics.

of strength in areas of public employment. It also made municipal work or relief for the unemployed a necessity to prevent their being drafted as a strikebreaking force. For these reasons the new unionists, like practically all organizations of unskilled workers, began at once to take a direct interest in politics. West Ham, 'the cradle of new unionism,' naturally enough became an early centre of Labour politics.[11] In 1889 three unionists, all with Lib-Lab connections, were elected to the town council. When Will Thorne joined the council with a declaration of loyalty to the Social Democratic Federation (SDF) in 1891, he symbolized the arrival of a powerful new voice in borough politics. The drafting of Keir Hardie to Thorne's West Ham South constituency, and support for this Labour candidate by a *de facto* alliance of Liberal, temperance, Irish nationalist, and trade unionist forces, first displayed the possibilities for independent Labour dominance within a larger coalition.[12]

Despite the national significance of Hardie's victory (including its catalysis of the Independent Labour Party [ILP] in 1893), within West Ham the most dynamic political forces remained centred around Thorne's Gasworkers and the SDF. Born in 1857 of parents who were both brickmakers, and having put in a twelve hour working day as early as age six, Thorne personified a common code of class experience and identity. Settling in Canning Town after securing employment at the nearby Beckton Gas Works, Thorne in quick succession joined the local SDF branch and signed a teetotal pledge. While the latter suggested his self-discipline, it was the former which defined his entry into the wider world of labour and political radicalism. Through the SDF, Thorne encountered the leading socialist propagandists of his day, including Eleanor Marx Aveling, who would teach him to write and continue to serve as a close counsellor to the

---

11. Socialist and independent labour political strength can be directly correlated to the resurgent industrial strength of the unstable Gasworkers' Union. From its weakest point in 1896 (it still had 1400 members in West Ham alone), union membership surged upwards of 3000 men during the period June-August, 1898. West Ham *Guardian*, Aug. 20, 1898; Paul Thompson, pp. 101-102.

12. On Hardie in West Ham, see Fred Reid, *Keir Hardie: The Making of a Socialist* (London, 1978), pp. 127-55.

gasworkers' union.[13] Friends and enemies alike thought of Thorne as a tough, battling underdog. As early as 1889, Dockers' leader Ben Tillett found in Thorne 'all the sturdy qualities of [Zola's] peasant hero.'[14]

Since 1891, when he had refused to attend the mayor's hospitality luncheon for newly elected councilmen, Thorne had carried the banner of political advance against the old order. In 1892 he urged the labouring population to 'make no distinction between the two parties as from a labour standpoint, they are one and the same.' In a hostile council from 1891 to 1898, he fought for twenty-eight resolutions to raise the pay of Corporation employees, losing all but one.[15] Yet, he was clearly making headway. By 1893 the Gasworkers had already placed eighteen representatives on municipal councils, school boards, and boards of Guardians. In 1894 the formation of the United Socialist and Labour Council at a meeting of thirty representatives of the SDF, ILP, and West Ham Trades Council marked a significant advance in political organization. Although Keir Hardie lost his parliamentary seat (and subsequently turned away from London) due to Liberal defections in 1895, the local forces of the Labour opposition continued to coalesce. By 1896 labour unity had resulted in a functioning Labour 'party' of seven on the council. The election of 1897 boosted the delegation's strength to eleven, and in that year what now was known as the 'Labour Group' took on more prescribed dimensions, centring around the endorsement of its candidates by the Trades Council, which represented 7500 West Ham workers.[16]

If in the preceding years the socialist and labour forces had made steady progress, still, on the eve of the biggest poll in the borough's history, 'Nobody anticipated such a complete rout

13. Giles and Lisanne Radice, *Will Thorne: Constructive Militant* (London, 1974), pp. 22-25.

14. West Ham *Herald*, March 4, 1899; Paul Thompson, p. 128.

15. Paul Thompson, pp. 102, 128; West Ham *Citizen*, April 21, 1899; West Ham *Herald*, March 4, 1899.

16. West Ham *Guardian*, Sept. 22, 1894; Kenneth O. Morgan, *Keir Hardie: Radical and Socialist* (London, 1975), pp. 79-83; West Ham *Guardian*, Jan. 8, 1898; *Justice*, April 2, 1898; West Ham *Herald*, Nov. 11, 1897.

of the old parties by the new one.' Yet, at the end of November 1898, in an electoral process stretching over three weeks (council elections Nov. 1 followed by aldermanic and resulting bye-elections), twenty-seven Labour Group councillors – Thorne dubbed them 'the gallant twenty-seven' – sat as a majority of three in the council chamber. The impact of the ballot upon both ends of popular opinion was stunning. Even those who had most continually belittled the socialists' efforts now exaggerated their accomplishment as a result of their own paranoia. To the *Stratford Express* it was as if the town were at the receiving end of the Great Crusade. 'They have had a gospel to preach, a principle to fight for, and they have fought for it as men who had a faith. Against them was a disorganized crowd; people at sixes and sevens; men with no great and fundamental principle to bind them together, with no enthusiasm – most of them with no public spirit. How could the crowd hope to beat the disciplined army?' The socialists did nothing to minimize their victory, calm their opponents, or deny that the millennium was indeed approaching. The SDF's *Justice* congratulated West Ham as the 'Roubaix of England, so far as socialist control of municipal affairs is concerned,' and, unable to conceal a special, sectarian pleasure, it added, 'Who will say that London lags behind the provinces now?'[17]

Independent Labour forces in West Ham benefitted at once from the agitation within their own ranks and the exceptional lethargy of their opponents. Until shaken by the labour onslaught, local government in West Ham had been carried on in a cosy, clublike atmosphere. Small businessmen and shopkeepers predominated as office-holders, and as late as 1897 the Mayor could calm quarrelling councillors with a 'sailor-like phrase "be men."'[18] The town council was for years

---

17. A measure of grassroots excitement is evidenced in the fact that the local Labour candidates of South West Ham in 1898 out-polled even their 1895 Parliamentary candidate – Hardie – by 150 votes. Stratford *Express*, Nov. 5, 1898; *Justice*, Nov. 12, 1898. Jules Guesde and the Parti Ouvrier Francais established an enduring socialist political presence in the textile town of Roubaix beginning in the 1890s. See Patricia Hilden, *Working Women and Socialist Politics in France, 1880-1914: A Regional Study* (London, 1986); West Ham *Herald*, Nov. 29, 1898.

18. West Ham *Guardian*, May 1, 1898.

disinclined to positive action in the general welfare. When in 1895 the lack of enforcement of the Smoke Nuisance Act was brought to the council's attention, Councillor Rippen, a Liberal, brushed the complaint aside, asking, 'Where would West Ham be but for the factories?'[19] Even the stolid West Ham *Guardian* had grown critical of the council by the beginning of 1898. Its January 1 edition cautioned against adopting an arrogant, indifferent attitude to the problems of the poor in the borough. And evidence does suggest that the Old Gang had fallen into particularly indolent and even corrupt ways. It was no wonder that spontaneous cries of 'old buffers' and 'scoundrels!' rang out increasingly from both gallery and council chamber proper.[20]

Like the Conservatives, the Liberals made no attempt to tackle municipal programmes seriously; they prepared no programme of their own and did not even resubmit the municipal programme that they had discussed a few years before. Their chief interest was in the national scene, and the rise of Labour fostered in them a plaintive self-pity. In November, 1898, the regular Liberal columnist of the radical, pro-temperance *Herald* was lamenting, 'Where can be found a group of animated Liberal politicians who are ready to wage war for the faith of their fathers? The answer is nowhere . . . The official Liberal is being lost in the crowd. He has neither captain, chart, nor compass.'[21]

---

19. West Ham *Herald*, July 23, 1898.

20. For example, Council time was taken up in arguing over which of two competing firms should receive a municipal contract. The owners of both firms sat on the council, not even feigning objectivity; yet when the vote came an inattentive Councillor Page, one of the two affected, managed mistakenly to cast his vote for the other man's firm. Alderman Smith, shortly before the November elections, was charged with feeding inferior meal to the Corporation horses, a task for which he had the contract. The only communication at election time of Ald. Hay, former West Ham mayor, to the people of the district was an on-the-scene journalistic account of his success at deer-hunting in the forests of Germany. West Ham *Guardian*, July 8, 1898.

21. West Ham *Herald*, Aug. 27, Nov. 12, 1898. The deep cultural barrier between the traditional parties and the labouring population of West Ham was exemplified in the mid-summer social sponsored by the Forest Gate Liberal and Radical Association:

'The outing took place in splendid weather and the arrangements

In striking contrast to the air of complacency in traditional ruling circles, the Labour forces, sparked by the extraordinary energy of the socialist organizations, were in high gear during the election period. One measure of Labour's political enthusiasm is reflected in the fact that while Thorne was elected in 1894 with 860 votes, three years later the same district returned him with more than 2000 votes. Within the council the Labour members shrewdly forced divisions on proposals which they could not win but which would advertise their policy for the campaign. Outside, delegates of the United Socialist and Labour Council addressed more than one hundred electoral meetings. In July the West Ham Workers' Supply Association was founded, and by November the profits from its cooperative bakery were helping to defer campaign costs.[22]

Analysis of the campaign in two diverse wards indicates that the West Ham election neatly foreshadowed the later, national pattern of Labour reliance on the cultivation of a manual working-class constituency with simultaneous if distinct appeals to the professional middle class. Canning Town ward in South West Ham was one of the real bastions of organized labour and socialism in the borough. Not surprisingly, the Labour Group represented by Charles Skelton and Richard Mansfield of the SDF and Charles Pert, ILP member and skilled mechanic (one of two Labour Group candidates from the Amalgamated Society of Engineers, reflecting the politicization of this 'old union' following the lockout of 1897), here pushed most unambiguously their open identification with the immediate economic interests of the labouring classes. The first plank in their platform called for

---

were generally a success . . . The idea of brakes was a happy one, and enabled parties to be arranged more in accordance with individual tastes than obtains in the case of larger vehicles. It is a pleasure to record the great improvement in the cricket match . . . Some of the party had cause of complaint about the tea, or rather, the serving of it; provisions were ample, I am informed, but they were in the wrong place – being in the kitchen instead of in the tea room. There were some who had a thoroughly good tea, others also – after a long and tedious wait – while several had scarcely any at all. For those few unfortunate ones everybody was truly sorry [West Ham *Guardian*, July 23, 1898].'

---

22. West Ham *Herald*, Nov. 11, 1897; Nov. 29, 1898.

the establishment of a Works Department, to carry out all Corporation projects at trade union wages and hours, and 'municipal workshops,' with no sub-contracting allowed. The second demand was that work be found for the unemployed in the borough during the winter. Thirdly, they demanded new municipal housing together with a house-to-house sanitary inspection of all dwellings in the borough and the appointment of women sanitary inspectors. The construction of new public baths and a washhouse in the ward also received prominent attention, and the socialists promised to employ council labour in removing fish offal from the streets. Municipalization of services, a key plank of middle-class reformers and Fabian socialists, was thrown in near the bottom of the Canning Town programme where in one breath was urged the municipalization not only of trams, gas, and water (common Progressive concerns) but also markets, bakeries, and the liquor traffic. The rest of the programme called for new free library branches (plank seven), municipal control of the police (plank eight), and, at the bottom, paying last respects to an old SDF principle, the elimination of the aldermanic bench, which in a few days would become the crux of Labour control of the council. In his campaign, Skelton, General Secretary of the Crane Driver's Union, added a demand for free courses at the newly-opened Technical Institute for every worker in the borough.[23]

The Stratford High Street ward offered a different challenge. A motley contrast of some of the best shops in the borough, sections of the Great Eastern Railway system (including the homes of its skilled employees), and dwellings of unskilled matchbox and jute workers, the constituency demanded a pluralistic campaign from any party which hoped to conquer it. In this respect Walter Scott of the ILP and [J. J.] Terrett of the SDF were obliging not only in their electoral programme but also in their contrasting personal appeals. Scott, a school teacher backed by the West Ham Teachers' Association in his council campaign, came from a Liberal family. His father had founded the Stratford Cooperative Society, and he himself was prominent in the Socialist Sunday School movement, as well as the ILP, which he served as secretary. His melodious voice entertained many audiences in

---

23. Radice, p. 52; West Ham *Herald*, Oct. 29, 1898.

the borough on light occasions. In life style, though a secularist, Scott was undoubtedly closer to the Nonconformist liberals of North West Ham than to his proletarian and Marxist friends to the south.[24]

Joe Terrett was hardly so respectable. Though probably from a lower middle-class family (he had been accepted at the Brewers' Company School), Terrett followed the unruly reputation of his Forest of Dean upbringing. Returning from travels in South America, he threw himself at age eighteen into the dock and gasworker battles of 1889 and, in fact, sustained a head wound which scarred him for life. In 1891 Terrett travelled to Lancashire and became a moving spirit of the Eight Hours agitation, delivering some eight hundred lectures for the SDF in two years. Upon moving to Newington in South London, Terrett was elected a vestryman in 1893. Told that he was unqualified to hold office since he had lived in the district for only three days and assessed a fine of fifty pounds for every vote he delivered, Terrett did not leave the parish until he was fired from his job and evicted physically from the vestry board after amassing a fine of L10,000. In 1895 Terrett brought his formidable speaking talents to West Ham, and in 1898, employed as a meatpacker at Smithfields, he ran amicably with the school teacher Scott as 'Socialist, Labour, and Trade Unionist candidates.'[25]

The socialist electoral manifesto in Stratford did not contradict that in Canning Town. Housing of the working classes and a new fair wage clause to ensure trade union conditions on all municipal contracts were again top priority items, but the approach to the issues was modified. On the housing question, for example, there was a direct appeal both to the social conscience of those who could appreciate 'what poverty, misery, bad surroundings, and insanitation mean to the mass of the working people' and to the pocket books of rate-payers by emphasizing the economies that had been achieved by other cities in their housing programmes. In the same manner, the Fair Labour Clause was proposed so that only 'first-rate' employers would handle municipal projects. In Stratford

---

24. Howarth and Wilson, pp. 32-33; Paul Thompson, p. 132; West Ham *Herald*, Feb. 11, 1898.

25. Ibid.

no reference was made to the Works Department or to the elimination of sub-contractors. Scott and Terrett were careful to address their appeal 'to every class of reformer':

> To the Radical and Progressive, because the only party on the West Ham Town Council carrying out a similar policy to the Progressives on the London County Council is the Labour Group; to the Temperance advocate, because healthier homes means greater sobriety; to the Trades Unionist, because united political action must now largely supersede isolated individual action; to the Socialist, because in municipal progress and development will be found the line of least resistance to the political, social, and industrial emancipation of the working masses.[26]

Besides adopting a programme to fit a coalition of interests among the West Ham population, Labour Group candidates took advantage of one issue which fell neatly into their lap at election time. In late summer of 1898, East London was hit by a serious water shortage. When the East London Water Company denied all responsibility in the face of a growing popular outcry and was defended by *The Times*, opposition forces were handed an easy target. The evidence suggests that in West Ham, at least, the Labour Group took the initiative and received credit for proposing a municipal water supply as well as other vital community services. London SDF leaders, including H. M. Hyndman, George Lansbury, and Will Thorne, were all active in making the most of the company's negligence, and in West Ham, although both socialists and a group of Liberals called public meetings on the issue, only the Labour meeting drew a crowd. The issue, of tangible and universal concern to the people of the borough, was also important in that it proved that the socialists could really deal with a practical problem. Councillor Davis commented, 'It is strange that we are forced to go to "the dreamers" for a remedy.'[27] The *Guardian* had some justification for attributing the Labour Group victory on November 1 to 'taking advantage of the water question and playing it for all it was worth.'[28]

---

26. Election manifesto, 1898, Stratford Library archives; *Justice*, Feb. 19, 1898; West Ham *Herald*, Sept. 11, 1898.

27. West Ham *Herald*, Sept. 11, 1898.

28. West Ham *Guardian*, Nov. 5, 1898.

Yet, for all the political artfulness responsible for Labour's victory, some larger element of social process was clearly also operating in West Ham.[29] The feeling expressed within the labouring community in November 1898 was not simply of one horse being traded for another, better leaders replacing lesser ones, or even enlightened government challenging stagnation. Rather, the elections of 1898 were viewed as a popular upsurge, a demand for power by people who felt that until then they had been ruled and manipulated by their social betters. 'Let 'em all come!' sang out the election posters of Labour candidates on November 1. 'Let 'em orl kum,' chimed the sympathetic West Ham *Herald* before the aldermanic bye elections. The crowd of men and women who marched by torchlight to Stratford the night of November 1 sang no hymns but rather a boisterous rendition of 'England Arise' and 'The Marseillaise.' Moreover, the expansive, rather than defensive, spirit of the hour was further evident in one Stratford poster:

> Fellow electors! In this grand fight of poverty against insolent wealth; of the dejected and downtrodden against the powerful and the strong; we confidently ask you to stand on the side of labour, progress, and reform.[30]

Class feeling in West Ham, of course, had only to be stirred, not invented. The growing assertiveness of Labour partisans was in part a reaction to the scorn with which they had long been treated by the established political interests. A middle-class convert to the workers' cause of the 1890's would later recall with bitterness, 'They regarded us as rebels, they called us an uneducated crowd.'[31] In every issue leading up to the elections, the Tory *Guardian* poured out a steady stream

---

29. For a convincing argument re. the 'politically determined' quality of Labour's rise to power, see Cronin, p. 15.

30. West Ham *Herald*, Nov. 19, 1898; *Justice*, Oct. 22, 1898. Years later, Jack Jones, West Ham gasworker and SDF member, would carry this same class-edged tone to Parliament. In his maiden speech, when interrupted for beginning with the word 'Gentlemen' instead of addressing the Chair, Jones formally apologized and retracted the compliment. George Caunt, *Two M.P.'s From the Gas Works* (Manuscript, Stratford Reference Library archives, 1969), p. 13.

31. Author interview with Cuthbert St. Clair Collins, July 31, 1969, at the Franciscan Mission in Plaistow.

of personal abuse against the working-class socialist candidates, particularly dwelling on their lack of education and rough ungrammatical language. It contrasted these 'wild . . . empty-headed fools' with the 'men of grit and understanding . . . the educated, whose successful careers mark them as fit and proper to control financial and local matters.'[32]

Analytically, the initiatives of the West Ham Labour Group appear more assertive and dynamic than insular and defensive. To be sure, Stedman Jones does touch appropriate chords in emphasizing the coalition character of Labour's moments of political success as well as the leadership's rhetorical cultivation and accentuation of the cultural 'distance of the working class from the classes above it.'[33] Turn-of-the-century Labour's preoccupation with class was 'dense' (again to use Stedman Jones' terms) enough, but was it really so 'inward looking' and accepting of a 'permanent social hierarchy'?[34] Class identity was occurring as an element not of stasis but of *political change* in West Ham, and there is ample evidence of a sense of opening, of hopes for social integration and community advance, rather than mere 'consolation.' The rhetoric of class was no empty shell but a vehicle for re-politicizing the community culture.

Nor was the exuberance and determination of the Labour effort a case of election day fever. The Labour Group would meet for up to five hours every other Monday night, the day before a council meeting which would last at least that long. Working men who would have to rise at four or five in the morning might not get home until eleven-thirty for two nights in a row (for those councillors who attended regular SDF meetings it was three or four nights a week); and at least once they were required to miss a day's work and a day's pay to attend to political business. Several workers who held no elected position were important permanent fixtures in the galleries and often sharper than the Labour Group councillors themselves in rebutting a Moderate's arguments. Community interest remained high. Two thousand people turned

---

32. West Ham *Guardian*, Oct. 22, 1898; West Ham *Herald*, Feb. 5, 1898; West Ham *Citizen*, May 6, 1899.

33. Stedman Jones, p. 237.

34. Stedman Jones, pp. 236-37.

out at an open-air meeting just to hear two Labour councillors attack each other as liars. Every Sunday large crowds would flock to Wanstead Flats, Beckton Road Recreation Grounds, and Stratford Grove to hear Joe Terrett or Walter Godbold hold forth on 'socialism and the iniquities of the capitalist state.' It is hard to conceive how a group could devote so much effort for so little reward had it not been that they felt themselves to be agents of a historic social breakthrough.[35]

This was the bulwark of Labour politics in West Ham: the elemental and robust identification with the working-class that was both cultural and political. Its most determined voice was undoubtedly the Social Democratic Federation. Eleven of the Labour Group of twenty-seven were formal members of the SDF, of whom six came from the unskilled unions.[36]

---

35. Collins interview. Cm. Keir Hardie at the founding conference of the ILP in 1893: 'The Labour movement is not an organisation. It is neither a programme nor a constitution but the expression of a great principle – the determination of the workers to be the arbiters of their own destiny. There are not in this meeting any of the great ones nor learned ones amongst the sons of men, and therein lies the hope of the Labour movement.' *Report of the First Annual Conference of the Independent Labour Party* (Bradford, 1893), p. 3; cm. also J. B. Priestley's complaint about Yorkshire labour politics: 'I cannot help feeling that [Fred] Jowett and his later ILP group clung far too tenaciously to their old convictions that socialism would be created solely by a working-class movement . . . They tended to believe that one class-conscious manual worker was worth a dozen middle-class converts to Socialism, even though all the evidence pointed the other way.' E. P. Thompson, 'Homage to Tom Maguire,' *Essays in Labour History* (London, 1960), p. 301.

36. A typical London SDF branch included in its membership a number of respectable artisans, several general labourers, and 'a number of middle-class men' including 'one intellectual' who would normally take but a small part in branch affairs. Sunday propaganda meetings were 'like revivalist meetings' and would open and close with a song. Judging from the make-up of those SDF members who came to prominence on the town council, the West Ham SDF seems to fit this picture pretty closely. The SDF members of the Labour Group included: gasworkers, Thorne, Richard Mansfield, Joe Terrett, and (future M.P.) Arthur Hayday; casual dock or brickyard labourers, George Bissell and a man called Davis; West Ham *Citizen* publisher, Martin Judge; Board of Trade engineer, James Fraser; lawyer, Saunders Jacobs; minister-publisher William Ward; and the middle-class George Coe, about whose background all we know is that he came from a Liberal Radical

Contradicting their common historiographic representation, these men were not for the most part sectarian and impractical. They collected rent statistics and reported on sanitary conditions of municipal dwellings. The employment committee helped men find jobs in a project that foreshadowed the official Labour Bureau. SDF representatives on the West Ham Burial Board made an 'improvement in drawing up the water from the graves, which is much appreciated by the gravediggers.'[37] And they attempted without success to remove the word 'Pauper' from burial board documents.[38]

Had the SDF tradition of class combative socialism been the sole tradition represented in the West Ham Labour Group, it would have been a significant force to reckon with in the borough but not a vital threat to the political status quo. It controlled several seats in South West Ham and continued to do so in the period of Labour's misfortunes after 1900. However, the Labour Group's success, as we have seen, required a melding of the rhetoric of class polarization with other interests and sensibilities. An early recognition of this fact is evident in the abandonment sometime after 1894 of the clause calling for the socialization of the means of production which the SDF-controlled Trades Council had once demanded of endorsed candidates. By 1898 various observers were commenting on the outstretched hand which the SDF was extending to other groups. As Proletaire (ILP columnist for the influential West Ham *Herald*) put it, 'Revolutionary Socialism, sobered by municipal experience shorn of mere rancour for rancour's sake, has found its place as a powerful progressive factor.'[39]

In building a political coalition, it was the West Ham ILP, not the SDF, which made the most effective bridge to middle-class opinion. The connection was most tangibly made at the university settlement, Mansfield House, in Canning Town. Of the five London settlements, Mansfield House corres-

---

Radical background and continued to champion the anti-vivisection cause before local socialist groups. Paul Thompson, pp. 127-28; West Ham *Citizen*, April 29, 1899.

---

37. *Justice*, Jan. 21, 1899.

38. Ibid.; West Ham *Herald*, Oct. 6, 1894; Jan. 1, 1898.

39. West Ham *Herald*, Oct. 22, 1898.

ponded most closely to Toynbee Hall in its non-sectarian religious atmosphere.[40] In addition to such welfare projects as a lodging house for the homeless and a free legal services for the poor, Mansfield House was active in borough politics throughout the 1890s, successfully backing candidates for the school board and the Board of Guardians. It created its own committees on public health, the Poor Law, and other issues and hosted a controversial political speakers' series, where questions like 'The Cost of Capitalism' were debated. The settlement not only arranged the initial unity talks for the socialist forces, but in 1898 its warden, Percy Alden, led the Labour candidates in a sweep of Plaistow ward.[41]

In his social outlook Alden was what the West Ham *Guardian* disparagingly labelled 'a kid-gloved sort of socialist.'[42] A convert at Balliol College to the New Liberalist thinking of T. H. Green and Benjamin Jowett, Alden enjoyed a close connection with J. A. Hobson, J. Ramsey MacDonald, and other 'ethical socialists' who openly identified the labour movement with their hopes for 'a just and humane ordering of industrial life.'[43] In addition to its moral and religious inspiration, Alden's thinking clearly also bore the mark of social *noblesse oblige*: 'The settlement has been called upon to fill the gap which the absence of men of leisure and education has left in our poorer districts.'[44] A willing custodian of 'rational recreation' for the less fortunate, Alden believed that 'the

---

40. K. S. Inglis, *Churches and the Working Classes in Victorian England* (London, 1954), pp. 159, 166.

41. West Ham *Herald*, Oct. 22, 1898; Standish Meacham, *A Life Apart: The English Working Class, 1890-1914* (Cambridge, MA, 1977), p. 80. The political activism of Mansfield House prompted the conservative West Ham *Guardian*'s quip that 'social work as interpreted by some of the elected officials is something largely resembling SOCIALIST WORK,' and objected that 'funds of charitable people . . . should be used in any way to help the return to local bodies of doctrinaire young men freshly imported from Oxford.' (March 5, 1898).

42. West Ham *Guardian*, March 5, 1898.

43. J. Boyle, *Viscount Samuel* (London, 1957), p. 34; Lord Elton, *The Life of James Ramsey McDonald, 1886-1919* (London, 1934), p. 94.

44. Percy Alden, 'Settlements in Relation to Local Administration,' in Alden, ed., *University and Social Settlements* (London, 1898), p. 28; cm. Meacham, pp. 1-23.

working classes, and especially the very poor, need to be treated as children in the matter of amusements . . . Free concerts, free lectures, free picture exhibitions will gradually make a difference.'[45]

Alden's 'philosophical socialism' (for he did not formally join the ILP but maintained his official Liberal affiliation) equipped him well as the chief interpreter of the labour movement to a middle class public. While Alden likely shared the basic ambition of Toynbee Hall founder, Samuel Barnett, 'to mitigate class suspicion,' he also found sufficient practical reasons why the progressive-inclined professional should co-operate with the Labour forces:

> To begin with he [the Labour man] is probably an educationalist, and is willing to spend money on our schools. He believes in free libraries, technical instruction, proper sanitation, well-built houses, recreation grounds, public baths, pure water, well-paved streets: In all these things [the settlement leader] is at one with the Labour member, and is in all probability more effective in the effort he makes.[46]

As early as 1894 Alden had disassociated himself from the Liberals formerly in control of Mansfield House and 'made it settlement policy to support all honest and intelligent labour candidates.'[47] Links with the ILP were fashioned through the personal friendship of Alden and MacDonald and reinforced by the activism of Edith Kerrison, a staunch Congregational-ist, who worked at the Women's Settlement and served on the Board of Guardians as an avowed ILP socialist. In 1895 she represented South West Ham at the national ILP conference and two years later directed the Socialist Sunday School.[48]

The variations within West Ham socialism were tempera-mental as well as organizational and ideological. Cuthbert St. Clair Collins, a later-day convert to the West Ham ILP,

---

45. Chris Waters, *British Socialists and the Politics of Popular Culture, 1884-1914* (Stanford, 1990), p. 84.

46. Alden, p. 30; West Ham *Guardian*, March 5, 1898.

47. Paul Thompson, p. 24; Inglis, p. 166; Alden later served as an executive member of the Fabian Society and was elected Liberal/Progressive MP for Tottenham in 1906. Chris Waters, *British Socialists and the Politics of Popular culture, 1884-1914* (Stanford, 1990), p. 83.

48. Elton, p. 108; West Ham *Herald*, Dec. 10, 1898; April 1, 1899; Henry Pelling, *The Origins of the Labour Party, 1880–1900* (London, 1954), p. 144.

remembered Alden as a man who 'wouldn't upset people if he could help it.' Loosely linking Alden with the ILP group, Collins contrasted these 'gentle Labour people' to local SDF leaders like Thorne, Terrett, and Jack Jones, whom he recalled as 'big men, fighters, men who would stand no nonsense from anybody.'[49]

An important precondition to Labour Group success was cooperation between the two socialist organizations. Despite the many frictions which arose between other constituents of the Labour Group coalition, the SDF-ILP relationship in 1898-1899 seems to have been remarkably clam. Working together on the North West Ham Socialist Council (probably an extension or equivalent of the United Socialist and Labour Council), they prepared plans for a borough crematorium, argued with the school board about the amount of play allowed at the Fyfield Truant School, worked for an extension of swimming instruction for girls in the Poor Law Union schools, and visited ministers to ask them to preach special sermons for May Day. In January 1899, the SDF and ILP jointly initiated the West Ham Anti-High-Rents League as part of a larger East End movement. Meeting in the Canning Town ILP hall, they elected as president a member of the Forest Gate SDF and as vice-president a member of the South West Ham ILP. At the national ILP conferences of 1899 and 1900 West Ham delegates were among those calling for closer organizational ties with the SDF. In 1899 George Rule,

---

49. Cuthbert St. Clair Collins interview, op. cit. Born into a Tory ship captain's family in Poplar in 1881, Collins was personally converted to socialism by Edith Nesbit, wife of Fabian Society treasurer, Hubert Bland. When the Fabians urged their members to make contact with the Labour movement, Collins joined the West Ham ILP and soon became a close associate of Edith Kerrison and Rebecca Cheetham at Mansfield House. He was elected to the town council in 1922 and mayor of West Ham in 1935. To be sure, the appeal of the ILP in West Ham was not limited to the educated middle class. Among ILP councillors in 1898, for example, were, in addition to the aforementioned schoolteacher, Walter Scott, and skilled mechanic, Robert Ambrose: printer-publisher Walter Godbold, bricklayer Robert Ambrose, and Catholic dockworker William Devaney. In addition, the lawyer, Saunders Jacobs, and minister-publisher, William Ward, were claimed by both the ILP and SDF. West Ham *Guardian*, Jan. 29, 1898; West Ham *Herald*, Oct. 7, 14, 1899; Nov. 19, 1898; on the SDF vs. ILP social composition in London, generally, see Paul Thompson, p. 234.

representing North West Ham, seconded a resolution calling for a fusion of the two groups. Each time Saunders Jacobs spoke at the conference of 1900 it was to suggest either amalgamation with the SDF or closer alliance with trade unions. He pointedly exonerated the SDF members he knew from the sectarianism of the national office.[50]

The labour forces of West Ham, had, of course, to reach beyond the influence of specifically socialist organizations. Perhaps the easiest political marriage was between the Labour Group and the Irish Nationalist League (joined by the Catholic Electoral Association in 1899). The League, which had been an important element in Keir Hardie's parliamentary victory earlier in the decade, returned two of its members – including Thomas Scanlon, a compositor who ran as a 'Catholic and Socialist' – to the borough council in 1898, while at least two other socialists also depended on its support. So solicitous of the Irish vote were the secularist leaders of the Labour Group that in 1899 they backed a Catholic candidate in Upton ward who ran on the heretical ticket of 'No Fads! No Theories!! No Extravagance!!!'[51]

Finally, in addition to its major organizational ties, the Labour Group coalition attracted a mixture of individual members comprising diverse ideological 'progressives' and rank opportunists. Coming from the middle or upper classes, their ranks included radical secularists, temperance advocates, and two plain 'Labour' men. John East, a builder and house agent, was an active primitive methodist who received (as did Alden and Godbold) the electoral support of the Temperance Union. Jesse Weaver Smith, former secretary of the Forest Gate and Upton Liberal and Radical Association, ran with the enthusiastic endorsement of the West Ham Teachers' Association, of which he was a prominent member. Richard Athey, whose employment apparently alternated between a decorating business and skilled work at the GER works, nursed a large personal constituency among non-union railway workers. And John Henry Bethell was an uncrusading Liberal, clearly seeking labour support for his parliamentary ambitions. A director of Barclay's Bank, a

---

50. West Ham *Herald*, Jan. 7, 28, 1899; April 8, 1899.

51. Election manifestos, Stratford Library archives.

member of both the National Liberal and the Reform clubs, Bethell would fail in 1900 to be elected in West Ham but succeed in 1906 at Romford. He later became a knight and a peer. While regularly listing his achievements in *Who's Who*, the first Baron Romford neglected to mention his membership in the nation's first Labour council.[52]

Middle-class sympathy for the Labour Group tended naturally to congeal around the progressive, class-conciliative aspects of its message. To the West Ham *Herald*, the reformers' most importance voice of non-socialist support, 'The Labour Party and the Socialists are but upholding the flag that the false Progressives have deserted.' The paper noted the similarity between the Labour Group platform and the 1891 Newcastle programme of the Liberal Party, including the common calls for self-administered municipal work at trade union rates. *London*, expressing the views of the Progressives on the London County Council, likewise supported the Labour Group by likening it to the London Party and stressing its plans for public baths, a free library, sanitary inspection, and municipalization of transportation, all measures for which there was substantial popular and middle-class support.[53]

Strife came quickly to the Labour Group, but not so quickly as to deny it the fulfilment of many of its municipal promises. Binding its members to vote as a bloc according to majority rule, the Group first endorsed six resolutions (the first one called for a reduction in electricians' hours) prepared by the local trades council. Next, the Group undermined the council's committee structure by offering a disproportionate number of committee assignments to socialists and trade unionists and reactivating a Works Committee to prepare an ambitious new municipal labour-employer policy. In the next breadth, the Labour Group transferred paid Corporation advertisements (hitherto given to both the *Herald* and *Guardian*, most widely read of the local newspapers) from the conservative press to the struggling socialist labour weekly, the *Citizen*.[54]

52. *Who's Who, 1907, 1908 . . . 1945* (London, 1907, 1908, . . . 1945); West Ham *Herald*, Oct. 29, 1898; Stratford *Express*, Oct. 15, 1898.

53. *Herald*, Nov. 19, 1898; West Ham *Guardian*, Nov. 26, 1898.

54. West Ham *Guardian*, Nov. 4, 1899.

Perhaps the single most radical change of 1898-1899 was the re-establishment of the municipal Works Department. In early December the council passed a resolution that the Department take over, in principle, 'all council work.' Three months later the council set the following conditions for all public projects: trade union membership, the eight-hour day, a forty-eight hour week, twenty shillings per week minimum wage, paid Labour Day holidays on May 1, and a two week annual holiday. The conditions amounted to an average increase of one shilling ninepence per week per employee. For carmen it meant a reduction of four to six hours work a day for the same pay. The so-called Labour Clause not only demanded payment of wages for all borough Corporation work, but also insisted that if outside contractors were required, they must submit to union conditions on projects both in and out of West Ham. From the sidelines William Crow protested, 'That sort of thing turns the council into a trade union.'[55]

Even after the Works Department was created, questions remained as to the vigour with which public work would be pursued and the impact of municipal supervision on actual work organization. In early February it came time to let a major contract for the Plaistow Fever Hospital. Prodded by the Works Committee, Lewis Angell, the borough engineer, submitted an estimate on behalf of 'direct work' lower than the estimates of contending outside firms. Brushing aside the doubts of older borough authorities, the council accepted the municipal bid. The Labour Group answered the second question even more emphatically. When workers complained in April about the stable manager and the borough engineer, they were both dismissed in favour of men with more pronounced trade union sympathies. Overall, the Labour Group was responsible for adding several hundred workers to a one-thousand-person-plus municipal payroll.[56]

The same spirit which counselled a hard line on matters relevant to organized workers could dictate indifference to other issues. In January, 1899, several West Ham manufac-

---

55. West Ham *Guardian*, Dec. 17, 1898; West Ham *Herald*, Feb. 18, 1898, Oct. 14, 1899.

56. Howarth and Wilson, pp. 119-20, 180-83; West Ham *Herald*, April 22, May 5, July 15, 1899.

turers came to the council asking for help in submitting a parliamentary bill which would authorize a loan for industrial development of the Lea Backwater Area, the largely unusable backside of Canning Town. Unenthusiastic and divided on the issue (some thought it would detract from the limited borrowing power available for municipal housing), the socialists gave the scheme the lowest of priorities. 'We are not going to try to please everybody,' said Councillor Coe. 'We shall have all our work cut out to please the workers who elected us.' Proletaire seconded this view: 'I am inclined to think that the first labour parliament will find a worthier niche in history than to go down to the memory of mankind as a body of men, who, having survived the desert and arrived in the land of milk and honey, did not know on which side their bread was buttered when they got there.'[57]

Besides the Works Department, Council's legislative attention was focused on housing and employment. The Labour Group quickly authorized construction of two rows of municipal housing 'distinctly better than the bulk of the surrounding property.' Later in 1899 the council gave approval for three hundred more units to be built on 1000 acres of land acquired by the Corporation if the rate-payers approved in a borough referendum. The Labour Group also ordered the first local house-to-house sanitary inspection. Although incapable of full enforcement, this order had some effect as both the number of homes inspected and the number of notices served on landlords for defective property doubled in the first nine months of 1898-1899 over the figures of the preceding year.[58]

In other matters as well a not so subtle difference in emphasis was manifest in municipal policy. For the first time outside a severe depression, for example, Council offered direct relief work, including the paving of streets and cleaning of schools. A further difference in the application of relief funds was the wage – seven-pence per hour, the minimum union scale. Council could initiate other projects but not see them through to fulfilment. The list of legislation submitted as private acts of Parliament from West Ham, 1898, was the

57. West Ham *Herald*, Jan. 21, 1899; Howarth and Wilson, p. 119.

58. West Ham *Herald*, Oct. 14, 1899.

longest in the borough's history, including requests for authority to purchase and work municipal tramways, to supply electricity to houses, to buy land for a new recreation ground, and to raise a loan for new municipal baths.[59] The Labour Group also endorsed the quality-of-life and self-improvement issues associated with ethical socialist and Liberal-Radical members. They began negotiations for a new municipal library. They erected a bandstand in Wanstead Flats and arranged for summer and winter concerts. They held an art exhibit at the Technical Institute, and Will Thorne spoke at the opening ceremony:

> He said he was not a critic in art or of pictures. Most of his life had been spent in driving a wheelbarrow and a shovel . . . But he re-echoed the hope that West Ham might before long have a permanent art exhibition.[60]

The first year of local Labour 'rule' in Britain offered a fair representation of Labour's larger political agenda. Did the Labour vision, as Stedman Jones suggests, really represent an historical abdication of demands for 'power' in favour of 'welfare'? Unlike the Chartists, to be sure, the new Labour movement was making no demand on the 'form of [the] state.'[61] On the other hand, the dismissal of positive demands on the state as mere 'welfare' misses the significance of the contemporary contest over the uses of the resources and authority of the state. The Labour movement offered the chance to influence, and even direct, the planning of one's immediate environment. Like their municipal socialist contemporaries in France, local Labour militants might well be described as 'creating a protected terrain within which class organizations and working class culture could survive.'[62] The

---

59. Howarth and Wilson, p. 367; West Ham *Citizen*, Jan. 13, 1899; Donald McDougall, ed., *Fifty Years a Borough, 1886-1936: The Story of West Ham* (London, 1936), p. 85.

60. West Ham *Herald*, Jan. 14, April 1, 1899.

61. Stedman Jones, p. 238.

62. Joan Wallach Scott, 'Social history and the history of socialism: French socialist municipalities in the 1890s,' *Mouvement Social* 111 (1980), p. 147. Scott's larger argument about the replacement of older working-class 'fraternal' imagery with 'family' metaphors in municipal socialism is worth further exploration in the British context.

victor in such a contest might justly claim a tangible measure of 'empowerment.'

The fragile nature of Labour 'power' was, in any case, quickly demonstrated. For all of its connectedness to economic-centred issues, it is ironic that working-class unity should first fall victim to a distinctly cultural controversy. In early January 1899, Conservative Councillor Boardman, acting on behalf of one of his more zealous constituents, moved that the *Freethinker*, G. W. Foote's secularist publication, be removed from the table of the Stratford Library. The Labour Group, knowing that the magazine had been in the library for years and eager to get on with other business, rejected the complaint. It happened, in fact, that the *Freethinker* had been laid on the library table only by a librarian's mistake. It belonged behind a screen where it could be taken out only upon request. But the damage was done. Panic swept the religious institutions of the·borough; the spectre of SDF atheism was denounced universally from Protestant and Catholic pulpits. Rather than fending off an attack on freedom of the press, the Labour Group appeared to have taken a provocative cultural initiative.[63]

Among local socialists, the issue provoked an equally strong Jacobin reaction. A letter to the *Herald* asked, 'Are we the workers (not the middle-men and the psalmsinging, Bible-preaching brigade) to be told what we may be allowed to read, and what we are not to read, by the people who in all ages have been the greatest obstacles to all progress?' People referred scornfully to the YMCA as the Young Men's Chloroforming Association. To Proletaire the whole question was 'a stupid, senseless, and unimportant' burden, 'a movement . . . promoted not by religious advocates but by Labour's foes.' A dozen trade unions sent petitions to the council insisting that the magazine remain on the table.[64]

While the leadership of the Labour Group was at first inclined to maintain an adamant position, Thorne temporized by supporting a poll of citizens on the issue, while freeing individual council members from majority discipline. Within weeks passions had abated until the question of the

---

63. West Ham *Herald*, Jan. 14, 21, 28, 1899.

64. West Ham *Herald*, Jan. 18, Feb. 4, 1899.

cost of the poll aroused as much concern as the original issue. In March the council quietly dropped the poll, and the *Freethinker* returned to its former resting place behind the screen. Alderman Kelly's public disassociation from the 'Socialists and Atheists' was the only internal scar left by the episode.[65]

Soon after, however, the problem of 'sectionalism' – Hobsbawm's diagnosis for many of Labour's more recent problems – split West Ham Labour's prime constituency. The main trouble centred around implementation of the Labour Clause. The first conflict pitted the aggressive new unionists on the Trades Council against the workers of the Great Eastern Railway, seventy-five percent of them non-union. A crisis broke in early May when a handful of non-unionized workmen belonging to the provocative Free Labour Association refused to procure union cards at the Bethell Avenue housing site even after being solicited personally by Will Thorne. When the other workers, led by Jack Jones, threatened to strike, the Works Committee fired the non-union men. The issue might have rested there had it not been for Councillor Athey. Athey was champion of the Railway workers. Since his election to the Labour Group he had pushed vigorously for baths and better housing for workers, but he did not fit easily into a subordinate position in the ruling circles. Chafing over what he perceived as earlier slights from Thorne, he now seized on the firing to launch a vendetta against the Labour Group leader. Within the council he accused Thorne of violating a resolution allowing unionists and non-unionists to work together at the housing site. Raising the spectre of 'forced trade unionism,' Athey told an enthusiastic rally outside the Great Eastern Gates that it was Thorne's intention 'to supplant the northern men with men from the south.' He dared Thorne to appear at his fiefdom and said that they would 'roll him in the mud.' Thorne went to the rally, but he had only the chance to say that Athey had 'made one of the biggest mistakes of his life in attacking Will Thorne,' before he was heckled and jostled away.[66]

65. West Ham *Herald*, Feb. 4, March, 4, 1899.

66. West Ham *Citizen*, May 6, 1899; West Ham *Herald*, April 1, May 6, 1899; re. Athey's trade union affiliation, cf. Paul Thompson, pp.

But Thorne was disinclined to surrender. At mass meetings at the Grove and Beckton Road, he offered to accept Athey's challenge that they both resign their seats on the council and contest them at the next municipal election. When Athey called a special town council meeting, Thorne, a skilled in-fighter, had eleven letters sent to the council from trade unions (including one from the London branch of Athey's own Amalgamated Society of Railway Servants) condemning Athey's actions. When the decision of the Works Committee was supported by the entire Labour Group except Athey, he backed off from his electoral challenge to Thorne. But the bitterness on both sides was deep. And beyond the person-alities lay a serious split in the desires of the borough's workers. Athey formally withdrew from the Labour Group. For the rest of the year he served as a lightning rod for criticism of the Labour Group with polemical attacks on 'Little Willie' and the socialists ('They are humbugs; they are cowards').[67]

The dissatisfaction of the ASE (Amalgamated Society of Engineers) with Thorne's leadership, though expressed in less vindictive terms, was no less grave, for it questioned the good faith of Group policy towards the working men of the bor-ough. If Athey and his supporters objected to the rigorous enforcement of the Labour Class, the ASE charged that it was too lax. In September the ASE filed a special complaint with the Trades Council. In 1898 the union had given Labour strong electoral support because Thorne and his followers had spoken out firmly against the Ferranti firm during a bitter and unsuccessful strike for union recognition. Yet once La-bour had attained power, it had accepted the Ferranti bid for the borough's new electric power station. 'Sold again!' was the natural reaction of the skilled engineers, who were un-touched by programmes assisting the unemployed and muni-cipal workers.[68]

For Thorne the Ferranti issue was only the most dramatic of the immovable obstacles he had come up against in trying to

67. West Ham *Herald*, May 6, June 17, Oct. 7, 1899.

68. West Ham *Herald*, Sept. 23, 1899.

implement the Labour Clause at a municipal level. From the beginning he faced a cabal of the major manufacturers. Whether it was the use of a steam roller or the construction of a costly lighting system, no reputable engineering contractor in England would agree to meet the demand for trade union conditions in the Labour Clause. Friction among sections of the borough's workers was exacerbated when a firm agreed to pay skilled workers the union wage but not to pay more to the labourers. In the case of the power station, Ferranti was apparently the most technically qualified firm, its offer was the cheapest, and no other offer fully met the trade union conditions. Furthermore, if electric light was not installed soon, the borough would remain, according to Thorne, 'at the mercy of the gas monopolists and gas extortionists.' But the logic of Thorne's position did not convince the engineers. The day after Ferranti was given the contract by the council, Councillor Pert said simply, 'If ever a man gave his cause away, he did on Monday night.'[69]

The limited reach of municipal authority hurt Labour in other ways as well. Approaching new elections in November 1899, the Labour Group stumbled on the question of ward redistricting. On the eve of their departure from office the Moderates had passed a resolution over the protest of labour members to redistrict the borough into twelve wards rather than four. The Labour Group appealed desperately to the Privy Council to stop the proceedings, but, not surprisingly, Lord Salisbury's government was none too sympathetic. From Labour's point of view smaller wards seemed likely to give an advantage to well known and wealthy candidates living in the wards, weakening an across-the-borough appeal to working-class interest. In addition, smaller districts increased the importance of detailed canvassing, one of several electioneering techniques which British Labour forces were notoriously slow to master.[70] On the surface of the matter, however, the issue put the Group in the embarrassing position of opposing more direct representation. They also lost ground in a futile effort to defy the authority of the Privy Council by

69. West Ham *Citizen*, May 13, 27, 1899.

70. *Justice*, Nov. 11, 1899; on Labour's difficulties with local registration work, generally, see Ross McKibbin, *The Evolution of the Labour Party* (London, 1974), pp. 8-9.

refusing to cooperate in the re-drawing of districts until threatened with an arbitrary arrangement and legal proceedings. The vacillation of the Group on the issue provoked one reader of the *Herald* to suggest, 'They are fast losing what little common sense they may have been supposed to possess.'[71]

Another blow was dealt to labour's political prospects when the *Herald* changed owners. In March 1899, Councillor Ward protested that he had been driven out of his interest in the publishing company, Ward, Whiteway, and Co., for his political activities; but a more plausible explanation was that Whiteway, 'a gentleman from West London with a taste for antiquarian research,' had saved the paper from bankruptcy. In any case the *Herald* soon adopted a more middle-of-the-road position. Proletaire's column was discontinued; in May he turned up in the pages of the *Citizen* attacking his old home which he said now 'panders to the advertisers at every turn.'[72] In early October the *Herald* was incorporated into the larger South Essex *Mail*, and the proceedings of the West Ham Town Council ceased to attract the attention they had formerly received. Labour had lost its most effective publicist.

Left to its own devices the Labour Group might have crippled itself by its internal divisions and its inability to cope with outside pressures. As it happened, it did not get the chance. Anticipating similar developments in national politics, the presence of a Labour Party in West Ham united Liberals and Conservatives for the first time in a new municipal organization of their own. In July of 1899 a collection of manufacturers, Liberals and Conservatives long active in municipal affairs, and a good portion of the leading local clergy, formed the Municipal Alliance, headed by A. F. Hills, managing director of the Thames Iron Works. By November they had developed a common programme and endorsed a full field of twelve candidates for the municipal elections.[73] Initial socialist reaction to the Alliance was a smug I-told-you-so. As a local militant told the *Herald*, 'As soon as the proletariat . . . stepped into the political arena to do their

71. West Ham *Herald*, Aug. 15, 1899.

72. West Ham *Citizen*, May 13, 27, 1899.

73. West Ham *Herald*, July 29, Oct. 27, 1899.

own work for themselves, [it was predictable that] the sham parties of the capitalist class, Liberal and Tory would unite against them.' Jack Lane of the ASE 'did not blame the other side for making the issue clear; if they were wise they would fight for all they were worth.'[74]

However, the issues and choices in 1899 were not made so clear. The Municipal Alliance did not seek to accentuate class divisions, but to befuddle them. Appealing to the corporatist, pre-partisan tradition of local electioneering, the Alliance called itself, 'Non-Political, Non-Partisan, and Non-Sectarian,' and even suggested that it might conceivably support a few socialists. The formation of the new municipal party was justified as a reaction to 'the American caucus spirit' which had grown up in the town council. The first item on its platform was, therefore, 'absolute equality of treatment to all, without distinction of party, creed, or class.'[75] The *Herald* (now *South Essex Mail*) subtly endorsed the alliance appeal in instructing its readers, 'Let no politics weigh in the voting . . . vote for the men.' Appropriating the more middle-class oriented themes of the labour programme (proper sanitary conditions, good roads, municipal water supply), the Alliance sought to divide progressive reformers from the socialist bloc.[76]

The Alliance also beckoned directly to the working man. It agreed to support trade union rates of pay, sanitary houses and sanitary streets. In his campaign against Will Thorne in 1900, John Byford supported municipalization of gas, water, and trams 'if properly managed.' He was in favour of building Corporation houses 'if carried out on strict business lines [i.e. no burden on rates].' He warned of a rise in rents if the socialists were returned to office. Appealing to the self-interests of distinct constituency groups, he accused Thorne of neglecting the needs of Tidal Basin ward in appeasing the northerners by building the first baths on Romford Road in

---

74. West Ham *Herald*, August 27, Oct. 28, 1899.

75. West Ham *Guardian*, Oct. 22, 1899.

76. Stratford *Express*, Oct. 28, 1899; West Ham *Guardian*, July 29, Sept. 2, Oct. 28, 1899; West Ham *Herald*, Oct. 14, 1899; *South Essex Mail*, Oct. 28, 1899; on the further development of the Municipal Alliance, see Paul Thompson, p. 83.

Stratford.[77] Byford favoured class conciliation. That the Thames Iron Works, of which Mr. Hills was the leading figure and Byford a foreman, was concurrently engaging in experiments with 'scientific management' further substantiates the image of change from a haughty paternalism to more subtle persuasion in elite relationships with the local working class. Hills had just begun his 'Good Fellowship' system at the plant, including a work-study and piece work bonus plan, in order to achieve a rise in productivity in exchange for an eight hour day for his workers.[78]

In November 1899, in the largest municipal poll ever recorded in West Ham, the Municipal Alliance captured four council seats from the Labour Group. The election effectively deprived Labour of control over the council and gave the disaffected 'Athey' group (effectively wielding five votes) the key to power. Over the next year, the Municipal Alliance consolidated its control. Amidst the jingoist fever accompanying the Boer War, both Thorne and the Liberal Bethell, running with mutual political endorsements, were defeated in the parliamentary elections of 1900. In November of that year the Labour Group was reduced to seventeen in a Council of forty-eight members. Thorne temporarily lost his seat to Byford, and Cornelius Mansfield regained his. By 1903 the Labour Group had slipped to fifteen seats. In 1906 it had only eleven places, all in South West Ham, and these, except for Godbold, were 'under the grip of the SDF.'[79]

As the old interests reestablished their position in the town's government, the progressive edge of the Alliance wore thin. In 1900 the new majority required a permit for all meetings to be held in Stratford Grove, successfully resisted a

---

77. West Ham *Guardian*, Oct. 27, 1900; Howarth and Wilson, pp. 162-63.

78. West Ham *Citizen*, May 13, 1899; *South Essex Mail*, Nov. 18, 1899.

79. *Justice*, Nov. 3, 1900. The 1899 election drew 15,000 out of a possible 36,000 electors, or 42% turnout, still less than the 52% turnout for the parliamentary election of 1900; *South Essex Mail*, Nov. 3, 1900; Nov. 9, 1901; Nov. 9, 1902; Nov. 7, 1903; Nov. 5, 1904; Nov. 4, 1905; Nov. 3, 1906. Even the Liberals were eventually driven away from the Alliance policies. By 1901 a few Progressives began to run as 'Independents'; West Ham *Citizen*, Jan. 27, 1900; *West Ham Tribune, A Socialist and Labour Journal*, Nov. 1901; West Ham *Citizen*, Jan. 13, 1900; *South Essex Mail*, Nov. 3, 1906.

housing plan proposed by the Labour Group in a borough referendum, and reduced relief benefits from seven-pence to four-pence.[80] The next year some 200 workers were laid off the municipal payroll, and the Works Department succumbed to neglect. By 1907 the labour clause enforcement of trade union contracts was lax; the eight-hour day had been abandoned, the May Day holiday cancelled, and borough minimum wage lowered. With bitter hyperbole, an SDF councillor called West Ham 'the most reactionary borough in England.'[81]

Various factors contributed to Labour's electoral tailspin. At a technical level, the twelve ward scheme did indeed take its toll. The Poor Law overseers, left to prepare new electoral lists after the ward change, undoubtedly overlooked many eligible voters who did not take the initiative themselves to make sure that they were registered. Of a possible 2000 lodger votes, for example, which should have formed the backbone of Labour support, only fifty were on the rolls. While the socialists had publicly opposed re-districting, the fact that they made no effort in 1899 to restore the disenfranchised to the electoral lists, nor engaged in concerted canvassing, suggests that they largely failed to grasp its significance.[82]

Within the borough, worker sectionalism had also played a deleterious role. Conflicts of interest and of personalities, symbolized in the Ferranti and Athey episodes, had narrowed the attitude of each labour body to an impatient demand for immediate self-remuneration. According to Joe Terrett of the SDF, the treatment of municipal workers had aroused an intense jealousy on the part of other labourers in the borough. 'Here am I,' he thinks, 'slaving for twenty-four s. a week and I am paying that chap twenty-eight s. to loiter about the roads.'[83] Similarly, defeat of a borough housing referendum in 1900 by a vote 6193 to 5602 likely signalled a rejection not only from middle-class ratepayers but from those workers who calculated that they could not afford municipal rents.[84] In

---

80. West Ham *Citizen*, Jan. 13, 1900.

81. Labour election manifestos, Stratford Library archives, 1900-1907.

82. Paul Thompson, p. 134; *Justice*, Nov. 3, 1900.

83. *Justice*, Nov. 11, 1899.

84. John Wesley Marriott, 'London Over the Border: A Study of West

a final example of the triumph of particular over general interests, in 1900 the Labour Group did not even bother to back a candidate in the railroad district. William Sanders, an ILP observer from Battersea, warned his followers in 1902 that the 'subtle spirit of Tanamyism [sic], which is fatal to democratic progress, could be introduced into municipal life. That this is no mere supposition of evils is proved by the history of the Labour party in West Ham.'[85]

Although its initial victory was based on an appeal to a plurality of culture, traditions, and expectations, the Labour Group, once it came to power, was clearly the victim of the dominant culture it represented. General complaints of Labour 'extravagance' and the service of 'a privileged few' masked a middle-class reaction against a political agenda clearly tilted towards redistributing power and a degree of wealth into lower-class hands. The Stratford *Express* pronounced the 1900 electoral defeats a verdict on 'the extreme rashness' of Labour rule. 'For the next ten years the Labour Group might have ruled West Ham if they had shown moderation and fairness. But they cried 'full steam ahead' and they have run among the brakers.[86]

Finally, the cultural cleavage in the borough also left its mark. Local ILP representative Walter Godbold, for example, cited the *Freethinker* issue as the fundamental reason for the defeat in West Ham. Shortly before the November elections, a Mr. Sparks of the Secular Society was impolitic enough to revive the moribund issue with a letter offering a second, free subscription to the *Freethinker* for the library. 'Does he belong to the Municipal Alliance?' asked one Labour man, with plaintive facetiousness.[87]

The decline of Labour's appeal must not be exaggerated. In the poorest wards of South West Ham they established a base which they never surrendered, and at times they could rise again to the spirit of 1898. When Thorne came back from his

Ham During Rapid Growth, 1840-1910' (Ph. Diss., Cambridge, 1984), pp. 164-66.

---

85. W. Sanders, *The Political Re-Organization of the People* (London, 1902), pp. 104-105; see Pelling, pp. 124-125.

86. Stratford *Express*, Nov. 3, 1900.

87. West Ham *Herald*, Oct. 14, 1899.

rebuff in the regular ballot of 1900 to contest a bye-election in Canning Town, he garnered a smashing majority in the biggest turnout yet recorded in a single-ward election in West Ham.[88] Indeed, when Labour was propelled back into a working majority in the election of 1910, it was accomplished by a sweep of the poorer, new unionist wards of South West Ham and without any support at all from the more socially mixed wards of the northern half of the town.[89]

Nevertheless, it appears that the initial setback of the Labour Group contributed for a time to an overall loss of morale as well as votes among the independent labour forces. For not only had the Municipal Alliance picked off the marginal Labour or Radical sympathizer, but even among the socialist councillors and their labouring-class constituency there had developed a general weariness coupled with increased self-indulgence. The lackadaisical attitude of the councillors at the end of 1899 was noted by several observers. Terrett accused his fellow Labour candidates of having 'given away' High Street and Hudsons wards (together lost by fifty-three votes) by their indifference. Robert Ambrose, one of the accused, admitted his offence. He was tired. He said that he had lost several jobs during the year because of the demands of council work. 'After what I have done on their behalf if the workers don't care to vote for me, they need not. I am quite content.' Even Will Thorne appeared to have lowered his expectations of what could be accomplished at the municipal level. Attending only twelve of eighteen meetings in 1899-1900, he neglected council duties at a time when firm discipline was most important if the Labour bloc was to maintain its municipal legislative power. Instead of concentrating on the power levers of the council and the task of rebuilding Labour's electoral strength, Thorne set out in vain to get the ceremonial post of mayor.[90]

Undoubtedly contributing to the problems of electoral mobilization and the inner turmoil of sectionalism, frustra-

---

88. *Justice*, Nov. 17, 1900; West Ham *Herald*, Nov. 24, 1900; West Ham *Guardian*, Nov. 3, 1900. Thorne defeated his opponent in the 1900 bye-election 1397 to 953, a 70% increase over the previous year's turnout for the Labour candidate in the Canning Town ward.

89. McKibbin, *Evolution of the Labour Party*, p. 10.

90. West Ham *Citizen*, Nov. 11, 1899; West Ham *Herald*, Nov. 11, 1899.

tion with the political process – what others might call the 'crisis of social democracy' – also began early in West Ham. In April, 1899, the Fabians called a conference of labour representatives from all over England in Leeds. Sidney Webb offered a characteristic appeal to municipal efficiency: 'Socialist representatives won influence and respect for their creed and adherents to their views, not by windy declamation or abuse, but by actually demonstrating that municipal action carried out on their lines was more generally profitable to the ratepayers than municipal apathy of the old-fashioned Liberal or Individualist.' Walter Godbold represented the West Ham ILP at the conference. There was no sign that he agreed with a message that flew in the face of the expansionist, class-based rhetoric which formed the hub of the West Ham labour triumph. Yet Godbold openly confessed that he and his allies had no clear idea of what direction the council's work should take once it had achieved its initial goals. 'In West Ham,' said Godbold, 'we are now hard up for a programme . . . Almost every item on our labour scheme had been realized. We should be glad to receive suggestions for a new programme.'[91]

The SDF did not have any more answers than Godbold, but for them the situation was more serious. The Social Democrats had sought, after all, to differentiate their programme from that of middle-class reformers who looked more towards efficiency than social justice. *Justice* thus attacked the collaborationist stance towards the LCC of Bernard Shaw and John Burns as 'living in a fool's paradise.'[92] But in actual practice, as SDF activist, William Sanders, later admitted, 'Our scoffing did not deter us from following Fabian methods.'[93] The SDF was in a difficult position, rhetorically preparing for class war while groping electorally for some vague social resolution.

Not surprisingly, the quandary surrounding the theory and policy of the SDF at the national level appeared in the West Ham chapter as well. Socialists like Joe Terrett and Martin Judge could agree with Sidney Webb that 'socialism was

---

91. P. Poirier, *Advent of the Labour Party* (New York, 1958), p. 92; *The Municipal Journal and London*, VIII, April 7, 1899.

92. *Justice*, Feb. 2, 1895.

93. Sanders, *Earlier Socialist Days*, p. 70.

rapidly accommodating itself to the Englishman's innate distaste for theories.' Intellectually, they might identify with the 'municipal socialist' for whom the aim was 'to enlarge the sphere of public employment by municipalizing as many monopolies as possible.' Still, there was some ambiguity. The ballot, more than a mere instrument of improvement, was supposed to be an agent of liberation, a means, as Judge put it, 'to shake off this thraldom.' Terrett, likewise, had sounded impatient at election time. 'Remember,' he told the voters, 'this is your last chance. You will not have such a one for a long time. It is NOW or NEVER! Do your duty and the reign of the sweater and the landlord is at an end!' The SDF maintained simultaneously a strategy of qualitative change through electoral policies and a more militant rhetoric tinged with references to revolutionary struggle. Both positions were rendered hollow when the Labour Group was forced to stand by patiently while the Local Government Board arbitrarily refused loans for municipal baths and housing, or when the Privy Council sliced the borough up into twelve wards against the majority decision of the town council, or when plural voting defeated a housing scheme.[94]

But such a disparity between a theory of class struggle and a politics of practical coalition-building was not the SDF's main problem. The larger theoretical framework could always be shoved aside in favour of more consensual arguments for immediate ends. It was less easy, however, to negotiate the appeal to class culture on the one hand with the determination to achieve and retain electoral power on the other. Appealing for solidarity in the ranks on the basis of class separateness, how was one at the same time to strive successfully for political integration? If the SDF was able to establish a loyal political base in West Ham, it was because of its affinity with important aspects of working-class culture: namely, smoldering resentment of upper-class pretensions, emphasis on manliness and self-respect, pride in one's immediate community, and the traditional sanction of crowd action to enforce justice. The weakness of the SDF lay in its inability to make these qualities the basis of an ongoing practical politics. James E.

94. West Ham *Citizen*, July 22, 1899; *Justice*, Oct. 22, 1898; West Ham *Herald*, Dec. 16, 1899, April 7, 1900.

Cronin's location of the 'key problem' in modern British working-class history seems remarkably apposite.[95]

The tension between cultural inclination and political necessity is best embodied in Joe Terrett. When he talked in the abstract about paths towards socialism he might well agree with the calm, rational advance proposed by the Webbite Fabians and Progressives. When he reacted to them in flesh and blood, however, the compatibility ended abruptly. He referred scornfully to the class position of the Progressives on the London County Council in calling them 'politicians whom the Yankees called mugwumps.' 'They professed all sorts of sympathy with the people but they do nothing.' He tended to assess other socialists not so much by their political beliefs as by the attitude they assumed towards popular struggle. Terrett clung to the same scale of virtues as did James Sexton, leader of the Liverpool dockers, who distinguished G. B. Shaw from his colleagues – 'He was a fighter and that was the last thing the Fabians could claim to be.' He accused most philosophers of being 'moral cowards,' and he instinctually attacked intellectuals for their deficient virility.[96]

In practice the members of the Labour Group could not hide the contradictions in their approach to municipal politics. At times in responding to the broader, cultural impulses they fit only uncomfortably into the institutional framework. Indeed, foreshadowing the famous confrontation of Poplar's Labour Guardians with the law some twenty years later, West Ham's Labour representatives betrayed their own frustrations in following the niceties of parliamentary procedure.[97] In 1894 Richard Athey (who undoubtedly would have been hard pressed if asked for a theoretical justification) appeared in aldermanic gown on a Sunday to open the Stratford Green to children in direct defiance of a recent statute restricting its use. Martin Judge, the theoretician of the force of the ballot,

---

95. Cronin, p. 15.

96. West Ham *Citizen*, July 8, 1899.

97. In 1921, led by Mayor George Lansbury (who notably looked to West Ham as a model of municipal socialism), thirty Labour members of the Poplar borough council spent six weeks in jail for refusing to levy 'unequal' poor law rates. George Lansbury, *My Life* (New York, 1930), p. 163; Noreen Branson, *Poplarism, 1919-1925: George Lansbury and the Councillors' Revolt* (London, 1979).

once became so upset with the insensibility of the board of Guardians that he publicly threatened them with 'the power of Beckton Road.' Even the *Herald*'s Proletaire, who warned working class councillors about the political danger of using slang in the council chamber, could not always restrain himself. On one occasion, he allowed, it would have given him 'unholy joy . . . if Godbold's constituents . . . had trouped into the chamber at the following meeting of the council, to do for themselves what their representatives were prevented from doing.'[98] Similarly frustrated by the snail's pace of housing reform, one West Ham militant urged Labour supporters to abandon 'constitutional methods':

> While you are waiting there is that tendency for the movement to fizzle out. It will do so whether left in the Liberal, Tory, or Social Democratic hands. Let a few thousands decline paying their rent, and the landlord will be powerless to act . . . More could be done at one blow than all the tinkering and patching that the council will be capable of in ten years.[99]

The restraints on direct action seem to have lessened after the Labour Group lost its slim council majority. When the Municipal Alliance acted to clear the galleries at Council meetings in 1900, it provoked a visceral response. At the next meeting a crowd assembled outside the town hall; and when they were refused admittance, Joe Terrett pulled out a crowbar and broke open the lock, letting them in. Percy Alden disassociated himself from the act, but the socialists supported Terrett. And the unpredictable Athey agreed: 'While force was used on one side, it must be used on the other.'[100] A few years later Ben Cunningham, an SDF councillor, joined the cause of the Plaistow 'land-grabbers' on trial for having seized a piece of uncultivated wasteland and set up camp. Cunningham's motivation for this drastic step was not based on accepted political doctrine or strategy. As he explained:

> Continually for many years, and more especially during the last few months, I have had this cry ringing in my ears – men whom I know, often with large families, saying to me when I met them, 'Cannot you do something for us, Ben?' or 'When are you going to find us some work?

98. West Ham *Herald*, August 13, 1898.

99. West Ham *Herald*, Dec. 31, 1899.

100. West Ham *Herald*, Dec. 15, 1900.

For God's sake, Ben, help us' – until I said to myself, 'I must do something. I can stand it no longer.'[101]

The Labour Group did indeed return from the Edens of perfection to the point that society had reached. The socialists who determined its course worked within the municipal institutions, exploiting what authority they possessed and bearing the consequent frustrations. But their behaviour implied less a full-hearted embrace of due process than an ambivalent acceptance of one of the terrains of struggle available for the construction of social democracy. Rather than naive denizens of Gladstonian liberalism, the West Ham Labour people appear, in retrospect, as rather precocious pioneers in what would remain a most sobering twentieth century project.

'The Labour Party,' historian Ross McKibbon concludes in a recent essay, 'was not free to choose between Marxism and reformism but only between varieties of reformism.'[102] The West Ham experience studied here appears to bear on two aspects of McKibbon's statement. First, I hope that this essay has helped to elucidate two of the axes of contemporary labour reformism. A politics of class solidarity offered one potential building block toward progressive municipal reforms enhancing worker welfare and the power of organized labour. At the same time, however, both SDF and ILP partisans reached out in a cross-class appeal to community-mindedness, tempering images of inherent social conflict with those of civic responsibility and urban improvement. Tensions immediately beset such reformist paradigms: the limits of local legislative authority, problems of coalition building, and issues of taxation and administration bedevilled the translation of either political vision into political reality.

The historical implications of this split within Labour reform sensibilities have yet to be fully worked out. On the one hand, it conjures up themes which Chris Waters has recently explored in elucidating the problematic connections between

---

101. 'The "Land-Grabbers" in Plaistow, Why We Formed Triangle Camp,' pamphlet, Stratford archives; Thorne, p. 179; Ben Turner, *Labour's Turning Point*, p. 129.

102. McKibbin, *Ideologies of Class*, p. 41.

the socialist political project and popular culture. The ILP-Mansfield House types in West Ham perhaps best fit Waters' characterization of 'municipal Puritans' (as applied to the Progressives on the London County Council). Yet, both branches of the West Ham socialist tradition (that is, the SDF and the ILP) partook in the genteel ideals of rational recreation and cultural self-improvement. Jointly repudiating a 'philanthropic paternalism' identified with the old parties – while substituting for it a high culture agenda of their own – the socialist-Labour vanguard split with Liberals and Progressives mainly on the 'class' project: was the working-class an agent to be cultivated or a condition to be alleviated as soon as possible? Labour in West Ham thus tried to have it both ways – popular culture *and* refinement. Social-evangelical liberalism in West Ham was balanced by an open appeal to working-class pride, a sense of self-worth – and social entitlement – unconnected to the trappings of refined status. It was notably not a West Ham man who said, 'I would, if elected, oppose back-to-back houses . . . scientists of the highest character are against back-to-back houses, and having lived in them, I appreciate their wisdom and judgement.' Nor would the Labour representative have lasted long there who could admit to 'getting tired of working-class boots, working-class trains, working-class houses, and working-class margerine.'[103]

The West Ham experience, in short, points to the rediscovery of the 'forward march of Labour' within complex, contemporary negotiations of class and cultural identities. Working-'class' identity, a much embattled concept within recent historiographical literature, gains renewed relevancy in this case in assessing contemporary political events. Class identity was arguably an unstable yet quite conscious part of the political mix making for socialist or independent Labour candidatures during the period. If an older popular radicalism (or what Patrick Joyce calls populism) tempered by a statist social democratic vision represent two prongs of the political tradition ultimately institutionalized by the Labour Party, the evidence from West Ham suggests that a politicized class identity constituted a third major component. We are not

---

103. Waters, pp. 131-56, quotations, 144-45; John Burns at the inaugural conference of the L.R.C. in 1900 as quoted in Philip Snowden, *An Autobiography* (London, 1934), p. 91; Paul Thompson, p. 129.

likely to understand the tradition – for the 'creation' itself would not stand – without allowing for working-class consciousness itself as part and parcel of what Alastair J. Reid has labelled 'a dynamic recomposition of popular radicalism.'[104]

The other noteworthy aspect of McKibbon's 'discovery' of inevitable Labour reformism is that it would have come as little surprise even to many British marxists at the turn of the century. The West Ham operatives, at least, were intensely pragmatic people, willingly subjugating their own millennial faiths to the demands of getting something accomplished in the here and now. Had they been confronted at the time with charges of bourgeois 'hegemony', we can only guess at their response.[105] 'Mate, can you do better?' might express the polite end of such an encounter. Recognition of the limits of their situation served *them* not as a farewell but as an invitation to political engagement. Perhaps this lesson is worth re-learning.

---

104. Patrick Joyce, *Visions of the People: Industrial England and the Question of Class, 1848-1914* (Cambridge, 1991); Alastair J. Reid, 'Old Unionism Reconsidered: The Radicalism of Robert Knight, 1870-1900,' in Eugenio F. Biagini and Alastair J. Reid, *Currents of Radicalism: Popular Radicalism, Organised Labour and Party Politics in Britain, 1850-1914* (Cambridge 1991), p. 243. For an excellent case study of a variant 'recomposition' to that described for West Ham, see Pat Thane on J. Ramsey MacDonald in 'Labour and Local Politics: Radicalism, Democracy and Social Reform, 1880-1914,' in Biagini and Reid, pp. 244-270.

105. Marriott, pp. 161, 169, 186, makes just such a claim. The West Ham Labour Group, he charges, 'failed to transform the nature of the discourse,' 'was never able to overcome the structural and ideological restraints that it faced,' and ultimately offered a programme 'that largely accorded with the interests of the bourgeoisie and petit bourgeoisie.'

Chapter Ten

Feminist, Socialist, Antiwar Agitator: Sylvia Pankhurst and the Great War

Barbara Winslow

When war broke out in August 1914, Sylvia Pankhurst, the English suffragette, was in Dublin compiling a firsthand report about English atrocities in Ireland for her newspaper, the *Woman's Dreadnought*.[1] Devastated by the news of war, Pankhurst 'could not realise its full horror.'[2] She had known that war was imminent; Keir Hardie, her mentor and lover, had warned her of the impending catastrophe, but she had been so embroiled in the struggle for the vote that thoughts about war – or, more important, about antiwar organizing – were pushed to the side. Knowing that it was coming, how-ever, in no way softened the blow.

The First World War brought tremendous changes for Sylvia Pankhurst. The women's suffrage movement, to which she had dedicated her life, collapsed, and women who had been involved in the struggle for the vote were now divided amongst themselves on the issue of supporting or opposing the war. Sylvia's mother, Emmeline, and older sister, Christabel, militantly supported England's war effort, and the differences among the Pankhursts over the struggle for women's suffrage became intractable when it came to the issue of war.

---

1. I would like to thank the International Institute for Social History for their kind permission to quote from Sylvia Pankhurst's unpublished works. I would like to also thank Ian Bullock, Stephanie Golden, Lucia Jones, Wilhelmina H. Schreuder, and Joan Smith for their help.

2. S. Pankhurst *The Home Front* (1932), p. 11.

The socialist movement, both in England and internationally, was thrown into confusion. The movement had long condemned wars as a means by which ruling classes solved their internal domestic problems at the expense of the working class. Prior to 1914, socialists, radical trade unionists, and most feminists shared Pankhurst's pacifism. The Second International, an international organization of socialist parties, had resolved that, if war broke out, it was the duty of socialists not to support their government's belligerency; it called for workers of all involved countries to go out on strike against war. However, when fighting did break out, many socialists and feminists abandoned their principles of 'sisterhood' and 'international working class solidarity' to support their own national ruling class against workers and 'sisters' of other nations.

Women have always played a central role in the history of peace campaigning, though there has been little written by official peace historians and standard women's movement historians. The links between feminism and anti-militarism have just recently been explored in Jill Liddington's *The Long Road to Greenham: Feminism and Anti-Militarism in Britain Since 1820*, and Sandi Cooper's *Patriotic Pacifism: Waging War on War in Europe, 1815-1914*. Sylvia Pankhurst played a unique wartime role as a socialist feminist, turning her tremendous suffrage energy toward antiwar agitation and alleviating oppressive wartime conditions. All this activity was an attempt to make feminism and anti-militarism relevant, even integral, to working women's lives.

In Britain, the war created a social crisis that revolutionized Pankhurst and her organization, the East London Federation of the Suffragettes (ELFS). Between 1914 and 1917, the ELFS made a shift of which Pankhurst was not fully aware. It changed from a political organization that mobilized women to fight for political demands for themselves to a feminist social-welfare organization that attempted to provide the sort of relief that government should have provided to alleviate the misery caused by the war. The organization's demand for suffrage also changed from votes for women to universal suffrage. An indication of this change of emphasis is that, in March 1916, the ELFS was renamed Workers' Suffrage

Federation (WSF). By the end of the war, however, Pankhurst's experiences fighting against the horrors of the war and government repression even greater than in the days of suffrage militancy had led her to a revolutionary political position. She came to the conclusion that her organization should not be trying to provide resources for the East End but rather be fighting for a socialist and feminist restructuring of society. During the war years, Pankhurst emerged as one of Britain's leading revolutionary antiwar agitators. In 1918, the organization's name and focus changed again; this time it became the Workers' Socialist Federation (WSF) and was no longer an East End-based organization but a national federation with branches in England and Scotland.

Given the widespread collapse of socialist and pacifist ideals once war had broken out, the first task facing Sylvia Pankhurst was to convince the ELFS that it must oppose the war. Some of the members and officers – Jessie Payne and Norah Smyth, for example – supported England's cause. Pankhurst's fierce and uncompromising opposition to the war and her determination to impose her position on the ELFS cost her dearly in terms of members. Smyth and Payne changed their positions about the war and remained in the ELFS but others left. As the East End began to feel wartime hardships, however, the original outburst of patriotism dissipated, and the ELFS/WSF won new recruits. Even so, there were no more than a few hundred people actively involved in the ELFS/WSF during wartime.[3]

The problems of membership were discussed at federation meetings quite openly. East Londoners were faced with the disincentive of intolerable conditions brought on by war. For example, in October 1916 and again in September 1917, it was reported to be difficult to get people to meetings because of the bombing of the East End. Outdoor meetings were slightly more successful, as were indoor and outdoor meetings held in provincial towns.[4]

---

3. This count is based on the Minute Books of the ELFS/WSF. At no time do they record the specifics of membership. Sylvia Pankhurst's papers (SP) are at the International Institute for Social History (IISH) in Amsterdam, the Netherlands.

4. Minute Book of the Bow Branch, October 16, 1917, November 17, 1917,

During the war years, Pankhurst attracted a remarkable group of women socialist organizers and agitators. Emma Boyce was a roving organizer for the ELFS/WSF. An early member of the ILP, she joined the ELFS in the beginning years of the war. She had twelve children, of whom four survived, and three of these fought in the war. In her fifties, when she worked with the ELF, she was a tireless activist, speaking sometimes five times a week and travelling around the country. She spent time organizing in Newcastle and Glasgow. Being an organizer could be dangerous work. I. Renson, a colleague, described a particular incident:

> When we were in Reading, me and my brother witnessed the breaking up of a 'Stop the War' meeting in the Market Place in about September 1918 by soldiers. The meeting was organized by the ILP and the chief speaker was Mrs. Boyce of Hackney. Soon after this elderly lady got on to the platform, it was pushed over and she fell off backwards, but she appeared to have been caught by her friends who were behind her.[5]

Boyce was elected a Hackney Labour councillor in 1918, and after 1923 served as the governor of the London Maternity Hospital.

Another new member was Jessie Stephens, a Glaswegian who had been active in the militant suffragette movement as well as in the ILP and the Socialist Sunday schools, organizations that mixed socialism and Christianity. When war broke out, she went to London, hoping to find a job, and met Pankhurst, who immediately asked her to work for the ELFS. Stephens, only twenty at the time, went back to Glasgow to think about Pankhurst's offer, finally deciding to take it. The Stephens family was very poor, and Jessie did not have the train fare to go back to London, but one night her mother defied her husband and secretly gave Jessie the fare.[6] After the young woman had spent some time in London, Pankhurst sent her out to organize the provincial cities. Stephens later described her work:

IISH P.P. 8211b.

---

5. Ken Weller, *Don't Be A Soldier: The Radical Anti-War Movement in North London, 1914-1918* (1985), p. 75.

6. 'Interview With Jessie Stephens,' *Spare Rib Reader* (1982), pp. 558-59.

There were two of us, Mrs. Boyce, a working woman who'd brought up a family of twelve kids and was going around the country, just like me. She gave me lots of hints as what to do. She says, 'always take with you a pound of candles because you'll find in some places no light, when you'll want to read in your bed and you can't . . .'

When I was working for Sylvia I got thirty bob a week and it wasn't enough sometimes to pay my digs when I was travelling through the country. But I used to go to the ILP branches as well – freelance, of course, because none of us were on salary – we had to depend on the branches to pay us what they could . . .[7]

Stephens was also successful as a fund raiser for the ELFS/WSF. She stayed on until spring 1917, when she became an ILP organizer for Bermondsey. Stephens respected and enjoyed working with Pankhurst, whom she said 'could charm when she liked, but at the core was inclined to be as autocratic as her mother and elder sister Christabel.'[8] Like so many others, Stephens continued her political activism after she left Pankhurst's organization. She participated in the birth control movement and was the first woman president of the Bristol Trades Council. In 1975, when she was interviewed by *Spare Rib*, the English feminist magazine, Stephens was eighty-one and still active in the Trades Union Congress.[9]

Still another activist was Lillian Thring, a militant suffragette from London who in 1911 moved to Melbourne, Australia, where she came into contact with revolutionaries and joined the Industrial Workers of the World (IWW). She was famous for being a brilliant public speaker. Married in 1913, she lived briefly in the Sudan and then returned in 1915 to England, where she joined the ELFS/WSF. She was especially active in the 'Hands Off Russia' campaign and the Workers' Committee Movement. As an alumna of the WSF, Thring was active in the thirties, forties, and fifties in the Communist party, the ILP, and the antifascist and trade union movements.[10]

Upon the outbreak of war, the ELFS had to rearrange its priorities. When its executive committee met to discuss the wartime emergency, it decided that it had three options: to

7. Ibid.

8. Ibid.

9. Ibid.

10. Ken Weller, *Don't Be A Soldier*, p. 78.

continue suffragette activities as if nothing had happened; to try and alleviate suffering in the East End; and 'to make capital out of the situation,' meaning to exploit the issue of the war in order to gain new members.[11] Suffrage work took a backseat to defending the East End: the executive committee voted for the second choice. However, given Pankhurst's passionate pacifism, the federation did all it could to make political capital out the wartime catastrophe. Pankhurst was aware of her political isolation; she could 'not say much against the war at present as so many people have relations in it, that they will not listen yet.'[12] It was not until 1915, when antiwar sentiment was developing, that the WSF took a clear antiwar position.

During the first two years of the war, the ELFS/WSF was largely responsible for initiating what antiwar activity existed in London. Its tactics were similar to those used during the suffrage agitation. Meetings were usually held at the East India Dock Gates and followed by a procession in Victoria Park. Even though most of the demonstrations were large, with numbers of soldiers and sailors participating, they were smaller than the suffragette demonstrations had been, and they were met with greater hostility.[13] Melvina Walker, who lived in Poplar two doors away from the recruiting office on East India Dock Road, wrote that Dock Road was an extremely good spot to have chosen for that office, for it was a 'parade ground for the unemployed.'[14] The dock gates, once the sacred ground of socialist agitators, became a platform for recruiters. Pankhurst travelled to Glasgow in October 1914, becoming one of the first suffragettes to speak out against the war. At a well-attended meeting sponsored by the ILP, she said that peace must be made by the people and not by the diplomats.[15] In December, along with a hundred other prominent English women, she signed an open Christmas letter, published in *Jus Suffragi*, an international women's suffrage publication, from the 'British Women to the Women of

11. ELFS Executive Committee Minutes, August 6, 1914, IISH P.P.

12. Ibid.

13. Minute Book of the WSF, January 6, 1917, IISH P.P. 82II 9.

14. *Woman's Dreadnought*, March 17, 1917.

15. *Glasgow Herald*, October 29, 1914.

Germany and Austria,' which said, 'We are with you in this sisterhood of sorrow.'[16]

The war began with a volunteer army – in keeping with Liberal ideas of individual freedom. But by 1915 the realities of trench warfare had led not only to an increased need for new recruits, but also to a need to discipline the civilian population. Early in 1915 there were strikes of engineering workers in Glasgow and dockers in Liverpool as workers decided they had a right to share in the increased profits that their extra war work was creating. The government secured draconian legislation designed to get more recruits into the armed forces and to better discipline the workers in defence-related industries. The Defence of the Realm Act (DORA), passed in August 1914, was continually amended. Under DORA it was illegal to spread information 'likely to cause disaffection or alarm' to anyone in the military or among the civilian population. Suspects could be arrested without a warrant. Power was given to search anyone's premises at any time and to seize documents or anything the government deemed suspect. Furthermore, civilians arrested under DORA could be tried by military court-martial.[17] In May 1915, the government passed the Munitions Act, which regulated the lives of all workers employed by the munitions industry. Finally, after 1915, the government began to pass a long series of acts designed to 'soften up' the British public and to get it ready for 'Prussian' type conscription in 1916, then full conscription in 1918. Pankhurst and a growing number of socialists campaigned against military conscription for men and industrial conscription for women. They especially objected to the fact that only labouring people – workers and the military – were being conscripted, not capital, essential services, and supplies.[18]

Pankhurst was particularly appalled by section 40d of the Defence of the Realm Act. This made it compulsory for women suspected of being prostitutes to be inspected for venereal diseases and illegal for infected women to have sexual intercourse with a member of the H.M. Forces. Pank-

---

16. *Labour Leader*, December 24, 1914.

17. Pankhurst, *The Home Front*, p. 36.

18. Ibid., p. 185.

hurst argued that this act would make innocent women susceptible to blackmail and false imprisonment; it punished women and led men to believe that, since they were automatically absolved from any guilt in transmitting venereal diseases, prostitution was right and necessary.[19] Yet feminists who had earlier campaigned against the Contagious Diseases Acts until they were suspended in 1883 – with the exception of the Women's Freedom League – remained silent about this and other new versions of repressive legislation.

The government also rushed through the National Register Act, which made it compulsory for all citizens to supply detailed particulars of their lives and their trade or profession. Penalties were imposed on anyone who did not register or who falsely claimed to have registered.[20] Pankhurst, the ELFS, and other trade union and radical groups opposed the Act because they saw it as the first step toward conscription. In July 1915, the ELFS announced it would march through London protesting the Register Act and the conditions of sweated labour. Pankhurst had written to Lloyd George asking him to meet this deputation, whose objective was to call attention not just to the registration of workers, but also to the high cost of food and coal and to the low level of women's wages: it would also demand equal pay for equal work. For this march Pankhurst had no support from official representatives of organized labour or from working women's groups such as the Women's Trade Union League. Unable to get Trafalgar Square, she settled for a small indoor meeting. According to the sympathetic socialist *Daily Herald*, the demonstration was hurt by bad weather and poor attendance.[21]

The next month, August 1915, the ELFS also staged a demonstration opposing registration which won support from a large number of prominent individuals and organizations such as the Suffragette Crusaders, the United Suffragists, the Amalgamated Society of Toolmakers, Engineers and Machinists, the BSP, and the National Union of Gasworkers.

---

19. *Workers' Dreadnought*, April 13, 1918; April 20, 1918.

20. Pankhurst, *The Home Front*, p. 186.

21. *Daily Herald*, August 21, 1915.

Speaking at the rally were Charlotte Despard, George Lansbury, Bessie Ward of the London section of the Shop Assistants' Union, Julia Scurr, Pankhurst, Charlotte Drake and Edith Sharpe of the ELFS, W.I. Appleton of the General Federation of Trade Unions, Margaretta Hicks of the National Women's Council, and Miss L. Rothwell of the Women's Trade Union League.[22] This demonstration was large and well received. Pankhurst, speaking for the ELFS, said that the register had been initiated 'solely for the purpose of exploiting the workers and [would] be used for that object.' She went on to denounce war profiteering and women's sweated labour, finally saying that she would refuse to sign the register, for she, like millions of Englishwomen, still did not have the vote.[23] The demonstration had no effect on the government, which later that year passed a bill that called upon men to 'attest' that they would undertake military service if and when they were called upon to do so. Known as the Derby scheme, this was the last attempt to keep recruitment on a voluntary basis. (Conscription for single men was introduced in January 1916, and universal manhood conscription in May 1916.)

It was at a large demonstration against conscription, in September 1915, that Sylvia heard about the death of Keir Hardie. This was the greatest emotional devastation she had experienced since the death of her adored father in 1897. 'I was not faint, but stunned and stricken . . . [T]he world was dreary and grey, and Life was pitilessly cruel.'[24] The entire October 16 issue of the *Women's Dreadnought* was devoted to Hardie. Sylvia's pencilled draft of his obituary says that 'Keir Hardie has been the greatest human being of our time.'[25]

The ELFS/WFS continued its opposition to conscription. In December 1915 the ELFS, represented by Charlotte Drake, Emma Boyce and Eugenia Bouvier, participated in a No Conscription Conference held under the auspices of the Poplar and Hackney Trade Councils.[26] This meeting led to a

22. *East London Observer*, August 14, 1915.

23. Ibid., August 21, 1914.

24. Pankhurst, *The Home Front*, 230.

25. IISH P.P. 64 (60).

26. *Woman's Dreadnought*, January 1, 1916.

major demonstration, on January 9, 1916, with two thousand people attending. Speaking for the federation were Drake, Walker, and Bouvier.[27] The rally, however, was far smaller than the earlier No Conscription Rally. In the same month, the ELFS/WFS began to lobby MPs in the vain hope of convincing them not to vote for conscription.

Because of the imminence of conscription, other radical and socialist groups began for the first time to work with the ELFS/WSF in antiwar, anti-repression activities. In February 1916, the ELFS/WFS, the ILP, and the newly formed No-Conscription Fellowship held a meeting that five hundred people attended. Melvina Walker spoke for the federation, and according to the *East London Observer*:

> She dealt with the evils of conscription from the working woman's point of view and suggested that if they did not actively oppose it now it would not be very long before the women of England were conscripted and sent to make bombs by which other mothers' sons would be slaughtered.[28]

On March 1, at another meeting sponsored jointly with the Forest Gate and District branch of the No Conscription Fellowship, Emma Boyce spoke out for the federation against conscription. With three sons in uniform, she argued that, if military conscription was introduced, industrial conscription and the crushing of the workers would be next. Also that week, Nellie Best, a woman unknown to Pankhurst, was imprisoned for violation of DORA. Hundreds of women organized by the ELFS/WFS demonstrated against her imprisonment.[29]

The newly renamed Workers' Suffrage Federation organized a demonstration the second week of March 1916 in Trafalgar Square which demanded 'human suffrage' and repeal of DORA, the Munitions Act, and conscription. New provisions under DORA enabled the Army Council or the Admiralty to occupy factories that employed vital workers and to requisition and to regulate their output. The Munitions Act, passed in May, was supposed to come into force in July 1916. In making provisions for the settlement of labour disputes in munitions works, the Act proscribed strikes. In

---

27. Ibid., January 15, 1915.

28. *East London Observer*, February 19, 1916.

29. Ibid., March 3, 1916.

order to prevent wages from increasing when workers moved from plant to plant, workers were forbidden to leave their place of work. The Act also provided for limitations on profits and established Munitions Tribunals to deal with offences committed under the act. As the government took over more and more industries and series, the scope of the Act was further extended.

The focus of the Trafalgar Square demonstration, held April 8, 1916, was to oppose the full scope of the government's repressive legislation.[30] The WSF worked hard to build support for the demonstration. Norah Smyth went to the Dockers' Union for support; similarly, Mrs. Walts visited the Gasworkers. Miss Beamish approached the Canning Town ILP. the BSP, and the Shoreditch Trade Council.[31] On March 12, Mrs. Drake and twenty other members were arrested in the east London area called the Isle of Dogs for sticking publicity posters on walls. The posters said 'War is Murder' and 'The Soldiers in the Trenches are Longing for Peace.'[32] The demonstration, numbering some twenty thousand, was perhaps the largest of the antiwar protests to date. The WSF led a large contingent on the familiar six-mile route from Bow to Poplar to Trafalgar Square. On the platform were leading members and supporters of the WFS: Pankhurst, Charlotte Drake, Melvina Walker, Dr. Tchaykovsky, and Eva Gore-Booth. Also speaking was a Glasgow city councillor, Mr. Taylor, who reported on the engineers' strike that was sweeping the Clydeside and the situation of workers who had been arrested under DORA.[33] Despite the presence of a large number of hostile soldiers and sailors who threw red dye and physically assaulted some of the speakers, the demonstration was an indication of growing opposition to war and the wartime conditions.

In April, the WSF[34] issued a leaflet which was distributed to women in the East End. It warned:

---

30. *Woman's Dreadnought*, April 15, 1916.

31. WSF Minutes, March 27, 1916, IISH P.P. 8211b.

32. Annual General Report, 1916, IISH P.P.

33. *East London Observer*, April 6, 1916.

34. In March 1916 the ELFS changed its name to the Workers' Suffrage Federation.

In a few days conscription will be the law of the land. Can the mothers realise what this means? Do they realise that henceforth every boy born of an English mother will be branded with the mark of Cain? For let nobody be deceived by this lying tale of conscription for the operation of the war. It has come to stay. Are we going to strike a blow for freedom and right? If so that blow must be struck at once. Now is the time to act. Now is the time to work.[35]

True to its promise, the WSF continued antiwar agitation throughout 1916. In June, it called a Woman's Convention Against Conscription, where it was decided to ask Prime Minister Asquith to receive a deputation of working women – consisting of most of the women who had met with him in 1914 to argue for women's suffrage – who would explain why they opposed conscription.[36] Asquith, of course, did not agree to the demands of the WSF. Conscription and DORA were far too important to the success of the war effort. In all probability, he knew that even though the WSF could organize demonstrations, it was not as large as the ELFS had been in the pre-war suffragette days. Furthermore, he was aware that the East End, like the rest of the country, was divided on the issue of the war and that most working people would support the government rather than the WSF.

In December, the WSF held a well-attended open-air peace rally at the East India Dock Gates that ended with several arrests. A young man was speaking against the war when a group of angry men began asking why he was not in uniform. The men tried to throw him off the stage. The police, who had done nothing to protect the speakers, ordered the meeting to end. Pankhurst, Walker, and Charlotte Drake began to speak. The police then arrested them as well as Minnie and Edgar Lansbury, the daughter-in-law and son of George Lansbury, claiming that it was for their own good. The crowds were very hostile, explained a sergeant named Loftus, and they wanted to throw Pankhurst in the river.[37] The charges were later dropped.

---

35. *East London Observer*, April 8, 1916.

36. *Woman's Dreadnought*, June 10, 1916.

37. *Woman's Dreadnought*, December 23, 1916; IISH P.P. WSF Minutes, December 18, 1916; *East London Observer*, December 23, 1916.

With the inevitable passage of conscription, the WSF turned to the peace campaign, which had already been initiated by Helen Crawfurd and Agnes Dollan, ILP women in Glasgow. They thought about bringing working women from the provinces to march upon Parliament, but it proved too expensive.[38] The organization also sent its members on a 'peace canvass' in the East End, which met with little success. It continued to hold open-air and antiwar meetings in the East End, especially by the dock gates. more and more it found itself in demonstrations with socialist organizations such as the BSP and the ILP.

Pankhurst attended the 1917 Labour party conference where Labour delegates shouted abuse at WSF women.[39] She was a delegate at the 1918 Labour party conference, where she moved the British Socialist party's resolution that the Labour party withdraw from the government because of Liberal-Tory support for the war. Again, she was rudely treated, and her motion lost.[40] It was these wartime experiences with the Labour party which convinced her of its bankruptcy and of the futility of working with it.

Pankhurst's antiwar activity was not solely confined to the East End. She also worked with women from the earlier suffrage campaign. Contrary to popular thinking – which Pankhurst herself helped create in *The Home Front*, a highly personal account of her experiences during the First World War – not all women in the suffrage movement supported the war. In fact, many of them opposed it, and those who had been involved in the Women's Congress, an international organization of feminists, formed the British section of the Women's International League in late April 1915.[41] Pankhurst

---

38. Pankhurst to George Lansbury, June 1917, Lansbury Papers, London School of Economics.

39. *Daily Herald*, September 1, 1917.

40. *The Call*, August 8, 1918.

41. Ann Wiltsher, *Most Dangerous Women: Feminist Peace Campaigners of the Great War* (1985), p. 1. Sylvia Pankhurst, *The Home Front*, 271, refers accusingly to the 'WPSU with its women sticking out white feathers into the buttonholes of reluctant men, and brandishing little placards with the slogan "intern them all" . . .' This has been accepted as truth. David Doughey, the archivist at the Fawcett Library, told me

attended a preliminary meeting in London and was elected to the executive committee. She moved that the title be changed to the Women's International Peace League and that women who were not British citizens be allowed to join. The resolution was defeated.[42] She was very critical of the WIL; some of her feelings, no doubt, were due to the fact that many of its leaders had been involved in the non-militant National Union of Women Suffrage Societies, and she considered them politically timid. For its part, the WIL was cautious and did not wish to be associated with radicals.[43]

The monthly WIL meetings lasted from 10 a.m. to 6 p.m., and Pankhurst would return to the East End exhausted. In October 1915, there was a discussion as to whether the ELFS should formally affiliate with the WIL. Despite her criticisms of it, Pankhurst argued that the League was 'the best and most ambitious interpretation of the women's movement today,' pointing out that the ELFS was 'more advanced than most of the others [women's groups] who belong to the League and our mission is to lead them.' She further suggested an East End branch of the WIL. Charlotte Drake argued that affiliation would be too great a drain on the federation, but Pankhurst's motion carried.[44] In any event it turned out that the WSF had too few members; five thousand were required for affiliation.[45] Pankhurst resigned personally from the WIL in 1917, when it refused to support one of its own members, Emily Hobhouse, who had been strip-searched and called a traitor by the British government after travelling to Belgium to investigate the truth of British stories about German atrocities.[46]

Pankhurst's relationship with the WIL shows that she did not want herself or the ELFS to be 'insular' (as she argued at the October 1915 executive committee meeting), even if this

in December 1988 that there was no corroboration for this story of the white feathers.

42. Pankhurst, *The Home Front*, p. 153.

43. Wiltsher, *Most Dangerous Women*, p. 133.

44. Minute Book, October 18, 1915, IISH P.P. 821c.

45. December 20, 1915, IISH P.P. 8211b.

46. Wiltsher, *Most Dangerous Women*, p. 133.

meant working with middle-class women and former opponents within the suffrage movement.[47] She had her differences and impatience with the WIL: for example, the League had refused to support the demonstration protesting Nellie Best's sentence for violating the DORA (Mrs. Swanwick, WIL chair, told Pankhurst that she 'didn't think the sentence was severe . . . [I]t might have been death').[48] Yet Pankhurst was uncharacteristically charitable about its work. 'It carried no fiery cross; but tried in a quiet way, sincerely, if at times haltingly, to understand the causes of war, and to advance the cause of peace by negotiation, and the enfranchisement of women.'[49]

During the war, Pankhurst emerged as one of the leading socialist antiwar agitators. In September 1915, she spoke at an antiwar, anti-conscription rally of six hundred to seven hundred people in Bristol.[50] In July 1915, when miners in South Wales successfully struck in defiance of the Munitions Act, Pankhurst took up their cause. She spoke at meetings in South Wales and later wrote regular articles for the *Rhondda Socialist*. The ILP wanted to run Robert Smillie, the miners' leader, for Parliament in Keir Hardie's old district, and the ILP asked her if she would like to campaign for him. The general membership of the WSF voted unanimously that Pankhurst should do this, for Smillie was a suffragist, supported trade union rights, and opposed conscription. Another motivation for Sylvia Pankhurst to campaign for the miners' leader was, no doubt, that her mother and older sister actively opposed Smillie because of his opposition to the war and conscription.[51] In 1915, she also took a dangerous trip to speak in Belfast; crossing the Irish Sea was risky during the war since German U-boats were always on patrol.[52]

---

47. Memo, October 18, 1915, IISH P.P. 821e.

48. Pankhurst, *The Home Front*, p. 292.

49. Ibid., 153.

50. *Daily Herald*, September 4, 1915.

51. Minute Book of the General Membership, October 18, 1915, IISH P.P. 621c.

52. Gretta Cousins to Hannah Sheehy Skeffington, n.d. 1915, National Library Dublin, 22.672.

In 1916, Pankhurst spoke at several meetings in Glasgow with George Lansbury and John MacLean, the pioneering Scottish Marxist and leading revolutionary on the 'Red Clyde.' She praised and defended women who had successfully organized a rent strike. Speaking in opposition to Emmeline and Christabel's industrial campaign, she warned shop stewards to stand firm against profiteering and conscription; they should beware, she said, of the dilution of their jobs by unskilled workers, who would be forced to do their work for a fraction of their proper wages. She also urged strike action when necessary, even though it was illegal.[53] In May 1917, schoolchildren in Burston, Norfolk went on strike, set up their own strike school, and invited Pankhurst to come and speak.[54]

Still, none of this antiwar agitation influenced the Labour party, the coalition government in power, or any significant number of people in the East End either to join the ELFS/WSF or to adopt many of its antiwar positions. The ELFS/WSF was a small organization working with other small organizations and battling wartime patriotism as well as the general conservatism of the East End. Nonetheless, a small group of dedicated activists kept the issues of peace and opposition to government repression alive during this difficult political period.

During the war, Pankhurst became caught up in the contradictions of the organization she had built. Unlike other socialists who opposed the war, she had an organization that she could immediately mobilize to do consistent antiwar work – she was not an individual voice at the East End dock gates. But her organization had been built, for the most part, on the issue of women's suffrage (albeit in the context of other social issues), and it was embedded in one community. During the war, Sylvia found herself creating many social welfare agencies – substitutes for government agencies that did not exist – in order to serve the pressing needs of the women of the East End. She also found herself in a dilemma similar to that which faced the shop stewards' movement or the engineers during the war: do you consistently oppose the war, or do you

53. *The Call*, July 6, 1916.
54. *Woman's Dreadnought*, May 19 and 26, 1917.

campaign for better wages and working conditions for workers in war production? Pankhurst came to the same conclusion as the shop stewards and engineers: she fought for the rights of the community, which in her case meant advocating equal pay for equal work for women war workers.

Her concern simultaneously to continue antiwar, anticonscription, and peace agitation – as well as a limited amount of suffrage agitation – and to build social welfare agencies and to organize women workers pulled her in many different directions. In order to maintain its social work agencies, the ELFS/WSF had to appeal for money to middle-class supporters of the suffrage movement. At the same time, many members of the organization became antiwar activists and took stands opposing those of their affluent supporters. Meanwhile the ELFS/WSF was losing its exclusive East End base and gradually becoming a national organization through the *Dreadnought*, which was reaching a wider audience.

The ELFS/WSF expended much of its energy in the area of public relief.[55] It was this work that shifted the federation's focus. While it lobbied Parliament, wrote exposés in the press, and pressured individuals to do something about the conditions of women workers, the ELFS/WSF did not spend equal amounts of time and energy trying to organize these women to change their working and living conditions. The federation set up day-care centres and nurseries, communal restaurants, baby clinics, and other types of services for the people of the East End; and while all these were invaluable to those who benefited from them, they constituted a departure from the old suffragette tactic of organizing thousands of people to force the government to provide the necessary services. As the organization spent more time and energy providing community services, the ELFS/WSF lost a great deal of its earlier strength. Emma Boyce astutely commented that by 1917 the federation seemed more like 'a charity organization with suffrage tacked on.'[56]

---

55. In *The Home Front*, Pankhurst does not mention that other groups, in particular the Women's Freedom League and the United Suffragists, did similar feminist social work in the East End. These stories need to be written.

56. Minutes of the General Meeting of the WSF, January 15, 1917, IISH

The decision to devote so much time and effort to providing services was mainly a response to the real needs of East End women. Melvina Walker, for example, told how Poplar women were faced with a shortage of many commodities during the war, especially sugar. Yet the dockers were unloading tons of sugar into the warehouses. Women of the ELFS/WSF went to see the president of the Board of Trade, but got nowhere. Walker also described the desperate potato shortage, which led women to get up at five in the morning and wait all day in line, quite often only to be turned away empty-handed. They then had to face the prospect of spending the night in 'dug out' bomb shelters. Crowds of women ran past Walker's door, carrying their babies, rugs, and cushions to the Blackwall Tunnel, where they stayed until daybreak. The tunnel they fled to for protection against bombs also sheltered wagon-loads of munitions awaiting shipment. People were sometimes maimed or killed when the horses went wild, frightened by the explosions of the bombs.[57]

The work that was done, even though it led to greater problems, was an indication of the strong socialist and feminist convictions of the federation. Food became an increasingly important issue as the war progressed; the food lines, the profiteering and cheating by the rich, rubbed the working class's nose in the shortages. On 8 August, 1914, the *Dreadnought* had called for a No Rent Strike '[u]ntil the government controls the food supply.'[58] However, the No Rent Strike was soon dropped. On August 24 Sylvia wrote Hannah Sheehy Skeffington, the Irish suffragette, that 'we are postponing the No Rent Strike until things get more acute as only a proportion of people are ready for it yet, but of course we still go on with our suffrage work.'[59] As soon as war was declared, the federation had met and adopted a programme of nationalization of food supplies – a programme that showed its concern for working women and workers'

P.P.

57. *Woman's Dreadnought*, January 27, 1917.

58. *Woman's Dreadnought*, August 8, 1914.

59. Pankhurst to Hannah Sheehy Skeffington, August 24, 1914, National Library Dublin, MS222, 666(v).

control. One federation member, Mary Phillips, urged direct action. She said that the ELFS should go to the shops and buy food at the old prices, or take it forcibly if the shopkeepers refused to sell at low prices. Sylvia claimed that this was already being done by women in the East End.[60]

Throughout the war, the federation campaigned alone and also with other groups to control food prices. In August 1914, Pankhurst and Mrs. Drake were at the Poplar Dock Gates calling for government control of food supply in consultation with working-class women, equal pay for equal work, and the vote.[61] In November 1914, the National Women's Council of the British Socialist Party agreed to form a joint food-supply committee with the ELFS, the Women's Industrial Council, and the Rugby Housewives Committee.[62] A few months later the ELFS and the Poplar Trades and Labour Council organized a deputation to Asquith concerning food prices. The federation was represented by Julia Scurr and Walter Mackay; to Poplar councillors, J. Bands and S. March, spoke for the council. Nothing came of the deputation.[63]

In April 1915, the ELFS, along with the London Trades Council and the British Socialist Party, secured the London Opera House for a meeting to discuss food distribution.[64] Also in that month, a food deputation met with the mayor of Poplar, A. H. Warren, calling for the nationalization of food. Charlotte Drake advocated communal kitchens for factory workers and schoolchildren; Pankhurst told the mayor that if the food supply was not nationalized, there would be general unrest. The deputation ended with the presentation of a number of resolutions: an end to private trading in food; food supply to be administered by the town or county councils; the introduction of rationing; municipal distribution of food with a ticket system for rationing; county councils to be in charge of the mills and food preserving factories; and national buying of food for the civilian population as well as for the military. (There were also other resolutions not directly concerned

60. Pankhurst, *The Home Front*, p. 29.

61. *Daily Herald*, August 24, 1914.

62. *Justice*, November 5, 1914.

63. *East London Observer*, February 20, 1915.

64. *Daily Herald*, April 17, 1915.

with food, including a call for peace negotiations and a demand for votes for all.[65]) In June 1915, the ELFS further elaborated on its proposals for food distribution with another series of resolutions calling for, among other things:

> An advisory committee consisting of 1/3 merchants, 1/3 representatives of working women, housekeepers and the principal consumers of the nation, [that] shall be appointed to formulate and carry out the proposals for safeguarding the supplies and limiting the prices of food and milk. This committee shall have the power to fix both prices and profits.[66]

In spite of these numerous conferences, deputations and demonstrations, none of the plans put forward by the WSF were adopted. It was not that the population was unconcerned with the food crisis. The problem for the WSF was that there was no working-class movement demonstrating and striking around these issues. The activities of the federation seemed almost like forms of 'resolutionary' socialism or feminism because they did not have broad, organized support to back them up. With this failure to influence state policy, and given that the federation was committed to bettering the lives of working-class women, it is not surprising that it then attempted itself to set up the necessary social welfare services.

One of the first services set up by the federation was communal cost price restaurants. Pankhurst thought communal restaurants were an important step toward the emancipation of women in her vision of an egalitarian society.

> 'Cost price restaurants!' The phrase sprang into my mind. Cost price or under cost price mattered not. The name should be a slogan against profiteering and carry no stigma of charity . . . Communal restaurants supplying first rate food at cost price were in line with our hope of emancipating the mother from the too multifarious and largely conflicting labours of the home.[67]

Two restaurants were set up. Wood from George Lansbury's timber yard was made into tables by his son, Edgar, and members of the Rebels' Social and Political Union.[68] Dinner (the midday meal) cost 2d. (one penny for children) and supper 1d.; they were free for those who could not afford

65. *Woman's Dreadnought*, April 17, 1915.

66. *East London Observer*, June 3, 1915.

67. Pankhurst, *The Home Front*, pp. 42-43.

68. Ibid.

this.[69] In one day, the cost price restaurants served 400 people, averaging 150 people at a sitting.[70] This is a sizable number when one considers how small the membership of the federation was and how meagre its resources. But popular as the restaurants were, they served only a tiny fraction of the community. Furthermore, there is no indication that the federation made recruits or won people to its activities through the restaurants. Thus, although the federation's stress on feeding the working class communally had a degree of success, it did not inspire working-class women to organize and demand that the government set up communal restaurants everywhere.

The ELFS/WSF also set up a Distress Bureau in the Women's Hall in Bow, where members answered questions about food, rent, and pensions. The idea for this came about because Pankhurst and Lansbury sat on the local committees of the National Distress Bureau. They were appalled at the complacency of the local authorities and the apathy of the councillors. In the *Dreadnought*, Sylvia attacked the snooping investigators who judged whether or not women were 'worthy' of allowances.[71] The Distress Bureau fought on behalf of those people who were evicted from their homes for being unable to pay their rents. It also secured the release of several people in prison, helped others through the problems of unemployment, and secured separation allowances for many wives of soldiers and sailors. The need was so great that bureaus were set up in Bromley, Canning Town, and Poplar.[72]

In response to conditions resulting from the war – including housing cutbacks, lack of separation allowances, and food scarcity (combined with the inefficiency of established bodies which distributed relief) – Pankhurst set up the League of Rights for Soldiers' and Sailors' Wives and Relatives in 1915. She approached George Lansbury with the idea, hoping to involve sympathetic trade unionists and socialists, albeit in a minimal capacity. The federation would be responsible for the routine day-to-day work, and in this way it did, in fact,

---

69. *Woman's Dreadnought*, August 23, 1914.

70. *Woman's Dreadnought*, April 17, 1915.

71. *Woman's Dreadnought*, January 2, 1915.

72. Ibid.

succeed in involving women in the struggle for their rights.
Many soldiers' and sailors' wives became honorary secretaries in branches of the League of Rights. Pankhurst persuaded Mrs. Lansbury to be the honorary secretary of the
League but she was so overwhelmed by chores and children
that she never had any time to do the work.[73] So Sylvia
persuaded George Lansbury's daughter-in-law, Minnie Lansbury, to give up teaching and replace her mother-in-law as
honorary secretary. Minnie devoted all her time to the
League, and she and Pankhurst hoped that in time it would
become a national body and take over the role of the inadequate Soldiers' and Sailors' Families Association.[74] However,
this organization was not accompanied by the flashy success of
the suffrage days. The meetings were attended by 'quiet,
earnest little women, who joined the organization with diffi-
dence and in modest numbers. The dark streets were a
growing deterrent.'[75] The League of Rights existed as an
unofficial pressure group throughout the war and was still
advertising (in the *Dreadnought*) its meetings in Wal-
thamstow and East Ham as late as 1918 and 1919. But by then
its main functions were being handled by the other ex-
servicemen's organizations.

Other community services were established by the federation, including a baby clinic and day nursery. For 3*d*. a day
(including food), working mothers were able to leave their
children in the care of the ELFS/WSF.[76] The clinic was able to
hold only about thirty children, but in 1915 the WSF took
over an old pub called the Gunmaker's Arms, renamed it the
'Mothers' Arms,' and turned it into a day-care centre and

73. Pankhurst, *The Home Front*, p. 131.

74. Ibid. Nellie Rathbone, Sylvia's secretary, claims it was she, not Lansbury, who did all the work for Pankhurst in this respect: 'She started
this thing and I did all the work . . . [S]o the soldiers and sailors wives
and relatives came to see me and I got such intimate information about
their family life . . . [Y]ou know I spent my time writing to the War
office and goodness knows . . . [Y]ou see, they were stranded . . .
[T]hey had no money coming through.' (Nellie Rathbone interview,
1972, University of Warwick, Coventry.)

75. Pankhurst, *The Home Front*, p. 132.

76. *Daily Herald*, October 17, 1914.

nursery run by Montessori methods.[77] Milk centres were also organized by the federation. The milk – or money for the milk – came from the generosity of people outside the community. At the Women's Hall in Bow, about a thousand nursing mothers received a quart of milk and dinner every night.[78] Unfortunately, there were problems with the milk centres. Many of the babies were often so ill that they were unable to digest the milk. One of the nurses was accused of buying Nestle milk and selling it to the mothers at a profit. She was constantly arguing about the price of milk with the women who used the centre and was also suspected of stealing money and other items from the 'Mothers' Arms.'[79]

The ELFS/WSF was particularly concerned with child welfare, an issue with which Pankhurst would involve herself for many years. One plan urged by the federation was to send the poor children of the East End to live in the country for the duration of the war. There they would be exposed to the benefits of country life and their health would improve.[80] (This plan was adopted by the national government during the Second World War.) The federation also proposed to the Poplar Council that it set up more maternity and infant centres, and this was accepted.[81] Every Christmas the ELFS/WSF organized a large party for the children of the East End, attended by six hundred or so members and friends of the federation, mostly working women and children. The success of the party was not completely due to the people of the East End. Maude Arncliff Sennett, formerly a constitutional suffragist, helped arrange for gifts to be sent to the ELFS/WSF and claimed that the food and gifts had all been provided by wealthy sympathizers.[82] Later, when political disagreements arose at a 1916 suffrage meeting, Sennett complained that

77. *Woman's Dreadnought*, January 2, 1915.

78. *East London Observer*, October 24, 1914.

79. WSF Finance Committee, January 19, 1918, IISH P.P.

80. *East London Observer*, June 12, 1915.

81. Minutes of the Poplar Council, November, 1914, Poplar Borough Hall.

82. Maud Sennett, *The Child* (London: C.W. Daniel & Company, Ltd., 1938), p. 110.

Pankhurst and the East End women were not appreciative enough of their wealthy benefactresses.[83]

Here again we see the dilemmas facing Pankhurst. She was forced to scrounge from her mother's wealthy friends for money and supplies for her projects rather than rely on the East End community to develop programmes and services based upon their own resources. What is remarkable is that the ELFS did not change its political positions in order to appease its richer and more conservative sources. Pankhurst also faced contradictions in her attempts to organize working women. The first initiatives taken against unemployment were straightforward, but as war increased the demand for labour, women were employed in order to release men for the army. The ELFS/WSF found itself both opposing the war and fighting for the working women who replaced the men who had been drafted.

One wartime institution particularly galled the ELFS/WSF: the Queen Mary's Workrooms. These had been set up in 1914 to give unemployed women useful work, although at abysmal rates of pay. Pankhurst wrote to the Queen on behalf of the ELFS, pointing out that in the workrooms bearing her name women were forced to work long hours at less than 3d. an hour. She urged that women with children be given 10s. extra and 5s. per child.[84] The ELFS considered these Workrooms a disgrace and called them the 'Queen Mary's Sweatshops.' They were disbanded in 1915 because war work had all but liquidated unemployment. In the meantime, the ELFS campaigned vigorously against them, but with little success or support. Pankhurst and Julia Scurr served on the Poplar Relief Committees and used those positions as a way to expose the conditions in the workrooms. They called upon Susan Lawrence and Mary Macarthur, two leading trade unionists and government officials who sat on government committees, to organize a strike in protest against the setting up of sweated shops.[85] Both refused.

In an attempt to counter the sweated shops and provide work for unemployed women, the ELFS decided to establish

---

83. Ibid.

84. *Daily Herald*, September 9, 1914.

85. Pankhurst, *The Home Front*, p. 58.

its own model factories. A boot-and-shoe factory, and later a toy factory, were set up in 1914. Fifty-nine people were employed at the toy factory, which was run on a cooperative basis: everyone was paid 5*d*. an hour or 11*s*. a week, and no one made a profit.[86] The boot-and-shoe factory never paid for itself; it was subsidized by wealthy supporters of the ELFS. As with many of her projects, Pankhurst found herself begging for support from women she knew in WSPU days. She even spent one miserable weekend – trying to get support from England's wealthy – at the home of Lady Astor, the first woman to serve as a Member of Parliament.[87] Here again she came up against a contradiction: without the contributions of rich supporters, the cooperative factories could not have continued; Lady Astor later wrote to Pankhurst that she never would have invited her to the Astor mansion, nor aided the toy factory, had she been aware of Pankhurst's pacifist and socialist beliefs.[88]

The toy factory prospered, though arguments arose over its method of operation. It was run by a Polish woman, Mrs. Hercbergova, whose commercial expertise outweighed her socialist and feminist ideas of industrial organization. She opposed the WSF's belief that the factory should have a definite constitution and be run by a committee made up of its workers. Mrs. Hercbergova wanted business management to be separate from this committee. The WSF decided that a special factory committee should be formed: outside people might be elected to it, but only those who held either socialist or cooperative viewpoints.[89]

The factories were set up to provide needed employment as well as to bring money into the East End, but in fact they in no way helped the community's problems of unemployment and poverty. Nor, as with users of the cost price restaurants, is there any indication that the people employed in the workrooms joined the federation or were involved in any kind of agitation. Rather than setting up workrooms which totally

---

86. *Woman's Dreadnought*, January 2, 1915.

87. Pankhurst, *The Home Front*, pp. 142-146.

88. Ibid, 150. Lady Astor had probably confused Sylvia with her better known sister Christabel.

89. Memo, November 2, 1917, IISH P.P. 82IIa.

depended upon the support and generosity of the rich, it might have been better for the ELFS to organize working and unemployed women to fight for their rights as workers – for better pay and working conditions and for more jobs.

After 1915, the WSF no longer had to deal with the question of massive unemployment for women because thousands were entering the work force, and this created a new set of problems. The WSF's issues became the abolition of sweating, the protection of women workers, the upgrading and training of women, and the securing of equal pay. The *Dreadnought* played a role in exposing their horrendous working conditions: in Limehouse, for example, one food factory was housed in a dank, steaming basement; ironically, the factory made turtle soup for the royal family.[90] The federation's propaganda and agitation concerning working conditions received some sympathetic attention. The Labour party, women's organizations, trade unions, and the Liberal and Conservative government claimed that they wanted to do all they could to ensure safe, decent working conditions for the women who were making soldiers' uniforms or munitions. In other words, they wanted to improve the conditions of women war workers in order to win the war. However, while the efforts of the WSF brought attention to the true position of women in industry, it was not able to bring about any real improvements.

As soon as women's war work registration was announced, in March 1915, Pankhurst called for a women's conference to discuss the problems of women workers. She also wrote to Lloyd George demanding that the government enforce equal pay legislation. Pankhurst thought she had wrung a concession from the government. But Lloyd George's response was deliberately vague, promising only that 'if the women turn out the same quantity of work as men employed on the same job, they will receive exactly the same pay.'[91] A few months later, the WSF called for demonstrations protesting the Registration Act as well as the conditions of women workers. Again Pankhurst wrote to Lloyd George asking him to receive a

---

90. Sheila Rowbotham, *Hidden from History* (New York: Pantheon, 1973), p. 116.

91. Pankhurst, *The Home Front*, p. 159.

deputation, and announced that the WSF would lobby individual M.P.s. However, the call was for the most part ignored by the labour officials, the Women's Trade Union League, and the Women's Labour League, and the Lloyd George government refused to meet with it.[92]

In August 1915, attending a conference on Women's Organizations and the War called by the government, Walker and Pankhurst demanded that it live up to Lloyd George's promise to pay women workers the same as men. Both Lloyd George and Walter Runciman, the president of the Board of Trade, refused to answer. Pankhurst and Walker were isolated at this conference; even Pankhurst admitted that most of the women present looked upon the WSF as disrupters.[93] Some months later, in March 1916, Pankhurst wrote again to the Prime Minister asking that he receive a deputation from the WSF that would address him on the question of equal pay for women workers. In her letter, Pankhurst pointed out that neither the Home Office nor the Board of Trade had included any mention of equal pay for women workers in its latest report on women's war work. Also, only four out of thirteen appointed members of the advisory committee on this question were women; and of these four, none represented working women and one had been notorious for opposing women's suffrage.[94]

Again, the limitations of Pankhurst's work are evident. It might have been better for the WSF to concentrate on convincing women munitions workers rather than Runciman and Lloyd George that they deserved equal pay. Had there been an organization of women workers calling for equal pay, backed up with strikes, rallies, and demonstrations, perhaps more could have been accomplished. Other socialist, trade union, and women's organizations did little on behalf of women warworkers, however.

In spite of the enormous tasks Pankhurst took on for herself to oppose the war, she never abandoned the struggle for women's suffrage and neither did the ELFS/WSF. During the war, the ELFS/WSF remained the only organization that

---

92. *Woman's Dreadnought*, July 24, 1915.

93. Pankhurst, *The Home Front*, p. 161.

94. *East London Observer*, March 18, 1916.

consistently pressured the government to grant votes to *all* women. Whether in the food antiwar, or sweated industries deputations, the demand for votes for all women and men was always included. Pankhurst angered many former suffragettes and suffragists in her determination to give all adults the vote. At a Caxton Hall suffrage meeting in 1916, she and the WSF argued for adult suffrage. The majority voted against the WSF.[95] Nevertheless, the WSF continued suffrage agitation, although with new allies. The British Socialist Party, for example, which had condemned the suffragettes during the height of militancy, praised the WSF, observed that 'Sylvia comes on like one resurrected,' and promised their support.[96]

This new support arose because it was clear that the new Franchise Bill drawn up by the government in 1916 was intended to give the vote to women over thirty who were either householders or married to householders. This meant that the suffrage would be extended to those women who were probably more conservative than younger, propertyless women. The very fact that franchise legislation was being presented to Parliament at this time was a result of increasing public pressure for soldiers to be enfranchised. Also, the existing occupational qualifications for voting deprived many munitions workers of the vote, since they moved around the country doing vital war work. This seemed grossly unfair to many people. On top of this was the feeling that all working men had contributed equally to the war effort and that therefore the property qualification should be abolished. Thus there was a growing demand for votes for all men, to which was added a demand for votes for some women. To have given all women over twenty-one the vote would have made them a majority, and this the government would not allow. In a letter to *The Call*, Pankhurst clearly pointed out why socialists could not support the Franchise Bill:

1. A woman is not to vote until 30 years of age, though the adult age is 21 . . .

2. A woman is on a property basis when enfranchised.

3. A woman loses both her Parliamentary and her local government vote if she or her husband accept Poor Law Relief; her husband

---

95. Maud Sennet, *The Child*, p. 110.

96. *The Call*, July 6, 1916.

retaining his Parliamentary and losing his local government vote if he accepts Poor Law Relief.

4. A woman loses her local government vote if she ceases to live with her husband, i.e. if he deserts her, she loses her vote, he retains his.

5. Conscientious objectors to military service are to be disenfranchised.[97]

Even though they were not committed to women's suffrage, the BSP, sections of the Labour party, and other radical and some suffrage groups opposed this blatantly discriminatory suffrage bill and were willing to work against it with Pankhurst to avoid its electoral results. But only a minority of suffragists were interested in adult suffrage. At a WSF executive meeting in April 1917, Nora Smyth said that the WSF 'had turned the middle-class against us by our attitude toward adult suffrage.'[98] This was the major reason for the change in name in March 1916 from East London Federation of the Suffragettes to Workers' Suffrage Federation. The WSF opposed the wording of the Franchise Bill: it excluded men because of poverty and their political beliefs, it discriminated against working-class women, and it excluded women because they happened to be young, poor, widowed, or deserted. Only a law that simply gave the franchise to every person over twenty-one would be acceptable, and it was decided that the federation's name should reflect this. The federation members also hoped that the increasing sense of grievance felt by men who could not vote would prompt them to want to join an organization that fought for their rights. The new name was also more appropriate to an organization of women and men, and one which increasingly was involved in struggles other than specifically women's rights issues. As Pankhurst wrote in the *Dreadnought*, 'the battle for human suffrage is part of the great struggle for upward human evolution, in the course of which dominance and compulsion, exploitation and poverty will be abolished.'[99]

Following a meeting called by Emmeline Pethick-Lawrence, Pankhurst's friend and sister suffragette, under the auspices of the Women's International League, the National Council of Adult Suffrage was formed. But although it

---

97. Ibid, December 6, 1917.

98. WSF Committee Meeting, April 16, 1917, IISH P.P. 48.

99. *Woman's Dreadnought*, January 22, 1916.

was formally committed to adult suffrage, it was inactive and the WSF disaffiliated in November 1917.[100] With George Lansbury and other Labour leaders, the WSF then formed the Adult Suffrage Joint Committee. This consisted of four WSF members, three trade unionists, and one member of the BSP.[101] Pankhurst believed that such an organization was necessary because the women's suffrage movement had disintegrated. The WSF introduced a resolution in May 1917 that shows its strong socialist/feminist position on suffrage:

> We the undersigned workers, realising that if a woman can cast a shell, she can cast a vote, and that women whether in industry or as wives and mothers, have their full share of the world's work, whether or not in peace or war, call upon the government to introduce not a Registration Bill, but a Franchise Bill to give a vote to any woman and man of full age.[102]

The days of massive suffrage agitation, however, were over. The Franchise Bill was passed in 1918. Pankhurst stood in opposition to some of her former suffragette comrades, including her mother and sister, who had said that soldiers should vote and women should wait.

Pankhurst's transformation from a pacifist suffragette to a socialist antiwar agitator also involved her commitment to the Irish struggle for independence. On Easter Sunday, 1916, Irish socialists and nationalists staged an abortive rising against the British government. Pankhurst and the WSF defended the rising and argued against British rule in Ireland, while the other socialist groups either denounced the rebels or were silent.[103] Pankhurst dispatched Patricia Lynch an extraordinary member of the WSF, to Dublin to cover the rising for the *Dreadnought*. Lynch pulled off a spectacular journalistic coup. Only eighteen, she was the first British person to go to Dublin after the rebellion. The city was closed off by the British Army, but Lynch was determined to get a firsthand account for the *Dreadnought*. On the train to Ireland, she met a sympathetic army officer who let her pose as his sister. She was thus able to evade the English authorities, who were

---

100. WSF Committee Meeting, May 5, 1917, IISH P.P. 8211b.

101. Ibid., June 19, 1917.

102. Ibid.

103. *Woman's Dreadnought*, April 22, 1916.

insistant upon maintaining a news blackout and detaining and arresting all those who were sympathetic to the Irish rebels.[104] Lynch's story published in the *Dreadnought*, generated so much interest that the issue sold out. New copies were printed, and eventually the story was reissued as a pamphlet. (The British government had it suppressed in the United States.)[105]

Pankhurst's support of and contribution to the struggle for Irish freedom were not forgotten. Fifteen years after the rising, Hannah Sheehy Skeffington, an Irish pacifist and feminist whose husband, Francis, had been shot in the back by English soldiers after the rising, expressed her feelings about Pankhurst's work:

> I know no English rebel who understands the Irish situation and the international so well. The comments and the sympathy of some English on Ireland just drive me mad at times as they show such a blind spot where we are concerned, in fact, friends are the worst! Your paper *Dreadnought* was always fine on this and other war matters.[106]

The influence of the *Dreadnought* also contributed to Pankhurst's growing reputation as an antiwar militant. The *Dreadnought*'s unique depth of its coverage in comparison with the other socialist newspapers made it arguably the most influential antiwar newspaper in England. In December 1914, Pankhurst was the first English socialist to reprint the analysis by the German Marxist, Karl Liebknecht, that the First World War was caused by imperialists fighting over the world market.[107] In 1917, the *Dreadnought* published the famous letter from the English poet Siegfried Sassoon, M.C. Third Battalion, Royal Welsh Fusiliers, to his commanding officer:

---

104. Raymond Challinor, *The Origins of British Bolshevism* (London: Croom Helm, 1977), p. 169.

105. Patricia Lynch, *Rebel Ireland*, WSF Publication, 1916. The American government suppressed the pamphlet because of its revolutionary content and the sympathy it would receive from the millions of Irish in the United States.

106. Hannah Sheehy Skeffington to Sylvia Pankhurst, 1932, National Library, Dublin.

107. *Woman's Dreadnought*, December 26, 1914.

> I am making this statement as an act of wilful defiance of military authority, because I believe that the war is being deliberately prolonged by those who have the power to end it.
>
> I am a soldier, convinced that I am acting on behalf of the soldiers. I believe that this war, upon which I entered as a war of defence, has now become a war of aggression.[108]

The paper demanded nationalization of food as the only means to alleviate hunger. It consistently argued against all repressive measures taken by the government. It also encouraged industrial and military sabotage, as well as a peace referendum for the troops. Not surprisingly, the paper was raided by British authorities in 1916 and 1918.[109] When editions of the *Dreadnought* carried articles about British atrocities in Ireland, the paper was not allowed into Ireland.[110] Pankhurst always had difficulties raising money for the paper and, more important, finding a printer who would risk printing possibly seditious materials.

As the full horror and destructiveness of the international slaughter began to hit home, Pankhurst's antiwar propaganda began to reach more receptive ears. But events in Russia were the ultimate catalyst in the transformation of Pankhurst and the WSF. One of the first British revolutionaries to speak out in favour of the Bolsheviks, she did so consistently and enthusiastically. She demanded that Britain negotiate a peace with Germany on Russia's terms with no annexations and no indemnities. The Russian revolution boosted the growing militancy in Britain's factories, and the WSF found itself being swept along on a swelling tide of revolutionary unrest. Indicating the changing mood, in July 1917 the *Women's Dreadnought* was renamed the *Workers' Dreadnought*. The SLP welcomed the change. Its paper, *Solidarity*, wrote,

> Woman and worker are synonymous terms so there is nothing very startling about the alteration of the title of the bright little rebel paper, the *Woman's Dreadnought* . . . Miss Sylvia Pankhurst has succeeded in making the *W.D.* a real force in Labour politics and we wish her every success.[111]

---

108. Ibid., July 28, 1917.

109. WSF Minutes, October 12, 1917, IISH, P.P.; *Woman's Dreadnought*, January 31, 1917.

110. WSF Minutes, December 12, 1916, IISH, P.P.

111. *Solidarity*, July, 1917.

By 1918 Pankhurst was interested in forming her own revolutionary organization, the Workers' Socialist Federation, in opposition to the BSP and the ILP.

By the time of the armistice, Sylvia Pankhurst's beliefs were changing with the same remarkable speed as were the events surrounding her. She summed up this transformation in 1920 in an impassioned speech to a judge who was about to sentence her to jail:

> Because I had been a suffragette and had fought for the cause of women, the women came to me and asked me to help them. I had dying babies brought to me. I had to start clinics and find accommodation for people whose fathers were fighting for the capitalist governments of their country. I used to sit up all night writing, begging for money for these people. We had good families of people coming to my house without a penny, and with six or seven children, and I opened two penny restaurants where you could get two penny meals. These expenses used to pass through my hands. I used to spend £150 a week on that. But I know it is all palliatives. It will not do any good really. I want to change the system. I am going to fight it if it kills me.[112]

The war, the Easter Rising, and the Russian Revolution overturned Sylvia Pankhurst's world. Her participation in the antiwar struggles helped forge her new revolutionary ideals. Her work in the East End of London was dedicated to women emancipating themselves from the ravages of poverty, overwork, ill health, powerlessness, and war. Sylvia Pankhurst was no longer a socialist suffragette but a feminist revolutionary dedicated to the struggle for socialism, internationalism, and peace.

---

112. Sylvia Pankhurst's *Appeal*, p. 32, IISH P.P. 40.

Chapter Eleven

On the Waterfront: Black, Italian and Irish Longshoremen in the New York Harbour Strike of 1919

Calvin Winslow

'The working class and the employing class have nothing in common,' says the I.W.W. preamble. This is wrong. They have the A.F. of L. in common.

John Reed, 'The Convention of the Dead,'
The Liberator, August, 1919

The New York longshoremen's strike began in Brooklyn, early in the morning, October 7, 1919. The strike spread to the Chelsea piers in Manhattan, then engulfed the Habour, closing 700 miles of waterfront, and stranding 650 ships. Forty to seventy thousand longshoremen struck – it was agreed that it was impossible accurately to estimate the size of this vast waterfront workforce. The longshoremen were then joined by tens of thousands of others, workers from dozens of harbour trades, so that by the week's end, 150,000 workers were idled, in what was perhaps the largest habour strike ever.

This great strike, of course, took place in the year of great strikes. 'The year 1919 was like none other in American history,' writes Melvyn Dubofsky.[1] There were 3,630 strikes recorded, involving 4,160,000 workers. The year began with a

1. Melvyn Dubofsky, 'Abortive Reform: The Wilson Administration and Organized Labor, 1913-1920,' in *Work, Community and Power*, James E. Cronin and Carmen Sirianni, (Philadelphia, 1983), p. 213. I would like to thank Professor Dubofsky for suggesting the topic of this essay. I would like to acknowledge the support of the Michael Harrington Center at Queens College/CUNY, in particular Kathleen Donovan. Thanks also to Priscilla Murolo and Barney Pace.

general strike in Seattle, included a strike by the Boston police, and ended with nationwide walkouts by steelworkers and coal miners. The 1919 strikes were the culmination of a decade-long strike wave, a decade of unprecedented industrial conflict in the United States.[2] This conflict was not interrupted by the war; in fact wartime conditions seemed to favour labour's advance. This was certainly the case on the New York waterfront, where the longshoremen's union, the International Longshoremen's Association (I.L.A.), scarcely 6,000 strong in 1914, emerged from the war years with 40,000 members, organized in 54 local unions along the New York Habour waterfront.[3]

The strikes of this period were marked by mass-involvement and direct action.[4] They reflected the growth of class consciousness among American workers and the development of a radical spirit. New solidarities were constructed, and ethnic isolation diminished. Managerial authority was frequently challenged, and even where the issues at stake were strictly 'pure and simple' (that is, wages, hours, working conditions), the conflicts often spilled out of the workplace and into working class neighbourhoods. At the same time, the American Federation of Labour (A.F.L.), the dominant labour organization in the United States, was itself challenged, as increasing numbers of workers came to reject its traditions and practice – conservatism, collaboration with the employers and the state, and its strict insistence on the sanctity of contracts, on jurisdictional division by craft, and on the authority of the trade union leaders.

This was true in Seattle in 1919 where not just managerial but civil authority itself was challenged, as workers assumed, temporarily at least, control over the health and safety of the entire city. It was also true in Pittsburgh where representatives of the Interchurch World Movement, investigating the steel

---

2. See David Montgomery, 'The New Unionism and the Transformation of Workers' Consciousness in America, 1919-22,' in *Workers Control in America*, 91-112, New York, 1979. Also David Montgomery, 'New Tendencies In Union Struggles and Strategies in Europe and the United States,' in Cronin and Sirianni, *op. cit.*, pp. 88-116.

3. Charles Barnes, *The Longshoremen* (New York, 1915), p. 125, Brooklyn *Eagle*, October 12, 1919.

4. See Montgomery, *op. cit.*, pp. 91-112.

strike, found that the Slavic steel workers were 'radical' and impatient with the conservative pleas of their union leaders.[5] In West Virginia, coal miners, whose strikes continued well into the 1920s, were sometimes insurrectionary, at one point organizing themselves into an army 10,000 strong for an armed assault on non-union Logan County. Working class crowds engaged strike breakers and the police in the streets. There were crowds of looters in Boston. In Cleveland, on May Day, workers and socialists fought all day with police and vigilantes. In New York, the port was shut down three times in 1919 *before* the long strike of the longshoremen began in October. In each case, steps were taken to unite the marine and waterfront workers, long divided by a host of crafts and unions, into an industrial federation.[6]

Government labour policy during the war tended to favour labour's advance, though the Wilson administration carefully sought collaboration with the 'responsible' trade unionists, the conservative leaders of the A.F.L. Wartime industrial and labour boards promoted uninterrupted production, and the impact of this policy often meant significant gains for American unions – growth in membership, recognition, bargaining rights, participation on the labour boards themselves. But this situation changed dramatically at the war's end. In the spring and summer of 1919, government policy shifted to containing inflation and 'the high cost of living' – consumer prices had doubled during the war.[7] The administration now made wage restraint the central feature of its labour policy and instructed those wartime labour boards not already disbanded to resist concessions to the unions. This was the goal

---

5. Commission of Inquiry, Interchurch World Movement, *Report on the Steel Strike of 1919* (New York, 1920) p. 161.

6. The longshoremen's strike was the fourth major strike in the Harbour in 1919. The *Nation*, commenting on New York City's 'labor crisis,' noted that 'harbor workers are awaiting the findings of the War Labor Board with the . . . comfortable knowledge that at a day's notice they can tie up the whole vast traffic of New York Harbor.' The *Nation*, February 1, 1919. 'With trade unionists,' wrote J. B. S. Hardman, commenting on the 1919 strikes, 'as with everyone else, the appetite comes with the eating.' J. B. S. Hardman, 'Postscript to Ten Years of the Labor Movement,' *American Labor Dynamics*, (New York, 1928) p. 23.

7. See Melvyn Dubofsky, *op. cit.* on federal labor policies in this period.

of the U.S. Shipping Board's National Adjustment Commission, which oversaw industrial relations on the nation's waterfronts and piers; it sought to maintain wartime wage rates. The employers favoured this shift and they set out to increase the productivity of labour, which they claimed had fallen sharply during the war. The victory of the Republican Party in the Congressional elections emboldened them; they sought to halt labour's advance, if not roll it back. By the end of 1919, the reestablishment of the open shop was central to their agenda. The issues for the workers varied, yet wages and the cost of living were crucial. On the New York waterfront, it was the wage award of the National Adjustment Commission which sparked the great strike.

The fall of 1919 marked the expiration of the wartime waterfront wage agreements. The U.S. Shipping Board reconstituted its National Adjustment Commission in midsummer to consider the future of Longshoremen's wages and working conditions. The top leaders of the I.L.A., T. V. O'Connor, the International President, and Joseph Ryan, the New York District leader, were members of the Commission. They were joined by William Z. Ripley, a Harvard economist, who chaired the Commission, and two shipping company executives, Frederick Toppin and Oakley Wood.[8] The Commission issued its 'award' on October 6, after lengthy hearings. It recalled President Wilson's reaction to the wage demands of the railway shopmen and reiterated the 'soundness of this policy' – wage restraint. Nevertheless, the Commissioners noted, 'We are . . . so deeply impressed with the hardships under which the longshoremen, with unsteady and casual employment, are now living, that we cannot resist a partial and immediate compliance with their demands. We therefore, even in the face of the President's appeal, award an increase in Deepsea rate of five cents per hour for day work, and ten cents an hour for overtime work, effective from October 1, 1919.' O'Connor and Ryan dissented on the specifics of the wage award but signed the agreement.[9] The longshoremen had wanted $1.00 an hour for an eight hour day

8. 'Award of the National Adjustment Commission,' (October 6, 1919), R. G. 32, U. S. Shipping Board, National Archives, Washington D.C. (NARA)

9. *Ibid.*

and $2.00 an hour for overtime. The award was greeted with an explosion of anger. Longshoremen called it the 'Woolworth Award' – five and ten.[10] Italian longshoremen in Brooklyn struck on October 5th in anticipation of the award, returned to work, then struck again, this time taking picket lines to Chelsea, the stronghold of the Irish dockers and the centre of the union in New York. They found support. When John Riley, an I.L.A. district leader, waded into a crowd of strikers on a Chelsea pier, ordering them to work, he was beaten bloody and left unconscious in a mud puddle. 'Mobs,' reported the New York *Times*, 'now rule the waterfront.'[11]

The strike was a bold adventure, a remarkable display of industrial power. It involved virtually every longshoreman who worked in the Harbour, uniting Irish and Italians, blacks, Hungarians, Swedes, Russians. It effectively stopped shipping for nearly one month; traffic was not back to normal for six weeks. At the end of October, the *Times* reported 'more than 600 vessels tied up in the Harbour – the largest number of ships ever known to be here at one time – 540 steamships, fifty passenger liners . . . More than 100 ships anchored along Red Hook . . .'[12] William Ripley estimated the cost of strike at more than one million dollars a day.[13]

The authorities feared the strike would spread, and in fact there was a major strike in New Orleans, the nation's second busiest port, as well as turmoil on the Pacific Coast.[14] But there is little evidence of a direct connection linking these conflicts – aside from the I.L.A., whose international officers feverishly sought to quell them. Nevertheless, there was solidarity in the Harbour. Sixteen thousand marine workers,

---

10. New York *Call*, October 8, 1919. The N.A.C. established the basic day of eight hours, a rate of $.65 per hour regular time and $1.00 per hour overtime for deep-sea longshoremen in October, 1918. See Benjamin M. Squires, 'The Strike of the Longshoremen at the Port of New York,' *Monthly Labor Review*, vol. IX, December, 1919, p. 101.

11. New York *Times*, October 10, 1919.

12. New York *Times*, October 30, 1919.

13. 'Records of the National Adjustment Commission,' *op. cit.*, p. 21.

14. See Eric Arnesen, *Waterfront Workers of New Orleans* (New York, 1991), pp. 230-232. On the situation of the Pacific Coast, see Bruce Nelson, *Workers on the Waterfront* (Urbana and Chicago, 1988).

led by the Marine Workers' Affiliation, joined the strike, as
did ten thousand railway express workers. The *Times* estimated 100,000 workers idle at the end of the first week. The
socialist New York *Call* estimated 150,000.[15]

The strikers met a chorus of condemnation. T. V. O'Connor immediately ordered them back to work. 'This is not a
strike,' he insisted; it was the work of 'the Italian element,
aided by German sympathizers,' men from '166 Sackett
Street in Brooklyn,' – the headquarters of the Industrial
Workers of the World (I.W.W.)[16] Samuel Gompers, the
President of the A.F.L., wired O'Connor that the strike was a
violation of 'the fundamental principle of the American
Federation of Labour. The agreement to abide by the award
was a sacred contract to accept it.'[17] The press discovered a
'bolshevik conspiracy,' led by foreigners, chiefly Italians,
members of the I.W.W. Its partisanship was extreme, as each
day it condemned the strikers, listed the names and addresses
of alleged I.W.W. members, and announced the strike
broken.[18]

---

15. New York *Times*, October 12, 1919. New York *Call*, October 12, 1919;
     New York *World*, October 12, 1919. The *World* reported the following
     figures: longshoremen, 60,000; clerks, bookkeepers, scalers,
     teamsters, 60,000; deckhands, bridgemen, oilers, 2,400; captains and
     pilots, 4,000; engineers, 5,000; railway expressmen, 10,000; total,
     141,400. Ernest Poole in his novel, *The Harbor*, features a woman
     strike leader, a clerk. Ernest Poole, *The Harbor* (New York 1915). I
     found no such workers featured amongst the strikers, but the *Herald*
     reported '300 women employed on and off the piers affiliated with the
     I.L.A. joined the strikers.' N. Y. *Herald*, October 10, 1919.

16. New York *Times*, October 10, 1919.

17. AFL Records, The Samuel Gompers Era, 'Longshoremen,' Reel 39.
     Others joined this chorus, including Secretary of Labor, William B.
     Wilson, Ben Tillet, the General Secretary of the British dockers,
     Thomas Edison and Frederick Toppin, Vice-president of the
     International Mercantile Marine, who praised the role of T. V.
     O'Connor, the man 'who stood between this country and Bolshevism.'
     New York *Call*, October 22, 1919.

18. According to the *Call*, 'The strike of the longshoremen has presented
     the capitalist press with an unusual opportunity to lie from day to day.
     In headlines, in news stories and editorials, efforts have been made to
     divide their forces, to sow suspicion in their ranks, to support any
     tendency of some to surrender, and always to lend their influence to

The strike in fact was a rebellion of rank and file longshoremen, who walked off their jobs with little leadership and less
organization. The issue was not bolshevism but wages, though
the strike was radical and a departure for workers not involved in a major dispute since 1907. The longshoremen
maintained their demand for $1.00 an hour regular and $2.00
an hour overtime pay to the very end; indeed, even when they
returned, they stubbornly rejected the 'Woolworth Award,'
saying dignity demanded that they work at the previous rates.

There are several other features of the strike worth noting.
Two sometime longshoremen and union leaders, Richard
Butler and Paolo 'Paul Kelley' Vacarrelli, the first a saloon
keeper, the second a small-time gangster, gained notoriety
both during the strike and in subsequent accounts of it. They
sought to capture the leadership of the strike and negotiate a
settlement, thereby reestablishing themselves as waterfront
union leaders. They were joined by Tammany Hall in the
person of the Mayor, John Hylan, who also claimed to
support the longshoremen, if not the strike, and promised
compromise. The I.W.W., which did not lead the strike,
came to play a significant role, though this was confined to
Brooklyn and, to a lesser degree, New Jersey. The I.W.W.
emerged in the middle days of the strike, when the longshoremen were increasingly under attack on the Brooklyn waterfront, both from the police and from strikebreakers. The
I.W.W. played an important role in the street fighting along
the docks and in the longshoremen's neighbourhoods, as the
strikers desperately sought to keep the strike alive.

The strike ended in the first week of November. It failed for
many reasons; certainly the odds were overwhelming – the
unwavering opposition of the union leadership, the shipping
companies, and the federal government. Federal soldiers
actually entered the Harbour in the second week of the strike,
though their presence was mostly symbolic. They confined
their activities to the army terminals and never directly confronted the strikers. The strikers themselves were undoubtedly exhausted by this conflict, as must have been their
families, existing a month without wages or strike benefits.

---

break the strike. From day to day they have reported the strikers going
back to work, only to have the men give the lie to these assertions.'
October 24, 1919.

This essay is intended to address two deficiencies. First, inexplicably, the New York longshoremen of 1919 have been largely ignored, by social and labour historians as well as others. Second, and more importantly, when the 1919 strike does appear in historical literature, it is consistently misinterpreted. Most often, the strike is mentioned as a prelude, as an introduction to some other subject – crime on the waterfront, for example, or corruption in the trade union movement. When the strike is considered in its own right, it is often as a negative illustration – an example of the consequences of ethnic and racial division, or of the power of trade union leaders.[19] Thus, the longshoremen became victims again, not only of omission, but of determinisms which render their actual experience irrelevant. Contemporaries saw things otherwise and considered the strike to be of the utmost importance, and not simply because of its sheer size. The *Nation* featured the New York longshoremen in a commentary on workers and the new unionism and considered these strikers, among others, as examples of '. . . the common man, forgetting the old sanctions, and losing faith in the old leadership . . . experiencing a new access of self-confidence, or at least a new recklessness to take changes . . .'[20] The *Call* saw the longshoremen as prominent in the struggle for industrial unionism in the tumultuous autumn of 1919, pointing to their numbers and the fact that they had '. . . tied up the busiest port in the world.'[21] The defeat of the longshoremen – a chapter in the defeat of industrial unionism in 1919 – is no excuse for regulating them to the status of historical nonentities, or second-class citizens, capable only of bit parts in other peoples' stories.

The problem of interpreting the longshoremen's strike also involves the conflict between O'Connor and his supporters

---

19. See, for example, Daniel Bell, 'Racket-Ridden Longshoremen,' *The End of Ideology* (New York, 1962) pp. 175-209.

20. *The Nation*, October 25, 1919.

21. New York *Call*, October 10, 1919. In 1919 the longshoremen seemed quite capable of creating an industrial union. They may have been newcomers, lacking in tradition, but on October, 1919, they appeared powerful, because dock labour's 'capacity to strike is powerful.' See E. J. Hobsbawm, 'National Unions at the Waterside,' *Labouring Men*, (New York 1967), p. 242.

among the district I.L.A. officers, and their opponents, Butler, Vacarrelli, and their supporters. An interpretation of the strike based on an analysis of this conflict emerged during the strike itself and was then developed in some detail immediately following the strike. Benjamin M. Squires, the Secretary of the National Adjustment Commission, in his article, 'The Strike of the Longshoremen at the Port of New York,' summed up his position and that of the Commission: 'The conclusion is forced, therefore, that factional differences played an important role in inducing the men to violate their agreement.' Moreover, Squires concluded, 'the evidence is clear that the walkout was not an indignant protest against an unjust award' but was instead an 'opportunity' for people who pursued 'personal aggrandizement' – namely Butler and Vacarrelli.[22] Most subsequent interpretation has been a variation on this theme.[23]

This explanation will not stand. Certainly, Butler, Vacarrelli and others in the New York district challenged the International officers during the course of the strike – there is no evidence they called the walkout. But this tells us nothing about the most important features of the strike. It does not explain the angry explosion of the longshoremen or their ability to spread the strike throughout the harbour within hours of the announcement of the award. Nor does it explain the tenacious resistance of virtually every section of the longshoremen, occupational, geographical, ethnic and racial, as they held out for more than a month. It does not explain the antipathy toward the union leaders or the appeal of industrial unionism. And it does not explain the movement for unity at the base – a more or less conscious movement to overcome divisions, with the goal, however vaguely felt or put, of

---

22. Benjamin M. Squires, *op. cit.*, pp. 110, 114.

23. See, for example, Charles P. Larrowe, *Shape-Up and Hiring Hall: A Comparison of Hiring Methods and Labor Relations on the New York and Seattle Waterfronts*, (Berkeley and Los Angeles, 1955) pp. 1-48. See also the more recent account of New York longshoremen in Howard Kimeldorf, *Reds or Rackets* (Berkeley and Los Angeles, 1988) pp. 46-49. Kimeldorf seems to dismiss the activity of the rank and file longshoremen, whom he apparently considers divided and conservative, and thus, it seems to me, misunderstands the situation in New York in 1919.

winning their wage demands as a step towards transforming their union, their work, and their lives. Finally, factionalism does not explain the radicalism of the strike – Butler and Vacarrelli were by no means radicals – or the sentiments that permitted such an audacious strike in the first place, held it firm, allowed for the intervention of the I.W.W., and carried people into the streets when all else failed.[24] In order to understand these features, we must indeed consider the events from the bottom, including the nature of the long-shoremen's work, their neighbourhoods, their union, and the relationship of the workers to their union leaders. We must also consider them, not separately, but as part of the move-ment of American workers in 1919, sharing its weaknesses, to be sure, but also its potential.

★   ★   ★   ★

'No place could be more appropriate for an A.F.L. Convention than Atlantic City – a pleasure resort without industry; a place where delegates would not be embarrassed by the presence of toiling masses – where no strike could occur to mar the harmony of the proceedings. The Convention would be safe in the Coney Island of the Rich.'

John Reed, 'The Convention of the Dead'

Casual work, the shape, and grinding toil united the long-shoremen, as did the abuse of the employers and the conde-scension of contemporary observers. Casual labour was the system of labour in the Harbour; the 'shape-up' was the method of hiring. While the shape is not strictly central to the argument here, it was crucial to the companies and the union, and the longshoremen. According to the shippers and the

24. Bruce Nelson identifies this radicalism as a 'mood' the components of which included syndicalism and industrial unionism. He writes, 'But industrial unionism, the quest for One Big Union, the various moves toward amalgamation and federation among craft unions – all of this made sense to growing numbers of workers for whom the ballot, the union label, and the unabashed class collaboration of labor statesmen had become blunt instruments indeed.' Nelson, *op. cit.*, p. 7. Contemporary observers of the longshoremen found evidence of this 'mood' on the New York waterfront. The young E. Franklin Frazier found this in his 1921 study of Black workers on the New York waterfront, who, 'during the war,' were 'affected by the wave of radicalism.' This radicalism, it was reported to Frazier, sometimes went 'to foolish extremes.' Franklin Frazier, 'The Negro Longshoremen.' (1921), unpublished ms., Russell Sage Foundation, p. 55.

leaders of the I.L.A., this system was dictated by the Harbour itself and the nature of the industry. Shippers' profits depended on a fast turnaround, but the sea, the tides and the traffic made planning impossible. The industry compensated with casual labour – the more the better. 'The ship must sail on time.'[25] The shape was the method of hiring casual labour. It gave the foreman the choice of whom to hire, when, and for how long, and it all but guaranteed his authority. While it often divided the longshoremen, literally setting them at one another, sometimes violently, it was also a key element in their common experience, as important in many ways as their work.

When a ship arrived at a pier, the longshoremen gathered, usually in a semi-circle at the head of the pier. There the foreman looked for and then hired the 'best men,' the 'good gangs,' though never too regularly, lest the others become discouraged and the surplus disappear. The cruelty of this system was always apparent. On the relatively well-organized Chelsea piers, John Riley estimated that 2,500 men might be hired on a 'normal day,' but twice that number would shape-up, 5,000 men or more, according to Riley.[26] Those not chosen

---

25. See Ernest Poole, 'The Ship Must Sail On Time', *Everybody's Magazine*, 19 (August 1908), pp. 176-186.

26. *Commission on Industrial Relations*, Vol. III (Washington 1916) (Hereafter *CIR*), p. 2054. In South Brooklyn, longshoremen routinely shaped twice. 'It was very, very bad,' recalled Rosario Ferrintino. Thousands of men would gather in Columbia Street, often overflowing up Carroll, President and Union Streets, where the police were always on hand – to keep order. 'They harassed men,' according to Ferrintino, 'They beat them with sticks.' Between five and six in the morning, foremen arrived, looking for specialists and favoured gangs. Once the locations of the work were discovered, or announced, the longshoremen would stampede to those piers to shape again. 'The foreman might announce he needs 100 men,' said Ferrintino. 'Down at the pier there are 1,000.' 'Italian Longshoremen,' CUNY Oral History Project, Tamiment Library.

Hoboken, across the Hudson, was better organized, according to Charles Kiern, a longshoreman who also edited the Hudson County *Socialist*, 'in his spare time'. The union was better organized as well, 'We might say 100%,' he told the Industrial Commission. But when the foremen gave out the preference checks, they sometimes used fire hoses to protect themselves from the crush of the men. 'Yes,' said Kiern, he also saw them use 'clubs.' 'Well, not over the head, but on the legs . . .

would wait for another shape, or a third, and again the next day if the work continued. Some might be taken on for an hour or two, then 'knocked off' to wait again. The average longshoremen shaped six or seven days a week, but worked at best three or four. Once hired, the longshoreman worked, if possible, until the job was done.

The work of the longshoremen was heavy and dangerous. Charles Barnes, the authority on this subject, considered that 'It is probable that there is no other heavy physical work which is accompanied with so much overtime and such long stretches of toil without interruption.'[27] Work on the piers varied, of course; there were white collar workers, clerks and checkers; there were skilled specialists, repairmen, scalers, horse fitters, riggers. There were also the most casual of the casuals, the 'shenangos,' the marginal workers and drifters who eked out an existence on the waterfront. The more typical longshoremen, however, did heavy, monotonous hauling in and out of the holds of ships – 220 pound sacks of potatoes, 280 pound sacks of sugar, lumber, machinery, bananas. They were, according to Montgomery, the 'human machines' of the piers and they were often the only machines on the primitive New York docks.[28] 'Nowhere,' reported the *Times* in 1914, 'is there such a lack of mechanism for economy and efficiency in handling cargoes.'[29] There were, as late as 1914, according to Frederick Ridgway, a superintendent for the International Merchant Marine, no moving cranes in the New York Harbour.[30] So humans were 'forced to push and pull enormous weights, aided only by the most elementary inclines, pulleys, winches, hooks and screws, and above all, by their own teamwork.'[31]

---

to keep them back. To see the men they wanted.' *CIR, III, op. cit.*, p. 2117.

---

27. Barnes, *op. cit.*, p. 130.

28. David Montgomery, *The Fall of the House of Labor*, (Cambridge, 1987), p. 61. In the Chapter, 'The Common Laborers,' Montgomery includes a very useful section on longshoremen.

29. Quoted in *CIR*, III, *op. cit.*, p. 2067.

30. *Ibid.*, p. 2081.

31. Montgomery, *op. cit.*, p. 97.

Timothy Carroll, a Liverpool docker who came to New York 'to make his fortune,' discovered 'Chinese labour' instead, reporting he often carried 280 pound sacks of flour up to fourteen hours.[32] Dennis Delaney, a New York longshoreman for 24 years, testified, 'After working day and night, longshoremen . . . are ordered back again under a penalty, "Don't come any more if you don't come back".'[33] Sometimes, according to Charles Kiern, '. . . men work 20, 30, I have seen them work over 40 hours in a stretch'.[34] 'One day he will almost work his life out, and the next two or three days have nothing to do, except when he has a few spare coins to go to the saloon and spend it.'[35]

On the piers, the men were driven, cursed at by the foremen, called 'donkeys' and worse, and always pressed to 'work faster.' 'They are trying to rush the life out of us,' said William Flynn. 'They are killing people . . .'[36] Work in the coastal trade was considered the worst; work in Chelsea was often said to be the best. But, according to Kiern, not everyone agreed. 'I have heard today about the best dock in the city being the White Star dock. The men generally don't consider the best dock where the work is so Taylored that they work a man's life out of him in ten years.'[37]

The New York longshoremen were frequently investigated and the resulting reports included accounts of 'hopelessness' and 'despair' in their homes and neighbourhoods. The report of the Mayor's Committee found 'serious evils' in the dockside neighbourhoods, chief among these being 'the constant manufacture of paupers' creating burdens for others and adding to the dangerous classes. These 'evils' 'permeated the life of the city.'[38] Such reports were at best condescending,

---

32. *CIR*, III, *op. cit.*, p. 2104.

33. *Ibid.*, p. 53.

34. *Ibid.*, p. 430.

35. *Ibid.*, p. 2122.

36. 'Records of National Adjustment Commission,' *op. cit.*, pp. 446-7.

37. *CIR*, III, *op. cit.*, p. 2117. The men quoted were rank-and-file longshoremen invited to testify to the Commission and the National Adjustment Commission.

38. Mayor's Committee on Unemployment, 'Report on Dock Employ-

emphasizing the powerlessness of the longshoremen, yet they also reveal the realism, conditioned by fatalism, of the workers. E. Franklin Frazier's account of black longshoremen emphasized 'fear and hopelessness' but also called attention to the 'fatalism' of these workers, as well as the pride with which they bore their 'burdens'.[39] The reformers were frustrated by this fatalism and the longshoreman's apparent 'economism' of wage demands and trade unionism. The Mayor's Committee attempted to explain the longshoreman's lack of interest in the reorganization of waterfront work with reference to 'the independence of spirit of the longshoremen,' but complained of their 'reluctance . . . to consider anything in the nature of change . . . unless won by themselves . . .'[40] This, of course, involved a matter of perspective. Pressed on why the longshoremen made no demands for the regulation of hours – the central issue for longshoremen and their families, according to the Committee – John Riley responded: 'The reason we do not do anything in regard to that is because we are not powerful enough. I understand we need it,' he continued, 'but there are lots of things we need . . .'[41]

★　★　★　★

Business men from all over the country, agents of Chambers of Commerce and manufacturer's associations, Mr. Easley of the Civic Federation – all these were in attendance at the thirty-ninth Convention of the American Federation of Labor at Atlantic City. The Mayor, a local real estate shark, welcomed the gathering, saying, 'We want no convention that doesn't contain men and women one hundred per cent American.'
John Reed, 'The Convention of the Dead'

What divided the longshoremen was all too obvious. There were workers of dozens of ethnicities on the waterfront, but three groups predominated in 1919 – Irish, Italians and blacks. The longshoremen lived, for the most part, where they worked. In Manhattan, they were in great concentrations along what was then called the North River, in New Jersey in Hoboken and Jersey City, and in Brooklyn from Wallabout

Employment in New York City,' (October 1916), p. 12.

---

39. Frazier, *op. cit.*, p. 9.
40. Mayor's Committee, *op. cit.*, p. 28.
41. *CIR*, III, *op. cit.*, p. 2064.

along the shoreline to the Bush Terminals. Chelsea, in Manhattan, was the centre of a band of neighbourhoods that stretched from Chambers Street toward midtown. The Irish lived there, cramped in between streets and warehouses, in neighbourhoods known for big families and saloons. These streets gave the longshoremen the reputation as 'loafers, drinkers, and brawlers.'[42] They were the most hopeless in the city, according to social worker, Mary Oakly Bay.[43]

But if the West side neighbourhoods were the city's 'most hopeless,' what of the others, in particular those of the Italians, who by 1919 were the majority of longshoremen? What of the black longshoremen, struggling to defend and expand their position on the waterfront? Franklin Frazier visited these blacks in Columbus Hill and found them living in 'dilapidated' four room flats, with 'rusty mail boxes, broken bells, ruined tiles, disfigured walls and general dirtiness . . .' He found that fifty percent of these men he questioned were idle three months of each year or more. The result was desperately low income, despite relatively high wages, high especially compared to the average wage of black workers.[44]

The Italians lived in Brooklyn, in South Brooklyn – 'the Italian Quarter' – adjacent to the Erie and Atlantic basins, and southward along the waterfront to the Bush Terminal piers and Bay Ridge. The Italians first came to the Habour, as strikebreakers, in the time of the 'big strike', the revolt of the longshoremen led by the Knights of Labour in 1887. Their numbers grew through the nineties and into the twentieth century, until by the time of Barnes' study they were half the longshoremen.[45] Their communities constituted, in the words of Frederick Hersey, a manager at the Bush Terminal in

---

42. Charles Barnes, *The Longshoremen* (New York, 1915), p. 13. Most investigators rejected this view. For example, Arthur McFarland, a writer concerned with longshore conditions, told the Commissioners, 'Their work is hard, desperately hard, and they are driven at it, and yet they have kept their heads high.' *CIR*, III, p. 2154.

43. Bay, a social worker from Pottstown, Pennsylvania, came to work in New York in the district from Chambers Street to Fourteenth Street, an area 'almost exclusively made up of the families of longshoremen.' *CIR*, III, pp. 2138-2139.

44. Frazier, *op. cit.*, pp. 40-45.

45. Barnes, *op. cit.*, p. 5.

Brooklyn, 'a reserve.' 'The greater part of the Italian labor comes from a district of its own, and it is very easy to draw from that district.'[46] Some 'longshoremen' had no neighbourhoods at all, notably the coal bargemen and their families who lived on their barges. Here descriptions of conditions match the dark drama of Poole's *Harbor*.[47] Whole families lived in single cabins ten feet wide, travelling wherever the barges went. Mary Bay estimated 4,000 children lived on these barges, unschooled and raised by illiterate parents.

Longshoremen, from separate ethnic groups, then, tended to live in separate neighbourhoods, be employed on separate piers, work in separate gangs, and belong to separate local unions. On the docks and in the union this was not exactly 'Jim Crow' – there were too many exceptions, too much variety in the patterns. And, as apologists for the union were quick to point out, the Italians were the first to organize their own locals, and there were companies, such as the Kerr Line, which hired only Italians.[48]

But the fact remains that the union was organized in a way which not only followed the patterns of racial and ethnic division in the city and in the industry, but also reinforced them. The Irish, for example, were not simply immigrants. They included second and third generation 'Americans' of Irish descent as well, people susceptible to the racial nativism of 1919, the year of race riots in Chicago and elsewhere, and also of a new assertiveness among blacks. In this context, it is important to remember that Italians were not only newcomers, they were also not considered 'white'. The division of the union into ethnic locals, therefore, was not simply a convenience, but was a reflection of the racial/ethnic hierarchy in American society. Many black longshoremen believed they were only tolerated in the union because 'the Negro inside the union could be controlled.'[49] 'We are in the

---

46. *CIR*, III, p. 2095.

47. Ernest Poole, *op. cit.* This is a novel about New York Harbour which culminates in a general harbour strike, presumably led by I.W.W.-type revolutionaries. It is very interesting to compare and contrast this fictional account with the actualities of the Habour and the 1919 strike.

48. Frazier, *op. cit.*, p. 31.

49. *Ibid.*

union today,' said the leader of a Brooklyn local, 'because the white man had to take us in for his own protection. Outside the Organization the Negro could scab on the white man. Inside he can't. In return for this we get a share of the work, the protection of the union contract and organization support.'[50]

Black workers also entered the industry as strikebreakers, and in times of severe labour shortage. They came on to the Ward Line piers in 1895 during a strike and stayed. They secured work on the Mallory Line in 1899, again during a strike though in the face of 'a race riot' – that is, an organized attack by whites – and 'not . . . without paying with blood.'[51] In the second decade of the century, blacks increased their numbers ten-fold, so that by 1919 there were 5,000 black longshoremen in the deep-water trade, a result of the wartime labour shortage and the exodus of blacks from the South.[52] Blacks organized their own locals, for example, locals 873 and 879 in Brooklyn, and they were the great majority in local 968, set up in 1917 specifically to bring the newcomers into the union. Black longshoremen opposed discrimination on the piers and in the union. Still, many favoured all black locals as the only way to have a voice in the union.

Their demand for a black organizer was typical of their problem, as was their attempt to get the I.L.A. to adopt a resolution in opposition to discrimination. At the 1919 I.L.A. Convention in Galveston, Maurice Stephney and two other black delegates from local 873 in Brooklyn spoke in favour of this motion. They were met with a wall of opposition, led by the leadership of the New York district. Patrick Connors denied there was discrimination in New York. James McGuire considered the issue 'nothing more than a radical

---

50. Sterling Spero and Abram Harris, *The Black Worker* (New York, 1931), pp. 199-200.

51. Frazier, *op. cit.*, p. 4.

52. *Ibid.*, p. 3. Sterling Spero and Abram Harris, *op. cit.*, p. 105. According to Spero and Harris, 'The leaders of Negro longshoremen in New York like the leaders in Hampton Roads, prefer to have the members of their race join their own locals because it gives them direct representation and power and influence in both district and international councils which they would not have if they remained minorities scattered in various white locals.'

move.' President T.V. O'Connor denied that blacks were discriminated against within the union, though 'there are one or two companies who do not hire colored men but we have no right to tell any employer what race they shall employ as long as they are union men.'[53]

Nevertheless, the black longshoremen interviewed by Frazier 'were unanimous in declaring they were discriminated against,' and several feared a 'race riot' would be the only result of pressing their demands. They found 'the greatest antagonism' to be 'on the part of the Irish.' The Italians, 'the first to admit Negroes,' showed 'less racial antipathy,' but even they were 'assimilating . . . the prejudices of the white men, in order apparently to insure their own standing.'[54] Some black longshoremen even distrusted their own officers and for a similar reason – 'getting too close to the white men.'[55] Still, of 82 black longshoremen interviewed by Frazier, 80 said they favoured unions 'unconditionally.'[56] 'The majority of the men,' he concluded, 'realized that the increases in earnings and improvement of working conditions had come through organization as represented by unions.'[57]

The attitudes of the Italian longshoremen were not investigated, and this is an area where much useful work can be done. The Chelsea Irish are somewhat better known, though here too there is not an abundance of information. We know much more about the views of the leaders than those of the rank and file. And of course not all Irish longshoremen lived in Chelsea; thousands lived in Brooklyn and still others in Hoboken and Jersey City. Certainly the Irish feared for their position on the waterfront and believed they had most to lose. Nevertheless, the black men cautioned that 'during hard times . . . common misfortune softens the prejudice even of the Irish.'[58] They seem to have grudgingly accepted the Italians, if only for their numbers, and to the degree that they

---

53. 'Proceedings of the Twenty-Fifth Convention,' International Longshoremen's Association, July, 1919, pp. 526-529.

54. Frazier, *op. cit.*, p. 27.

55. *Ibid.*, p. 29.

56. *Ibid.*

57. *Ibid.*, p. 27.

58. *Ibid.*

stayed in Brooklyn – T.V. O'Connor was enraged during the strike when the 'Italian element' came 'over the bridge'. One gets the impression that the Irish believed the union belonged to them, though by 1914, union policy was to recruit all longshoremen, regardless of race or nationality.[59]

There was little to mediate the racism of the Irish; socialism, for example, made scant headway in Irish neighbourhoods. Charles Leinenweber called the Irish 'the missing factor' in the New York socialist movement.[60] They were also missing in the fight for industrial unionism, for many of the same reasons. If the rank and file Irish longshoremen were able to challenge the ethnocentrism and conservatism of their communities and union leaders in the course of the 1919 strike – which, to a considerable degree, they did – they were not able to close the door on Tammany. Irish workers, according to Leinenweber, were 'highly susceptible to the appeals of machine politics,' while their leaders were 'closely tied to Tammany Hall,' the ruling Democratic Party machine.[61]

The New York longshoremen, then, were thoroughly divided, most importantly along lines of race and ethnicity, and this division was institutionalized in the I.L.A. Of course, these workers travelled, worked other jobs, served in the

---

59. 'Records of National Adjustment Commission,' (October 11, 1919), *op. cit.*, p. 82. For a recent account of workers, unions and immigration, see John Bodnar, *The Transplanted* (Bloomington, 1985), pp. 85-116. For Italian immigrants, see Edwin Fenton, *Immigrants and Unions: Italians and American Labor, 1870-1920* (New York, 1975). A more provocative account is Donna Rae Gabaccia, *Militants and Migrants: Rural Sicilians Become American Workers* (New Brunswick and London, 1988). On Irish conservatism, see Kerby A. Miller, 'Class, Culture and Immigrant Group Identity: The Case of Irish-American Ethnicity,' pp. 96-129, in Virginia Yans-McLaughlin, ed., *Immigration Reconsidered* (New York, 1990). David Brundage offers an interesting alternative in 'The 1920 New York Dockers' Boycott: Class, Gender, Race and Irish-American Nationalism' (Unpublished 1992).

60. Charles Leinenweber, 'The Class and Ethnic Bases of New York City Socialism, 1904-1915,' *Labor History*, Winter, 1981. See also, Leinenweber, 'The American Socialist Party and the "New Immigrants,"' *Science and society*, Vol. XXXII, No. 1, 1968.

61. Leinenweber, *Ibid.*, p. 47.

armed forces. We do not have to accept Daniel Bell's description of the Irish as 'an isolated mass' facing the 'other ethnic masses of the city' to recognize the fundamental fact of division.[62] All the more significant, then, is the degree of solidarity that developed in the conflict of 1919 among Irish, Italian and black strikers.

★ ★ ★ ★

Externally there was little to differentiate the assembly from the annual convention of the National Association of Car Manufacturers, which was meeting at the same time in another hall . . . More than a third of the delegates were themselves employers of labor; all but a few were well-to-do. Even the newspapers commented on the display of diamonds . . . These were the officials of the great national and international unions.

John Reed, 'The Convention of the Dead'

The I.L.A originated in the Middle West. It was founded in 1892, in Detroit, Michigan. It was from the start an aggressive union which worried A.F.L. leaders by pursuing not only longshoremen but other Great Lakes marine workers as well. It grew rapidly in the first years of the century, winning the closed shop by guaranteeing employers a steady labour supply and ruthlessly crushing wildcat strikes. When O'Connor became president in 1908, he made peace with the A.F.L. but continued the tradition of denying local unions autonomy and opposing strikes, even when this resulted in the charge – on the Great Lakes – that the I.L.A. was a company union.[63]

The I.L.A. established itself in New York as a step in its campaign to become a national union. It came in the aftermath of the 1907 strike, a bitter dispute involving 30,000 longshoremen, which ended in defeat and demoralization within the union, the Longshoremen's Union Protective Association (L.U.P.A.), which the I.L.A. absorbed in 1913. This merger, according to Barnes, resulted in a union representing just 6,000 workers.[64] By the war's end, however, the I.L.A. was well established on the waterfront, 40,000 strong. In addition, it had won, via the wartime labour boards, higher

---

62. Bell, *op. cit.*, p. 192.

63. See John R. Commons, 'The Longshoremen of the Great Lakes,' *Labor and Administration* (New York, 1913), pp. 267-268. See also Maud Russell, *Men Along the Shore: The ILA and Its History* (New York, 1966).

64. Barnes, *op. cit.*, p. 125.

wages and the eight hour day. In return, it had delivered peace on the piers.

Nevertheless, New York longshoremen invariably compared themselves unfavourably with other longshoremen. The New Orleans dockers were 'better organized' – 'they are all union men down there'; Pacific Coast longshoremen were higher paid – '80 cents an hour' and the 'Frisco men worked shorter hours.'[65] Moreover, the New York longshoremen were nearly unanimous in believing that their real wages had fallen dramatically as a result of the wartime cost of living and that they were able to sustain themselves only by working excessive hours.[66]

The position of the I.L.A. in New York, consequently, was somewhat tenuous, as was that of the International's president, T. V. O'Connor. He was an outsider, born in Buffalo, a Great Lakes tugboat captain. Still, he insisted on running the district with an iron hand, he was ruthless with oppositionists, and he detested radicals. 'We wiped out the I.W.W. . . . . in this organization,' he told the National Adjustment Commission meeting that was convened just after the strike began. It was no secret that this attack on the I.W.W. had been carried out in collaboration with the shipping companies and the government.[67] O'Connor boasted that he had never sanctioned a longshoremen's strike and said, in the midst of the 1919 strike, 'If everyone of the 40,000 longshoremen of New

---

65. 'Records of the National Adjustment Commission', *op. cit.*, p. 465.

66. See David Montgomery, 'New Tendencies in Union Struggles and Strategies in Europe and the United States, 1916-1922,' in James E. Cronin and Carmen Sivianni, *op. cit.*, pp. 90, 91.

67. 'Investigation Case Files,' Bureau of Investigation, O.G. 690, August 25, 1915, NARA. At a N.A.C. meeting in Washington, D.C. in December, 1917, Professor Carlton Parker presented a proposal for ending the influence of the I.W.W. of Puget Sound. Parker calculated 'there are approximately 800 I.W.W. working on the waterfront.' O'Connor asked for the names: 'If we can get the names of the men who are members of the I.W.W., we will either tear up their card or will expel them from our organization.' 'Records of the N.A.C.', *op. cit.*, December 1917. Parker was a professor at the University of Washington and author of *The Casual Laborer* (New York 1920).

York vote to remain on strike, I will still refuse to endorse or support the action.'[68]

O'Connor's New York lieutenants were much like him, Irishmen, conservative and patriotic, loyal to O'Connor and loyal to the A.F.L. They believed in the sanctity of contracts. The Galveston convention, they argued, had unanimously agreed to submit the longshoremen's case to the N.A.C. They were obligated to abide by its decision. They insisted on the authority of the union leaders. This explains the formalism of their endorsement of O'Connor's statement that 'This is not a strike. It is not sanctioned. No strike benefits have been issued.'[69] They delivered labour in return for recognition and bargaining rights. It was in this context that they accepted, even supported, the shape-up, casual work and Jim Crow. Just as O'Connor left it to the shipper to hire whom he chose, even if this meant the exclusion of black longshoremen – 'as long as they are union men' – so his New York organizer, William Holt, left working conditions to the employer. When John Commons of the Commission on Industrial Relations, pressing Holt on the possibility of 'equalizing work', asked, 'You don't try to see every man has a fair return?' Holt responded, 'All we try to see is that he hires all union men.'[70] This, it seems, is what contemporaries referred to as 'job trust' unionism, and in this the I.L.A. leaders were not so exceptional.[71]

Richard Butler and Paolo Vacarrelli might have looked rather good in this context; Butler had actually been a long-shoreman in his youth, though O'Connor charged he had not worked on the waterfront in fifteen years. Vacarrelli, the leader of the garbage scow trimmers, played a minor role in the development of the Marine Workers' Affiliation, a federation of the Harbour's craft unions. Yet Butler, a mid-town saloon keeper, was at best in and out of the union. His

---

68. New York *Call*, October 19, 1919.

69. New York *Times*, October 10, 1919.

70. *CIR. op. cit.*, p. 2195. Commons was the founder of the Wisconsin School of Labor History.

71. John Reed, 'The Convention of the Dead,' The *Liberator*, September, 1919. 'Job trust' refers to Reed's charge that the A.F.L.'s business was selling labour or at least acting primarily as a broker of labour.

detective agency, the Kenmore Agency, seemed to have been organized to provide union musclemen with gun permits. John Riley, an O'Connor supporter, said that 'The only good thing Richard T. ever did for the organization was when he sold L.U.P.A. to it' – allegedly for $400.[72] Vacarrelli owned the Packard Transportation Agency and was accused at the 1919 Galveston Convention of also being a partner in the Santaro Construction Company, and, thus 'an employer of labor.' Vacarrelli ran a saloon in Great Jones Street and was widely believed to be a gangster.[73]

Justice Department agents consulted Ralph Easley of the National Civic Federation concerning these men. Easley turned to Hugh Frayne, the A.F.L.'s national organizer, for information and was assured that O'Connor was 'absolutely to be relied upon.' Vacarrelli, according to Frayne, was 'a notorious character in the city' but had 'played absolutely fair' and had 'a clean slate' since his election as vice president of the I.L.A. Butler, however, was 'an undesirable citizen' and 'not to be trusted in any way.' The agent's report included a memo which noted that Vacarrelli was 'very popular in the Harbor movement' and that he had edited two patriotic journals, *The Loyal Labor Legion Review* and *Uncle Sam*. Butler and Vacarrelli challenged O'Connor at the 1917 and 1919 I.L.A. Conventions, but the 1919 Convention ended with O'Connor firmly in control, Butler defeated, and Vacarrelli unseated as Seventh International Vice President.[74] It is interesting to note that the federal Bureau of Investigation continued to be concerned with these men, even after the

---

72. 'Proceedings of the Twenty-fifth Convention,' International Longshoremen's Association, *op. cit.*, pp. 24-28.

73. *Ibid.*, p. 53. Louis Adamic reported that Vacarrelli, 'a gorilla of great prowess,' had shifted to the musicians union (M.M.P.U.) in 1924 where his job was to 'terrorize performers outside the union.' Louis Adamic, *Dynamite: The Story of Class Violence in America* (New York, 1931), p. 338.

74. 'Investigation Case Files,' Bureau of Investigation, *op. cit.*, O.G. 48655. Barnes, *op. cit.*, p. 9. In 1917, at the Toledo convention, Butler ran against O'Connor with Vacarrelli's support, but lost when Vacarrelli switched sides. At the Galveston Convention, the three men traded charges: O'Connor attacked the Kenmore Agency; Butler charged O'Connor with breaking strikes in Cleveland; Vacarrelli's businesses were condemned.

strike. In May, 1919, J. Edgar Hoover requested a 'special
. . . discreet undercover investigation to T. V. O'Connor,'
'ascertaining if this individual has any radical tendencies.'[75]

There was, then, factionalism in the New York I.L.A. –
rather exotic factionalism, even by A.F.L. standards. This
merits attention.[76] But the gulf between O'Connor (and his
district supporters) and the rank and file was far more important. Butler and Vacarrelli tried to fill the vacuum but were
only partly successful. They did not control events. The rank-
and-file longshoremen did. And while they were united on
just one issue – wages – it is clear that they saw wages as the
vehicle for transforming their lives and the fight for wages as
the occasion to take control of their union. Here their actions
fitted the pattern of the industrial conflict of 1919.

★ ★ ★ ★

> It was impossible to keep out all information. The One Big Union
> movement in Canada and the West, industrial unionism in its various
> manifestations, The Seattle Strike, The Winnipeg Strike – all these beat
> upon the Convention and surged up within it. They had to be, and were,
> brought out, denounced and scotched, without debate.
>
> John Reed, 'The Convention of the Dead'

George Speed, a member of the I.W.W.'s executive board,
spoke for the Wobblies in New York in the chaotic first days of
the strike. Speed arrived in the city just before the strike
began. He had recently been released from Leavenworth, the
federal penitentiary where he had been imprisoned with
William Haywood and the 100 I.W.W. leaders convicted in
Chicago. The longshoremen's strike, he told the *Call*, was
'spontaneous.' 'The men tumbled out over the heads of their
union officials . . .' It was 'a wonderful manifestation of
power on the part of the longshoremen who had for so long
been docile . . .'[77]

Strikers themselves came forward to make the same point.
John Gunlach, a Hoboken longshoreman, speaking to the
N.A.C., which had been reconvened in emergency session in

---

75. *Ibid.*, p. 30.

76. The factionalism merits attention but not glamourization. See, for
    example, Bell's description of Butler, 'a fabulous West Side character.'
    op. cit., p. 188. See also Butler's own sensationalist account in *Dock
    Walloper* (New York 1933).

77. New York *Call*, October 12, 1919.

New York, criticized the International officers for 'shoving the award down their throats.' 'The men rebelled against that . . . They are out for justice.' How could the press, he asked, 'vilify the men who have been out for only one purpose, to get a decent living . . . to make it possible for them to live a decent life, as well as for their families.'[78] Walter Bell, the black leader of local 968, pleaded with the commissioners: 'You cannot question the loyalty of the men of my race (coloured) . . . The I.W.W. and the Bolsheviks, I do not think I would know one of them if I saw them.' 'I wish you would consider this, that the five and ten cents you have offered to these men, is more an insult than it is justice.'[79]

The *Call* reported that 'The rank-and-file of the unions involved in the big harbor strike of New York, which has taken on a triangular aspect, [are] in complete control of the situation, having taken it into their own hands following open defiance to all leaders.'[80] It concluded: 'Industrial unionism, that is the issue . . . in the rank and file strike of 60,000 longshoremen, which had tied up the busiest harbor in the world . . .'[81] *The Nation*, under the headline, 'The Revolt of the Rank and File,' called attention to events from Seattle and San Francisco to Pittsburgh, where Mr. Gompers was 'compelled' to 'call a steel strike' lest control pass into the hands of the I.W.W.s and other 'radicals'. In New York, this revolt 'brought about the longshoremen's strike and kept the men out in defiance of union officials . . . which the international officers, even though the employers worked hand in glove with them, were completely unable to control.'[82]

The strike was a remarkable display of industrial power. At the end of October it was still a standoff. The *Call* wrote that

78. 'Records of the National Adjustment Commission,' Conference After Strike, *op. cit.*, p. 554.

79. *Ibid.*, pp. 56, 57.

80. New York *Call*, October 15, 1919.

81. *Ibid.*, October 10, 1919.

82. The *Nation*, October 25, 1919. Industrial unionism is not synonymous with rank-and-file power. But industrial unionism, it seems to me, was absolutely essential if workers were going to take control of their unions and mount an effective challenge to employers in settings such as New York Harbour.

'practically every foot of pier space along the entire water-front of New York is occupied by vessels awaiting loading or unloading. Vessels unable to find pier accommodation are jamming the lower anchorage space. All along the Jersey Shore are loaded ships coming in and steaming up the Hudson as a result of the strike . . .'[83] The longshoremen maintained their demand for $1.00 an hour and $2.00 overtime, made additional demands and formalized their rejection of the international leadership. When Mayor John Hylan established a 'Conciliation Committee' to settle the strike, the longshoremen turned to it with demands which groups of local officers and rank and file longshoremen appear to have formulated. The Mayor's Committee met with this 'grievance committee,' which also presented an addendum from 'the Brooklyn longshoremen.' The grievance committee, which included Italians and blacks as well as Irish, presented a list demanding an eight hour day, a forty-four hour week, over-time on Saturday afternoons, and no Sunday work what-soever. They demanded that 'all men who handle coal receive ten cents per hour extra' and that 'there shall be at all times a basket or box to take out of the ships hold all men who may be hurt, immediately, so that he may get first aid.' The grievance committee specifically included the demand of 'the delegates representing the Brooklyn locals' that 'their conditions be exactly the same as in New York.' Moreover, they demanded that 'every working man on a ship, whether he be Coastwise or Deep Sea, be considered as longshore workers.' The committee concluded by stating that' no man will return to work until every local, no matter what the craft is, is satisfied.'[84]

The rank-and-file character of the strike, and the degree to which the conflict was changing the consciousness of the strikers, was illustrated in series of mass meetings. On Octo-

---

83. New York *Call*, October 15, 1919.

84. New York City Municipal Archives, Records of Mayor John Hylan, file 'Longshoremen.' 'Secretary Wilson of the Department of Labor announced today [Oct. 18] the appointment of Mayor Hylan of New York, F. Paul Vacarrelli of New York, and James L. Hughes, Immigration Commissioner at Philadelphia, as a special Conciliation Commission to attempt to settle the longshoremen's strike in New York.' N.Y. *Times*, October 19, 1919.

ber 9, the International called a meeting at Tammany Hall, with the purpose of organizing the men back to work. But the thousands of longshoremen attending overwhelmed the officers in a tumultuous show of support for the strike. On October 12, the international officers called another meeting; they presented a series of influential speakers with the hope of regaining control of, or at least dividing the workers. But this meeting, attended by an overflow crowd of 3,000 at the Cooper Union, 'became from the outset, a wild repudiation of all union leadership.'[85] The rally got off to a bad start when the chairman was heckled by strikers who 'wanted a real longshoreman in the chair.' 'A telegram from Samuel Gompers was received with catcalls and then ignored.'[86] Ben Tillet said he was speaking for British dockers when he said he could not support the strikers, because 'the strike was unauthorized and without sanction of the Union.'[87] Hugh Frayne said he came personally to represent Gompers and the A.F.L., as he attempted to bring the crowd under control. He implored them 'to respect the traditions that have been the bulwark of organized labor.' He warned them to 'be considerate and just and calm,' saying that 'foolish action should not be used to destroy the labor movement.' 'We are not organized simply for ourselves,' he argued. 'We must consider other questions . . . Americanism demands that we listen to all sides. It is not a question of what is best for us, but what is best for our country.'[88] To this point, the longshoremen listened, but when O'Connor then appeared, they 'booed and hissed . . . until his plight was pitiable.' 'You double-crossed us.' 'You called us I.W.W.s,' they shouted. 'Now listen,' O'Connor tried to explain, 'About the I.W.W. business . . . I was misquoted, I never said it.' 'But,' he continued, 'there is an element here that doesn't want this strike settled, an element of agitators . . . an Italian element . . .'[89] 'Why pick on the Italians,' interrupted a striker. The jeering lasted five minutes. O'Connor continued in vain 'to beg, plead, cajole

---

85. Brooklyn, *Eagle*, October 14, 1919.

86. New York *Times*, October 14, 1919.

87. New York *Call*, October 14, 1919.

88. *Ibid.*

89. *Ibid.*

and threaten' the strikers until, at midnight, he turned the meeting over to Joseph Ryan, the district leader, whose motion that the men immediately return to work was drowned in opposition.[90]

The following week, yet another mass meeting was held, this time organized by Mayor Hylan and the Conciliation Committee. Hylan praised the strikers and denounced O'Connor, to the pleasure of the thousands of strikers in attendance. But when he concluded, 'I want you to go back to work tomorrow morning,' 'No, No!' was the response, 'loud enough to be heard by the many who could not gain admission and the hundreds of passersby on busy 14th Street, followed by clamorous applause.'[91] 'I came here to tell you that local 915 will not go back to work until we get a uniform scale of wages,' cried William Smith. 'We are working under the worst conditions of any class in the world,' shouted another striker. 'When I read that 25,000 Italians were going back to work,' said a delegate named Macolli, 'I said then and I say now it was a lie,' referring to constant press reports of back-to-work movements. 'That is synonymous to calling us scabs,' he continued, 'We must get what we want.' 'We will stay out until we get it,' came a shout in Italian. Then delegate Bell asked for the floor: 'The Negro in New York is suffering more now than any other in the city. You don't know of the high rentals imposed upon us in the Harlem section. It is really a disgrace. But let me tell you and the men in this hall that the Negro will stick with the men and do as they do.' The *Call* reported that this brief statement got more applause than any other. Finally, Thomas Welden, an 'old man' with a 'ringing voice,' representing riggers' local 783, concluded the demonstration by saying, 'We have got the shipping interests just where we want them . . . Why then should we go back to work?'[92] The Mayor then turned the meeting over to Paolo Vacarrelli, who was greeted with enthusiasm. The strikers

approved his stand for labor's rights; his attack on everybody standing in their way; he praised the solidarity of the rank and file . . . Four times he tried to swing the Italians to his side . . . twice he spoke to them in

---

90. *Ibid.*

91. *Ibid.*, October 22, 1919.

92. *Ibid.*

Italian and once he translated the Mayor's statement to their own language. But they overwhelmingly disapproved his recommendation to return pending a promise by the board for a reopening of their case . . . reference to going back to work repeatedly brought the same old 'No!'[93]

There seem to have been scores of local meetings, such as 'the enthusiastic meeting' of local 838, held at its headquarters on Union Street in Brooklyn, where 150 members 'voted unanimously to back up the dock strike after listening to speeches by Salvatore Mangiamale, president of the local, and other officers. The speeches were all in Italian.'[94] A meeting of 1,200 New Jersey longshoremen at St. Mary's Hall in Hoboken became a brawl when O'Connor, Ryan, and a group of armed bodyguards forced their way in, refusing to show their credentials to the men at the door. When a fight ensued and the bodyguards began attacking the strikers, shots were fired and the intruders were chased from the area. Some were arrested by Hoboken police. Ryan and several others were charged with 'riot' and possession of concealed weapons in Records Court, where the Recorder said he 'considered it a very serious state of affairs when gunmen and hoodlums from New York cross the river to break up a perfectly peaceable meeting in Hoboken.' The *Call* reported that the meeting reached no conclusion, but none of the city's 1,000 longshoremen were at work the following morning.[95]

Perhaps the most remarkable rally was held in Brooklyn, on October 18, in Pilgrim Hall on Court Street. There 3,000 members of locals 37, 346, 903, 923, and 929 'howled down all mention of I.L.A, leaders,' according to the reporter present, 'and roundly cheered speakers who have been identified by union men as I.W.W. high-lights among the Brooklyn longshoremen.' The *Eagle* reporter, who called this rally an 'ugly turn of events,' estimated that the locals represented there involved 17,000 longshoremen and that only three Brooklyn locals were absent. 'The speakers,' according to the *Eagle*, charged the officials of the I.L.A. with 'forcing the members

---

93. *Ibid.* The *Eagle* called Vacarrelli a 'picturesque survival of the old East Side gangsters . . .' October 6, 1919. The *World* described 'his necktie and fingers sparkling with diamonds.' New York *World*, October 22, 1919.

94. Bureau of Investigation, 'Case Files,' *op. cit.*, O.G. 690.

95. New York *Call*, October 23, 1919.

of local 808 to go back to work at the point of a pistol.' They also attacked 'the capitalist press' for reporting that '20,000 Brooklyn dockmen' had gone back to work. The strikers voted to 'stay out on the streets until their demands were met' and then 'cheered at the top of their lungs.' The meeting was conducted in Italian, with an interpreter for those present who spoke only English. The *Eagle* report also noted that 'I.W.W. agitation was clearly the purpose of the speakers . . . and their agents circulated through the audience.'[96]

This meeting reflected the growing influence of the Wobblies in Brooklyn. When an *Eagle* reporter investigated the Brooklyn I.W.W., he had no difficulty locating its headquarters. 'It does not attempt to hide itself. It is in a congested Italian neighborhood. In a window above an Italian fruit and vegetable store is a large colored sign reading "Industrial Workers of the World."' The reporter entered the building and climbed the stairs to find a small room, 'not altogether clean, but clean enough,' occupied by two or three dozen men, 'talking volubly, but without disorder, in Italian. These men, although they wore black and dark-colored suits and usually no collars, gave an altogether clean impression . . .'[97]

The Wobblies 'laughed' at O'Connor's charge that they led the strike: 'I wish it were,' said one,

> but we had nothing to do with it . . . The longshoremen of the New York and Brooklyn waterfronts became disgusted with the methods employed by the officers of the I.L.A. That's the explanation . . . The circular [referred to by O'Connor as evidence] had nothing to do with it. It was too late . . . Men came to the headquarters without solicitation and asked that we organize them. A meeting was held here on Tuesday night, and it was decided to print the circulars. We distributed some of them Wednesday morning, but found that practically all the men were already on strike. So all the posters are still here [pointing to them].

---

96. Brooklyn *Eagle*, October 19, 1919. The situation in Brooklyn was considerably different from that in Manhattan, where, for example, a Seattle Wobblie, identified as William Rooney, was well received when he spoke to the first big Tammany Hall meeting – until he said 'union labor should have no leaders,' was identified as an I.W.W. member, and was chased from the building. Socialist speakers outside the Cooper Union rally were also chased away, while inside, John Riley was able to have a motion passed 'repudiating the I.W.W.' The *Call*, October 14, 1919.

97. Brooklyn *Eagle*, October 12, 1919.

Then the reporter spoke to longshoremen gathered on the street outside. They were 'indignant'. 'They had been promised a dollar an hour . . . and all they received was a five cent increase . . .' They claimed that 'all the delegates were crooked, all the I.L.A. delegates . . . [who] would steal, steal, steal the money and the opportunities of the men . . .'[98] A subsequent *Eagle* report described times when there would be 'thousands of Italian longshoremen' surrounding the little Sackett Street I.W.W. hall in apparently spontaneous, informal strike rallies.[99]

The I.W.W. did not lead the strike; the denials were true. The I.W.W. in New York, according to the *One Big Union Monthly*, had experienced 'a little trouble' in October, but 'we expect to settle it,' said a report from the Marine Transport Workers Industrial Union #8, the I.W.W. organization for longshoremen and marine workers.[100] This is not surprising, for the I.W.W. in 1919 was still the target of fierce repression and the chief victim of the 'red scare.' It had in most places been reduced to an organization which was forced to concentrate on the defence of its own members – George Speed was in New York to help raise support for 'class war prisoners.' Fred Thompson remembers the New York district 'as a center of disputes,' but also recalled that in 1919 few branches were in a position to do more than 'offer moral support . . . [and] cheer workers on. Leadership was out of the question.'[101] Nevertheless, the press and the authorities seemed utterly incapable of grasping this. The press exaggerated I.W.W. involvement until the end. Even when it switched to the Vacarrelli/Butler argument, it continued to emphasize I.W.W. involvement in strike violence, especially on the Brooklyn waterfront.[102] The Bureau of Investigation

98. *Ibid.*

99. *Ibid.*, October 20, 1919.

100. *One Big Union Monthly*, series I, Vol. I, November, 1919.

101. Fred Thompson, conversation with C. W., June, 1986. Thompson was an I.W.W. member in 1919. Dubofsky writes, 'In that sense, the I.W.W. from 1919 to 1923 was a radical fellowship and not a functioning labor organization.' Melvyn Dubofsky, *We Shall Be All* (New York, 1969), p. 473.

102. New York *Times*, October 17, 1919; October 23, 1919.

relentlessly pursued signs of the I.W.W. on the waterfront, even though its final report was somewhat sceptical of the I.W.W. leadership theory.

The War Department's Military Intelligence also attributed the strike to the I.W.W. According to Intelligence Officer Thomas Crockett, Major, 'I am reliably informed that James Stott, I.W.W. Marine Transport Workers, New York, is responsible for the longshoremen's strike. Stott extreme radical.'[103] Another officer, H. A. Strauss, also a Major, offered a rather more sophisticated, though equally wrong, version of this: 'The fight in the longshoremen's union is between O'Connor and conservative labour against Vacarrelli and his I.W.W. element, the same as the steel strike is a fight between Gompers on the one hand and Foster and Fitzpatrick on the other.'[104] Another Strauss report warned of collaboration between the I.W.W. and the editors of the *Messenger* Magazine, a journal of black radicals, 'in regard to organization among the colored race.'[105] Strauss was concerned with 'the radical element' in Hoboken, as well, whose members 'are to a great extent German, but as yet it is impossible for me to state whether German interests and money are behind the strike.'[106]

These accounts of radical activity were greatly exaggerated but not without significance. The war had severely weakened the American left, in particular the I.W.W., whose most active members were jailed, subjected to endless legal proceedings, intimidated into retreat and even lynched.[107] The Communist parties, of course, were little more than isolated sects and just weeks old. They issued proclamations hailing the longshoremen, calling for the 'Dictatorship of the Workers,' and posted these in the vicinities of the piers.[108] The

---

103. Department of Justice, R.G. 60 Glasser File, NARA, October 11, 1919.

104. *Ibid.*, October 23, 1919.

105. *Ibid.*, October 25, 1919.

106. *Ibid.*, October 23, 1919.

107. Wesley Everest, an I.W.W. member and World War I veteran, was lynched in Centralia, Washington, on Armistice Day, November 11, 1919.

108. Bureau of Investigation, 'Investigation Case Files,' O.G. 690.

left's absence was certainly a factor in the strike. As Hardman noted, assessing the 1919 strikes, a great weakness of the workers' movements was that 'there was no radical political party in the field which would seek to give the movement centralized and sustained political guidance.'[109] The I.W.W. in New York, with all its weaknesses, attempted to fill this vacuum. While its press and its strike circulars were often vague and remote, its members and sympathizers pressed the strike in the streets. They criticized Butler and Vacarrelli as 'corrupt politicians' and they consistently championed industrial unionism. They played an important role among the Italian strikers, and this was a significant achievement. In November, they reported having recruited 1,200 longshoremen during the strike. They had an Italian organizer, 'Fellow Worker Bobba,' in the field, and they were distributing two flyers, 'Your Organization' and 'After the Strike.'[110]

Once it was clear that neither O'Connor nor a 'red scare' would get the longshoremen back to work, the authorities set about breaking the strike in three ways. First, Secretary of Labor Wilson announced the appointment of the Special Conciliation Commission, led by the Mayor, John Hylan, who was joined by Vacarrelli and James L. Hughes, Immigration Commissioner at Philadelphia. The Commission was denounced by O'Connor and Ryan, who said there was 'nothing to mediate and nothing to conciliate.'[111] It was also criticized by Ripley and the N.A.C. staff. Benjamin Squires asserted that the Commission prolonged the strike by encouraging 'the belief that a more liberal settlement was in sight.'[112] At most, the Commission may have succeeded in removing O'Connor from the centre of the dispute. It gave Vacarrelli a platform and it provided Butler an arena. Vacarrelli seems to have been satisfied with this. He consistently claimed not to have inspired the strike, saying that he first heard of it from reading the paper. His criticism of O'Connor and Ryan was that they misled the longshoremen into believing they could win a

---

109. Hardman, *op. cit.*, p. 12.

110. *Rebel Worker*, November, 1919: *New Solidarity*, November 15, 1919, November 22, 1919.

111. New York *Times*, October 19, 1919.

112. B. M. Squires, *op. cit.*, p. 112.

substantial wage gain. Butler used the Commission to press for his compromise on wages, but little ever came of this. He joined the call for 'all out war' at the height of the strike, but his intention seems to have been to get the strikers to accept an offer of 85 cents from the Conciliation Commission, claim a victory, and regain his prominence in the union. The authorities, however, were determined not to give anything at all.[113]

Second, the federal Government made a show of force, sending soldiers into the Harbour, though chiefly to the army docks. The *Call* reported that the first soldiers involved in the strike were 'regulars' who unloaded the army transport, *Northern Pacific*, at Hoboken. 'Thousands of striking long-shoremen stood by and silently watched the uniformed men unload the vessel.'[114] On October 21, J. J. O'Hare, a captain with military intelligence, noted that the 12th U.S. Infantry had arrived in New York on the transport, *George Washington*. 'This organization was ordered to this port,' he wrote, 'for the purpose of doing longshoremen's work, due to the longshoremen's strike in New York City.'[115] He also reported that 48 officers and 247 privates were being sent to the army piers at Bush Terminals, South Brooklyn. He advised that 'the presence of federal troops in New York City for this duty is a cause of considerable comment in the press of last evening and this morning, and was also a cause for the protest of the Mayor of the City of New York to the Secretary of War.' He concluded, however, that 'It is not believed that the presence of federal troops in New York City will be the cause of any particular disturbance.'[116] This conclusion seems to have been borne out. The striking longshoremen were no doubt angered and discouraged, but apart from the Mayor's protest there was little impact, though O'Hare did report that there had been 'some discontent among the enlisted personnel of this

---

113. New York *Times*, October 27, 1919. Meeting on October 26 of grievance committee. At this meeting, William Smith, the committee secretary, declared that the vote to call a general strike might mean an amalgamation with miners and railroad men.

114. New York *Call*, October 13, 1919.

115. Department of Justice, Glasser File, *op. cit.*, October 21, 1919.

116. *Ibid.*

regiment, because they were assigned to this character of work.'[117]

Third, the shippers increasingly resorted to using strike-breakers, chiefly along the East River and in South Brooklyn, though also in New Jersey but rarely in Manhattan – in the latter place presumably because the union was strongest there, it was Irish, and the potential for widespread disruption as well as political damage was greater. In Brooklyn, the use of strikebreakers, plus the attempts of small groups of workers to return, led to a series of street confrontations. On October 14, for example, the South Brooklyn waterfront was reported to be 'tight as a drum' but only after a 'crowd of 1,000 strikers gathered at the docks and marched up 13th Street to stop strikebreakers.'[118] The *Call* reported that on October 15, 'When some members of local 808 appeared at the foot of 1st Avenue to go to work, more than 1,000 strikers were there to make a street protest.'[119] The following day there was 'a violent disorder on the East River,' during which four men were shot and another man stabbed in a confrontation between strikers, strikebreakers and police.[120] On the same day the *Times* reported violence at the United Fruit Company docks in Brooklyn where 'non-union workers' were attempting to unload the steamship *San Mateo*: 'A squad of strikers managed to get at them and a free-for-all fight followed.' The same report included an account of fighting, including shots fired, at the Greenpoint Ferry. The *Times* believed that 'radicals' were the cause of these incidents and noted that one of the strikers arrested had 'an I.W.W. card.'[121] According to the Brooklyn *Eagle*, 'Along the Greenpoint docks, so serious is the danger of riots, strong-arm men have been imported to protect workers. There are 800 stevedores keeping in operation six of the twelve docks there and they are being protected by a delegation of ex-service men recruited in Oklahoma . . . These men have guns and ammunition and are excellent rifle

117. *Ibid.*, October 22, 1919.

118. Brooklyn *Standard Union*, October 14, 1919.

119. *Call*, October 16, 1919.

120. *Ibid.*, October 17, 1919.

121. New York *Times*, October 18, 1919.

and pistol shots.'[122] Asked about the violence, T. V. O'Connor responded that as there was no strike, he didn't consider 'strikebreaking' to be an issue. 'The violence,' he said, 'was further evidence of intimidation by reds. These men are mostly Italian,' he said, 'the foreign element . . .'[123]

On October 16th 'A riot nearly occurred,' according to the *Call* 'when a truck carrying several Negro dockworkers to Pier 15 on the East River' was confronted by strikers who declared that 'Negroes returning to work . . . would inevitably lead to "race riots."'[124] On the 18th 'there was an encounter between about 1,000 strikers and the police . . . the police say they were forced to use their sticks to disperse the crowd.'[125] On the 22nd there was fighting at the Ward Line's Pier 18 between 'strikers and colored gangs.'[126] On the same say, 'Large groups of longshoremen were on the waterfront,' the *Times* reported, with 'raiding parties' attacking the United Fruit piers, 'which operate on the open-shop principle' and have been working 'right along in spite of the strike.'[127] 'The most serious clash . . . since the strike began,' according to the *Times*, took place on 2nd Avenue near 42nd Street, at the Bush Terminals. The *Eagle* said this was a place where large numbers of strikers 'meet every morning, usually to harass the workers as they report to the docks.'[128] This time '1,000 or more Italian longshoremen' attacked strikebreakers and the police, many of them calling for 'a war to the finish on the waterfront.'[129] The *Call* estimated 2,000 longshoremen involved.[130] Bureau of Investigation Agent Anderson heard calls 'in Italian and English' that brought 'hundreds' out of the

---

122. Brooklyn *Eagle*, October 18, 1919.

123. New York *Call*, October 16, 1919.

124. *Ibid.*, October 17, 1919.

125. *Ibid.*, October 19, 1919.

126. Brooklyn *Standard Union*, October 22, 1919.

127. New York *Times*, October 23, 1919.

128. Brooklyn *Eagle*, October 28, 1919.

129. New York *Times*, October 28, 1919.

130. New York *Call*, October 28, 1919.

neighbourhood.[131] The *Times* said '100 shots' were fired in the battle, which lasted an hour.[132] Anderson noted that 'Nobody seems to know how the fight started, but all at once the streets were covered with fighting men.'[133] The press routinely linked the I.W.W. and this violence, for its own purposes, of course. Still, it would be difficult to imagine that I.W.W. members were not on the front lines.

This represents a selective account of the conflict on the Brooklyn waterfront, a conflict which raged every day for more than two weeks along the piers and in the working class neighbourhoods adjacent to them. Many thousands of workers were involved. The employers, responding in kind to this 'fight to the finish,' formally announced on October 28 their intention to 'break the strike' and return to the 'open shop' throughout the Harbour.[134] The longshoremen's resistance indicated their fierce refusal to be driven back into 'the system.'

The Irish locals in Chelsea refused as stubbornly, though not as violently, as did the New Jersey longshoremen. It is impossible to say just why the strike broke in the first days of November. There were increasing reports of longshoremen in fear of starving, searching the city in desperation for work. Certainly, strikers must have been exhausted.[135] The government and the shippers remained enormously confident, never blinking. Mayor Hylan, often discouraged, kept his door open, as Vacarrelli and Butler searched for a way to get the men back – and claim the victory. On November 5, at a meeting called by the Mayor, the Chelsea longshoremen voted to return to work; the Brooklyn and New Jersey locals followed, though there were scattered disruptions in the port for two weeks. The vote followed the Mayor's 'final' plea, supported by Butler and Vacarrelli. The longshoremen, even at this point, however, remained defiant, insisting they were

131. Bureau of Investigation, 'Investigation Case Files,' *op. cit.*, O.G. 690.

132. New York *Times*, October 28, 1919.

133. Bureau of Investigation, *op. cit.*, O.G. 690.

134. New York *World*, October 29, 1919.

135. New York *Call*, November 4, 1919.

returning on the basis of the pre-award wages and conditions.[136]

The great strikes of 1919 were nearly all lost, so there is little point in speculating about alternative outcomes to the longshoremen's strike. Still, there is a difference worth noting. Other workers would achieve industrial unionism, though a generation later, in the turbulence of the thirties. The New York longshoremen never would. There was not another major strike on the waterfront for 26 years. In the 1950s the veteran labour journalist, Mary Heaton Vorse, could still write of 'the shape up, favoritism,' and casual work – "No matter how long he's worked on the docks, every man is hired fresh every day" – and deprivation and the 'threat of unemployment.' She could still call attention to collaboration of the union leadership and the shippers, to Joseph Ryan, 'the president for life of the International Longshoremen's Association,' and his belief that 'the system' as 'best suited for the port of New York,' and to thousands of 'anonymous longshoremen,' again in 'revolt,' still 'living for the day of liberation' from this 'system.'[137]

Much has been written here about the power of the New York longshoremen in 1919, about their capacity to organize and to struggle in an effort to overcome staggering obstacles. Something more should be said about their leaders. The International Officers of the I.L.A., led by O'Connor and Ryan, clung tenaciously to their control of the union, despite the overwhelming opposition of the New York members. In doing this they were supported, even praised, by the shipping companies, by their colleagues on the National Adjustment Commission and at the Shipping Board, and by the leaders of the American Federation of Labor. Moreover, they reaped great rewards. O'Connor went on to become Chairman of the U.S. Shipping Board, though he maintained the title 'Honorary President' of the longshoremen's union.[138] Ryan did in fact

136. New York *Call*, October 6, 1919.

137. Mary Heaton Vorse, 'The Pirate's Nest of New York,' in *Rebel Pen*, Dee Garrison, ed. (New York 1985), pp. 213-233.

138. William Ripley sent this note to O'Connor after the strike. 'I expect to be in Washington for a week soon and may drop in on you . . . Or would you take dinner with me some night at the Cosmos Club, and

become 'President for Life.' But he also served as Vice-president of the New York State Federation of Labor, A.F.L., for more than twenty years. And he was President of the Central Labor Council of Greater New York City for ten years, 1929-1938.[139] The 'small-time criminals,' Vacarrelli and Butler, faded away; in their place came crime and corruption on a grand scale.

There have been many explanations of why the mob came to be so deeply entrenched in the Harbour and of how the longshoremen's union came to be so corrupt. That is not the subject here. One should say, though, that its triumph must not be seen as inevitable, even in the sea of corruption that was New York City. The rank-and-file longshoremen fought heroically – there is no other word, no matter how unfashionable it may have become – in a year of heroic struggles, for a kind of unionism which would have presented enormous obstacles to the criminals and the shippers, as well as to corruption in the trade union movement itself. The still-birth of industrial unionism on the waterfront in New York was a great tragedy in a year of working class defeat.

---

have a smoke afterwards, recalling the old times?' 'Records of National Adjustment Commission' (C. 1923) *op. cit.*

---

139. Gary Fink, ed., *Biographical Dictionary of American Labor*, pp. 444, 497. Charles Larrowe suggests that the I.L.A. officials were hardened by their experience during the strike, and that in part they established control attacking 'local autonomy' and establishing 'cordial relations with city officials.' *Shape-Up and Hiring Hall* (Berkeley and Los Angeles, 1955), pp. 14-15.

Chapter Twelve

Fear and Hope in the Nuclear Age
Robert Malcolmson

'War itself is not unnatural, only the modern weapons of war are unnatural. The weapons dominate us. The pilot is the tool of his plane, the gunner of his gun. That is what makes modern war a new predicament.' (Charles Ritchie, a Canadian diplomat in London, 13 May 1940)

'. . . [atomic] war is unthinkable but not impossible, and therefore we must think about it.' (Bernard Brodie, writer on military affairs, 1947)

'I think a revolution has occurred . . . through the introduction of nuclear weapons into the arsenal of warfare. For from the beginning of history to the end of the Second World War, there existed a rational relationship between violence as a means of foreign policy, and the ends of foreign policy . . . This rational relationship . . . has been destroyed by the possibility of all-out nuclear war.' (Hans J. Morgenthau, a political scientist, 1961)[1]

In March 1947, Mass-Observation, the research organization that studied British attitudes and social behaviour, enquired into public opinion on the atomic bomb and its effect on world affairs. Two of the replies to these enquiries pointed to a fundamental clash in outlook concerning this remarkable new weapon.

---

1. Charles Ritchie, *The Siren Years: A Canadian Diplomat Abroad, 1937-1945* (Toronto, 1974), p. 51; Bernard Brodie, 'The Security Problem in the Light of Atomic Energy', in Quincy Wright, ed., *A Foreign Policy for the United States* (Chicago, 1947), p. 91; and Hans J. Morgenthau, in *Commentary*, October 1961, p. 280. About a quarter of this essay draws on evidence or arguments previously published in my book *Beyond Nuclear Thinking* (McGill-Queen's University Press, 1990). I am grateful to the editors of this Press for permission to reuse this material. Thanks are also due to the Advisory Research Committee of Queen's University for timely financial support for research in 1991-92.

One respondent thought that, 'Having had the Bomb thrust upon us, we can but put up some show of control through International Treaty and Commission, and thus put off the evil day for as long as possible.'[2] This classic pessimism was similarly voiced by others. Controls might be attempted, and perhaps a few of them might even work, at least for a while. (In fact, during the previous year, 1946, there had been not only much political talk about the international control of atomic energy but also some thoughtful proposals as to how to achieve this control, of which the Acheson-Lilienthal plan was the most substantial and serious.)[3] But pessimists doubted then and would continue to doubt that controls could work beyond the short-term. The new-found destructive power of atomic weaponry could not, it was supposed, be suppressed indefinitely. Perhaps it could be managed for a while – a few years, a few decades, a few generations – but surely not for ever. Such lethal power in the hands of mere humans, fallible and often irrational, frequently inept and prone to violence, was bound some day to erupt, with cataclysmic consequences.[4] This was a view that highlighted the dark side of human nature and that led, if it led to any positive

---

2. University of Sussex Library, The Tom Harrison Mass-Observation Archive, Directive Replies 1947 (February/March), file E-L, N1523.

3. Richard G. Hewlett and Oscar E. Anderson, *The New World, 1939/1946: A History of the United States Atomic Energy Commission, Vol. I* (University Park, PA, 1962), chap. 15.

4. Such cataclysms were foreseen by a few military men, who endeavoured to reconcile the prospect of atomic war with their professional commitments. In *Bombing and Strategy: The Fallacy of Total War* (London, n.d. [c.1946]), Admiral Sir Gerald Dickens foresaw the enhancement of naval power (for him, a good thing) as a result of the development of long-range sea-based missiles, armed with atomic warheads. But he acknowledged that such atomic warfare might serve no rational purpose. 'While we hope that war of such an insane pattern will never be fought we can at least hope that if it did [occur] we should be able to extract a mighty retribution before we went under – with everyone else.' Here too was pessimism, informed by fatalism, for wars, he assumed, were integral to the human condition. 'Wars came to us with Original Sin. When we sin no more as individuals no one, presumably, will want to make war. As things are, all we can do is, by moral and physical means together, to lessen the chances of war and, *when it comes*, to soften its impact to the world wherever this is possible.' (pp. 66-67: emphasis added)

policy (if often led to a resigned fatalism), to an advocacy of disarmament. Disarmament, some of its supporters conceded, involved risks. But what could be worse than the prospect of universal death? What horrors could exceed the obliteration of all that humanity had laboured to create through civilization?

Another respondent to Mass-Observation, a sergeant posted in Germany, took a different and more hopeful line. He wondered if the atomic bomb, because of its remarkable destructiveness, 'might prove . . . to be a blessing in disguise.' The bomb, he thought, tended to force a choice between extremes: either 'we must live in peace or it means total destruction.' The crippling cost of war was bound to make peace more appealing – indeed, vastly more appealing. He also emphasized 'the fact of common fear. If no other means can ever bring about peace, it might be the fear of atomic warfare and the consequent suicide of mankind, which may prompt nations to live peacefully together. This would be the Atom Bomb's greatest boon.'[5] This argument, stressing the positive role of fear as redefined by the nuclear threat, had been developed shortly after Hiroshima by the American economist, Jacob Viner. He pointed out that

> for the most part wars arise out of mutual fear of peace, out of fear of loss of national independence or of other nationally treasured objectives unless war is resorted to, more than out of love of war or than out of lust for war booty. Countries most often go to war because they fear the consequences of remaining at peace . . . By adding to the horror of war and therefore to the attractiveness of peace, the discovery of the atomic bomb will aid instead of hinder the diplomacy of peace.

The bomb, in short, would in his view subvert the logic of war and fortify the logic of peace.[6]

---

5. University of Sussex Library, The Tom Harrison Mass-Observation Archive, Directive Replies 1947 (February/March), file E-L, N1292. Two other respondents offered similar views. 'The atom-bomb's contribution to the peace parleys is probably that its horror has a steadying effect', thought one; another remarked that the bomb's 'only redeeming feature is that in fear of it the urgency of Peacemaking may be appreciated.' (Respectively: box of male replies, unidentified files, N1457; and file of unidentified informants, sex unknown, N1441.)

6. Jacob Viner, 'The Implications of the Atomic Bomb for International Relations', *Proceedings of the American Philosophical Society*, vol 90,

Fear, then, was proposed as the foundation for (perhaps) permanent peace. This supposition became central to arguments in favour of, or at least accepting of, nuclear weapons. In the past war had been in some sense a rational political option, for in many circumstances the benefits of war had been expected to exceed the costs of war. In the nuclear age, however, this would probably not be the case. War with nuclear weapons held out the prospect of all loss and no gain. It promised a battlefield outcome with losers but no winners. Nuclear war, it increasingly came to be said, was unthinkable. The prospect that any war between the great powers might involve the use of nuclear weapons meant that each of these powerful states would have reason to exercise exceptional prudence and self-restraint in the effort to avoid war.

Nuclear weapons could, and some said they should, be seen as instruments of peace. The very fact of their existence would surely *spoil* the rationale of great-power warfare. This became a widely held position. As Air Marshall Sir John Slessor put it in 1956, 'I believe that the hydrogen bomb in the armouries of the world brings a message not of despair but of hope – hope and even confidence that no one will ever again resort to major war as an instrument of policy.'[7] The incentives to preserve the peace were seen to be now overwhelming. Disputes would have to be settled in other ways. Modern weapons had become so destructive that their actual military use would be inconceivable. Military force, it was asserted, would henceforth exist entirely or almost entirely to avert war, not to fight it. The world's political future would depend, then, not on disarmament, but rather on nuclear deterrence. Slessor pursued this argument further in a book published in 1962:

> What we have to abolish is war itself. I have hammered away at the point for some years now . . . that modern science *has* abolished war – total war as I have known it twice in my time, and the unthinkable horrors of a future great war – *provided* only that we do not throw away the nuclear weapon prematurely.
> The prime and conclusive justification of that weapon is not that it will be used, but that it will *not* be used. Nor, as long as it exists, will any other

---

no. 1 (January 1946), p. 57.

---

7. Sir John Slessor, *The Central Blue: Recollections and Reflections* (London, 1956), p. 537.

weapons have to be used in another great war. I have already attempted to explain that the item on the credit side of nuclear armaments – and it is an overwhelming one – is that with them war can never again be profitable by any stretch of the imagination.[8]

Nuclear armaments, according to this thinking, were a force for peace. Their inherent threats could be turned to good ends. Preserving and strengthening the deterrence of aggression by virtue of the threat of nuclear destruction became the crucial declared objectives of both military strategy and, more generally, the pursuit of national security.

This brief and rather schematic account involves a high degree of compression and simplification. It ignores – in Britain, the United States, and other Western nations – the muddled thinking, the uncertainties, the ups and downs in anxiety, the oscillations between fear and hope (or even feistiness), the contradictory impulses (such as Bertrand Russell, the critic of modern warfare, toying in the later 1940s with the idea of a preventative nuclear war against the Soviet Union),[9] the paths considered but not taken, the missed opportunities, the perplexities and confusion that sometimes afflicted decision-makers. A nuclear arms race had in fact been predicted *before* any atomic device was ever exploded. In June 1945 a number of knowledgeable scientists attached to the Manhattan Project warned of the likely consequence of a unilateral first-use of the atomic bomb by the United States. Arguing for restraint by Washington and an active search for international control of atomic energy, they predicted that,

> If no efficient international agreement is achieved, the race for nuclear armaments will be on in earnest not later than the morning after our first demonstration of the existence of nuclear weapons. After this, it might take other nations three or four years to overcome our present head start, and eight to ten years to draw even with us if we continue to do intensive work in this field.[10]

---

8. Sir John Slessor, *What Price Coexistence? A Policy for the Western Alliance* (London, 1962), p. 52.

9. Alan Ryan, *Bertrand Russell: A Political Life* (London, 1990), pp. 177-181; and Ronald W. Clark, *The Life of Bertrand Russell* (New York, 1976), chap. 19.

10. 'The Franck Report, June 11, 1945', printed as an appendix to Alice Kimball Smith, *A Peril and a Hope: The Scientists' Movement in*

The prospect of another power drawing level, which in fact took only slightly longer than these scientists predicted, meant that the United States would eventually risk becoming naked to annihilating attack, just as other nations (as the Kremlin in particular would notice) were soon to become naked to American attack. Already in 1945 this was the foreseeable consequence of introducing nuclear weapons into a politically anarchical world.

Despite a few warnings against overdependence on nuclear weapons for its security, the United States came to champion the bomb as the centrepiece of its strategy for peace, especially after the outbreak of war in Korea in 1950. The sources of the period are full of explicit assertions as to the centrality of the nuclear threat as an instrument of peace. Indeed, there can be little doubt as to the muscularity of America's nuclear posture. Some claims were almost celebratory. For example, in a major speech delivered in October 1951, the chairman of the U.S. Atomic Energy Commission, Gordon Dean, sought to justify his country's growing reliance on nuclear weapons and explicitly tied together American world leadership, moral virtue, and the atomic bomb. He spoke of 'the noble ideas of freedom and human dignity to which mankind has always aspired and which have reached their greatest fruition here in our own country.' 'Today', he continued, 'the United States stands before the world with the lamp of liberty raised high in one hand and the atomic bomb in the other.' To those who questioned this joining together of virtue and the bomb, Dean gave the following answer:

> In essence, we have taken the position as a nation that war is bad, and aggression is bad, and any weapon that serves to prevent war and aggression, or to stop aggression once it has been undertaken, is good . . . [A]ny other position would in all likelihood mean the end, not only of our freedom and our way of life, but of all the noble ideals to which man has aspired through the ages.[11]

America: 1945-47 (Cambridge, MA, 1970), p. 376.

---

11. Roger M. Anders, ed., *Forging the Atomic Shield: Excerpts from the Office Diary of Gordon E. Dean* (Chapel Hill, NC, 1987), appendix, pp. 279-80.

The atomic bomb was perceived as a major advantage for America in its struggle with major adversaries; and as Secretary of Defense Robert Lovett remarked in a memorandum of 16 May 1952, 'we place no limit on the extent of the use of atomic or any other weapons, nor do we believe that the use of large numbers of atomic weapons against an enemy would have an adverse effect on neutrals or potential allies.'[12] As Dean and Lovett and many others saw it, the radical evil of dictatorial communism, combined with the exceptional moral stature of America, justified the central role of atomic weapons in the free world's pursuit of peace and security.

In the Cold War climate of the early and mid 1950s, the bomb was no longer seen as such a fearful thing, as it had been during the months immediately after Hiroshima. Consider, for example, a mundane incident that nicely reveals something of the changing postwar political mood. In September 1950 the *New York Times* reported that a musical record entitled 'Old Man Atom', which had been composed by a Los Angeles newspaperman in 1945, shortly after Hiroshima, was being withdrawn from distribution by R.C.A.-Victor and Columbia Records, apparently because 'pressure had been brought on them on the ground that the song followed the Communist party "peace line".' The message of the song, it was said, which had previously been entitled 'Talking Atomic Blues', was that 'the atomic bomb endangers all people everywhere and that we must have peace in the world or we will all be in pieces.' This message was unacceptable to influential pressure groups who argued that the song 'parroted the Communist line on peace and reflected the propaganda for the Stockholm "peace petition"' and thus should not be available for public consumption.[13] Learning to Love the Bomb: this was a flippant phrase of the time that embodied a measure of truth. In an April 1954 editorial, 'Facing Up to the Bomb', the *New York Times* gave voice to opinion that by then was commonplace:

---

12. *Foreign Relations of the United States, 1952-1954, vol. II, part 2: National Security Affairs* (Washington, DC: U.S. Government Printing Office, 1984), pp. 934-35.

13. *New York Times*, 1 September 1950, p. 4.

Though Soviet Russia has mastered the secret of both atomic and hydrogen explosions, the United States and through it all free nations have the lead at present in the production of atomic and hydrogen weapons, and this fact increases the strength of the free world and therewith the chances of world peace.[14]

Satisfaction was expressed about the possession of this superior destructive power.

By the mid 1950s nuclear weapons were at the heart of America's pursuit of security, and the size of this arsenal was growing rapidly. Documents were produced to guide the nation's security policy and these official documents were explicit in their articulation of the centrality of the nuclear threat. According to one such statement in 1957:

It is the policy of the United States to place main, but not sole, reliance on nuclear weapons; to integrate nuclear weapons with other weapons in the arsenal of the United States; to consider them as conventional weapons from a military point of view; and to use them when required to achieve national objectives.

Some resistance to this policy of relying heavily on nuclear weapons was anticipated, especially abroad. Thus another clause of this statement recommended that the 'United States should continue efforts to persuade its allies to recognize nuclear weapons as an integral part of the arsenal of the Free World and the need for their prompt and selective use when required.'[15] The U.S. Secretary of Defense, in conversation with the British Secretary of State on 28 August 1959, was blunt about his nation's nuclear-dependency: 'the whole of United States strategy was conditioned to nuclear weapons.'[16] There was little disposition for nuclear restraint. The bomb was represented as a source of hope for free peoples. And as with most good things that technology had brought forth, it came to be mass-produced. In 1950 the United States possessed perhaps 300 to 500 fission weapons. A decade later the

14. Ibid., 6 April 1954, p. 28.

15. *Foreign Relations of the United States, 1955-1957, vol. XIX: National Security Policy* (Washington, DC: U.S. Government Printing Office, 1990), p. 511 (from NSC 5707/8, June 1957). At a meeting in the White House in May of 1956, President Eisenhower had said that 'He felt that in the emphasis he has given on the atomic weapons lies the greatest safety and security for our country.' (Ibid., p. 314.)

16. Public Record Office, FO 371, no. 140551 (IAD 44/10).

American arsenal comprised around 18,000 nuclear war-heads and was still growing (though 'quality' was soon to be given priority over crude quantity).[17]

By the mid 1950s the United States had committed itself to a heavily nuclearized world. It would be only a slight exag-geration to say that, by the 1960s, nuclear weapons – and increasingly Soviet as well as American weapons – were almost everywhere: at sea and under the sea, in the air, on land, in various countries, occasionally under the land (as mines). Attempts were made to give this nuclearized world an air of normalcy, and the words 'security' and 'deterrence' were reiterated with impressive frequency.

'Deterrence' has been probably the most oft-repeated con-cept of the nuclear age. Nuclear weapons, it was said again and again, existed to deter. Formidable efforts were con-tinually being made to *strengthen deterrence*. New weapons were repeatedly deployed in its name. In fact, virtually all innovations in nuclear weaponry – the H-bomb, ballistic missiles, cruise missiles, multiple warheads (MIRVs), preci-sion guidance systems, 'stealth' technologies – were justified on the grounds that they would enhance deterrence and thus better prevent the outbreak of war. Deterrence theory in its various elaborations became a staple component of security and strategic studies. The speeches and sound-bites of politi-cians, defence officials, and military planners were held aloft in part by the language of deterrence, which provided the essential rationale for much Cold War policy and expenditure on weaponry. Nuclear war might well be a nasty business, should it regrettably come about. But the nuclear threat, *our* nuclear threat, a threat that had to be constantly fortified, was needed to keep the adversary at bay, to deter communist aggression, to encourage one's allies and friends, and to offset the alleged formidable advantages of the communist camp in military manpower and conventional firepower.

Several judgments can be offered about the early years of the atomic age. First, while the atomic bomb was obviously a revolutionary weapon with extraordinary implications, the

---

17. Thomas B. Cochran, William M. Arkin, and Milton M. Hoenig, *Nuclear Weapons Databook, vol. I: U.S. Nuclear Forces and Capabilities* (Cambridge, MA, 1984), p. 15.

emphasis on air-atomic power was in many respects a continuation of the Anglo-American policies of strategic air
power that had been pursued during World War Two. These
policies had endorsed the mass bombing of civilian targets.
They had rejected the distinction between combatants and
non-combatants. They had sought to undermine civilian morale and the enemy's social fabric by more-or-less indiscriminate destruction from the air. The bombers' objectives were
to create panic, to cause terror, to 'dehouse' industrial
workers, and, if possible, to damage war-related industries
that were located in these cities (this was commonly more an
ancillary than a central goal). During 1943, 1944, and early
1945, tens of thousands of German and Japanese civilians,
mostly women and children, were killed in air raids that were
designed to obliterate large swathes of enemy cities (the raids
on Hamburg in July 1943, Dresden in February 1945, and
Tokyo in March 1945 were among the most destructive). The
significance of these bombings for the eventual allied victory
has been much debated and continues to be controversial, but
there is no doubt about their legacy. The experience of total
war between 1939 and 1945 included a tradition of saturation
bombing, of wholesale destruction from the air. This tradition
was eminently compatible with the even more destructive
capabilities of airpower that were revealed in the summer of
1945. And it led logically to the strategy of air-atomic superiority that was becoming self-conscious American policy by
the end of the 1940s. Postwar atomic strategy was very much
built on what had happened immediately before.[18]

Second, American policy choices during the decade after
1945 were, perhaps, neither particularly unusual nor particularly surprising. For most Americans the atomic bomb
was new-found power, and power, of course, was to be used:
used to induce others to align themselves more closely with

18. Among the most useful works on strategic bombing are the following:
Martin Middlebrook, *The Nuremburg Raid, 30-31 March 1944*
(London, 1973); idem, *The Battle of Hamburg: Allied Bomber Forces
against a German City in 1943* (London, 1980); Max Hastings, *Bomber
Command* (New York, 1979); Ronald Schaffer, *Wings of Judgment:
American Bombing in World War II* (New York, 1985); and Michael S.
Sherry, 'Was 1945 a break in history?', *Bulletin of the Atomic Scientists*,
July/August 1987, pp. 12-15, and *The Rise of American Air Power: The
Creation of Armageddon* (New Haven, CT, 1987).

the American position, used as a persuader, used as a 'tool of peace'. The bomb was seen by most people, certainly from 1947 and sometimes before, as an American advantage, an advantage that ought to be exploited (in a good sense) in the interest of national security and strengthening the United States agenda for an orderly and prosperous postwar world. There was nothing especially remarkable in these views. They were unexceptional views for a great power that was determined to secure its immediate interests and struggling to find the means to do so in a time of radical change and upheaval.

In many respects the United States during the early atomic age was responding in a conventional manner to an extraordinary situation. And the problems it faced deserve to be sympathetically appreciated. The United States had *suddenly* become the foremost global power – it had never before had to manage such world-wide interests. The atomic bomb had *suddenly* appeared on the world scene – there were no precedents for dealing with such a powerful weapon. The colossal tumult of 1939-1945 meant that American statesmen and diplomats were bound to be scrambling to cope with radically redefined realities almost everywhere. They were often uncertain, even baffled; and they were not always able or disposed to think through the longer-term implications of their actions. One of the most astute interpreters of the atomic age, Bernard Brodie, once said of the nuclear weapons policies of his country, 'I see no reason to believe that any other government placed in comparable circumstances would very likely have done better.'[19] Considering the political records of other great powers in this and previous centuries and their affection for the tools of violence, it would be hard to quarrel with this judgment.

Third, American nuclear strategy can only be properly understood in relation to the Stalinist character of its chief adversary. While Washington's eventual heavy reliance on nuclear weapons was in some sense historically logical and understandable, the acuteness of this dependency was partly a consequence of the acuteness of Stalinist repression and dogmatism, especially in eastern and central Europe. The

---

19. U.C.L.A. Research Library, Bernard Brodie Papers, Box 20, file 13 (Munich Conference, February 1968), typescript paper on 'Nuclear Strategy in Its Political Context', p. 1.

heavy hand of Stalinism, whether in Hungary or Czechoslo-
vakia or Berlin, was hardly conducive to those habits of
compromise, flexibility, and accommodation that were essential to any sort of postwar political settlement. Stalinist rule
was mostly by force, little by consent. It aroused fear, hatred,
and (among most of its subjects) sullen acquiescence. It
presented a face to the outside world that was rarely attractive
and often repellent. The extremities of Stalinism made the
extreme American dependency on nuclear weapons easier to
swallow and to justify. The bomb was spoken of as the
absolute weapon; the Soviet Union – or 'world communism' –
was considered to be an absolute evil. The argument was
made that the Stalinist threat, which was seen as a fundamental attack on civilized values, could be adequately met *only* by
the nuclear threat (which was said by a few people at that time
and was regarded by many people after as at least an equal
peril to mankind). This was an argument that most people in
the 1950s found plausible, persuasive, even self-evident. It is
noteworthy that during the two years immediately after
Hiroshima, when Soviet-American relations were often difficult and strained but certainly not without hope, Washington
gave little priority to its atomic arsenal, which numbered
around a dozen bombs in mid-1947. It was only after 1947,
when Stalin pressed for an even harsher agenda in his sphere
of influence, that the United States became deeply committed, even adamantly committed, to the nuclearization of
its national security policy.

Fourth, most of the crucial decisions about nuclear
weapons and their development had been made by 1960. The
essential structure of the American nuclear presence – the
arsenal of bombers, submarine-based missiles, land-based
missiles, and tactical weapons – was already determined by
1960. The changes effected afterwards, during the 1960s,
1970s, and 1980s, were relatively much less important. The
quantities of weapons that existed in the Reagan years were
much the same as the quantities in the early 1960s. As
Herbert York, a prominent military scientist of long experience, observed in 1987: 'at the end of the Eisenhower administration we had plans, largely backed by solid commitments,
for a strategic nuclear delivery force consisting of about 2,400
vehicles, just slightly more than we had in the mid-1980s, a

quarter century later.' 'The remarkable thing about' the numbers of nuclear warheads, he said, and about other nuclear numbers as well, 'is how much they changed during the Eisenhower administration and how little they changed since.'[20] The nuclearization of American policy was a rapid, early, and precipitous development in the nuclear age. Little more than a dozen years after Hiroshima, the United States was locked into a structure of nuclear dependency that would prove to be highly resistant to future revision.

Fifth and finally, this massive nuclear buildup meant that, even if the United States did not in fact come to possess an actual preemptive first-strike capability (and some Air Force officers thought that it had), the Soviet Union certainly had grounds for fearing this American nuclear predominance. From Moscow's point of view, a preemptive U.S. nuclear strike could not be ruled out. Soviet leaders were not at liberty to perceive America's mightily expanding nuclear arsenal as strictly defensive. In their eyes this arsenal was potentially offensive, perhaps even decisively offensive. They were certainly more attentive to its coercive implications than its alleged deterrent function, which was the core of Washington's declaratory policy. Soviet fear was certainly more real, and perhaps more understandable, than most American observers were prepared to allow. The principal practical outcome of this fear of American might was a massive Soviet buildup of nuclear armaments, which, with respect to long-range weapons, was especially pronounced in the 1960s.

The Cold War witnessed a kind of normalization of the status of nuclear weapons, which was particularly fostered by the members of NATO led by the United States. Nuclear weapons were made to seem rather ordinary. To use them, it was sometimes suggested, would not be all that remarkable (though loose talk along these lines, by over-candid officials, caused occasional agitated public reactions). Given the conscious and explicit adoption of a policy of nuclear dependence, such normalizing language was understandable but not cost-free. As Bernard Brodie pointed out in the late 1950s:

---

20. Herbert F. York, *Making Weapons, Talking Peace: A Physicist's Odyssey from Hiroshima to Geneva* (New York, 1987), p. 194.

although a considerable residue of anathema and horror for the use of nuclear weapons remains in the world today, it has been considerably eroded by repeated insistence, emanating mostly from the United States, that the use of nuclear weapons must be regarded as absolutely normal, natural, and right. Whether it was really in the American interest to attack the emotional resistances to using nuclear weapons was never soberly examined.[21]

Attentive observers could see the force of this scepticism. After all, here was the United States, the world's leading liberal-industrial nation, which, on the one hand, championed human rights and liberty and civilized values and, on the other hand, took *the* leading role in threatening nuclear devastation in order to preserve these rights and values and other interests deemed vital to the nation. Because of this official American position, the Soviet Union, from the start of the nuclear age, had often been able to stand on firmer intellectual ground in formulating its positions on the nuclear threat. Consider the views of one observer who touched on this delicate issue. Writing in 1951, Richard Stebbins, author of *The United States in World Affairs, 1950*, remarked perceptively on the Soviet peace campaign that was then being conducted against the 'immoral' atomic weapon. He, like most Americans, faulted this campaign (which indeed was heavily propagandistic) but conceded that 'it undoubtedly encouraged the popular revulsion against atomic warfare and thus tended to build up the psychological obstacles to the use of the atomic bomb by the United States.' He also noted the advantages the Soviets enjoyed in condemning nuclear weaponry: after 'they managed to develop an atomic bomb,' he thought, 'they were unlikely to make it the centrepiece of their strategy, still less to announce the fact to a shuddering world . . . [T]hey had everything to gain by playing upon the apprehensions which the American attitude had aroused in Western Europe and elsewhere.'[22] In later years the Soviet Union sometimes did choose to emulate America and flaunt its own nuclear missiles (rarely with any advantage to itself) –

---

21. Bernard Brodie, *Strategy in the Missile Age* (Princeton, NJ, 1959), p. 320.

22. Richard P. Stebbins, *The United States in World Affairs, 1950* (New York: Harper for the Council on Foreign Relations, 1951), pp. 158-59 and 64.

Nikita Khrushchev had a weakness for posturing of this sort. But by the 1980s the Soviet leadership under Mikhail Gorbachev was again emphasizing the sort of anti-nuclear sentiment that it had espoused three decades before.

A small incident from August 1960 testifies to the sensitivity found in Western capitals to informed criticisms of what had by then become established orthodoxy. In this case the critic was a member of Britain's political establishment, Lord Hailsham, Minister for Science in the Macmillan government. Hailsham, in a speech reported in the press, raised questions about the long-term merit of 'relying on mutual [nuclear] terror':

> Though it is true that such a balance of terror is efficient now, and may be efficient for years to come, yet viewing the matter against the backdrop of history I am solemnly convinced . . . that if we go on indefinitely experimenting with these weapons, manufacturing them and stockpiling them, boasting of their potentialities, and keeping them at instant readiness, sooner or later a situation will arise, sometime, somewhere, where one will go off. It may be the deliberate explosion of a sophisticated weapon by one of the major powers. It may be a misunderstanding, or the blunder of a trigger-happy subordinate. It might be the crude explosion of some clumsy and primitive nuclear device by some adventurer in the second or third rank of world powers who had clandestinely acquired and manufactured it for reasons of prestige. It might be 50 years from now – or it might be ten, or it might be two. But my youngest child is eight, and I would wish that he might live to a ripe old age, and that we might bequeath him a state of the world which will permit him to do so.[23]

These were the sorts of remarks Ministers of the Crown were *not* supposed to make. The Foreign Office received a letter of complaint from an official in the Ministry of Defence, who noted that Lord Hailsham's speech

> does lend itself, with little misrepresentation, to press reports which imply that H.M.G. believe that the possession of nuclear weapons is in itself dangerous and presumably more dangerous than would be the situation today if nobody had them.
>
> This is hardly in accordance with H.M.G.'s policy . . . that the West's possession of nuclear weapons, given the manifest determination to use them in retaliation, has successfully and will successfully continue to deter resort to aggression. Disarmament is stated to be one of H.M.G.'s principle [sic] aims, but nuclear disarmament should, H.M.G. believes, come at the end of a disarmament process which suggests, as is the case, that it is nuclear armaments that ensure security against aggression.

23. *Daily Sketch*, 11 August 1960.

The Ministry of Defence advised that, in future, ministerial speeches on these matters should better reflect government policy.[24]

Nuclear states became very protective of their special powers, and the management of these powers was conducted largely if not entirely out of the public eye. A book by John Simpson on 'the military atom' and its role in Anglo-American relations, published in 1983, was given an especially appropriate title: *The Independent Nuclear State*. This independent or at least semi-independent nuclear state was radically at odds with democratic principles. Its managers, the custodians and operators of the nuclear system, were assiduous in insisting on a high degree of autonomy for themselves and in resisting public enquiries into the exercise of their extraordinary powers. They resented such scrutiny and regarded it as intrusive, dangerous, perhaps even unpatriotic. Exposures, they suggested, might undermine national security and provide succour to the enemy.

Nuclear weapons establishments were able to claim for themselves a sort of sovereign authority. According to the political scientist Hans Morgenthau in 1962, the U.S. Atomic Energy Commission 'has become a kind of state within a state'.[25] Little was divulged. Concealment, secrecy, and silences abounded. Slogans and abstractions were offered in place of information. The principle of the accountability of the powerful was seriously eroded; the new nuclear elites

---

24. Public Record Office, FO 371, no. 149265 (IA 10/4), letter of 19 August 1960 from C. W. Wright to Peter Wilkinson.

25. Hans Morgenthau, 'Decision-making in the Nuclear Age', *Bulletin of the Atomic Scientists*, vol. 18 (December 1962), p. 8. For similar opinion from later years, see William M. Arkin and Richard W. Fieldhouse, *Nuclear Battlefields: Global Links in the Arms Race* (Cambridge, MA, 1985), pp. 144-5; and Janne E. Nolan, *Guardians of the Arsenal: The Politics of Nuclear Strategy* (New York, 1989), pp. 30-33. Thomas E. Murray, one of the five members of the Atomic Energy Commission between 1950 and 1957, recalled an incident from 1957 that testified to this preoccupation with secrecy. 'At that time I wished to convey certain factual information about the composition of our nuclear stockpile to certain members of the National Security Council, including the Secretary of State. It was ruled by the AEC that they had no "need to know" the facts I wished to present.' (Thomas E. Murray, *Nuclear Policy for War and Peace* [Cleveland and New York, 1960], p. 213.)

were for the most part answerable only to themselves. These threats to democracy had for years been foreseen, though they were usually deprecated by government and, when necessary, justified on the grounds of national security. One of the earliest warnings had been sounded by the historian E. L. Woodward, who suggested in late 1945 that 'We might do well . . . to ask ourselves what domestic safeguards, if any, may be available to us against the misuse of this tremendous concentration of power henceforward in the hands of the State.'[26] Forty years later an American political scientist, Robert Dahl, was pointing to some of the implications for democracies of such concentrations of power. 'Nuclear weapons', he thought, 'present a tragic paradox: No decisions can be more fateful for Americans, and for the world, than decisions about nuclear weapons. Yet these decisions have largely escaped the control of the democratic process.'[27]

The independence of the nuclear arm of the state involved for a few people remarkable creative freedom: the freedom for weapons laboratories to innovate and explore new ideas, the freedom for scientists to design new weapons and for others to promote them.[28] This has been particularly an American phenomenon and much of it is testimony to that nation's intellectual ferment, pluralism, technological optimism and exuberance, and comparatively unrestrained enterprise. In the United States, unlike the Soviet Union, the grassroots (scientists, private laboratories, mid-level officials) was the source of military ideas, initiative, and creative energy. A new military-scientific proposal, as Matthew Evangelista has argued in *Innovation and the Arms Race*, 'is pushed up through the bureaucracy until it attracts the attention of supporters in the Congress and the Executive. In this respect,

26. E. L. Woodward, *Some Political Consequences of the Atomic Bomb* (Toronto, 1945), p. 25.

27. Robert Dahl, *Controlling Nuclear Weapons: Democracy Versus Guardianship* (Syracuse, NY, 1985), p. 3.

28. Relevant evidence concerning the Lawrence Livermore National Laboratory in California may be found in two books by William J. Broad: *Star Warriors: A Penetrating Look Into the Lives of the Young Scientists Behind Our Space Age Weaponry* (New York, 1985); and *Teller's War: The Top-Secret Story Behind the Star Wars Deception* (New York, 1992).

a new weapon starts with a technological idea rather than as a response to a specific threat or as a means to fulfill a long-standing mission.'[29] These ideas tended to acquire their own momentum. Military-strategic rationales frequently emerged *after* a technology was discovered to be feasible, at which time the potential institutional possessors of this technology laboured to define missions that the newly-conceived hardware could be made to perform. The United States followed an engineering approach to nuclear strategy. The weapons that were procured were the weapons that science was able to conceive and produce, not those that strategy or doctrine called for.[30] Thomas E. Murray, an engineer and one of the Commissioners of the U.S. Atomic Energy Commission between 1950 and 1957, thought that 'It is the instinct of technology to exploit to the maximum the possibilities inherent in every discovery.'[31] It was this instinct, heightened by the inflamed American fears and hyperpatriotism of the 1950s, that drove the arms race to such extremes of lethality.

The momentum of weapons-making had a robust life of its own. This truth was demonstrated yet again in 1989 and shortly thereafter as the Cold War was liquidated. For even as the traditionally-conceived Soviet threat virtually vanished, and as NATO doctrines of nuclear war-fighting and first-use were reduced to absurdity, Western nuclear arsenals were at first merely trimmed. Reductions were confined mostly to those weapons that were obviously obsolete, or of marginal institutional importance, or intended for battlefield use and thus only congenial to those who believed in controlled and limited nuclear war. Nuclear testing, a crucial prerequisite for weapons modernization, continued to be championed by Washington. Fissionable material from dismantled weapons was being recycled into new armaments. Major nuclear weapons systems, along with Star Wars, remained high priority items in the Pentagon's budget (though this priority was under attack). Here was striking testimony to the autonomy

---

29. Matthew Evangelista, *Innovation and the Arms Race: How the United States and the Society Union Develop New Military Technologies* (Ithaca, NY, 1988), p.x.

30. Carl G. Jacobsen, ed., *Strategic Power: USA/USSR* (London, 1990), pp. 102 and 505.

31. Murray, *Nuclear Policy* (1960), p. 50.

of the nuclear state and its resilience in the face of sea-changes in world politics.

On 11 August 1945, the British Embassy in Washington presented its customary report to London on the news of the week. 'It has been', the despatch began, 'a tumultuous week of earth-shattering events.' The atomic bomb was on almost everyone's mind. 'The stories of the atomic bomb appealed to everything most typical in the American nature. The lurid fantasies of the comic strips seemed suddenly to have come true. Headlines sagged under the weight of the drama and the superlatives they had to carry.' Among the various public emotions there was, in the Embassy's apt phrase, 'a thrill of power' – and, the diplomats added, 'the instinctive pleasure at the thought of Japan cringing in abject surrender.'[32] This American thrill of power was hardly surprising: it was the fruit of total victory, made even more luxuriant by the spectacular manner of the final triumph. The bomb was exclusively in American hands. This fact should (it was generally thought) be used to good political effect – perhaps not used to the hilt, but certainly used to further the nation's agenda of peace, prosperity, justice, and security. If the bomb could be of service in advancing this agenda and in bringing about a new world order, then clearly (as most Americans saw it) the new weapon should not be denigrated or discarded.

Of course, not everyone believed this. There were sceptics, critics, pessimists, internationalists, and others who doubted the political utility of the bomb's destructive power and more still who feared the prospect of a nuclear arms race. But they lost the debates. By the early 1950s the bomb had been embraced as a tool of peace. It was seen as a source of hope for free peoples. Its existence became central to the conduct of the Cold War, which involved most crucially the containment of communism. Nuclear weapons, it was felt, could be mas-

---

32. H. G. Nicholas, ed., *Washington Despatches 1941-1945: Weekly Political Reports from the British Embassy* (Chicago, 1981), p. 598. The report noted at the same time that 'America's deep-rooted humanitarianism has begun to assert itself [with regard to the destruction caused by the atomic bombings] and this secondary revulsion has been very marked in private conversation although it has not yet appeared in the press.'

tered and properly controlled. They could be harnessed to the central cause of anti-communism. Detailed plans were worked out for the operational use of these weapons, in Europe, on the seas, in various other 'theatres'. There was in all this, as one historian has said of the 1950s, 'a certain cockiness about control capabilities'[33] and naiveté about America's capacity to manage an environment awash in nuclear technologies – technologies which, moreover, would increasingly be possessed by others. While there were moments of self-doubt and nervousness and even panic (such as 1957-58), America's mood was generally one of nuclear self-assurance. Sometimes this self-assurance caused alarm abroad, especially when it was seen as an indication of American complacency about the perils of nuclear war.[34] How close

---

33. Ronald W. Pruessen, 'John Foster Dulles and the Predicaments of Power', in Richard H. Immerman, ed., *John Foster Dulles and the Diplomacy of the Cold War* (Princeton, NJ, 1990), p. 36.

34. A letter of 13 November 1961 to Prime Minister Harold Macmillan from Philip Holland, Conservative M.P. for Acton, suggests the sort of concern that could arise in allied capitals. Holland was reporting the impressions of a constituent, a leading industrialist, who had spent time recently in the United States:

> He tells me that nine people in every ten with whom he spoke now take the view that survival of the majority of Americans in a future nuclear war is highly probable, and that such a war may well come within the next twelve months.
>
> Indeed the attitude of most Americans appeared to him to be that America would be well advised to fight Russia now before Russian superiority in missiles supercedes America's present superiority in manned aircraft. My informant likened this change in attitude over the past six months to the change in public attitude that took place in this country between Munich and the outbreak of the second World War.
>
> He also gained the impression that Americans regard the political miscalculation over Cuba [i.e., the Bay of Pigs invasion] as a military defeat and are anxious to redress the balance; they have an adolescent feeling that they cannot afford any further loss of face.
>
> It appeared to my informant that the whole pressure of the Government propaganda machine is conditioning the American public to an acceptance of global war. His fear is that this is beginning to rebound in public pressure on the American Government to adopt intractable attitudes.

Macmillan's reply discounted the weight of these 'more extreme

the United States (and, from around 1960, the Soviet Union) actually came during times of perceived crisis to using nuclear weapons is a question for continuing investigation.

If the arms race was a product of the Cold War, the massive buildup of nuclear weapons that actually occurred from around 1950 was primarily a consequence of the way in which the United States chose to pursue its rivalry with the Soviet Union. Certainly Stalin's ambitions, brutalities, and diplomatic clumsiness were a crucial stimulus to the climate of fear and animosity. But if Moscow determined much of the politics of the Cold War, particularly in central and western Europe, Washington tended to determine the currency of competitive exchange. This currency was heavily nuclear, and in pushing its early nuclear advantage so hard the United States almost certainly forced the Soviet Union to compete on the same terms: that is, to commit huge resources to creating its own nuclear arsenal, and to devise the same sort of threat of devastating power that the United States had already declared essential to its own security. America set the standard; and the standard it did set, of pursuing national security by means of the nuclear threat, was bound to be emulated by the other superpower. Perhaps there were possibilities in the mid and later 1950s that this nuclear buildup could have been more adequately contained and that the numbers of warheads could have been prevented from growing so dramatically. But these opportunities for restraint were lost; weapons production forged ahead; and, very broadly, the Soviets did during the decade after the Cuban missile crisis what the United States had done and proclaimed to be a good thing during the decade before. It might be excessive to propose that America had 'forced' the Soviet Union to construct a vast nuclear arsenal. But it would not be grossly excessive. For given the longstanding realities of power politics and great power rivalries, there was a predictable logic to the Kremlin's responses and to its determination not to remain a nuclear inferior.

So, a few decades later, when the politics underpinning the Cold War suddenly collapsed, the former Soviet Union presented to the world a landscape that bristled with nuclear weapons and the radioactive residues of a failed regime's 45-

elements' in American public life. (Public Record Office, FO 371, no. 156490, AU 1241/2.)

year quest for nuclear parity. This toxic aftermath was bound to outlive the Cold War by many years, even (in some respects) centuries or millennia. Some of this contamination might spread beyond the borders of the former Soviet Union.

Nor was the United States spared the consequences of its own championing of nuclear weapons, for it too (by now deeply in debt) confronted disposal and cleanup costs of possibly hundreds of billions of dollars, not to mention the long-term challenge of safely monitoring radioactive materials far into the future. Dozens of future generations would be obliged to contend with environmental hazards created in (it will seem to these future generations) the remote past, by peoples in two nation states during a period of tension lasting less than fifty years. The Cold War could be and was rapidly wound down. The nuclear age could not and will not be. Some of its wastes and contaminants were bound to endure, perhaps to be adequately managed, perhaps not. It will certainly be a very long time before future civilizations – civilizations with different interests, different dynamics, different languages – can safely ignore them. Indeed, special measures (most of them yet to be devised) will have to be taken to ensure that future peoples know of these enduring hazards, are duly warned, and have guidance on how to cope.[35]

Here, then, is a price that will have to be paid for depending on nuclear weapons to 'keep the peace', assuming that one accepts some of this standard argument in support of nuclear deterrence. Highlighting the nuclear threat was never cost-free, and the real costs of this strategy may be mostly for future consideration. These possible costs ought to be kept in mind when one confronts assertions that the West's 'victory' in the Cold War should be construed as a vindication of its longstanding emphasis on, as Sir John Slessor had put it, 'the great deterrent'. According to this argument, the U.S. nuclear arsenal had helped to win the Cold War and avoid a hot war. But it is not evident now and never has been evident that deterrence was dependent on such a massive nuclear commitment. Rather than constructing an arsenal of some 25,000 to 30,000 warheads (as each side eventually did), perhaps 500 or

---

35. For an early and popular discussion of some of these issues see Alan Burdick, 'The Last Cold-War Monument: Designing the "keep out" sign for a nuclear-waste site', *Harper's*, August 1992, pp. 62-67.

1,000 American warheads would have done just as well? Perhaps this much more modest but still very potent capacity for destruction would have been just as 'stabilizing' (even allowing some merit to the notion of the stability of deterrence)?[36] Perhaps it would have been more stabilizing and less hazardous than the stupendous capacity for overkill that was actually insisted upon by the United States in pursuit of its national security?

Future research, including research in the archives of the former Soviet Union, may help to clarify our thinking on such matters. But it seems unlikely that this research will demonstrate that such colossal overkill and such proliferation of nuclear weapons were necessary to keep the Kremlin in line. A more likely conclusion of further enquiries may be to question the West's embrace of the bomb, on the vast scale that actually occurred. Whatever these conclusions, they will surely depend heavily on future assessments of costs, which, given the nature of radioactivity, will not be fully known for a long time. As these costs do become known, their sources, in the anxieties and political experiences and decisions of the generation after World War Two, may be scrutinized with less complacency than they have heretofore.

---

36. A thoughtful defence of the 'stabilizing' impact of nuclear weapons is offered by John Lewis Gaddis, 'Nuclear Weapons, the End of the Cold War, and the Future of the International System', in Patrick J. Garrity and Steven A. Maaranen, eds., *Nuclear Weapons in the Changing World* (New York and London, 1992), especially pp. 18-22.

E.P. Thompson: A Select Bibliography

Harvey J. Kaye and Keith McClelland

Books and collected essays

William Morris: Romantic to Revolutionary, London, Lawrence & Wishart, 1955; rev. edn, London, Merlin, 1977.

The Making of the English Working Class, London, Victor Gollancz, 163; 2nd edn with a new postscript, Harmondsworth, Penguin, 1968; 3rd edn with a new preface, 1980.

Whigs and Hunters: The Origins of the Black Act, London, Allen Lane, 1975; reprinted with a new postscript, Harmondsworth, Penguin, 1977.

The Poverty of Theory and Other Essays, London, Merlin and New York, Monthly Review Press, 1978.

Writing by Candlelight, London, Merlin, 1980.

Zero Option, London, Merlin, 1982; in USA: *Beyond the Cold War*, New York, Pantheon, 1982.

Double Exposure, London, Merlin, 1985.

The Heavy Dancers, London, Merlin, 1985; in USA: *The Heavy Dancers*, New York, Pantheon, 1985. This edition incorporates *Double Exposure* but excludes selected essays of the British edition.

The Sykaos Papers, London, Bloomsbury and New York, Pantheon, 1988.

Customs in Common, London, Merlin, 1991.

Edited Works

There is a Spirit in Europe: A Memoir of Frank Thompson, with T. J. Thompson, London, Victor Gollancz, 1947.

The Railway: An Adventure in Construction, London, The British-Yugoslav Association, 1948.

Out of Apathy, London, Stevens & Sons/New Left Books, 1960.

The May Day Manifesto with Raymond Williams and Stuart Hall, rev. edn, ed. Raymond Williams, Harmondsworth, Penguin, 1968.

Warwick University Ltd, Harmondsworth, Penguin, 1970.

The Unknown Mayhew: Selections from the Morning Chronicle 1849-1850, with Eileen Yeo, London, Merlin, 1971.

Albion's Fatal Tree: Crime and Society in 18th-Century England, with Douglas Hay et al, London, Allen Lane, and New York, Pantheon, 1975.

Family and Inheritance: Rural Society in Western Europe, 1200-1800, with Jack Goody and Joan Thirsk, Cambridge, Cambridge University Press, 1976.

Protest and Survive, with Dan Smith, Harmondsworth, Penguin, 1980, rev. edn in USA, New York, Monthly Review Press, 1981.

Star Wars, Harmondsworth, Penguin, 1985.

Prospectus for a Habitable Planet, with Dan Smith, Harmondsworth, Penguin, 1987.

Two Poems, 'The Thresher's Labour' by Stephen Duck and 'The Woman's Labour' by Mary Collier, with Marian Sugden. Merlin, London, 1989.

Pamphlets

The Fascist Threat to Britain, 1947.

The Struggle for a Free Press, London, People's Press Printing Society, 1952.

The Communism of William Morris, a lecture by Edward Thompson given on 4 May 1959 in the Hall of the Art Workers' Guild, London, London, The William Morris Society, 1965.

Education and Experience, Fifth Mansbridge Memorial Lecture, 1968.

Homage to Salvador Allende [a poem], Spokesman Broadsheet, 30 September 1973.

Protest and Survive, CND/Bertrand Russell Peace Foundation, 1980.

Beyond the Cold War, Merlin, London, 1982.

Ferenc Köszegi and E.P. Thompson, *The New Hungarian Peace Movement*, END Special Report, London, Merlin, n.d. [1982]. (EPT wrote the Foreword and 'The "Normalisation" of Europe. A Lecture delivered in a private apartment in Budapest, 23 September 1982.')

The Defence of Britain, Merlin, London, 1983.

Infant and Emperor: Poems for Christmas, London, Merlin, 1983.

Star Wars: Self-Destruct Incorporated, with Ben Thompson, London, Merlin, 1985.

Articles and Essays

Note: All but a few book reviews have been excluded; those included are marked with an *.

Essays reprinted in the following collections have been excluded from this list: *Writing by Candlelight* (London: Merlin, 1980); *The Heavy Dancers* (London: Merlin, 1985).

'Poetry's not so easy', *Our Time*, June 1947.

'Comments on a People's Culture', *Our Time*, October 1947.

'Omladinska Pruga', in E. P. Thompson (ed.), *The Railway*, 1948,

'A New Poet', *Our Time*, June 1949.

'On the liberation of Seoul', [poem], *Arena*, 2 (6), 1951.
'The murder of William Morris', *Arena*, 2 (7), 1951.
'William Morris and the moral issues of today', *Arena*, 2 (8), 1951.
'Winter Wheat in Omsk', *World News*, 30 June 1956.
'Reply to George Matthews', *The Reasoner*, 1, July 1956.
'Through the smoke of Budapest', *The Reasoner*, 3, November 1956.
'Socialism and the intellectuals: a reply', *Universities and Left Review*, 2, 1957.
'Socialist Humanism', *The New Reasoner*, 1, 1957.
'God and King and Law',* *The New Reasoner*, 3, 1957-8 [On Peterloo]
'Agency and Choice', *The New Reasoner*, 5, 1958.
'Nato, neutralism and survival', *Universities and Left Review*, 4, 1958.
'Commitment in Politics', *Universities and Left Review*, 6, 1959.
'The New Left', *The New Reasoner*, 9, 1959.
'A Psessay in ephology', *The New Reasoner*, 10, 1959.
'Homage to Tom Maguire', in *Essays in Labour History*, ed. Asa Briggs and John Saville, London, Macmillan, 1960.
'At the point of decay' and 'Revolution', both in *Out of Apathy*, ed. E. P. Thompson (1960). ('Revolution' also appeared in *New Left Review*, 3, 1960.)
'Outside the Whale', in *Out of Apathy*, ed. E. P. Thompson (1960); repr. in E. P. Thompson, *The Poverty of Theory and Other Essays*.
'At the point of production', *New Left Review*, 1, 1960.
'Countermarching to Armageddon', *New Left Review*, 4, 1960.
'Revolution again! Or shut your ears and run', *New Left Review*, 6, 1960.
'The Long Revolution', *New Left Review*, 9-11, 1961.
'The Peculiarities of the English', *Socialist Register 1965*; repr. in E. P. Thompson, *The Poverty of Theory and Other Essays*.
'The book of numbers',* *The Times Literary Supplement*, 9 December 1965. (Anon.: review of Peter Laslett, *The World We Have Lost*.)
Preface to Staughton Lynd, *Class Conflict, Slavery, and the United States Constitution*, 1967.
'Glandular aggression', *New Society*, 19 January 1967.
'Time, work-discipline and industrial capitalism', *Past & Present*, 38, 1967.
'The political education of Henry Mayhew', *Victorian Studies*, 11, 1967.
'Introduction' to Frank Peel, *The Risings of the Luddites, Chartists and Plug-Drawers*, London, Frank Cass, 1968.
'Disenchantment or Default? A Lay Sermon', in Conor Cruise O'Brien and W. D. Vanech (eds), *Power and Consciousness*, New York, New York University Press, 1969, pp. 149-81.
'Mayhew and the *Morning Chronicle*', in E. P. Thompson and E. Yeo (eds), *The Unknown Mayhew*, 1971.
'Organizing the left', *The Times Literary Supplement*, 19 February 1971.
'The moral economy of the English crowd in the 18th century', *Past & Present*, 50, 1971.
'Rough Music: *le charivari anglais*', *Annales ESC*, 27, 1972.
'Anthropology and the discipline of historical context',* *Midland History*, 1 (1972). (Review of Keith Thomas, *Religion and the Decline of Magic* and A. Macfarlane, *The Family Life of Ralph Josselin*.)

'An Open Letter to Leszek Kolakowski', *Socialist Register 1973*; repr. in E. P. Thompson, *The Poverty of Theory and Other Essays*.

'Under the same roof-tree'*, *The Times Literary Supplement*, 4 May 1973. (Anon., review of P. Laslett (ed.), *Household and Family in Past Time*).

'Alexander Pope and the Windsor Blacks', *The Times Literary Supplement*, 7 September 1973.

'Testing class struggle',* *Times Higher Education Supplement*, 8 March 1974. (Review of John Foster, *Class Struggle and the Industrial Revolution*.)

'In citizens' bad books', *New Society*, 28 March 1974.

'Patrician society, plebeian culture', *Journal of Society History*, 7, 1974.

'A question of manners', *New Society*, 11 July 1974.

'A nice place to visit',* *New York Review of Books*, 6 February 1975. (Review of Raymond Williams, *The Country and the City*.)

'The crime of anonymity', in *Albion's Fatal Tree* (1975).

'Détente and dissent', in *Détente and Socialist Democracy: A discussion with Roy Medvedev*, ed. Ken Coates, Nottingham, Spokesman, 1975.

'The grid of inheritance: a comment', in *Family and Inheritance*, ed. Goody, Thirsk and Thompson, 1976.

'On history, sociology, and historical relevance',* *British Journal of Sociology*, 27 (2), 1976. (Review of Robert Moore, *Pitmen, Preachers and Politics*.)

'Modes de domination et révolutions en Angelterre', *Actes de la Recherche en Sciences Sociales*, 2, 1976.

'Interview with E. P. Thompson', *Radical History Review*, 3, 1976. (Repr. in *Visions of History. Interviews with E. P. Thompson et al*. New York, Pantheon, 1984.)

'Romanticism, utopianism and moralism: the case of William Morris', *New Left Review*, 99, 1976.

'Caudwell', in *Socialist Register 1977*, ed. R. Miliband and J. Saville, London, Merlin, 1977.

'Response to Tony Benn', in *The Just Society*, ed. Ken Coates and Fred Singleton, Nottingham, Spokesman, 1977.

'Folklore, anthropology, and social history', *Indian Historical Review*, III (2), 1977. (Repr. in England as 'A studies in labour history pamphlet', John L. Noyce, Brighton, 1979.)

'Happy families',* *New Society*, 8 September 1977. (Review of L. Stone, *The Family, Sex and Marriage in England 1500-1800*.)

'London', in *Interpreting Blake*, ed. M. Phillips, Cambridge, Cambridge University Press, 1978.

'Eighteenth-century English society: Class struggle without class?', *Social History*, 3 (2), 1978.

'The Poverty of Theory or An Orrery of Errors', in E. P. Thompson, *The Poverty of Theory and Other Essays*.

'Sold like a sheep for £1'*, *New Society*, 14 December 1978. (Review of George Rudé, *Protest and Punishment*.)

'Recovering the libertarian tradition', *The Leveller*, 22, January 1979. (Interview).

'Comment on "Common values? An argument"', *Stand*, 20 (2), 1979.

'The common people and the law', *New Society*, 24 July 1980.

'Danger of being too clever by half', *The Guardian*, 10 August 1980.

'Notes on exterminism, the last stage of civilization', *New Left Review*, 121, 1980. (Repr. in *Exterminism and Cold War*, ed. *New Left Review*, London, Verso, 1982. This volume also contains 'Europe, the weak link in the cold war'.)

'"Rough music" et charivari. Quelques réflexions complémentaires', in *Le Charivari*, ed. J. Le Goff and Jean-Claude Schmitt (Ecole des Hautes Etudes en Sciences Sociales Centre de Recherches Historiques. Civilisations et Sociétés, 67, Paris, Mouton, 1981).

'A Letter to America', *The Nation*, 24 January 1981.

'European Reborn. An interview with E. P. Thompson', *Peace News*, 15 May 1981.

'European Nuclear Disarmament: an interview with E. P. Thompson' (by Michael Kazin), *The Socialist Review*, 58, 1981.

'E. P. Thompson replies to Sabata', *New Statesman*, 4 May 1984.

'East and West Europe belong to the same culture' (a conversation between Thompson and George Konrad), *The Listener*, 13 June 1985.

'Why is Star Wars?' and 'Folly's Comet', in *Star Wars*, ed. E. P. Thompson, 1985.

'Letter to Americans' and 'The view from Oxford Street', in Mary Kaldor and Paul Anderson (eds), *Mad Dogs. The U.S. Raids on Libya*, London, Pluto Press with END, 1986.

E. J. Hobsbawm, Christopher Hill, Perry Anderson and E. P. Thompson, 'Agendas for Radical History', *Radical History Review*, 36, 1986.

'The reasons of the Yahoo', *Yale Review*, Summer 1986.

'The rituals of emnity', in *Prospectus for a Habitable Planet*, ed. E. P. Thompson and Dan Smith, 1987.

'Eighteenth-century Ranters: did they exist?', in *Reviewing the English Revolution*, ed. Geoff Eley and William Hunt, London, Verso, 1988.

'Wordsworth's crisis'*, *London Review of Books*,* 10 (22), 8 December 1988, pp. 3-6. (Review of Nicholas Roe, *Wordsworth and Coleridge: The Radical Years*.)

'Protest and revise'&, *END Journal*, 37 (1989). (Review of Richard Taylor, *Against the Bomb. The British Peace Movement, 1958–1965* and James Hinton, *Protests and Visions. Peace Politics in Twentieth-Century Britain*).

'When the war is over', *New Statesman & Society*, 26 January 1990.

'History Turns on a New Hinge: E.N.D. and the Beginning', *The Nation*, 29 January 1990.

'Our Mission Remains: Break Up the Blocs in Europe', *The Nation*, 13/20 August 1990.

'What's Next? – a symposium', *The Nation*, 23 September 1991.

'Homage to Tom McGrath', in *Thomas McGrath: Life and the Poem*, ed. Reginald Gibbons and Terrance Des Pres, Urbana, University of Illinois Press, 1992.

'Blake's Tone,*, *London Review of Books*, 28 January 1993. (Review of Jon Mee, *Dangerous Enthusiasm: William Blake and the Culture of Radicalism in the 1790s*).

Notes on Contributors

Victor Bailey is Associate Professor of Modern British History at the University of Kansas. He is editor of *Policing and Punishment in Nineteenth-Century Britain*, (1981) and of *Forged in Fire: The History of the Fire Brigades Union*, (1992) and author of *Delinquency and Citizenship: Reclaiming the Young Offender, 1914–1948*, (1987).

Leon Fink is professor of history at the University of North Carolina at Chapel Hill. He is the author of *In Search of the Working Class: Essays in American Labor History and Political Culture*, (1994) and co-author of *Upheaval in the Quiet Zone: A History of Hospital Workers' Union, Local 1199*, (1989)

Douglas Hay teaches the history of law and crime at Osgoode Hall Law School and in the Department of History at York University, Toronto. He was an editor of and contributor to *Albion's Fatal Tree*, (1975) and has co-edited three other books on the subject as well as contributing a number of major publications to other collections and to leading periodicals.

Harvey J. Kaye is the Ben and Joyce Rosenberg Professor of Social Change and Development at the University of Wisconsin, Green Bay. He is the author of *The British Marxist Historians*, (1984), *The Powers of the Past*, (1991) and *The Education of Desire*, (1992), and the editor of several works including, with Keith McClelland, *E.P. Thompson, Critical Perspectives*, (1989) and, with Mari Jo Buhle and Paul Buhle, *The American Radical*, (1984).

Peter Linebaugh was a contributor to *Albion's Fatal Tree*, (1975) and is the author of *The London Hanged* (1991). He has published numerous articles in the history of crime and on the London and Atlantic proletariat. He has taught at several American universities, at the Attica Correctional Facility in New York and at the Federal Penitentiary in Mirion, Illinois.

Robert Malcolmson is Professor of History and Chairman of the Department at Queen's University in Kingston, Ontario. He is the author of *Popular Recreations in English Society 1700–1850*, (1973), *Life and Labour in England 1700–1780*, (1981), *Nuclear Fallacies*, (1985) and *Beyond Nuclear Thinking*, (1990).

Keith McClelland teaches at the University of Reading and is the author of numerous articles in the field of British Labour history. With Harvey J. Kaye he edited *E.P. Thompson, Critical Perspectives*, (1990).

Alec Morley read History at Queen's University in Kingston, Ontario, where he studied with Edward Thompson in 1988. In recent years he has been engaged in development work in southern Africa.

J.M. Neeson is Associate Professor, Department of History, York University, Toronto. She is the author of *Commoners, Common Right, Enclosure and Social Change in England, 1700–1820*, (1993).

Sheila Rowbotham is a senior research fellow at Manchester University and a Simon Fellow. Her books include *Hidden from History*, (1973), *Women in Movement*, (1993) and *Homeworkers Worldwide*, (1993).

John Rule is Professor of History at the University of Southampton. He was a contributor to *Albion's Fatal Tree*, (1975) and is the author of *The Experience of Lzbour in Eighteenth-Century*, (1981), *The Labouring Classes in Early Industrial England, 1750–1850*, (1986) and of a two volume economic and social history of Hanovarian England, *The Vital Century, England's Developing Economy, 1714–1815* and *Albion's People English Society, 1714–1815*, (1992).

Peter Searby is a Fellow of Fitzwilliam College, Cambridge where until 1990 he taught history in the Faculty of Education. He has written on Victorian Coventry, on Chartism and on Victorian schooling. He is currently writing volume 3 (1750–1870) of the *History of the University of Cambridge*.

Barbara Winslow teaches in the Women's Studies Programme at Hunter College, City University of New York. She has completed a book on Sylvia Pankhurst and is writing a history of the women's liberation movement in Seattle. She is also the Executive Director of the Coordinating Committee for Women in the Historical Profession/Conference Group on Women's History.

Calvin Winslow teaches Labour Studies and directs labour projects at Queen's College, City University of New York. He was a contributor to *Albion's Fatal Tree* (1975).